stands [...] world lit[...]. It is read today both as history and for the brilliance of its style and reportorial skill.

Plutarch's scheme was to compare the lives of outstanding Greek figures with those of his own Roman compatriots, and his book placed Greek and Roman side by side. This selection from LIVES OF THE NOBLE ROMANS has been made as a companion volume to LIVES OF THE NOBLE GREEKS so that Plutarch's essential purpose could be perpetuated in this authoritative and inexpensive edition.

EDMUND FULLER teaches at Kent School. He is the author of three novels, *A Star Pointed North, Brothers Divided,* and *The Corridor,* and two books of critical essays, *Man in Modern Fiction* and *Books With Men Behind Them.* For Dell Laurel Editions Mr. Fuller has edited *Mark Twain: A Laurel Reader* and *Voltaire: A Laurel Reader.*

PLUTARCH

LIVES OF THE NOBLE ROMANS

A selection edited by

EDMUND FULLER

Translated by John Dryden

And Revised by Arthur Hugh Clough

A LAUREL CLASSIC

Published by
DELL PUBLISHING CO., INC.
750 Third Avenue
New York 17, N.Y.

Cover painting by Milton Glaser

First printing—December, 1959
Second printing—December, 1961
Third printing—January, 1963
Fourth printing February, 1964
Fifth printing—March, 1965

Printed in U.S.A.

Contents

Editor's Note

No more terse or telling summation has been made of the merits of Plutarch—first of the world's great biographers and model in this art to all succeeding times—than that of the distinguished classical scholar, Moses Hadas.

> It was after all Plutarch's main purpose in his *Lives* . . . to imbue his readers with Greek culture, which is embodied in Greek books; and if today a curious reader should ask for a single author who might communicate the fullest sense of the totality of classical culture, the answer would have to be Plutarch. . . . No author conveys a more complete sense of the political and intellectual climate of the Greco-Roman world. . . . He has indubitably had more European readers than any other pagan Greek and has been the greatest single channel for communicating to Europe a general sense of the men and manners of antiquity.
> —*Ancilla to Classical Reading*

All the Roman plays of Shakespeare are drawn heavily from Plutarch. The great French essayist, Montaigne, was his disciple and emulator. His influence has permeated Western culture. In Emerson's words: "We cannot read Plutarch without a tingling of blood."

In the opening paragraphs of the life of Timoleon (included in the companion volume to this one, *Lives of the Noble Greeks*) he makes his own statement of purpose.

> It was for the sake of others that I first commenced writing biographies; but I find myself proceeding and attaching myself to it for my own; the virtues of these great men serving me as a sort of looking-glass, in

which I may see how to adjust and adorn my own life. Indeed, it can be compared to nothing but daily living and associating together; we receive, as it were, in our inquiry, and entertain each successive guest, view—

"Their stature and their qualities,"

and select from their actions all that is noblest and worthiest to know. . . . My method . . . is, by the study of history, and by the familiarity acquired in writing, to habituate my memory to receive and retain images of the best and worthiest characters. I am thus enabled to free myself from any ignoble, base, or vicious impressions, contracted from the contagion of ill company that I may be unavoidably engaged in; by the remedy of turning my thoughts in a happy and calm temper to view these noble examples.

Yet, as scrupulous historian and portraitist, he gives us his figures in the round, as men compounded both of good and evil, folly and wisdom.

The complete *Lives* is an enormous volume, in which notable Greeks and Romans are set in juxtaposition for purposes of comparison, a scheme not perfectly preserved in the surviving text, as we have it. The present volume is a selection of ten of the *Lives of the Noble Romans,* chosen with consideration both of the most important figures and the finest specimens of Plutarch's literary qualities.

Five of these lives are unabridged. A shortened life of Marcellus is used to give us the major elements of his character and to add to the picture of the Roman struggle with Hannibal. But Marcellus chiefly serves as the source of Plutarch's notable pages about the extraordinary engines with which Archimedes defended Syracuse against the Romans, and to account for the ironic death of that great early scientist. The lives of Crassus, Caesar, Pompey, Cicero, and Antony jointly give us the drama of Rome's passing from a republic to an empire, undoubtedly the most dramatic, tumultuous, and decisive era in all Roman history. The lives of Caesar and Cicero are unabridged. Those of Crassus, Pompey, and Antony have been abridged particularly to avoid the repetition of material in these overlapping stories. In the case of Antony, the purpose also has been to highlight Plutarch's tremendous portrait of greatness destroyed by folly, especially as this culminates in the passionate and tragic liaison with Cleopatra. In these lives are the major sources of Shakespeare's *Julius Caesar* and *Antony and Cleopatra*.

In the companion volume, *Lives of the Noble Greeks*, may be found the lives of many of the Greeks whose careers Plutarch felt were analogous to those of certain of the Romans here included. Thus the reader may compare Theseus to Romulus, Alexander to Caesar, and Demosthenes to Cicero.

The ten lives in this volume provide us with the image of Rome from its mythic prehistory, through the days of the austerity and republican strength, to the height of its conquests and the collapse under the very weight and power of the state, of the forms and freedoms of republican government. Thus these lives outline for us the framework of a story larger than their actual compass. In their portrayals of human nature under the stresses and temptations of power, and of political and military dilemmas, they are rich in meaning for the modern world.

EDMUND FULLER

ROMULUS

From whom, and for what reason, the city of Rome, a name so great in glory, and famous in the mouths of all men, was so first called, authors do not agree. Some are of opinion that the Pelasgians, wandering over the greater part of the habitable world, and subduing numerous nations, fixed themselves here, and, from their own great *strength* in war, called the city Rome. Others, that at the taking of Troy, some few that escaped and met with shipping, put to sea, and driven by winds, were carried upon the coasts of Tuscany, and came to anchor off the mouth of the river Tiber, where their women, out of heart and weary with the sea, on its being proposed by one of the highest birth and best understanding amongst them, whose name was Roma, burnt the ships. With which act the men at first were angry, but afterwards, of necessity, seating themselves near Palatium, where things in a short while succeeded far better than they could hope, in that they found the country very good, and the people courteous, they not only did the lady Roma other honours, but added also this, of calling after her name the city which she had been the occasion of their founding. From this, they say, has come down that custom at Rome for women to salute their kinsmen and husbands with kisses; because these women, after they had burnt the ships, made use of such endearments when entreating and pacifying their husbands.

Some again say that Roma, from whom this city was so called, was daughter of Italus and Leucaria; or, by another account, of Telaphus, Hercules's son, and that she was married to Aeneas, or, according to others again to

Ascanius, Aeneas's son. Some tell us that Romanus, the son of Ulysses and Circe, built it; some, Romus, the son of Emathion, Diomede having sent him from Troy; and others, Romus, king of the Latins, after driving out the Tyrrhenians, who had come from Thessaly into Lydia, and from thence into Italy. Those very authors, too, who, in accordance with the safest account, make Romulus give the name of the city, yet differ concerning his birth and family. For some say, he was son to Aeneas and Dexithea, daughter of Phorbas, and was, with his brother Remus, in their infancy, carried into Italy, and being on the river when the waters came down in a flood, all the vessels were cast away except only that where the young children were, which being gently landed on a level bank of the river, they were both unexpectedly saved, and from them the place was called Rome. Some say, Roma, daughter of the Trojan lady above mentioned, was married to Latinus, Telemachus's son, and became mother to Romulus; others that Aemilia, daughter of Aeneas and Lavinia, had him by the god Mars; and others give you mere fables of his origin. For to Tarchetius, they say, king of Alba, who was a most wicked and cruel man, there appeared in his own house a strange vision, a male figure that rose out of a hearth, and stayed there for many days. There was an oracle of Tethys in Tuscany which Tarchetius consulted, and received an answer that a virgin should give herself to the apparition, and that a son should be born of her, highly renowned, eminent for valour, good fortune, and strength of body. Tarchetius told the prophecy to one of his own daughters, and commanded her to do this thing; which she avoiding as an indignity, sent her handmaid. Tarchetius, hearing this, in great anger imprisoned them both, purposing to put them to death, but being deterred from murder by the goddess Vesta in a dream, enjoined them for their punishment the working a web of cloth, in their chains as they were, which when they finished, they should be suffered to marry; but whatever they worked by day, Tarchetius commanded others to unravel in the night.

In the meantime, the waiting-woman was delivered of

two boys, whom Tarchetius gave into the hands of one Teratius, with command to destroy them; he, however, carried and laid them by the river side, where a wolf came and continued to suckle them, while birds of various sorts brought little morsels of food, which they put into their mouths; till a cowherd, spying them, was first strangely surprised, but, venturing to draw nearer, took the children up in his arms. Thus they were saved, and when they grew up, set upon Tarchetius and overcame him. This one Promathion says, who compiled a history of Italy.

But the story which is most believed and has the greatest number of vouchers was first published, in its chief particulars, amongst the Greeks by Diocles of Peparethus, whom Fabius Pictor also follows in most points. Here again there are variations, but in general outline it runs thus: the kings of Alba reigned in lineal descent from Aeneas, and the succession devolved at length upon two brothers, Numitor and Amulius. Amulius proposed to divide things into two equal shares, and set as equivalent to the kingdom the treasure and gold that were brought from Troy. Numitor chose the kingdom; but Amulius, having the money, and being able to do more with that than Numitor, took his kingdom from him with great ease, and, fearing lest his daughter might have children, made her a Vestal, bound in that condition forever to live a single and maiden life. This lady some call Ilia, others Rhea, and others Silvia; however, not long after, she was, contrary to the established laws of the Vestals, discovered to be with child, and should have suffered the most cruel punishment, had not Antho, the king's daughter, mediated with her father for her; nevertheless, she was confined, and debarred all company, that she might not be delivered without the king's knowledge. In time she brought forth two boys, of more than human size and beauty, whom Amulius, becoming yet more alarmed, commanded a servant to take and cast away; this man some call Faustulus, others say Faustulus was the man who brought them up. He put the children, however, in a small trough, and went towards the river with a design to cast them in; but, seeing the waters much swollen and coming violently down, was afraid to go nearer, and dropping the children near the bank, went away. The river overflowing, the flood at last bore up the trough, and, gently wafting it, landed them on a smooth piece of ground, which they now called Cermanus, formerly Germanus, perhaps from *Germani*, which signifies brothers.

Near this place grew a wild fig-tree, which they called Ruminalis, either from Romulus (as it is vulgarly thought), or from *ruminating*, because cattle did usually in the heat of the day seek cover under it, and there chew the cud; or better, from the suckling of these children there, for the ancients called the dug or teat of any creature *ruma;* and there is a tutelar goddess of the rearing of children whom they still call Rumilia, in sacrificing to whom they use no wine, but make libations of milk. While the infants lay here, history tells us, a she-wolf nursed them, and a woodpecker constantly fed and watched them; these creatures are esteemed holy to the god Mars; the woodpecker the Latins still especially worship and honour. Which things, as much as any, gave credit to what the mother of the children said, that their father was the god Mars; though some say that it was a mistake put upon her by Amulius, who himself had come to her dressed up in armour.

Others think that the first rise of this fable came from the children's nurse, through the ambiguity of her name; for the Latins not only called wolves *lupoe,* but also women of loose life; and such an one was the wife of Faustulus, who nurtured these children, Acca Larentia by name. To her the Romans offer sacrifices, and in the month of April the priest of Mars makes libations there; it is called the Larentian Feast.

Meantime Faustulus, Amulius's swineherd, brought up the children without any man's knowledge; or, as those say who wish to keep closer to probabilities, with the knowledge and secret assistance of Numitor; for it is said, they went to school at Gabii, and were well instructed in letters, and other accomplishments befitting their birth. And they were called Romulus and Remus (from *ruma,* the dug), as we had before, because they were found sucking the wolf. In their very infancy, the size and beauty of their bodies intimated their natural superiority; and when they grew up, they both proved brave and manly, attempting all enterprises that seemed hazardous, and showing in them a courage altogether undaunted. But Romulus seemed rather to act by counsel, and to show the sagacity of a statesman, and in all his dealings with their neighbours, whether relating to feeding of flocks or to hunting, gave the idea of being born rather to rule than to obey. To their comrades and inferiors they were therefore dear; but the king's servants, his bailiffs and overseers, as being in nothing better than themselves, they despised and slighted, nor were the least concerned at their commands and menaces. They used honest pastimes and liberal studies, not esteeming sloth and idleness honest and liberal, but rather such exercises as hunting and running, repelling robbers, taking of thieves, and delivering the wronged and oppressed from injury. For doing such things they became famous.

A quarrel occurring betwixt Numitor's and Amulius's cowherds, the latter, not enduring the driving away of their cattle by the others, fell upon them and put them to flight, and rescued the greatest part of the prey. At which Numitor being highly incensed, they little regarded it, but collected and took into their company a number of needy men and runaway slaves,—acts which looked like the first stages of rebellion. It so happened, that when Romulus was attending a sacrifice, being fond of sacred rites and divination, Numitor's herdsmen, meeting with Remus on a journey with few companions, fell upon him, and after some fighting, took him prisoner, carried him before Numitor, and there accused him. Numitor would not punish him himself, fearing his brother's anger, but went to Amulius, and desired justice, as he was Amulius's brother and was affronted by Amulius's servants. The men of Alba likewise resenting the thing, and thinking he had been dishonourably used, Amulius was induced to deliver Remus up into Numitor's hands, to use him as he thought fit. He therefore took and carried him home, and, being struck with admiration of the youth's person, in stature and strength of body exceeding all men, and perceiving in his very countenance the courage and force of his mind, which stood unsubdued and unmoved by his present circumstances, and hearing further that all the enterprises and actions of his life were answerable to what he saw of him, but chiefly, as it seemed, a divine influence aiding and directing the first steps that were to lead to great results, out of the mere thought of his mind, and casually, as it were, he put his hand upon the fact, and, in gentle terms and with a kind aspect, to inspire him with confidence and hope, asked him who he was, and whence he was derived. He, taking heart, spoke thus: "I will hide nothing from you, for you seem to be of a more princely temper than Amulius, in that you give a hearing and examine before you punish, while he condemns before the cause is heard. Formerly, then, we (for we are twins) thought ourselves the sons of Faustulus and Larentia, the king's servants; but since we have been accused and aspersed with calumnies, and brought in peril of our lives here before you, we hear great things of ourselves, the truth of which my present danger is likely to bring to the test. Our birth is said to have been secret, our fostering and nurture in our infancy still more strange; by birds and beasts, to whom we were cast out, we were fed, by the milk of a wolf and the morsels of a woodpecker, as we lay in a little trough by the side of the river. The trough is still in being, and is preserved, with brass plates round it, and an inscription in letters almost effaced, which may prove hereafter unavailing tokens to our parents when we are dead and gone." Numitor, upon these words, and computing the dates by the young man's looks, slighted not the hope that flattered him, but considered how to come at his daughter privately (for she was still kept under restraint), to talk with her concerning these matters.

Faustulus, hearing Remus was taken and delivered up, called on Romulus to assist in his rescue, informing him then plainly of the particulars of his birth, not but he had before given hints of it, and told as much as an attentive man might make no small conclusions from him; he himself, full of concern and fear of not coming in time, took

the trough, and ran instantly to Numitor; but giving a suspicion to some of the king's sentries at his gate, and being
gazed upon by them and perplexed with their questions, he
let it be seen that he was hiding the trough under his cloak.
By chance there was one among them who was at the ex-
posing of the children, and was employed in the office; he,
seeing the trough and knowing it by its make and inscription, guessed at the business, and, without further delay,
telling the king of it, brought in the man to be examined.
Faustulus, hard beset, did not show himself altogether proof
against terror; nor yet was he wholly forced out of all; confessed indeed the children were alive, but lived, he said, as
shepherds, a great way from Alba; he himself was going to
carry the trough to Ilia, who had often greatly desired to
see and handle it, for a confirmation of her hopes of her
children. As men generally do who are troubled in mind and
act either in fear or passion, it so fell out Amulius now did;
for he sent in haste as a messenger, a man, otherwise honest, and friendly to Numitor, with commands to learn from
Numitor whether any tidings were come to him of the children being alive. He, coming and seeing how little Remus
wanted of being received into the arms and embraces of
Numitor, both gave him surer confidence in his hope, and
advised them, with all expedition, to proceed to action; himself too joining and assisting them, and indeed, had they
wished it, the time would not have let them demur. For
Romulus was now come very near, and many of the citizens, out of fear and hatred of Amulius, were running out
to join him; besides, he brought great forces with him, divided into companies each of an hundred men, every captain carrying a small bundle of grass and shrubs tied to a
pole. The Latins call such bundles *manipuli*, and from
hence it is that in their armies they still call their captains
manipulares. Remus rousing the citizens within to revolt,
and Romulus making attacks from without, the tyrant, not
knowing either what to do, or what expedient to think of
for his security, in this perplexity and confusion was taken
and put to death. This narrative for the most part given by
Fabius and Diocles of Peparethus, who seem to be the

earliest historians of the foundation of Rome, is suspected
by some, because of its dramatic and fictitious appearance;
but it would not wholly be disbelieved, if men would remember what a poet fortune sometimes shows herself, and
consider that the Roman power would hardly have reached
so high a pitch without a divinely ordered origin, attended
with great and extraordinary circumstances.

Amulius now being dead and matters quietly disposed,
the two brothers would neither dwell in Alba without governing there, nor take the government into their own hands
during the life of their grandfather. Having therefore delivered the dominion up into his hands, and paid their mother
befitting honour, they resolved to live by themselves, and
build a city in the same place where they were in their infancy brought up. This seems the most honourable reason
for their departure; though perhaps it was necessary, having
such a body of slaves and fugitives collected about them,
either to come to nothing by dispersing them, or if not so,
then to live with them elsewhere. For that the inhabitants
of Alba did not think fugitives worthy of being received
and incorporated as citizens among them plainly appears
from the matter of the women, an attempt made not wantonly but of necessity, because they could not get wives by
good-will. For they certainly paid unusual respect and honour to those whom they thus forcibly seized.

Not long after the first foundation of the city, they
opened a sanctuary of refuge for all fugitives, which they
called the temple of the god Asylaeus, where they received
and protected all, delivering none back, neither the servant
to his master, the debtor to his creditor, nor the murderer
into the hands of the magistrate, saying it was a privileged
place, and they could so maintain it by an order of the holy
oracle; insomuch that the city grew presently very populous,
for they say, it consisted at first of no more than a thousand
houses. But of that hereafter.

Their minds being full bent upon building, there arose
presently a difference about the place. Romulus chose what
was called Roma Quadrata, or the Square Rome, and
would have the city there. Remus laid out a piece of ground

on the Aventine Mount, well fortified by nature, which was from him called Remonium, but now Rignarium. Concluding at last to decide the contest by a divination from a flight of birds, and placing themselves apart at some distance. Remus, they say, saw six vultures, and Romulus double that number; others say, Remus did truly see his number, and that Romulus feigned his, but when Remus came to him, that then he did indeed see twelve. Hence it is that the Romans, in their divinations from birds, chiefly regard the vulture, though Herodorus Ponticus relates that Hercules was always very joyful when a vulture appeared to him upon any action. For it is a creature the least hurtful of any, pernicious neither to corn, fruit-tree, nor cattle; it preys only upon carrion, and never kills or hurts any living thing; and as for birds, it touches not them, though they are dead, as being of its own species, whereas eagles, owls, and hawks mangle and kill their own fellow-creatures; yet, as Aeschylus says,—

"What bird is clean that preys on fellow bird?"

Besides, all other birds are, so to say, never out of our eyes; they let themselves be seen of us continually; but a vulture is a very rare sight, and you can seldom meet with a man that has seen their young; their rarity and infrequency has raised a strange opinion in some, that they come to us from some other world; as soothsayers ascribe a divine origination to all things not produced either of nature or of themselves.

When Remus knew the cheat, he was much displeased; and as Romulus was casting up a ditch, where he designed the foundation of the city-wall, he turned some pieces of the work to ridicule, and obstructed others; at last, as he was in contempt leaping over it, some say Romulus himself struck him, others Celer, one of his companions; he fell, however, and in the scuffle Faustulus also was slain, and Plistinus, who, being Faustulus's brother, story tells us, helped to bring up Romulus. Celer upon this fled instantly into Tuscany, and from him the Romans call all men that are swift of feet Celeres; and because Quintus Metellus, at his father's funeral, in a few days' time gave the people a show of gladiators, admiring his expedition in getting it ready, they gave him the name of Celer.

Romulus, having buried his brother Remus, together with with his two foster-fathers, on the mount Remonia, set to building his city; and sent for men out of Tuscany, who directed him by sacred usages and written rules in all the ceremonies to be observed, as in a religious rite. First, they dug a round trench about that which is now the Comitium, or Court of Assembly, and into it solemnly threw the first-fruits of all things either good by custom or necessary by nature; lastly, every man taking a small piece of earth of the country from whence he came, they all threw in promiscuously together. This trench they call, as they do the heavens, Mundus; making which their centre, they described the city in a circle round it. Then the founder fitted to a plough a brazen ploughshare, and, yoking together a bull and a cow, drove himself a deep line or furrow round the bounds; while the business of those that followed after was to see that whatever earth was thrown up should be turned all inwards towards the city; and not to let any clod lie outside. With this line they described the wall, and called it, by a contraction, Pomoerium, that is, *postmurum*, after or beside the wall; and where they designed to make a gate, there they took out the share, carried the plough over, and left a space; for which reason they consider the whole wall as holy, except where the gates are; for had they adjudged them also sacred, they could not, without offence to religion, have given free ingress and egress for the necessaries of human life, some of which are in themselves unclean. As for the day they began to build the city, it is universally agreed to have been the twenty-first of April, and that day the Romans annually keep holy, calling it their country's birthday.

The city now being built, Romulus enlisted all that were of age to bear arms into military companies, each company consisting of three thousand footmen and three hundred horse. These companies were called legions, because they were the choicest and most select of the people for fighting men. The rest of the multitude he called the people; an hundred of the most eminent he chose for counsellors; these he styled patricians, and their assembly the senate, which signifies a council of elders. The patricians, some say, were so called because they were the fathers of lawful children; others, because they could give a good account who their own fathers were, which not every one of the rabble that poured into the city at first could do; others, from patronage, their word for protection of inferiors, the origin of which they attribute to Patron, one of those that came over with Evander, who was a great protector and defender of the weak and needy. But perhaps the most probable judgment might be, that Romulus, esteeming it the duty of the chiefest and wealthiest men, with a fatherly care and concern to look after the meaner, and also encouraging the commonalty not to dread or be aggrieved at the honours of their superiors, but to love and respect them, and to think and call them their fathers, might from hence give them the name of patricians. For at this very time all foreigners give senators the style of lords; but the Romans, making use of a more honourable and less invidious name, call them Patres Conscripti; at first, indeed, simply Patres, but afterwards, more being added, Patres Conscripti. By this more imposing title he distinguished the senate from the populace; and in other ways separated the nobles and the commons,—calling them patrons, and these their clients,—by which means he created wonderful love and amity betwixt them, productive of great justice; in their dealings. For they were always their clients' counsellors in law cases, their advocates in courts of justice; in fine, their advisers and supporters in all affairs whatever. These again faithfully served their patrons, not only paying them all respect and deference, but also, in case of poverty, helping them to portion their daughters and pay off their debts; and for a patron to witness against his client, or a client against his patron, was what no law nor magistrate could enforce. In aftertimes, all other duties subsisting still between them, it was thought mean and dishonourable for the better sort to take money from their inferiors. And so much of these matters.

In the fourth month, after the city was built, as Fabius writes, the adventure of stealing the women was attempted; and some say Romulus himself, being naturally a martial man, and predisposed too, perhaps by certain oracles, to believe the fates had ordained the future growth and greatness of Rome should depend upon the benefit of war, upon these accounts first offered violence to the Sabines, since he took away only thirty virgins, more to give an occasion of war than out of any want of women. But this is not very probable; it would seem rather that, observing his city to be filled by a confluence of foreigners, a few of whom had wives, and that the multitude in general, consisting of a mixture of mean and obscure men, fell under contempt, and seemed to be of no long continuance together, and hoping farther, after the women were appeased, to make this injury in some measure an occasion of confederacy and mutual commerce with the Sabines, he took in hand this exploit after this manner. First, he gave it out as if he had found an altar of a certain god hid under ground; the god they called Consus, either the god of counsel (for they still call a consultation *consilium,* and their chief magistrates *consules,* namely, counsellors), or else the equestrian Neptune, for the altar is kept covered in the Circus Maximus at all other times, and only at horse-races is exposed to public view; others merely say that this god had his altar hid under ground because counsel ought to be secret and concealed. Upon discovery of this altar, Romulus, by proclamation, appointed a day for a splendid sacrifice, and for public games and shows, to entertain all sorts of people: many flocked thither, and he himself sat in front, amidst his nobles clad in purple. Now the signal for their falling on was to be whenever he rose and gathered up his robe and threw it over his body; his men stood all ready armed, with their eyes intent upon him, and when the sign was given, drawing their swords and falling on with a great shout, they ravished away the daughters of the Sabines,

they themselves flying without any let or hindrance. They
say there were but thirty taken, and from them the Curiae
or Fraternities were named; but Valerius Antias says five
hundred and twenty-seven, Juba, six hundred and eighty-
three virgins: which was indeed the greatest excuse Romulus could allege, namely, that they had taken no married
woman, save one only, Hersilia by name, and her too un-
knowingly; which showed that they did not commit this
rape wantonly, but with a design purely of forming alliance with their neighbours by the greatest and surest bonds.
This Hersilia some say Hostilius married, a most eminent
man among the Romans; others, Romulus himself, and that
she bore two children to him,—a daughter, by reason of
primogeniture called Prima, and one only son, whom, from
the great concourse of citizens to him at that time, he
called Aollius, and after ages Abillius. But Zenodotus the
Troezenian, in giving this account, is contradicted by many.

Among those who committed this rape upon the virgins,
there were, they say, as it so then happened, some of the
meaner sort of men, who were carrying off a damsel, excel-
ling all in beauty and comeliness and stature, whom when
some of superior rank that met them, attempted to take away,
they cried out they were carrying her to Talasius, a young
man, indeed, but brave and worthy; hearing that, they commended and applauded them loudly, and also some, turning back, accompanied them with good-will and pleasure,
shouting out the name of Talasius. Hence the Romans to
this very time, at their weddings, sing Talasius for their
nuptial word, as the Greeks do Hymenaeus, because they
say Talasius was very happy in his marriage. But Sextius
Sylla the Carthaginian, a man wanting neither learning nor
ingenuity, told me Romulus gave this word as a sign when
to begin the onset; everybody, therefore, who made
prize of a maiden, cried out, Talasius; and for that reason
the custom continues so now at marriages. But most are of
opinion (of whom Juba particularly is one) that this word
was used to new-married women by way of incitement to
good housewifery and *talasia* (spinning), as we say in
Greek, Greek words at that time not being as yet over-

powered by Italian. But if this be the case, and if the Romans did at the time use the word *talasia* as we do, a man might fancy a more probable reason of the custom. For when the Sabines, after the war against the Romans were reconciled, conditions were made concerning their women, that they should be obliged to do no other servile offices to their husbands but what concerned spinning; it was customary, therefore, ever after, at weddings, for those that gave the bride or escorted her or otherwise were present, sportingly to say Talasius, intimating that she was henceforth to serve in spinning and no more. It continues also a custom at this very day for the bride not of herself to pass her husband's threshold, but to be lifted over, in memory that the Sabine virgins were carried in by violence, and did not go in of their own will. Some say, too, the custom of parting the bride's hair with the head of a spear was in token their marriages began at first by war and acts of hostility.

This rape was committed on the eighteenth day of the month Sextillis, now called August, on which the solemnities of the Consualia are kept.

The Sabines were a numerous and martial people, but lived in small, unfortified villages, as it befitted, they thought, a colony of the Lacedaemonians to be bold and fearless; nevertheless, seeing themselves bound by such hostages to their good behaviour, and being solicitous for their daughters, they sent ambassadors to Romulus with fair and equitable requests, that he would return their young women and recall that act of violence, and afterwards, by persuasion and lawful means, seek friendly correspondence between both nations. Romulus would not part with the young women, yet proposed to the Sabines to enter into an alliance with them; upon which point some consulted and demurred long, but Acron, king of the Ceninenses, a man of high spirit and a good warrior, who had all along a jealousy of Romulus's bold attempts, and considering particularly, from this exploit upon the women, that he was growing formidable to all people, and indeed insufferable, were he not chastised, first rose up in arms, and with a powerful army advanced against him. Romulus likewise prepared to receive him; but when they came within sight and viewed each other, they made a challenge to fight a single duel, the armies standing by under arms, without participation. And Romulus, making a vow to Jupiter, if he should conquer, to carry, himself, and dedicate his adversary's armour to his honour, overcame him in combat, and a battle ensuing, routed his army also, and then took his city; but did those he found in it no injury, only commanded them to demolish the place and attend him to Rome, there to be admitted to all the privileges of citizens. And indeed there was nothing did more advance the greatness of Rome, than that she did always unite and incorporate those whom she conquered into herself. Romulus, that he might perform his vow in the most acceptable manner to Jupiter, and withall make the pomp of it delightful to the eye of the city, cut down a tall oak which he saw growing in the camp, which he trimmed to the shape of a trophy, and fastened on it Acron's whole suit of armour disposed in proper form; then he himself, girding his clothes about him, and crowning his head with a laurel garland, his hair gracefully flowing, carried the trophy resting erect upon his right shoulder, and so marched on, singing songs of triumph, and his whole army following after, the citizens all receiving him with acclamations of joy and wonder.

After the overthrow of the Ceninensians, the other Sabines still protracting the time in preparations, the people of Fidenae, Crustumerium, and Antemna joined their forces against the Romans; they in like manner were defeated in battle, and surrendered up to Romulus their cities to be seized, their lands and territories to be divided, and themselves to be transplanted to Rome. All the lands which Romulus acquired, he distributed among the citizens, except only what the parents of the stolen virgins had; these he suffered to possess their own. The rest of the Sabines, enraged hereat, choosing Tatius their captain, marched straight against Rome. The city was almost inaccessible, having for its fortress that which is now the Capitol, where a strong guard was placed, and Tarpeius their captain; not Tarpeia the virgin, as some say who would make Romulus a fool. But Tarpeia, daughter to the captain, coveting the golden bracelets she saw them wear, betrayed the fort into the Sabines' hands, and asked, in reward of her treachery, the things they wore on their left arms. Tatius conditioning thus with her, in the night she opened one of the gates, and received the Sabines. And truly Antigonus, it would seem, was not solitary in saying he loved betrayers, but hated those who had betrayed; nor Caesar, who told Rhymitalces the Thracian, that he loved the treason, but hated the traitor; but it is the general feeling of all who have occasion for wicked men's service, as people have for the poison of venomous beasts; they are glad of them while they are of use, and abhor their baseness when it is over. And so then did Tatius behave toward Tarpeia, for he commanded the Sabines, in regard to their contract, not to refuse her the least part of what they wore on their left arms; and he himself first took his bracelet off his arm, and threw that, together with his buckler, at her; and all the rest following, she, being borne down and quite buried with the multitude of gold and their shields, died under the weight and pressure of them; Tarpeius also himself, being prosecuted by Romulus, was found guilty of treason. Tarpeia afterwards was buried there, and the hill from her was called Tarpeius, until the reign of King Tarquin, who dedicated the place to Jupiter, at which time her bones were removed, and so it lost her name, except only that part of the Capitol which they still called the Tarpeian Rock, from which they used to cast down malefactors.

The Sabines being possessed of the hill, Romulus, in great fury, bade them battle, and Tatius was confident to accept it, perceiving, if they were overpowered, that they had behind them a secure retreat. The level in the middle, where they were to join battle, being surrounded with many little hills seemed to enforce both parties to a sharp and desperate conflict, by reason of the difficulties of the place, which had but a few outlets, inconvenient either for refuge or pursuit. It happened, too, the river having over-

flowed not many days before, there was left behind in the
plain, where now the forum stands, a deep blind mud and
slime, which, though it did not appear much to the eye,
and was not easily avoided, at bottom was deceitful and
dangerous; upon which the Sabines being unwarily about
to enter, met with a piece of good fortune; for Curtius, a
gallant man, eager of honour, and of aspiring thoughts, being mounted on horseback, was galloping on before the rest,
and mired his horse here, and endeavouring for a while,
by whip and spur and voice to disentangle him, but finding
it impossible, quitted him and saved himself; the place from
him to this very time is called the Curtian Lake. The Sabines, having avoided this danger, began the fight very
smartly, the fortune of the day being very dubious, though
many were slain; amongst whom was Hostilius, who, they
say, was husband to Hersilia, and grandfather to that Hostilius who reigned after Numa. There were many other
brief conflicts, we may suppose, but the most memorable
was the last, in which Romulus having received a wound
on his head by a stone, and being almost felled to the
ground by it, and disabled, the Romans gave way, and, being driven out of the level ground, fled towards the Palatium. Romulus, by this time recovering from his wound a
little, turned about to renew the battle, and, facing the fliers,
with a loud voice encouraged them to stand and fight. But
being overborne with numbers, and nobody daring to face
about, stretching out his hands to heaven, he prayed to
Jupiter to stop the army, and not to neglect, but maintain
the Roman cause, now in extreme danger. The prayer was
no sooner made, than shame and respect for their king
checked many; the fears of the fugitives changed suddenly
into confidence. The place they first stood at was where
now is the temple of Jupiter Stator (which may be translated the Stayer); there they rallied again into ranks and
repulsed the Sabines to the place called now Regia, and to
the temple of Vesta; where both parties, preparing to begin
a second battle, were prevented by a spectacle, strange to
behold, and defying description. For the daughters of the
Sabines, who had been carried off, came running, in great

confusion, some on this side, some on that, with miserable cries and lamentations, like creatures possessed, in the midst of the army and among the dead bodies, to come at their husbands and their fathers, some with their young babes in their arms, others their hair loose about their ears, but all calling, now upon the Sabines, now upon the Romans, in the most tender and endearing words. Hereupon both melted into compassion, and fell back, to make room for them betwixt the armies. The sight of the women carried sorrow and commiseration upon both sides into the hearts of all, but still more their words, which began with expostulation and upbraiding, and ended with entreaty and supplication.

"Wherein," say they, "have we injured or offended you, as to deserve such sufferings past and present? We were ravished away unjustly and violently by those whose now we are; that being done, we were so long neglected by our fathers, our brothers and countrymen, that time, having now by the strictest bonds united us to those we once mortally hated, has made it impossible for us not to tremble at the danger and weep at the death of the very men who once used violence to us. You did not come to vindicate our honour, while we were virgins, against our assailants; but do come now to force away wives from their husbands and mothers from their children, a succour more grievous to its wretched objects than the former betrayal and neglect of them. Which shall we call the worst, their love-making or your compassion? If you were making war upon any other occasion, for our sakes you ought to withhold your hands from those to whom we have made you fathers-in-law and grandsires. If it be for our own cause, then take us, and with us your sons-in-law and grandchildren. Restore to us our parents and kindred, but do not rob us of our children and husbands. Make us not, we entreat you, twice captives." Hersilia having spoken many such words as these, and the others earnestly praying, a truce was made, and the chief officers came to a parley; the women, in the meantime, brought and presented their husbands and children to their fathers and brothers; gave those that wanted

meat and drink, and carried the wounded home to be cured,
and showed also how much they governed within doors,
and how indulgent their husbands were to them, in demean-
ing themselves towards them with all kindness and respect
imaginable. Upon this, conditions were agreed upon, that
what women pleased might stay where they were, exempt,
as aforesaid, from all drudgery and labour but spinning;
that the Romans and Sabines should inhabit the city together; that the city should be called Rome from Romulus;
but the Romans, Quirites, from the country of Tatius; and
that they both should govern and command in common.
The place of the ratification is still called Comitium, from
coire to meet.

The city being thus doubled in number, an hundred of
the Sabines were elected senators, and the legions were increased to six thousand foot and six hundred horse; then
they divided the people into three tribes: the first, from
Romulus, named Ramnenses; the second from Tatius, Ta-
tienses; the third Luceres, from the *lucus,* or grove, where
the Asylum stood, whither many fled for sanctuary, and
were received into the city. And that they were just three,
the very name of *tribe* and *tribune* seems to show; each
tribe contained ten curiae, or brotherhoods, which, some
say, took their names from the Sabine women; but that
seems to be false, because many had their names from var-
rious places. Though it is true, they then constituted many
things in honour to the women; as to give them the way
wherever they met them; to speak no ill word in their presence; not to appear naked before them, or else be liable to
prosecution before the judge, of homicide; that their children should wear an ornament about their necks called the
bulla (because it was like a bubble), and the *praetexta,* a
gown edged with purple.

The princes did not immediately join in council together,
but at first each met with his own hundred; afterwards all
assembled together. Tatius dwelt where now the temple of
Moneta stands, and Romulus close by the steps, as they
call them, of the Fair Shore, near the descent from the
Mount Palatine to the Circus Maximus. There, they say,

grew the holy cornel tree, of which they report, that Romulus once, to try his strength, threw a dart from the Aventine Mount, the staff of which was made of cornel, which struck so deep into the ground, that no one of many that tried could pluck it up, and the soil being fertile, gave nourishment to the wood, which sent forth branches, and produced a cornel stock of considerable bigness. This did posterity preserve and worship as one of the most sacred things; and therefore walled it about; and if to any one it appeared not green nor flourishing, but inclining to pine and wither, he immediately made outcry to all he met, and they, like people hearing of a house on fire, with one accord would cry for water, and run from all parts with buckets full to the place. But when Caius Caesar, they say, was repairing the steps about it, some of the labourers digging too close, the roots were destroyed, and the tree withered.

The Sabines adopted the Roman months, of which whatever is remarkable is mentioned in the Life of Numa. Romulus, on the other hand adopted their long shields, and changed his own armour and that of all the Romans, who before wore round targets of the Argive pattern. Feasts and sacrifices they partook of in common, not abolishing any which either nation observed before, and instituting several new ones; of which one was the Matronalia, instituted in honour of the women, for their extinction of the war.

They say, too, Romulus was the first that consecrated holy fire, and instituted holy virgins to keep it, called vestals; others ascribe it to Numa Pompilius; agreeing, however, that Romulus was otherwise eminently religious, and skilled in divination, and for that reason carried the *lituus,* a crooked rod with which soothsayers describe the quarters of the heavens, when they sit to observe the flights of birds. This of his, being kept in the Palatium, was lost when the city was taken by the Gauls; and afterwards, that barbarous people being driven out, was found in the ruins, under a great heap of ashes, untouched by the fire, all things about it being consumed and burnt. He instituted also certain laws, one of which is somewhat severe, which suffers not a wife to leave her husband, but grants a husband power to turn off his wife, either upon poisoning her children, or counterfeiting his keys, or for adultery; but if the husband upon any other occasion put her away, he ordered one moiety of his estate to be given to the wife, the other to fall to the goddess Ceres; and whoever cast off his wife, to make an atonement by sacrifice to the gods of the dead. This, too, is observable as a singular thing in Romulus, that he appointed no punishment for real parricide, but called all murder so, thinking the one an accursed thing, but the other a thing impossible; and, for a long time, his judgment seemed to have been right; for in almost six hundred years together, nobody committed the like in Rome; and Lucius Hostius, after the wars of Hannibal, is recorded to have been the first parricide. Let this much suffice concerning these matters.

In the fifth year of the reign of Tatius, some of his friend and kinsmen, meeting ambassadors coming from Laurentum to Rome, attempted on the road to take away their money by force, and, upon their resistance, killed them. So great a villainy having been committed Romulus thought the malefactors ought at once to be punished, but Tatius shuffled off and deferred the execution of it; and this one thing was the beginning of open quarrel betwixt them; in all other respects they were very careful of their conduct, and administered affairs together with great unanimity. The relations of the slain, being debarred of lawful satisfaction by reason of Tatius, fell upon him as he was sacrificing with Romulus at Lavinium and slew him; but escorted Romulus home, commending and extolling him for a just prince. Romulus took the body of Tatius, and buried it very splendidly in the Aventine Mount, near the place called Armilustrium, but altogether neglected revenging his murder. Some authors write, that the city of Laurentum, fearing the consequences, delivered up the murderers of Tatius; but Romulus dismissed them, saying one murder was requited with another. This gave occasion of talk and jealousy, as if he were well pleased at the removal of his co-partner in the government. Nothing of these things, however, raised any sort of feud or disturbance among the Sabines; but some out of love to him, others out of fear of his power, some again reverencing him as a god, they all continued living peacefully in admiration and awe of him; many foreign nations, too, showed respect to Romulus; the Ancient Latins sent and entered into league and confederacy with him. Fidenae he took, a neighbouring city to Rome, by a party of horse, as some say, whom he sent before with commands to cut down the hinges of the gates, himself afterwards unexpectedly coming up.

The Roman cause gathering strength, their weaker neighbours shrunk away, and were thankful to be left untouched; but the stronger, out of fear or envy, thought they ought not to give way to Romulus, but to curb and put a stop to his growing greatness. The first were the Veientes, a people of Tuscany, who had large possessions, and dwelt in a spacious city; they took occasion to commence a war, by claiming Fidenae as belonging to them; a thing not only very unreasonable, but very ridiculous, that they, who did not assist them in the greatest extremities, but permitted them to be slain, should challenge their lands and houses when in the hands of others. But being scornfully retorted upon by Romulus in his answers, they divided themselves into two bodies; with one they attacked the garrison of Fidenae, the other marched against Romulus; that which went against Fidenae got the victory, and slew two thousand Romans; the other was worsted by Romulus, with the loss of eight thousand men. A fresh battle was fought near Fidenae, and here all men acknowledge the day's success to have been chiefly the work of Romulus himself, who showed the highest skill as well as courage, and seemed to manifest a strength and swiftness more than human. But what some write, that of fourteen thousand that fell that day, above half were slain by Romulus's own hand, verges too near to fable, and is, indeed, simply incredible; since even the Messenians are thought to go too far in saying that Aritomenes three times offered sacrifice for the death of a hundred enemies, Lacedaemonians, slain by himself. The army being thus routed, Romulus, suffering those that were left to make

their escape, led his forces against the city; they, having
suffered such great losses, did not venture to oppose, but,
humbly suing to him, made a league and friendship for an
hundred years; surrendering also a large district of land
called Septempagium, that is, the seven parts, as also their
salt-works upon the river, and fifty noblemen for hostages.
He made his triumph for this on the Ides of October, leading, among the rest of his many captives, the general of the
Veientes, an elderly man, but who had not, it seemed, acted
with the prudence of age; whence even now, in sacrifices
for victories, they lead an old man through the marketplace
to the Capitol, apparelled in purple, with a *bulla,* or child's
toy, tied to it, and the crier cries, *Sardians to be sold;* for
the Tuscans are said to be a colony of the Sardians, and
the Veientes are a city of Tuscany.

This was the last battle Romulus ever fought; afterwards
he, as most, nay all men, very few excepted, do, who are
raised by great and miraculous good-haps of fortune to
power and greatness, so, I say, did he; relying upon his
own great actions, and growing of an haughtier mind, he
forsook his popular behaviour for kingly arrogance, odious
to the people; to whom in particular the state which he as-
sumed was hateful. For he dressed in scarlet, with the
purple-bordered robe over it; he gave audience on a couch
of state, having always about him some young men called
Celeres, from their swiftness in doing commissions; there
went before him others with staves, to make room, with
leather thongs tied on their bodies, to bind on the moment whoever he commanded. The Latins formerly used
ligare in the same sense as now *alligare,* to bind, whence
the name *lictors,* for these officers, and *bacula,* or staves,
for their rods, because staves were then used. It is probable,
however, they were first called *litores,* afterwards, by putting in a *c, lictores,* or, in Greek, *liturgi,* or people's officers, for *leïtos* is still Greek for the commons, and *laös* for
the people in general.

But when, after the death of his grandfather Numitor in
Alba, the throne devolving upon Romulus, he, to court the
people, put the government into their own hands, and ap-

pointed an annual magistrate over the Albans, this taught
the great men of Rome to seek after a free and anti-mo-
narchical state, wherein all might in turn be subjects and
rulers. For neither were the patricians any longer admitted
to state affairs, only had the name and title left them, con-
vening in council rather for fashion's sake than advice,
where they heard in silence the king's commands, and so
departed, exceeding the commonalty only in hearing first
what was done. These and the like were matters of small
moment; but when he of his own accord parted among his
soldiers what lands were acquired by war, and restored the
Veientes their hostages, the senate neither consenting nor
approving of it, then, indeed, he seemed to put a great affront upon them; so that, on his sudden and strange disappearance a short while after, the senate fell under suspicion
and calumny. He disappeared on the Nones of July, as they
now call the month which was then Quintilis, leaving nothing of certainty to be related of his death; only the time, as
just mentioned, for on that day many ceremonies are still
performed in representation of what happened. Neither is
this uncertainty to be thought strange, seeing the manner of
the death of Scipio Africanus, who died at his own home
after supper, has been found capable neither of proof or dis-
proof; for some say he died a natural death, being of a sickly
habit; others that he poisoned himself; others again, that
his enemies, breaking in upon him in the night stifled him.
Yet Scipio's dead body lay open to be seen of all, and any
one, from his own observation, might form his suspicions
and conjectures, whereas Romulus, when he vanished, left
neither the least part of his body, nor any remnant of his
clothes to be seen. So that some fancied the senators, having
fallen upon him in the temple of Vulcan, cut his body into
pieces, and took each a part away in his bosom; others
think his disappearance was neither in the temple of Vulcan, nor with the senators only by, but that it came to pass
that, as he was haranguing the people without the city, near
a place called the Goat's Marsh, on a sudden strange and
unaccountable disorders and alterations took place in the
air; the face of the sun was darkened, and the day turned

into night, and that, too, no quiet, peaceable night, but
with terrible thunderings, and boisterous winds from all
quarters; during which the common people dispersed and
fled, but the senators kept close together. The tempest being
over and the light breaking out, when the people gathered
again, they missed and inquired for their king; the senators
suffered them not to search, or busy themselves about the
matter, but commanded them to honour and worship Romulus as one taken up to the gods, and about to be to them,
in the place of a good prince, now a propitious god. The
multitude, hearing this, went away believing and rejoicing in hopes of good things from him; but there were some,
who, canvassing the matter in a hostile temper, accused
and aspersed the patricians, as men that persuaded the people to believe ridiculous tales, when they themselves were
the murderers of the king.

Things being in this disorder, one, they say, of the patricians, of noble family and approved good character, and a
faithful and familiar friend of Romulus himself, having
come with him from Alba, Julius Proculus by name, presented himself in the forum; and, taking a most sacred oath,
protested before them all, that, as he was travelling on the
road, he had seen Romulus coming to meet him, looking
taller and comelier than ever, dressed in shining and flaming armour; and he, being affrighted at the apparition, said,
"Why, O king, or for what purpose have you abandoned
us to unjust and wicked surmises, and the whole city to be-
reavement and endless sorrow?" and that he made answer,
"It pleased the gods, O Proculus, that we, who came from
them, should remain so long a time amongst men as we did;
and, having built a city to be the greatest in the world for
empire and glory, should again return to heaven. But farewell; and tell the Romans, that, by the exercise of temperance and fortitude, they shall attain the height of human
power; we will be to you the propitious god Quirinus." This
seemed credible to the Romans, upon the honesty and oath
of the relater, and indeed, too, there mingled with it a certain divine passion, some preternatural influence similar to

possession by a divinity; nobody contradicted it, but, laying aside all jealousies and detractions, they prayed to Quirinus and saluted him as a god.

This is like some of the Greek fables. And many such improbabilities do your fabulous writers relate, deifying creatures naturally mortal; for though altogether to disown a divine nature in human virtue were impious and base, so again, to mix heaven with earth is ridiculous. Let us believe with Pindar, that—

> "All human bodies yield to Death's decree,
> The soul survives to all eternity."

For that alone is derived from the gods, thence comes, and thither returns; not with the body, but when most disengaged and separated from it, and when most entirely pure and clean and free from the flesh: for the most perfect soul, says Heraclitus, is a dry light, which flies out of the body as lightning breaks from a cloud; but that which is clogged and surfeited with body is like gross and humid incense, slow to kindle and ascend. We must not, therefore, contrary to nature, send the bodies, too, of good men to heaven; but we must really believe that, according to their divine nature and law, their virtue and their souls are translated out of men into heroes, out of heroes into demi-gods, out of demi-gods, after passing, as in the rite of initiation, through a final cleansing and sanctification, and so freeing themselves from all that pertains to mortality and sense, are thus, not by human decree, but really and according to right reason, elevated into gods admitted thus to the greatest and most blessed perfection.

Romulus's surname Quirinus, some say, is equivalent to Mars; others, that he was so called because the citizens were called Quirites; others, because the ancients called a dart or spear Quiris; thus, the statue of Juno resting on a spear is called Quiritis, and the dart in the Regia is addressed as Mars, and those that were distinguished in war were usually presented with a dart; that, therefore, Romu-

lus being a martial god, or a god of darts, was called
Quirinus. A temple is certainly built to his honour on the
mount called from him Quirinalis.

The day he vanished on is called the Flight of the People and the Nones of the Goats, because they go then out
of the city and sacrifice at the Goat's Marsh, and, as they
go, they shout out some of the Roman names, as Marcus,
Lucius, Caius, imitating the way in which they then fled
and called upon one another in that fright and hurry. It
was in the fifty-fourth year of his age and the thirty-eighth of
his reign that Romulus, they tell us, left the world.

NUMA POMPILIUS

Though the pedigrees of noble families of Rome go back in exact form as far as Numa Pompilius, yet there is great diversity amongst historians concerning the time in which he reigned; a certain writer called Clodius, in a book of his entitled Strictures on Chronology, avers that the ancient registers of Rome were lost when the city was sacked by the Gauls, and that those which are now extant were counterfeited, to flatter and serve the humour of some men who wished to have themselves derived from some ancient and noble lineage, though in reality with no claim to it. And though it be commonly reported that Numa was a scholar and a familiar acquaintance of Pythagoras, yet it is again contradicted by others, who affirm that he was acquainted with neither the Greek language nor learning, and that he was a person of natural talent and ability as of himself to attain to virtue, or else that he found some barbarian instructor superior to Pythagoras. Some affirm, also, that Pythagoras was not contemporary with Numa, but lived at least five generations after him; and that some other Pythagoras, a native of Sparta, who, in the sixteenth Olympiad, in the third year of which Numa became king, won a prize at the Olympic race, might, in his travel through Italy, have gained acquaintance with Numa, and assisted him in the constitution of his kingdom; whence it comes that many Laconian laws and customs appear amongst the Roman institutions. Yet, in any case, Numa was descended of the Sabines, who declare themselves to be a colony of the Lacedaemonians. And chronology, in general, is uncertain; especially when fixed by the lists of victors in the Olympic games, which were published at a late period by Hippias the Elean, and rest on no positive authority. Commencing, however, at a convenient point, we will proceed to give the most noticeable events that are recorded of the life of Numa.

It was the thirty-seventh year, counted from the foundation of Rome, when Romulus, then reigning, did, on the fifth day of the month of July, call the Caprotine None, offer a public sacrifice at the Goat's Marsh, in presence of the senate and people of Rome. Suddenly the sky was darkened, a thick cloud of storm and rain settled on the earth; the common people fled in affright, and were dispersed; and in this whirlwind Romulus disappeared, his body being never found either living or dead. A foul suspicion presently attached to the patricians, and rumours were current among the people as if that they, weary of kingly government, and exasperated of late by the imperious deportment of Romulus towards them, had plotted against his life and made him away, that so they might assume the authority and government into their own hands. This suspicion they sought to turn aside by decreeing divine honours to Romulus, as to one not dead but translated to a higher condition. And Proculus, a man of note, took oath that he saw Romulus caught up into heaven in his arms and vestments, and heard him, as he ascended, cry out that they should hereafter style him by the name of Quirinus.

This trouble, being appeased, was followed by another, about the election of a new king; for the minds of the original Romans and the new inhabitants were not as yet grown into that perfect unity of temper, but that there were diversities of factions amongst the commonalty and jealousies and emulations amongst the senators; for though all agreed that it was necessary to have a king, yet what person or of which nation was matter of dispute. For those who had been builders of the city with Romulus, and had already yielded a share of their lands and dwellings to the Sabines, were indignant at any pretension on their part to rule over their benefactors. On the other side, the Sabines could plausibly allege, that, at their king Tatius's decease, they had peaceably submitted to the sole command of Romulus; so now their turn was come to have a king chosen out of their own nation; nor did they esteem themselves to have combined with the Romans as inferiors, nor to have contributed less than they to the increase of Rome, which, without their numbers and association, could scarcely have merited the name of a city.

Thus did both parties argue and dispute their cause; but lest meanwhile discord, in the absence of all command, should occasion general confusion, it was agreed that the hundred and fifty senators should interchangeably execute the office of supreme magistrate, and each in succession, with the ensigns of royalty, should offer the solemn sacrifices and despatch public business for the space of six hours by day and six by night; which vicissitude and equal distribution of power would preclude all rivalry amongst the senators and envy from the people, when they should behold one, elevated to the degree of a king, levelled within the space of a day to the condition of a private citizen. This form of government is termed, by the Romans, interregnum. Nor yet could they, by this plausible and modest way of rule, escape suspicion and clamour of the vulgar, as though they were changing the form of government to an oligarchy, and designing to keep the supreme power in a sort of wardship under themselves, without ever proceeding to choose a king. Both parties came at length to the conclusion that the one should choose a king out of the body of the other; the Romans make a choice of a Sabine, or the Sabines name a Roman; this was esteemed the best expedient to put an end to all party spirit, and the prince who should be chosen would have an equal affection to the one party as his electors and to the other as his kinsmen. The Sabines remitted the choice to the original Romans, and they, too, on their part, were more inclinable to receive a Sabine king elected by themselves than to see a Roman exalted by the Sabines. Consultations being accordingly held, they named Numa Pompilius, of the Sabine race, a person of that high reputation for excellence, that, though he were not actually residing at Rome, yet he was no sooner nominated than accepted by the Sabines, with acclamation almost greater than that of the electors themselves.

The choice being declared and made known to the people, principal men of both parties were appointed to visit and entreat him, that he would accept the administration of the government. Numa resided at a famous city of the Sabines called Cures, whence the Romans and Sabines gave themselves the joint name of Quirites. Pomponius, an illustrious person, was his father, and he the youngest of his four sons, being (as it had been divinely ordered) born on the twenty-first day of April, the day of the foundation of Rome. He was endued with a soul rarely tempered by nature, and disposed to virtue, which he had yet more subdued by discipline, a severe life, and the study of philosophy; means which had not only succeeded in expelling the baser passions, but also the violent and rapacious temper which barbarians are apt to think highly of; true bravery, in his judgment, was regarded as consisting in the subjugation of our passions by reason.

He banished all luxury and softness from his own home, and while citizens alike and strangers found in him an incorruptible judge and counsellor, in private he devoted himself not to amusement or lucre, but to the worship of the immortal gods, and rational contemplation of their divine power and nature. So famous was he, that Tatius, the colleague of Romulus, chose him for his son-in-law, and gave him his only daughter, which, however, did not stimulate his vanity to desire to dwell with his father-in-law at Rome; he rather chose to inhabit with his Sabines, and cherish his own father in his old age; and Tatia, also, preferred the private conditions of her husband before the honours and splendour she might have enjoyed with her father. She is said to have died after she had been married thirteen years, and then Numa, leaving the conversation of the town, betook himself to a country life, and in a solitary manner frequented the groves and fields consecrated to the gods, passing his life in desert places. And this in particular gave occasion to the story about the goddess, namely, that Numa did not retire from human society out of any melancholy or disorder of mind, but because he had tasted the joys of more elevated intercourse, and, admitted to celestial wedlock in the love and converse of the goddess Egeria, had attained to blessedness, and to a divine wisdom.

The story evidently resembles those very ancient fables which the Phrygians have received and still recount of Attis, the Bithynians of Herodotus, the Arcadians of Endymion, not to mention several others who were thought blessed and beloved of the gods; nor does it seem strange if God, a lover, not of horses or birds, but men, should not disdain to dwell with the virtuous and converse with the wise and temperate soul, though it be altogether hard, indeed, to believe, that any god or daemon is capable of a sensual or bodily love and passion for any human form or beauty. Though, indeed, the wise Egyptians do not plausibly make the distinction, that it may be possible for a divine spirit so to apply itself to the nature of a woman, as to inbreed in her the first beginnings of generation, while on the other side they conclude it impossible for the male kind to have any intercourse or mixture by the body with any divinity, not considering, however, that what takes place on the one side must also take place on the other; intermixture, by force of terms, is reciprocal. Not that it is otherwise than befitting to suppose that the gods feel towards men affection, and love, in the sense of affection, and in the form of care and solicitude for their virtue and their good dispositions. And, therefore, it was no error of those who feigned, that Phorbas, Hyacinthus, and Admetus were beloved by Apollo; or that Hippolytus the Sicyonian was so much in his favour, that, as often as he sailed from Sicyon to Cirrha, the Pythian prophetess uttered this heroic verse expressive of the god's attention and joy:

"Now doth Hippolytus return again,
    And venture his dear life upon the main."

It is reported, also, that Pan became enamoured of Pindar for his verses, and the divine power rendered honour to Hesiod and Archilochus after their death for the sake of the Muses; there is a statement, also, that Aesculapius sojourned with Sophocles in his lifetime, of which many proofs still exist, and that, when he was dead, another deity took care for his funeral rites. And so if any credit may be given to these instances, why should we judge it incongruous, that a like spirit of the gods should visit Zaleucus, Minos, Zoroaster, Lycurgus, and Numa, the controllers of kingdoms, and the legislators for commonwealths? Nay, it may be reasonable to believe, that the gods, with a serious purpose, assist at the councils and serious debates of such men, to inspire and direct them; and visit poets and musicians, if at all in their more sportive moods; but for difference of opinion here, as Bacchylides said, "the road is broad." For there is no absurdity in the account also given, that Lycurgus and Numa, and other famous lawgivers, having the task of subduing perverse and refractory multitudes, and of introducing great innovations, themselves made this pretension to divine authority, which, if not true, assuredly was expedient for the interests of those it imposed upon.

Numa was about forty years of age when the ambassadors came to make him offers of the kingdom; the speakers were Proculus and Velesus, one or other of whom it had been thought the people would elect as their new king; the original Romans being for Proculus, and the Sabines for Velesus. Their speech was very short, supposing that, when they came to tender a kingdom, there needed little to persuade to an acceptance; but, contrary to their expectations, they found that they had to use many reasons and entreaties to induce one, that lived in peace and quietness, to accept the government of a city whose foundation and increase had been made, in a manner, in war. In presence of his father and his kinsman Marcius, he returned answer that "Every alteration of a man's life is dangerous to him; but madness only could induce one who needs nothing, and is satisfied with everything, to quit a life he is accustomed to; which, whatever else it is deficient in, at any rate has the advantage of certainty over one wholly doubtful and unknown. Though, indeed, the difficulties of this government cannot even be called unknown; Romulus, who first held it, did not escape the suspicion of having plotted against the life of his colleague Tatius; nor the senate the like accusation, of having treasonably murdered Romulus. Yet Romulus had the advantage to be thought divinely born and miraculously preserved and nurtured. My birth was mortal; I was reared and instructed by men that are known to you. The very points of my character that are most commended mark me as unfit to reign,—love of retirement and of studies inconsistent with business, a passion that has become inveterate in me for peace, for unwarlike occupations, and for the society of men whose meetings are but those of worship and of kindly intercourse, whose lives in general are spent upon their farms and their pastures. I should but be, methinks, a laughing-stock, while I should go about to inculcate the worship of the gods and give lessons in the love of justice and the abhorrence of violence and war, to a city whose needs are rather for a captain than for a king."

The Romans, perceiving by these words that he was declining to accept the kingdom, were the more instant and urgent with him that he would not forsake and desert them in this condition, and suffer them to relapse, as they must, into their former sedition and civil discord, there being no person on whom both parties could accord but on himself. And, at length, his father and Marcius, taking him aside, persuaded him to accept a gift so noble in itself, and tendered to him rather from heaven than from men. "Though," said they, "you neither desire riches, being content with what you have, nor court the fame of authority, as having already the more valuable fame of virtue, yet you will consider that government itself is a service of God, who now calls out into action your qualities of justice and wisdom, which were not meant to be left useless and unemployed. Cease, therefore, to avoid and turn your back upon an office which, to a wise man, is a field for great and honourable actions, for the magnificent worship of the gods, and for the introduction of habits of piety, which authority alone can effect amongst a people. Tatius, though a foreigner, was beloved, and the memory of Romulus has received divine honours; and who knows but that this people, being victorious, may be satiated with war, and, content with the trophies and spoils they have acquired, may be, above all things, desirous to have a pacific and justice-loving prince to lead them to good order and quiet? But if, indeed, their desires are uncontrollably and madly set on war, were it not better, then, to have the reins held by such a moderating hand as is able to divert the fury another way, and that your native city and the whole Sabine nation should possess in you a bond of goodwill and friendship with this young and growing power?"

With these reasons and persuasions several auspicious omens are said to have concurred, and the zeal, also, of his fellow-citizens, who, on understanding what message the Roman ambassadors had brought him, entreated him to accompany them, and to accept the kingdom as a means to unanimity and concord between the nations.

Numa, yielding to these inducements, having first performed divine sacrifice, proceeded to Rome, being met in his way by the senate and people, who, with an impatient desire, came forth to receive him; the women, also, welcomed him with joyful acclamations, and sacrifices were offered for him in all the temples, and so universal was the joy, that they seemed to be receiving, not a new king, but a new kingdom. In this manner he descended into the forum, where Spurius Vettius, whose turn it was to be interrex at that hour, put it to the vote; and all declared him king. Then the regalities and robes of authority were brought to him; but he refused to be invested with them until he had first consulted and been confirmed by the gods; so being accompanied by the priests and augurs, he ascended the Capitol, which at that time the Romans called the Tarpeian Hill. Then the chief of the augurs covered Numa's head, and turned his face towards the south, and, standing behind him, laid his right hand on his head, and prayed, turning his eyes every way, in expectation of some auspicious signal from the gods. It was wonderful, meantime, with what silence and devotion the multitude stood assembled in the forum, in similar expectation and suspense, till auspicious birds appeared and passed on the right. Then Numa, apparelling himself in his royal robes, descended from the hill to the people, by whom he was received and congratulated with shouts and acclamations of welcome, as a holy king, and beloved of all the gods.

The first thing he did at his entrance into government was to dismiss the band of three hundred men which had been Romulus's life-guard, called by him Celeres, saying that he would not distrust those who put confidence in him; nor rule over a people that distrusted him. The next thing he did was to add to the two priests of Jupiter and Mars a third in honour of Romulus, whom he called the Flamen Quirinalis. The Romans anciently called their priests Flamines, by corruption of the word Pilamines, from a certain cap which they wore, called Pileus. In those times Greek words were more mixed with the Latin than at present; thus also the royal robe, which is called Laena, Juba says, is the same as the Greek Chlaena; and that the name of Camillus, given to the boy with both his parents living, who serves in the temple of Jupiter, was taken from the name given by some Greeks to Mercury, denoting his office of attendance on the gods.

When Numa had, by such measures, won the favour and affection of the people, he set himself without delay to the task of bringing the hard and iron Roman temper to somewhat more of gentleness and equity. Plato's expression of a city in high fever was never more applicable than to Rome at that time; in its origin formed by daring and warlike spirits, whom bold and desperate adventure brought thither from every quarter, it had found in perpetual wars and incursions on its neighbours its after sustenance and means of growth, and in conflict with danger the source of new strength; like piles, which the blows of the hammer

serve to fix into the ground. Wherefore Numa, judging it
no slight undertaking to mollify and bend to peace the presumptuous and stubborn spirits of this people, began to
operate upon them with the sanctions of religion. He sacrificed often and used processions and religious dances, in
which most commonly he officiated in person; by such
combinations of solemnity with refined and humanising
pleasures, seeking to win over and mitigate their fiery and
warlike tempers. At times, also, he filled their imaginations
with religious terrors, professing that strange apparitions
had been seen, and dreadful voices heard; thus subduing and
humbling their minds by a sense of supernatural fears.

This method which Numa used made it believed that he
had been much conversant with Pythagoras; for in the philosophy of the one, as in the policy of the other, man's relations to the deity occupy a great place. It is said, also, that
the solemnity of his exterior garb and gestures was adopted
by him from the same feeling with Pythagoras. For it is
said of Pythagoras, that he had taught an eagle to come
at his call, and stoop down to him in his flight; and that, as
he passed among the people assembled at the Olympic
games, he showed them his golden thigh; besides many
other strange and miraculous seeming practices, on which
Timon the Philasian wrote the distich—

"Who, of the glory of a juggler proud,
    With solemn talk imposed upon the crowd."

In like manner Numa spoke of a certain goddess or
mountain nymph that was in love with him, and met him
in secret, as before related; and professed that he entertained familiar conversation with the Muses, to whose
teaching he ascribed the greatest part of his revelations;
and amongst them, above all, he recommended to the ven-
eration of the Romans one in particular, whom he named
Tacita, the silent; which he did perhaps in imitation and honour of the Pythagorean silence. His opinion, also, of images
is very agreeable to the doctrine of Pythagoras; who con-

ceived of the first principle of being as transcending sense and passion, invisible and incorrupt, and only to be apprehended by abstract intelligence. So Numa forbade the Romans to represent God in the form of man or beast, nor was there any painted or graven image of a deity admitted amongst them for the space of the first hundred and seventy years, all of which time their temples and chapels were kept free and pure from images; to such baser objects they deemed it impious to liken the highest, and all access to God impossible, except by the pure act of the intellect. His sacrifices, also, had great similitude to the ceremonial of Pythagoras, for they were not celebrated with effusion of blood, but consisted of flour, wine, and the least costly offerings. Other external proofs, too, are urged to show the connection Numa had with Pythagoras. The comic writer Epicharmus, an ancient author, and of the school of Pythagoras, in a book of his dedicated to Antenor, records that Pythagoras was made a freeman of Rome. Again, Numa gave to one of his four sons the name of Mamercus, which was the name of one of the sons of Pythagoras; from whence, as they say, sprang that ancient patrician family of the Aemilli, for that the king gave him in sport the surname of Aemilius, for his engaging and graceful manner in speaking. I remember, too, that when I was at Rome, I heard many say, that, when the oracle directed two statues to be raised, one to the wisest and another to the most valiant man in Greece, they erected two of brass, one representing Alcibiades, and the other Pythagoras.

But to pass by these matters, which are full of uncertainty and not so important as to be worth our time to insist on them, the original constitution of the priests, called Pontifices, is ascribed unto Numa, and he himself was, it is said, the first of them; and that they have the name of Pontifices from *potens*, powerful, because they attend the service of the gods, who have power to command over all. Others make the word refer to exceptions of impossible cases; the priests were to perform all the duties possible to them; if anything lay beyond their power, the exception was not to be cavilled at. The most common opinion is the most absurd, which derives this word from *pons*, and assigns the priests the title of bridge-makers. The sacrifices performed on the bridge were amongst the most sacred and ancient, and the keeping and repairing of the bridge attached, like any other public sacred office, to the priesthood. It was accounted not simply unlawful, but a positive sacrilege, to pull down the wooden bridge; which moreover is said, in obedience to an oracle, to have been built entirely of timber and fastened with wooden pins, without nails or cramps of iron. The stone bridge was built a very long time after when Aemilius was quaestor, and they do, indeed, say also that the wooden bridge was not so old as Numa's time, but was finished by Ancus Marcius, when he was king, who was the grandson of Numa by his daughter.

The office of Pontifex Maximus, or chief priest, was to declare and interpret the divine law, or rather, to preside over sacred rites; he not only prescribed rules for public ceremony, but regulated the sacrifices of private persons, not suffering them to vary from established custom, and giving information to every one of what was requisite for purposes of worship or supplication. He was also guardian of the vestal virgins, the institution of whom, and of their perpetual fire, was attributed to Numa, who, perhaps, fancied the charge of pure and uncorrupted flames would be fitly intrusted to chaste and unpolluted persons, or that fire, which consumes, but produces nothing, bears an analogy to the virgin estate. In Greece, wherever a perpetual holy fire is kept, as at Delphi and Athens, the charge of it is committed, not to virgins, but widows past the time of marriage. And in case by any accident it should happen that this fire became extinct, as the holy lamp was at Athens under the tyranny of Aristion, and at Delphi, when that temple was burnt by the Medes, as also in the time of the Mithridatic and Roman civil war, when not only the fire was extinguished, but the altar demolished, then, afterwards, in kindling this fire again, it was esteemed an impiety to light it from common sparks or flame, or from anything but the pure and unpolluted rays of the sun, which they usually effect by concave mirrors, of a figure formed by the revolution of an isosceles rectangular triangle, all the lines from the circumference of which meeting in a centre, by holding it in the light of the sun they can collect and concentrate all its rays at this one point of convergence; where the air will now become rarefied, and any light, dry, combustible matter will kindle as soon as applied, under the effect of the rays, which here acquired the substance and active force of fire. Some are of opinion that these vestals had no other business than the preservation of this fire; but others conceive that they were keepers of other divine secrets concealed from all but themselves, of which we have told all that may lawfully be asked or told, in the life of Camillus. Gegania and Verenia, it is recorded, were the names of the first two virgins consecrated and ordained by Numa; Canuleia and Tarpeia succeeded; Servius afterwards added two, and the number of four has continued to the present time.

The statutes prescribed by Numa for the vestals were these: that they should take a vow of virginity for the space of thirty years, the first ten of which they were to spend in learning their duties, the second ten in performing them, and the remaining ten in teaching and instructing others. Thus the whole term being completed, it was lawful for them to marry, and, leaving the sacred order, to choose any condition of life that pleased them; but this permission few, as they say, made use of; and in cases where they did so, it was observed that their change was not a happy one, but accompanied ever after with regret and melancholy; so that the greater number, from religious fears and scruples, forbore, and continued to old age and death in the strict observance of a single life.

For this condition he compensated by great privileges and prerogatives; as that they had power to make a will in the lifetime of their father; that they had a free administration of their own affairs without guardian or tutor, which was the privilege of women who were the mothers of three children; when they go abroad, they have the fasces carried before them; and if in their walks they chance to meet a criminal on his way to execution, it saves his life, upon oath made that the meeting was an accidental one, and not concerted or of set purpose. Any one who presses upon the chair on which they are carried, is put to death. If these vestals commit any minor fault, they are punishable by the high priest only, who scourges the offender, sometimes with her clothes off, in a dark place, with a curtain drawn between; but she that has broken her vow is buried alive near the gate called Collina, where a little mound of earth stands, inside the city, reaching some little distance, called in Latin *agger;* under it a narrow room is constructed, to which a descent is made by stairs; here they prepare a bed, and light a lamp, and leave a small quantity of victuals, such as bread, water, a pail of milk, and some oil; that so that body which had been consecrated and devoted to the most sacred service of religion might not be said to perish by such a death as famine. The culprit herself is put in a litter, which they cover over, and tie her down with cords on it, so that nothing she utters may be heard. They then take her to the forum; all people silently go out of the way as she passes, and such as follow accompany the bier with solemn and speechless sorrow; and indeed, there is not any spectacle more appalling, nor any day observed by the city with greater appearance of gloom and sadness. When they come to the place of execution, the officers loose the cords, and then the high priest, lifting his hands to heaven, pronounces certain prayers to himself before the act; then he brings out the prisoner, being still covered, and placing her upon the steps that lead down to the cell, turns away his face with the rest of the priests; the stairs are drawn up after she has gone down, and a quantity of earth is heaped up over the entrance to the cell, so as to prevent it from being distinguished from the rest of the mound. This is the punishment of those who break their vow of virginity.

It is said, also, that Numa built the temple of Vesta,

which was intended for a repository of the holy fire, of a circular form, not to represent the figure of the earth, as if that were the same as Vesta, but that of the general universe, in the center of which the Pythagoreans place the element of fire, and give it the name of Vesta and the unit; and do not hold that the earth is immovable, or that it is situated in the centre of the globe, but that it keeps a circular motion about the seat of fire, and is not in the number of the primary elements; in this agreeing with the opinion of Plato, who, they say, in his later life, conceived that the earth held a lateral position, and that the central and sovereign space was reserved for some nobler body.

There was yet a farther use of the priests, and that was to give people directions in the national usages at funeral rites. Numa taught them to regard these offices, not as a pollution, but as a duty paid to the gods below, into whose hands the better part of us is transmitted; especially they were to worship the goddess Libitina, who presided over all the ceremonies performed at burials; whether they meant hereby Proserpina, or, as the most learned of the Romans conceive, Venus, not inaptly attributing the beginning and end of man's life to the agency of one and the same deity. Numa also prescribed rules for regulating the days of mourning, according to certain times and ages. As, for example, a child of three years was not to be mourned for at all; one older, up to ten years, for as many months as it was years old; and the longest time of mourning for any person whatsoever was not to exceed the term of ten months; which was the time appointed for women that lost their husbands to continue in widowhood. If any married again before that time, by the laws of Numa, she was to sacrifice a cow big with calf.

Numa, also, was founder of several other orders of priests, two of which I shall mention, the Salii and the Fecials, which are among the clearest proofs of the devoutness and sanctity of his character. These Fecials, or guardians of peace, seem to have had their name from their office, which was to put a stop to disputes by conference and speech; for it was not allowable to take up arms until they had declared all hopes of accommodation to be at an end, for in Greek, too, we call it peace when disputes are settled by words, and not by force. The Romans commonly despatched the Fecials, or heralds, to those who had offered them injury, requesting satisfaction; and, in case they refused, they then called the gods to witness, and, with imprecations upon themselves and their country should they be acting unjustly, so declared war; against their will, or without their consent, it was lawful neither for soldier nor king to take up arms; the war was begun with them, and when they had first handed it over to the commander as a just quarrel, then his business was to deliberate of the manner and ways to carry it on. It is believed that the slaughter and destruction which the Gauls made of the Romans was a judgment on the city for neglect of this religious proceeding; for that when these barbarians besieged the Clusinians, Fabius Ambustus was despatched to their camp to negotiate peace for the besieged; and, on their returning a rude refusal, Fabius imagined that his office of ambassador was at an end, and, rashly engaging on the side of the Clusinians, challenged the bravest of the enemy to a single combat. It was the fortune of Fabius to kill his adversary, and to take his spoils; but when the Gauls discovered it, they sent a herald to Rome to complain against him; since, before war was declared, he had, against the law of nations, made a breach of the peace. The matter being debated in the senate, the Fecials were of opinion that Fabius ought to be consigned into the hands of the Gauls; but he, being forewarned of their judgment, fled to the people, by whose protection and favour he escaped the sentence. On this, the Gauls marched with their army to Rome, where having taken the capitol, they sacked the city. The particulars of all which are fully given in the history of Camillus.

The origin of the Salii is this. In the eighth year of the reign of Numa, a terrible pestilence, which traversed all Italy, ravaged likewise the city of Rome; and the citizens being in distress and despondent, a brazen target, they say, fell from heaven into the hands of Numa, who gave them this marvellous account of it: that Egeria and the Muses had assured him it was sent from heaven for the cure and safety of the city, and that, to keep it secure, he was ordered by them to make eleven others, so like in dimensions and form to the original that no thief should be able to distinguish the true from the counterfeit. He farther declared, that he was commanded to consecrate to the Muses the place, and the fields about it, where they had been chiefly wont to meet with him, and that the spring which watered the fields should be hallowed for the use of the vestal virgins, who were to wash and cleanse the penetralia of their sanctuary with those holy waters. The truth of all which was speedily verified by the cessation of the pestilence. Numa displayed the target to the artificers and bade them show their skill in making others like it; all despaired, until at length one Mamurius Veturius, an excellent workman, happily hit upon it, and made all so exactly the same that Numa himself was at a loss and could not distinguish. The keeping of these targets was committed to the charge of certain priests, called Salii, who did not receive their name, as some tell the story, from Salius, a dancing-master, born in Samothrace, or at Mantinea, who taught the way of dancing in arms; but more truly from that jumping dance which the Salii themselves use, when in the month of March they carry the sacred targets through the city; at which procession they are habited in short frocks of purple, girt with a broad belt studded with brass; on their heads they wear a brass helmet, and carry in their hands short daggers, which they clash every now and then against the targets. But the chief thing is the dance itself. They move with much grace, performing, in quick time and close order, various intricate figures, with a great display of strength and agility. The targets were called Ancilia from their form; for they are not made round, nor like proper targets, of a complete circumference, but are cut out into a wavy line, the ends of which are rounded off and turned in at the thickest part towards each other; so that their shape is curvilinear, or, in Greek, *ancylon;* or the name may come from *ancon,* the elbow, on which they are carried. Thus Juba writes, who is eager to make it Greek. But it might be, for that matter, from its having come down *ane-cathen,* from above; or from its *akesis,* or cure of diseases; or *auchmon lysis,* because it put an end to a drought; or from its *anaschesis,* or relief from calamities, which is the origin of the Athenian name Anaces, given to Castor and Pollux; if we must, that is, reduce it to Greek. The reward which Mamurius received for his art was to be mentioned and commemorated in the verses which the Salii sang, as they danced in their arms through the city; though some will have it that they do not say Veturium Mamuium, but Veterem Memoriam, ancient remembrance.

After Numa had in this manner instituted these several orders of priests, he erected, near the temple of Vesta, what is called to this day Regia, or king's house, where he spent the most part of his time performing divine service, instructing the priests, or conversing with them on sacred subjects. He had another house upon the Mount Quirinalis, the site of which they show to this day. In all public processions and solemn prayers, criers were sent before to give notice to the people that they should forbear their work, and rest. They say that the Pythagoreans did not allow people to worship and pray to their gods by the way, but would have them go out from their houses direct, with their minds set upon the duty, and Numa, in like manner, wished that his citizens should neither see nor hear any religious service in a perfunctory and inattentive manner, but, laying aside all other occupations, should apply their minds to religion as to a most serious business; and that the streets should be free from all noises and cries that accompany manual labour, and clear for the sacred solemnity. Some traces of this custom remain at Rome to this day, for, when the consul begins to take auspices or do sacrifice, they call out to the people, *Hoc age,* Attend to this, whereby the auditors then present are admonished to compose and recollect themselves. Many other of his precepts resemble those of the Pythagoreans. The Pythagoreans said, for example, "Thou shalt not make a peck-measure thy seat to sit on. Thou shalt not stir the fire with a sword. When thou goest out upon a journey, look not behind thee. When thou sacrificest to the celestial gods, let it be with an odd number, and when to the terrestrial, with even." The significance of each of which precepts they would not commonly disclose. So some of Numa's traditions have no obvious meaning. "Thou shalt not make libation to the gods of wine from an unpruned vine. No sacrifices shall be performed without meal. Turn round to pay adoration to the gods; sit after you have worshipped." The first two directions seem to denote the cultivation and subduing of the earth as a part of religion; and as to the turning which the worshippers are to use in divine adoration, it is said to represent the rotatory motion of the world. But, in my opinion, the meaning rather is, that the worshipper, since the temples front the east, enters with his back to the rising sun; there, faces round to the east, and so turns back to the god of the temple, by this circular movement referring the fulfilment of his prayers to both divinities. Unless, indeed, this change of posture may have a mystical meaning, like the Egyptian wheels, and signify to us the instability of human fortune, and that, in whatever way God changes and turns our lot and condition, we should rest contented, and accept it as right and fitting. They say, also, that the sitting after worship was to be by way of omen of their petitions being granted, and the blessing they asked assured to them. Again, as different courses of actions are divided by intervals of rest, they might seat themselves after the completion of what they had done, to seek favour of the gods for beginning something else. And this would very well suit with what we had before; the lawgiver wants to habituate us to make our petitions to the deity not by the way, and, as it were, in a hurry, when we have other things to do, but with time and leisure to attend to it. By such discipline and schooling in religion, the city passed insensibly into such a submissiveness of temper, and stood in such awe and reverence of the virtue of Numa, that they received, with an undoubted assurance, whatever he delivered though never so fabulous, and thought nothing incredible or impossible from him.

There goes a story that he once invited a great number of citizens to an entertainment, at which the dishes in which the meat was served were very homely and plain, and the repast itself poor and ordinary fare; the guests seated, he began to tell them that the goddess that consulted with him was then at that time come to him; when on a sudden the room was furnished with all sorts of costly drinking-vessels, and the tables loaded with rich meats, and a most sumptuous entertainment. But the dialogue which is reported to have passed between him and Jupiter surpasses all the fabulous legends that were ever invented. They say that before Mount Aventine was inhabited or enclosed within the walls of the city, two demigods, Picus and Faunus, frequented the springs and thick shades of that place; which might be two satyrs, or Pans except that they went about Italy playing the same sorts of tricks, by skill in drugs and magic, as are ascribed by the Greeks to the Dactyli of Mount Ida. Numa contrived one day to surprise these demigods, by mixing wine and honey in the waters of the spring of which they usually drank. On finding themselves ensnared, they changed themselves into various shapes, dropping their own form and assuming every kind of unusual and hideous appearance; but when they saw they were safely entrapped, and in no possibility of getting free, they revealed to him many secrets and future events; and particularly a charm for thunder and lightning, still in use, performed with onions and hair and pilchards. Some say they did not tell him the charm, but by their magic brought down Jupiter out of heaven; and that he then, in an angry manner answering the inquiries, told Numa, that, if he would charm the thunder and lightning, he must do it with heads. "How," said Numa, "with the heads of onions?" "No," replied Jupiter, "of men." But Numa, willing to elude the cruelty of this receipt, turned it another way, saying, "Your meaning is, the hairs of men's heads." "No," replied Jupiter, "with living"—"pilchards," said Numa, interrupting him. These answers he had learnt from Egeria. Jupiter returned again to heaven, pacified and *ileos,* or propitious. The place was, in remembrance of him, called Ilicium, from this Greek word; and the spell in this manner effected.

These stories, laughable as they are, show us the feelings which people then, by force of habit, entertained towards the deity. And Numa's own thoughts are said to have been fixed to that degree on divine objects, that he once, when a message was brought to him that "Enemies are approaching," answered with a smile, "And I am sacrificing." It was he, also, that built the temples of Faith and Terminus, and taught the Romans that the name of Faith was the most solemn oath that they could swear. They still use it; and to the god Terminus, or Boundary, they offer to this day both public and private sacrifices, upon the borders and stone-marks of their land; living victims now, though anciently those sacrifices were solemnised without blood; for Numa reasoned that the god of boundaries, who watched over peace, and testified to fair dealing, should have no concern with blood. It is very clear that it was this king who first prescribed bounds to the territory of Rome; for Romulus would but have openly betrayed how much he had encroached on his neighbours' lands, had he ever set limits to his own; for boundaries are, indeed, a defence to those who choose to observe them, but are only a testimony against the dishonesty of those who break through them. The truth is, the portion of lands which the Romans possessed at the beginning was very narrow, until Romulus enlarged them by war; all those acquisitions Numa now divided amongst the indigent commonalty, wishing to do away with that extreme want which is a compulsion to dishonesty, and, by turning the people to husbandry, to bring them, as well as their lands, into better order. For there is no employment that gives so keen and quick a relish for peace as husbandry and a country life, which leave in men all that kind of courage that makes them ready to fight in defence of their own, while it destroys the licence that breaks out into acts of injustice and rapacity. Numa, therefore, hoping agriculture would be a sort of charm to captivate the affections of his people to peace, and viewing it rather as a means to moral than to economical profit, divided all the lands into several parcels, to which he gave the name of *pagus,* or parish, and over every one of them he ordained chief overseers; and, taking a delight sometimes to inspect his colonies in person, he formed his judgment of every man's habits by the results; of which being witness himself, he preferred those to honours and employments who had done well, and by rebukes and reproaches incited the indolent and careless to improvement. But of all his measures the most commended was his distribution of the people by their trades into companies or guilds; for as the city consisted, or rather did not consist of, but was divided into, two different tribes, the diversity between which could not be effaced and in the meantime prevented all unity and caused perpetual tumult and ill-blood, reflecting how hard substances that do not readily mix when in the lump may, by being beaten into powder, in that minute form be combined, he resolved to divide the whole population into a number of small divisions, and thus hoped, by introducing other distinctions, to obliterate the original and great distinction, which would be lost among the smaller. So, distinguishing the whole people by the several arts and trades, he formed the companies of musicians, goldsmiths, carpenters, dyers, shoemakers, skinners, braziers, and potters; and all other handicraftsmen he composed and reduced into a single company, appointing every one their proper courts, councils, and religious observances. In this manner all factious distinctions began, for the first time, to pass out of use, no person any longer being either thought of or spoken of under the notion of a Sabine or a Roman, a Romulian or a Tatian; and the new division became a source of general harmony and intermixture.

He is also much to be commended for the repeal, or rather amendment, of that law which gives power to fathers to sell their children; he exempted such as were married, conditionally that it had been with the liking and consent of their parents; for it seemed a hard thing that a woman who had given herself in marriage to a man whom she judged free should afterwards find herself living with a slave.

He attempted, also, the formation of a calendar, not with absolute exactness, yet not without some scientific knowledge. During the reign of Romulus, they had let their months run on without any certain or equal term; some of them contained twenty days, others thirty-five, others more; they had no sort of knowledge of the inequality in the motions of the sun and moon; they only kept to the one rule that the whole course of the year contained three hundred and sixty days. Numa, calculating the difference between the lunar and the solar year at eleven days, for that the moon completed her anniversary course in three hundred and fifty-four days, and the sun in three hundred and sixty-five, to remedy this incongruity doubled the eleven days, and every other year added an intercalary month, to follow February, consisting of twenty-two days, and called by the Romans the month Mercedinus. This amendment, however, itself, in course of time, came to need other amendments. He also altered the order of the months; for March, which was reckoned the first he put into the third place; and January, which was the eleventh, he made the first; and February, which was the twelfth and last, the second. Many will have it, that it was Numa, also, who added the two months of January and February; for in the beginning they had had a year of ten months; as there are barbarians who count only three; the Arcadians, in Greece, had but four; the Acarnanians, six. The Egyptian year at first, they say, was of one month; afterwards, of four; and so, though they live in the newest of all countries, they have the credit of being a more ancient nation than any, and reckon, in their genealogies, a prodigious number of years, counting months, that is, as years. That the Romans, at first, comprehended the whole year within ten, and not twelve months, plainly appears by the name of the last, De-

cember, meaning the tenth month; and that March was
the first is likewise evident, for the fifth month after it was
called Quintilis, and the sixth Sextilis, and so the rest;
whereas, if January and February had, in this account,
preceded March, Quintilis would have been fifth in name
and seventh in reckoning. It was also natural that March,
dedicated to Mars, should be Romulus's first and April,
named from Venus, or Aphrodite, his second month; in it
they sacrifice to Venus, and the women bathe on the calends, or first day of it, with myrtle garlands on their heads.
But others, because of its being *p* and not *ph*, will not allow of the derivation of this word from Aphrodite, but say
it is called April from *aperio*, Latin for to open, because
that this month is high spring, and opens and discloses the
buds and flowers. The next is called May, from Maia, the
mother of Mercury, to whom it is sacred; then June follows, so called from Juno; some, however, derive them
from the two ages, old and young, *majores*, being their
name for older, and *juniores* for younger men. To the
other months they gave denominations according to their
order; so the fifth was called Quintilis, Sextilis the sixth,
and the rest, September, October, November, and December. Afterwards Quintilis received the name of Julius, from
Caesar, who defeated Pompey; as also Sextilis that of Augustus, from the second Caesar, who had that title. Domi-
tian, also, in imitation, gave the two other following
months his own names, of Germanicus and Domitianus;
but, on his being slain, they recovered their ancient denominations of September and October. The two last are
the only ones that have kept their names throughout without any alteration. Of the months which were added or
transposed in their order by Numa, February comes from
februa; and is as much as Purification month; in it they
make offerings to the dead, and celebrate the Lupercalia,
which, in most points, resembles a purification. January
was also called from Janus, and precedence given to it by
Numa before March, which was dedicated to the god
Mars; because, as I conceive, he wished to take every opportunity of intimating that the arts and studies of peace

are to be preferred before those of war. For this Janus, whether in remote antiquity he were a demigod or a king, was certainly a great lover of civil and social unity, and one who reclaimed men from brutal and savage living; for which reason they figure him with two faces, to represent the two states and conditions out of the one of which he brought mankind, to lead them into the other. His temple at Rome has two gates, which they call the gates of war, because they stand open in the time of war, and shut in the times of peace; of which latter there was very seldom an example, for, as the Roman empire was enlarged and extended, it was so encompassed with barbarous nations and enemies to be resisted, that it was seldom or never at peace. Only in the time of Augustus Caesar, after he had overcome Antony, this temple was shut; as likewise once before, when Marcus Atilius and Titus Manlius were consuls; but then it was not long before, wars breaking out, the gates were again opened. But, during the reign of Numa, those gates were never seen open a single day, but continued constantly shut for a space of forty-three years together; such an entire and universal cessation of war existed. For not only had the people of Rome itself been softened and charmed into a peaceful temper by the just and mild rule of a pacific prince, but even the neighbouring cities, as if some salubrious and gentle air had blown from Rome upon them, began to experience a change of feeling, and partook in the general longing for the sweets of peace and order, and for life employed in the quiet tillage of soil, bringing up of children, and worship of the gods. Festival days and sports, and the secure and peaceful interchange of friendly visits and hospitalities prevailed all through the whole of Italy. The love of virtue and justice flowed from Numa's wisdom as from a fountain, and the serenity of his spirit diffused itself, like a calm, on all sides; so that the hyperboles of poets were flat and tame to express what then existed; as that—

"Over the iron shield the spiders hangs their threads,"

or that—

"Rust eats the pointed spear and double-edged sword.
No more is heard the trumpet's brazen roar,
Sweet sleep is banished from our eyes no more."

For during the whole reign of Numa, there was neither
war, nor sedition, nor innovation in the state, nor any
envy or ill-will to his person, nor plot or conspiracy from
views of ambition. Either fear of the gods that were
thought to watch over him, or reverence for his virtue, or
divine felicity of fortune that in his days preserved human innocence, made his reign, by whatever means, a living example and verification of that saying which Plato,
long afterwards, ventured to pronounce, that the sole and
only hope of respite or remedy for human evils was in some
happy conjunction of events which should unite in a single
person the power of a king and the wisdom of a philosopher, so as to elevate virtue to control and mastery over
vice. The wise man is blessed in himself, and blessed also
are the auditors who can hear and receive those words
which flow from his mouth; and perhaps, too, there is no
need of compulsion or menaces to affect the multitude, for
the mere sight itself of a shining and conspicuous example
of virtue in the life of their prince will bring them spon-
taneously to virtue, and to a conformity with that blame-
less and blessed life of good-will and mutual concord, supported by temperance and justice, which is the highest
benefit that human means can confer; and he is the truest
ruler who can best introduce it into the hearts and practice
of his subjects. It is the praise of Numa that no one seems
ever to have discerned this so clearly as he.

As to his children and wives, there is a diversity of reports by several authors; some will have it that he never
had any other wife than Tatia; nor more children than one
daughter called Pompilia; others will have it that he left also
four sons, namely, Pompo, Pinus, Calphus, and Mamercus, every one of whom had issue, and from them descended the noble and illustrious families of Pomponii,

Pinarii, Calpurnii, and Mamerci, which for this reason took also the surname of Rex, or King. But there is a third set of writers who say that these pedigrees are but a piece of flattery used by writers who, to gain favour with these great families, made them fictitious genealogies from the lineage of Numa; and that Pompilia was not the daughter of Tatia, but Lucretia, another wife whom he married after he came to his kingdom; however, all of them agree in opinion that she was married to the son of that Marcius who persuaded him to accept the government, and accompanied him to Rome, where, as a mark of honour, he was chosen into the senate, and after the death of Numa, standing in competition with Tullus Hostilius for the kingdom, and being disappointed of the election, in discontent killed himself; his son Marcius, however, who had married Pompilia, continuing at Rome, was the father of Ancus Marcius, who succeeded Tullus Hostilius in the kingdom, and was but five years of age when Numa died.

Numa lived something above eighty years, and then, as Piso writes, was not taken out of the world by a sudden or acute disease, but died of old age and by a gradual and gentle decline. At his funeral all the glories of his life were consummated, when all the neighbouring states in alliance and amity with Rome met to honour and grace the rites of his interment with garlands and public presents; the senators carried the bier on which his corpse was laid, and the priests followed and accompanied the solemn procession; while a general crowd, in which women and children took part, followed with such cries and weeping as if they had bewailed the death and loss of some most dear relation taken away in the flower of age, and not an old and worn-out king. It is said that his body, by his particular command, was not burnt, but that they made, in conformity with his order, two stone coffins, and buried both under the hill Janiculum, in one of which his body was laid, and the other his sacred books, which, as the Greek legislators their tables, he had written out for himself, but had so long inculcated the contents of them, whilst he lived, into the minds and hearts of the priests, that their understandings became fully possessed with the whole spirit and purpose of them; and he therefore bade that they should be buried with his body, as though such holy precepts could not without irreverence be left to circulate in mere lifeless writings. For this very reason, they say, the Pythagoreans bade that their precepts should not be committed to paper, but rather preserved in the living memories of those who were worthy to receive them; and when some of their out-of-the-way and abstruse geometrical processes had been divulged to an unworthy person, they said the gods threatened to punish this wickedness and profanity by a signal and wide-spreading calamity. With these several instances concurring to show a similarity in the lives of Numa and Pythagoras, we may easily pardon those who seek to establish the fact of a real acquaintance between them.

Valerius Antias writes that the books which were buried in the aforesaid chest or coffin of stone were twelve volumes of holy writ and twelve others of Greek philosophy, and that about four hundred years afterwards, when P. Cornelius and M. Baebius were consuls, in a time of heavy rains, a violent torrent washed away the earth, and dislodged the chests of stone; and, their covers falling off, one of them was found wholly empty, without the least relic of any human body; in the other were the books before mentioned, which the praetor Petilius having read and perused, made oath in the senate, that, in his opinion, it was not fit for their contents to be made public to the people; whereupon the volumes were all carried to the Comitium, and there burnt.

It is the fortune of all good men that their virtue rises in glory after their deaths, and that the envy which evil men conceive against them never outlives them long; some have the happiness even to see it die before them; but in Numa's case, also, the fortunes of the succeeding kings served as foils to set off the brightness of his reputation. For after him there were five kings, the last of whom ended his old age in banishment, being deposed from his crown; of the other four, three were assassinated and murdered by treason; the other, who was Tullus Hostilius, that immediately succeeded Numa, derided his virtues, and especially his devotion to religious worship, as a cowardly and mean-spirited occupation, and diverted the minds of the people to war; but was checked in these youthful insolences, and was himself driven by an acute and tormenting disease into superstitions wholly different from Numa's piety, and left others also to participate in these terrors when he died by the stroke of a thunderbolt.

FABIUS

A son of Hercules and a nymph, of some woman of that country, who brought him forth on the banks of Tiber, was, it is said, the first Fabius, the founder of the numerous and distinguished family of the name. Others will have it that they were first called Fodii because the first of the race delighted in digging pitfalls for wild beasts, *fodere* being still the Latin for to dig, and *fossa* for a ditch, and that in process of time, by the change of the two letters, they grew to be called Fabii. But be these things true or false, certain it is that this family for a long time yielded a great number of eminent persons. Our Fabius, who was fourth in descent from that Fabius Rullus who first brought the honourable surname of Maximus into his family, was also, by way of personal nickname, called Verrucosus, from a wart on his upper lip; and in his childhood they in like manner named him Ovicula, or The Lamb, on account of his extreme mildness of temper. His slowness in speaking, his long labour and pains in learning, his deliberation in entering into the sports of other children, his easy submission to everybody, as if he had no will of his own, made those who judged superficially of him, the greater number, esteem him insensible and stupid; and few only saw that this tardiness proceeded from stability, and discerned the greatness of his mind, and the lionlikeness of his temper. But as soon as he came into employments, his virtues exerted and showed themselves; his reputed want of energy then was recognised by people in general as a freedom of passion; his slowness in words and actions, the effect of a true prudence; his want of rapidity and his sluggishness, as constancy and firmness.

Living in a great commonwealth, surrounded by many enemies, he saw the wisdom of inuring his body (nature's own weapon) to warlike exercises, and disciplining his tongue for public oratory in a style conformable to his life and character. His eloquence, indeed, had not much of popular ornament, nor empty artifice, but there was in it great weight of sense; it was strong and sententious, much after the way of Thucydides. We have yet extant his funeral oration upon the death of his son, who died consul, which he recited before the people.

He was five times consul, and in his first consulship had the honour of a triumph for the victory he gained over the Ligurians, whom he defeated in a set battle, and drove them to take shelter in the Alps, from whence they never after made any inroad or depredation upon their neighbours. After this, Hannibal came into Italy, who, at his first entrance, having gained a great battle near the river Trebia, traversed all Tuscany with his victorious army, and, desolating the country round about, filled Rome itself with astonishment and terror. Besides the more common signs of thunder and lightning then happening, the report of several unheard-of and utterly strange portents much increased the popular consternation. For it was said that some targets sweated blood; that at Antium, when they reaped their corn, many of the ears were filled with blood; that it had rained red-hot stones; that the Falerians had seen the heavens open and several scrolls falling down, in one of which was plainly written, "Mars himself stirs his arms." But these prodigies had no effect upon the impetuous and fiery temper of the consul Flaminius, whose natural promptness had been much heightened by his late unexpected victory over the Gauls, when he fought them contrary to the order of the senate and the advice of his colleague. Fabius, on the other side, thought it not seasonable to engage with the enemy; not that he much regarded the prodigies, which he thought too strange to be easily under-

stood, though many were alarmed by them; but in regard
that the Carthaginians were but few, and in want of money
and supplies, he deemed it best not to meet in the field a
general whose army had been tried in many encounters,
and whose object was a battle, but to send aid to their allies, control the movements of the various subject cities,
and let the force and vigour of Hannibal waste away and
expire, like a flame, for want of the aliment.

These weighty reasons did not prevail with Flaminius,
who protested he would never suffer the advance of the
enemy to the city, nor be reduced, like Camillus in former
time, to fight for Rome within the walls of Rome. Accordingly he ordered the tribunes to draw out the army into the
field; and though he himself, leaping on horseback to go
out, was no sooner mounted but the beast, without any apparent cause, fell into so violent a fit of trembling and
bounding that he cast his rider headlong on the ground; he
was no ways deterred, but proceeded as he had begun, and
marched forward up to Hannibal, who was posted near the
Lake Thrasymene in Tuscany. At the moment of this engagement, there happened so great an earthquake, that it
destroyed several towns, altered the course of rivers, and
carried off parts of high cliffs, yet such was the eagerness
of the combatants, that they were entirely insensible of it.

In this battle Flaminius fell, after many proofs of his
strength and courage, and round about him all the bravest
of the army; in the whole, fifteen thousand were killed, and
as many made prisoners. Hannibal, desirous to bestow funeral honours upon the body of Flaminius, made diligent
search after it, but could not find it among the dead, nor
was it ever known what became of it. Upon the former engagement near Trebia, neither the general who wrote, nor
the express who told the news, used straightforward and direct terms, nor related it otherwise than as a drawn battle,
with equal loss on either side; but on this occasion as soon
as Pomponius the praetor had the intelligence, he caused
the people to assemble, and, without disguising or dissem-
bling the matter, told them plainly, "We are beaten, O Romans, in a great battle; the consul Flaminius is killed; think,

therefore, what is to be done for your safety." Letting loose his news like a gate of wind upon an open sea, he threw the city into utter confusion: in such consternation, their thoughts found no support or stay. The danger at hand at last awakened their judgments into a resolution to choose a dictator, who by the sovereign authority of his office, and by his personal wisdom and courage, might be able to manage the public affairs. Their choice unanimously fell upon Fabius, whose character seemed equal to the greatness of the office; whose age was so far advanced as to give him experience, without taking from him the vigour of action; his body could execute what his soul designed; and his temper was a happy compound of confidence and cautiousness.

Fabius, being thus installed in the office of dictator, in the first place gave the command of the horse to Lucius Minucius; and next asked leave of the senate for himself, that in time of battle he might serve on horseback, which by an ancient law amongst the Romans was forbid to their generals; whether it were, that, placing their greatest strength in their foot, they would have their commanders-in-chief posted amongst them, or else to let them know, that, how great and absolute soever their authority were, the people and senate were still their masters, of whom they must ask leave. Fabius, however, to make the authority of his charge more observable, and to render the people more submissive and obedient to him, caused himself to be accompanied with the full body of four-and-twenty lictors; and, when the surviving consul came to visit him, sent him word to dismiss his lictors with their fasces, the ensigns of authority, and appear before him as a private person.

The first solemn action of his dictatorship was very fitly a religious one: an admonition to the people, that their late overthrow had not befallen them through want of courage in their soldiers, but through the neglect of divine ceremonies in the general. He therefore exhorted them not to fear the enemy, but by extraordinary honour to propitiate the gods. This he did, not to fill their minds with superstition, but by religious feeling to raise their courage, and lessen their fear of the enemy by inspiring the belief that Heaven was on their side. With this view, the secret prophecies called the Sibylline Books were consulted; sundry predictions found in them were said to refer to the fortunes and events of the time; but none except the consulter was informed. Presenting himself to the people, the dictator made a vow before them to offer in sacrifice the whole product of the next season, all Italy over, of the cows, goats, swine, sheep, both in the mountains and the plains; and to celebrate musical festivities with an expenditure of the precise sum of 333 sestertia and 333 denarii, with one-third of a denarius over. The sum total of which is, in our money, 83,583 drachmas and 2 obols. What the mystery might be in that exact number is not easy to determine, unless it were in honour of the perfection of the number three, as being the first of odd numbers, the first that contains in itself multiplication, with all other properties whatsoever belonging to numbers in general.

In this manner Fabius, having given the people better heart for the future, by making them believe that the gods took their side, for his own part placed his whole confidence in himself, believing that the gods bestowed victory and good fortune by the instrumentality of valour and of prudence; and thus prepared he set forth to oppose Hannibal, not with intention to fight him, but with the purpose of wearing out and wasting the vigour of his arms by lapse of time, of meeting his want of resources by superior means, by large numbers the smallness of his forces. With this design, he always encamped on the highest grounds, where the enemy's horse could have no access to him. Still he kept pace with them; when they marched he followed them; when they encamped he did the same, but at such a distance as not to be compelled to an engagement, and always keeping upon the hills, free from the insults of their horse; by which means he gave them no rest, but kept them in continual alarm.

But this his dilatory way gave occasion in his own camp for suspicion of want of courage; and this opinion prevailed yet more in Hannibal's army. Hannibal was himself the only man who was not deceived, who discerned his skill and detected his tactics, and saw, unless he could by art or force bring him to battle, that the Carthaginians, unable to use the arms in which they were superior, and suffering the continual drain of lives and treasure in which they were inferior, would in the end come to nothing. He resolved, therefore, with all the arts and subtleties of war to break his measures, and to bring Fabius to an engagement, like a cunning wrestler, watching every opportunity to get good hold and close with his adversary. He at one time attacked, and sought to distract his attention, tried to draw him off in various directions, and endeavoured in all ways to tempt him from his safe policy. All this artifice, though it had no effect upon the firm judgment and conviction of the dictator, yet upon the common soldier, and even upon the general of the horse himself, it had too great an operation: Minucius, unseasonably eager for action, bold and confident, humoured the soldiery, and himself contributed to fill them with wild eagerness and empty hopes, which they vented in reproaches upon Fabius, calling him Hannibal's pedagogue, since he did nothing else but follow him up and down and wait upon him. At the same time, they cried up Minucius for the only captain worthy to command the Romans; whose vanity and presumption rose so high in consequence, that he insolently jested at Fabius's encampment upon the mountains, saying that he seated them there as on a theatre, to behold the flames and desolation of their country. And he would sometimes ask the friends of the general, whether it were not his meaning, by thus leading them from mountain to mountain, to carry them at last (having no hopes on earth) up into heaven, or to hide them in the clouds from Hannibal's army? When his friends reported these things to the dictator, persuading him that, to avoid the general obloquy, he should engage the enemy, his answer was, "I should be more faint-hearted than they make me, if, through fear of idle reproaches, I should abandon my own convictions. It is no inglorious thing to have fear for the safety of our country, but to be turned from one's course by men's opinions, by blame, and by misrepresentation, shows a man unfit to hold an office such as this, which, by such conduct, he makes the slave of those whose errors it is his business to control."

An oversight of Hannibal occurred soon after. Desirous to refresh his horse in some good pasture-grounds, and to draw off his army, he ordered his guides to conduct him to the district of Casinum. They, mistaking his bad pronunciation, led him and his army to the town of Casilinum, on the frontier of Campania which the river Lothronus, called by the Romans Vulturnus, divides in two parts. The country around is enclosed by mountains, with a valley opening towards the sea, in which the river overflowing forms a quantity of marsh land with deep banks of sand, and discharges itself into the sea on a very unsafe and rough shore. While Hannibal was proceeding hither, Fabius, by his knowledge of the roads, succeeded in making his way around before him, and despatched four thousand choice men to seize the exit from it and stop him up, and lodged the rest of his army upon the neighbouring hills, in the most advantageous places; at the same time detaching a party of his lightest armed men to fall upon Hannibal's rear; which they did with such success, that they cut off eight hundred of them, and put the whole army in disorder. Hannibal, finding the error and the danger he was fallen into, immediately crucified the guides; but considered the enemy to be so advantageously posted, that there was no hope of breaking through them; while his soldiers began to be despondent and terrified, and to think themselves surrounded with embarrassments too difficult to be surmounted.

Thus reduced, Hannibal had recourse to stratagem; he caused two thousand head of oxen which he had in his camp to have torches or dry fagots well fastened to their horns, and lighting them in the beginning of the night, ordered the beasts to be driven on towards the heights commanding the passages out of the valley and the enemy's posts; when this was done, he made his army in the dark leisurely march after them. The oxen at first kept a slow orderly pace, and with their lighted heads resembled an army marching by night, astonishing the shepherds and herdsmen of the hills about. But when the fire burnt down the horns of the beasts to the quick, they no longer observed their sober pace, but unruly and wild with their pain, ran dispersed about, tossing their heads and scattering the fire round about them upon each other and setting light as they passed to the trees. This was a surprising spectacle to the Romans on guard upon the heights. Seeing flames which appeared to come from men advancing with torches, they were possessed with the alarm that the enemy was approaching in various quarters, and that they were being surrounded; and, quitting their post, abandoned the pass, and precipitately retired to their camp on the hills. They were no sooner gone, but the light-armed of Hannibal's men, according to his order, immediately seized the heights, and soon after the whole army, with all the baggage, came up and safely marched through the passes.

Fabius, before the night was over, quickly found out the trick; for some of the beasts fell into his hands; but for fear of an ambush in the dark, he kept his men all night to their arms in the camp. As soon as it was day, he attacked the enemy in the rear, where, after a good deal of skirmishing in the uneven ground, the disorder might have become general, but that Hannibal detached from his van a body of Spaniards, who, of themselves active and nimble, were accustomed to the climbing of mountains. These briskly attacked the Roman troops, who were in heavy armour, killed a good many, and left Fabius no longer in condition to follow the enemy. This action brought the extreme of obloquy and contempt upon the dictator; they said it was now manifest that he was not only inferior to his adversary, as they had always thought, in courage, but even in that conduct, foresight, and generalship, by which he had proposed to bring the war to an end.

And Hannibal, to enhance their anger against him, marched with his army close to the lands and possessions of Fabius, and, giving orders to his soldiers to burn and destroy all the country about, forbade them to do the least damage in the estates of the Roman general, and placed guards for their security. This, when reported at Rome, had the effect with the people which Hannibal desired. Their tribunes raised a thousand stories against him, chiefly at the instigation of Metilius, who, not so much out of hatred to him as out of friendship to Minucius, whose kinsman he was, thought by depressing Fabius to raise his friend. The senate on their part were also offended with him for the bargain he had made with Hannibal about the exchange of prisoners, the conditions of which were that, after exchange made of man for man, if any on either side remained, they should be redeemed at the price of two hundred and fifty drachmas a head. Upon the whole account, there remained two hundred and forty Romans unexchanged, and the senate now not only refused to allow money for the ransoms, but also reproached Fabius for making a contract, contrary to the honour and interest of the commonwealth, for redeeming men whose cowardice had put them in the hands of the enemy. Fabius heard and endured all this with invincible patience; and, having no money by him, and on the other side being resolved to keep his word with Hannibal and not to abandon the captives, he despatched his son to Rome to sell land, and to bring with him the price, sufficient to discharge the ransoms; which was punctually performed by his son and delivery accordingly made to him of the prisoners, amongst whom many, when they were released, made proposals to repay the money; which Fabius in all cases declined.

About this time, he was called to Rome by the priests, to assist, according to the duty of his office, at certain sacrifices, and was thus forced to leave the command of the army with Minucius; but before he parted, not only charged him as his commander-in-chief, but besought and entreated him not to come, in his absence, to a battle with Hannibal. His commands, entreaties, and advice were lost upon Minucius, for his back was no sooner turned but the new general immediately sought occasions to attack the enemy. And notice being brought him that Hannibal had sent out a great part of his army to forage, he fell upon a detachment of the remainder, doing great execution, and driving them to their very camp, with no little terror to the rest, who apprehended their breaking in upon them; and when Hannibal had recalled his scattered forces to the camp, he, nevertheless, without any loss, made his retreat, a success which aggravated his boldness and presumption, and filled the soldiers with rash confidence. The news spread to Rome, where Fabius, on being told it, said that what he most feared was Minucius's success; but the people, highly elated, hurried to the forum to listen to an address from Metilius the tribune, in which he infinitely extolled the valour of Minucius, and fell bitterly upon Fabius, accusing him for want not merely of courage, but even of loyalty; and not only him, but also many other eminent and considerable persons; saying that it was they that had brought the Carthaginians into Italy, with the design to destroy the liberty of the people; for which end they had at once put the supreme authority into the hands of a single person, who by his slowness and delays might give Hannibal leisure to establish himself in Italy, and the people of Carthage time and opportunity to supply him with fresh succours to complete his conquest.

Fabius came forward with no intention to answer the tribune, but only said, that they should expedite the sacrifices, that so he might speedily return to the army to punish Minucius, who had presumed to fight contrary to his orders; words which immediately possessed the people with the belief that Minucius stood in danger of his life. For it was in the power of the dictator to imprison and to put to death, and they feared that Fabius, of a mild temper in general, would be as hard to be appeased when once irritated, as he was slow to be provoked. Nobody dared to raise his voice in opposition; Metilius alone, whose office of tribune gave him security to say what he pleased (for in the time of a dictatorship that magistrateal one preserves his authority), boldly applied himself to the people in the behalf of Minucius; that they should not suffer him to be made a sacrifice to the enmity of Fabius, nor permit him to be destroyed, like the son of Manlius Torquatus,

who was beheaded by his father for a victory fought and
triumphantly won against order; he exhorted them to take
away from Fabius that absolute power of a dictator, and
to put it into more worthy hands, better able and more inclined to use it for the public good. These impressions very
much prevailed upon the people, though not so far as
wholly to dispossess Fabius of the dictatorship. But they
decreed that Minucius should have an equal authority with
the dictator in the conduct of the war; which was a thing
then without precedent, though a little later it was again
practised after the disaster at Cannae; when the dictator,
Marcus Junius, being with the army, they chose at Rome
Fabius Buteo dictator, that he might create new senators,
to supply the numerous places of those who were killed.
But as soon as, once acting in public, he had filled those
vacant places with a sufficient number, he immediately dismissed his lictors, and withdrew from all his attendance,
and mingling like a common person with the rest of the
people, quietly went about his own affairs in the forum.

The enemies of Fabius thought they had sufficiently
humiliated and subdued him by raising Minucius to be his
equal in authority; but they mistook the temper of the
man, who looked upon their folly as not his loss, but like
Diogenes, who, being told that some persons derided him,
made answer, "But I am not derided," meaning that only
those were really insulted on whom such insults made an
impression, so Fabius, with great tranquillity and uncon-
cern, submitted to what happened, and contributed a proof
to the argument of the philosophers that a just and good
man is not capable of being dishonoured. His only vexation arose from his fear lest this ill counsel, by supplying
opportunities to the diseased military ambition of his sub-
ordinate, should damage the public cause. Lest the rashness of Minucius should now at once run headlong into
some disaster, he returned back with all privacy and speed
to the army; where he found Minucius so elevated with his
new dignity, that, a joint-authority not contenting him, he
required by turns to have the command of the army every
other day. This Fabius rejected, but was contented that

the army should be divided; thinking each general singly would better command his part, than partially command the whole. The first and fourth legion he took for his own division, the second and third he delivered to Minucius; so also of the auxiliary forces each had an equal share.

Minucius, thus exalted, could not contain himself from boasting of his success in humiliating the high and powerful office of the dictatorship. Fabius quietly reminded him that it was, in all wisdom, Hannibal, and not Fabius, whom he had to combat; but if he must needs contend with his colleague, it had best be in diligence and care for the preservation of Rome; that it might not be said, a man so favoured by the people served them worse than he who had been ill-treated and disgraced by them.

The young general, despising these admonitions as the false humility of age, immediately removed with the body of his army, and encamped by himself. Hannibal, who was not ignorant of all these passages, lay watching his advantage from them. It happened that between his army and that of Minucius there was a certain eminence, which seemed a very advantageous and not difficult post to encamp upon; the level field around it appeared, from a distance, to be all smooth and even, though it had many inconsiderable ditches and dips in it, not discernible to the eye. Hannibal, had he pleased, could easily have possessed himself of this ground; but he had reserved it for a bait, or train, in proper season, to draw the Romans to an engagement. Now that Minucius and Fabius were divided, he thought the opportunity fair for his purpose; and, therefore, having in the night-time lodged a convenient number of his men in these ditches and hollow places, early in the morning he sent forth a small detachment, who, in the sight of Minucius, proceeded to possess themselves of the rising ground. According to his expectation, Minucius swallowed the bait, and first sends out his light troops, and after them some horse, to dislodge the enemy; and, at last, when he saw Hannibal in person advancing to the assistance of his men, marched down with his whole army drawn up. He engaged with the troops on the eminence, and sustained their missiles; the combat for some time was equal; but as soon as Hannibal perceived that the whole army was now sufficiently advanced within the toils he had set for them, so that their backs were open to his men whom he had posted in the hollows, he gave the signal; upon which they rushed forth from various quarters, and with loud cries furiously attacked Minucius in the rear. The surprise and the slaughter was great, and struck universal alarm and disorder through the whole army. Minucius himself lost all his confidence; he looked from officer to officer, and found all alike unprepared to face the danger, and yielding to a flight, which, however, could not end in safety. The Numidian horsemen were already in full victory riding about the plain, cutting down the fugitives.

Fabius was not ignorant of this danger of his countrymen; he foresaw what would happen from the rashness of Minucius, and the cunning of Hannibal; and, therefore, kept his men to their arms, in readiness to wait the event; nor would he trust to the reports of others, but he himself, in front of his camp, viewed all that passed. When, therefore, he saw the army of Minucius encompassed by the enemy, and that by their countenance and shifting their ground they appeared more disposed to flight than to resistance, with a great sigh, striking his hand upon his thigh, he said to those about him, "O Hercules! how much sooner than I expected, though later than he seemed to desire, hath Minucius destroyed himself!" He then commanded the ensigns to be led forward, and the army to follow, telling them, "We must make haste to rescue Minucius, who is a valiant man, and a lover of his country; and if he hath been too forward to engage the enemy, at another time we will tell him of it." Thus, at the head of his men, Fabius marched up to the enemy, and first cleared the plain of the Numidians; and next fell upon those who were charging the Romans in the rear, cutting down all that made opposition and obliging the rest to save themselves by a hasty retreat, lest they should be environed as the Romans had been. Hannibal, seeing so sudden a change of affairs, and Fabius, beyond the force of his age,

opening his way through the ranks up the hillside, that
he might join Minucius, warily forbore, sounded a retreat,
and drew off his men into their camp; while the Romans
on their part were no less contented to retire in safety. It is
reported that upon this occasion Hannibal said jestingly to
his friends: "Did not I tell you, that this cloud which always
hovered upon the mountains would, at some time or other,
come down with a storm upon us?"

Fabius, after his men had picked up the spoils of the
field, retired to his own camp, without saying any harsh or
reproachful thing to his colleague; who, also, in his part,
gathering his army together, spoke and said to them: "To
conduct great matters and never commit a fault is above
the force of human nature; but to learn and improve by the
faults we have committed, is that which becomes a good
and sensible man. Some reasons I may have to accuse fortune, but I have many more to thank her; for in a few
hours she hath cured a long mistake, and taught me that
I am not the man who should command others, but have
need of another to command me; and that we are not to
contend for victory over those to whom it is our advantage
to yield. Therefore in everything else henceforth the dictator must be your commander; only in showing gratitude
towards him I will still be your leader, and always be the
first to obey his orders." Having said this, he commanded
the Roman eagles to move forward, and all his men to
follow him to the camp of Fabius. The soldiers, then, as
he entered, stood amazed at the novelty of the sight, and
were anxious and doubtful what the meaning might be.
When he came near the dictator's tent, Fabius went forth
to meet him, on which he at once laid his standards at his
feet, calling him with a loud voice his father; while the
soldiers with him saluted the soldiers here as their patrons,
the term employed by freedmen to those who gave them
their liberty. After silence was obtained, Minucius said,
"You have this day, O dictator, obtained two victories; one
by your valour and conduct over Hannibal, and another
by your wisdom and goodness over your colleague; by one
victory you preserved, and by the other instructed us; and

when we were already suffering one shameful defeat from Hannibal, by another welcome one from you we were restored to honour and safety. I can address you by no nobler name than that of a kind father, though a father's beneficence falls short of that I have received from you. From a father I individually received the gift of life; to you I owe its preservation not for myself only, but for all these who are under me." After this, he threw himself into the arms of the dictator; and in the same manner the soldiers of each army embraced one another with gladness and tears of joy.

Not long after, Fabius laid down the dictatorship, and consuls were again created. Those who immediately succeeded observed the same method in managing the war, and avoided all occasions of fighting Hannibal in a pitched battle; they only succoured their allies, and preserved the towns from falling off to the enemy. But afterwards, when Terentius Varro, a man of obscure birth, but very popular and bold, had obtained the consulship, he soon made it appear that by his rashness and ignorance he would stake the whole commonwealth on the hazard. For it was his custom to declaim in all assemblies, that, as long as Rome employed generals like Fabius, there never would be an end of the war; vaunting that whenever he should get sight of the enemy, he would that same day free Italy from the strangers. With these promises he so prevailed, that he raised a greater army than had ever yet been sent out of Rome. There were enlisted eighty-eight thousand fighting men; but what gave confidence to the populace, only terrified the wise and experienced, and none more than Fabius; since if so great a body, and the flower of the Roman youth, should be cut off, they could not see any new resource for the safety of Rome. They addressed themselves, therefore, to the other consul, Aemilius Paulus, a man of great experience in war, but unpopular, and fearful also of the people, who once before upon some impeachment had condemned him; so that he needed encouragement to withstand his colleague's temerity. Fabius told him, if he would profitably serve his country, he must no less oppose Varro's ignorant eagerness than Hannibal's conscious readiness, since both alike conspired to decide the fate of Rome by a battle. "It is more reasonable," he said to him, "that you should believe me than Varro, in matters relating to Hannibal, when I tell you that if for this year you abstain from fighting with him, either his army will perish of itself, or else he will be glad to depart of his own will. This evidently appears, inasmuch as, notwithstanding his victories, none of the countries or towns of Italy came into him, and his army is not now the third part of what it was at first." To this Paulus is said to have replied, "Did I only consider myself, I should rather choose to be exposed to the weapons of Hannibal than once more to the suffrages of my fellow-citizens, who are urgent for what you disapprove; yet since the cause of Rome is at stake, I will rather seek in my conduct to please and obey Fabius than all the world besides."

These good measures were defeated by the importunity of Varro; whom, when they were both come to the army, nothing would content but a separate command, that each consul should have his day; and when his turn came, he posted his army close to Hannibal, at a village called Cannae, by the river Aufidus. It was no sooner day, but he set up the scarlet coat flying over his tent, which was the signal of battle. This boldness of the consul, and the numerousness of his army, double theirs, startled the Carthaginians; but Hannibal commanded them to their arms, and with a small train rode out to take a full prospect of the enemy as they were now forming in their ranks, from a rising ground not far distant. One of his followers, called Gisco, a Carthaginian of equal rank with himself, told him that the numbers of the enemy were astonishing; to which Hannibal replied with a serious countenance, "There is one thing, Gisco, yet more astonishing, which you take no notice of;" and when Gisco inquired what, answered, that "in all those great numbers before us, there is not one man called Gisco." This unexpected jest of their general made all the company laugh, and as they came down from the hill they told it to those whom they met, which caused a general laughter amongst them all, from which they were hardly able to recover themselves. The army, seeing Hannibal's attendants come back from viewing the enemy in such a laughing condition, concluded that it must be profound contempt of the enemy, that made their general at this moment indulge in such hilarity.

According to his usual manner, Hannibal employed stratagems to advantage himself. In the first place, he so drew up his men that the wind was at their backs, which at that time blew with a perfect storm of violence, and, sweeping over the great plains of sand, carried before it a cloud of dust over the Carthaginian army into the faces of the Romans, which much disturbed them in the fight. In the next place, all his best men he put into his wings; and in the body which was somewhat more advanced than the wings, placed the worst and the weakest of his army. He commanded those in the wings, that, when the enemy had made a thorough charge upon that middle advance body, which he knew would recoil, as not being able to withstand their shock, and when the Romans in their pursuit should be far enough engaged within the two wings, they should, both on the right and the left, charge them in the flank, and endeavour to encompass them. This appears to have been the chief cause of the Roman loss. Pressing upon Hannibal's front, which gave ground, they reduced the form of his army into a perfect half-moon, and gave ample opportunity to the captains of the chosen troops to charge them right and left on their flanks, and to cut off and destroy all who did not fall before the Carthaginian wings united in their rear. To this general calamity, it is also said, that a strange mistake among the cavalry much contributed. For the horse of Aemilius receiving a hurt and throwing his master, those about him immediately alighted to aid the consul; and the Roman troops, seeing their commanders thus quitting their horses, took it for a sign that they should all dismount and charge the enemy on foot. At the sight of this, Hannibal was heard to say, "This pleases me better than if they had been delivered to me bound hand and foot." For the particulars of this engagement, we refer our reader to those authors who have written at large upon the subject.

The consul Varro, with a thin company, fled to Venusia; Aemilius Paulus, unable any longer to oppose the flight of his men, or the pursuit of the enemy, his body all covered with wounds, and his soul no less wounded with grief, sat himself down upon a stone, expecting the kindness of a despatching blow. His face was so disfigured, and all his person so stained with blood, that his very friends and domestics passing by knew him not. At last Cornelius Lentulus, a young man of patrician race, perceiving who he was, alighted from his horse, and, tendering it to him, desired him to get up and save a life so necessary to the safety of the commonwealth, which, at this time, would dearly want so great a captain. But nothing could prevail upon him to accept of the offer; he obliged young Lentulus, with tears in his eyes, to remount his horse; then standing up, he gave him his hand, and commanded him to tell Fabius Maximus that Aemilius Paulus had followed his directions to his very last, and had not in the least deviated from those measures which were agreed between them; but that it was his hard fate to be overpowered by Varro in the first place, and secondly by Hannibal. Having despatched Lentulus with this commission, he marked where the slaughter was greatest, and there threw himself upon the swords of the enemy. In this battle it is reported that fifty thousand Romans were slain, four thousand prisoners taken in the field, and ten thousand in the camp of both consuls.

The friends of Hannibal earnestly persuaded him to follow up his victory, and pursue the flying Romans into the very gates of Rome, assuring him that in five days' time he might sup in the Capitol; nor is it easy to imagine what consideration hindered him from it. It would seem rather than some supernatural or divine intervention caused the hesitation and timidity which he now displayed, and which made Barcas, a Carthaginian, tell him with indignation, "You know, Hannibal, how to gain a victory, but not how to use it." Yet it produced a marvelous revolution in his affairs; he, who hitherto had not one town, market, or seaport in his possession, who had nothing for the subsistence of his men but what he pillaged from day to day, who had no place of retreat or basis of operation, but was roving, as it were, with a huge troop of banditti, now became master of the best provinces and towns of Italy, and of Capua itself, next to Rome the most flourishing and opulent city, all which came over to him, and submitted to his authority.

It is the saying of Euripides, that "a man is in ill-case when he must try a friend," and so neither, it would seem, is a state in a good one, when it needs an able general. And so it was with the Romans; the counsels and actions of Fabius, which, before the battle, they had branded as cowardice and fear, now, in the other extreme, they accounted to have been more than human wisdom; as though nothing but a divine power of intellect could have seen so far, and foretold contrary to the judgment of all others, a result which, even now it had arrived, was hardly credible. In him, therefore, they placed their whole remaining hopes; his wisdom was the sacred altar and temple to which they fled for refuge, and his counsels, more than anything, preserved them from dispersing and deserting their city, as in the time when the Gauls took possession of Rome. He, whom they esteemed fearful and pusillanimous when they were, as they thought, in a prosperous condition, was now the only man, in this general and unbounded dejection and confusion, who showed no fear, but walked the streets with an assured and serene countenance, addressed his fellow-citizens, checked the women's lamentations, and the public gatherings of those who wanted thus to vent their sorrows. He caused the senate to meet, he heartened up the magistrates, and was himself as the soul and life of every office.

He placed guards at the gates of the city to stop the frightened multitude from flying; he regulated and confined their mournings for their slain friends, both as to time and place; ordering that each family should perform such observances within private walls, and that they should continue only the space of one month, and then the whole city should be purified. The feast of Ceres happening to fall within this time, it was decreed that the solemnity should be intermitted, lest the fewness, and the sorrowful countenance of those who should celebrate it, might too much expose to the people the greatness of their loss; besides that, the worship most acceptable to the gods is that which comes from cheerful hearts. But those rites which were proper for appeasing their anger, and procuring auspicious signs and presages, were by the direction of the augurs carefully performed. Fabius Pictor, a near kinsman to Maximus, was sent to consult the oracle of Delphi; and about the same time, two vestals having been detected to have been violated, the one killed herself, and the other, according to custom, was buried alive.

Above all, let us admire the high spirit and equanimity of this Roman commonwealth; that when the consul Varro came beaten and flying home, full of shame and humiliation, after he had so disgracefully and calamitously managed their affairs, yet the whole senate and people went forth to meet him at the gates of the city, and received him with honour and respect. And, silence being commanded, the magistrates and chief of the senate, Fabius amongst them, commended him before the people, because he did not despair of the safety of the commonwealth, after so great a loss, but was come to take the government into his hands, to execute the laws, and aid his fellow-citizens in their prospect of future deliverance.

When word was brought to Rome that Hannibal, after the fight, had marched with his army into other parts of Italy, the hearts of the Romans began to revive, and they proceeded to send out generals and armies. The most distinguished commands were held by Fabius Maximus and Claudius Marcellus, both generals of great fame, though upon opposite grounds. For Marcellus, as we have set forth in his life, was a man of action and high spirit, ready and bold with his own hand, and, as Homer describes his warriors, fierce, and delighting in fights. Boldness, enterprise, and daring to match those of Hannibal, constituted his tactics, and marked his engagements. But Fabius adhered to his former principles, still persuaded that, by following

close and not fighting him, Hannibal and his army would at
last be tired out and consume, like a wrestler in too high
condition, whose very excess of strength makes him the
more likely suddenly to give way and lose it. Posidonius
tells us that the Romans called Marcellus their sword, and
Fabius their buckler; and that the vigour of the one, mixed
with the steadiness of the other, made a happy compound
that proved the salvation of Rome. So that Hannibal found
by experience that encountering the one, he met with a
rapid, impetuous river, which drove him back, and still
made some breach upon him; and by the other, though silently and quietly passing by him, he was insensibly washed
away and consumed; and, at last, was brought to this, that
he dreaded Marcellus when he was in motion, and Fabius
when he sat still. During the whole course of this war,
he had still to do with one or both of these generals; for
each of them was five times consul, and, as praetors or
proconsuls or consuls, they had always a part in the government of the army, till, at last, Marcellus fell into the trap
which Hannibal had laid for him, and was killed in his
fifth consulship. But all his craft and subtlety were unsuccessful upon Fabius, who only once was in some danger
of being caught, when counterfeit letters came to him from
the principal inhabitants of Metapontum, with promises
to deliver up their town if he would come before it with
his army, and intimations that they should expect him.
This train had almost drawn him in; he resolved to march
to them with part of his army, and was diverted only by
consulting the omens of the birds, which he found to be
inauspicious; and not long after it was discovered that the
letters had been forged by Hannibal, who, for his reception, had laid an ambush to entertain him. This, perhaps,
we must rather attribute to the favour of the gods than to
the prudence of Fabius.

In preserving the towns and allies from revolt by fair
and gentle treatment, and in not using rigour, or showing a
suspicion upon every light suggestion, his conduct was remarkable. It is told of him, that being informed of a certain Marsian, eminent for courage and good birth, who

had been speaking underhand with some of the soldiers about deserting, Fabius was so far from using severity against him, that he called for him, and told him he was sensible of the neglect that had been shown to his merit and good service, which, he said, was a great fault in the commanders who reward more by favour than by desert; "but henceforth, whenever you are aggrieved," said Fabius, "I shall consider it your fault, if you apply yourself to any one but to me"; and when he had so spoken, he bestowed an excellent horse, and other presents upon him; and, from that time forwards, there was not a faithfuller and more trusty man in the whole army. With good reason he judged, that, if those who have the government of horses and dogs endeavour by gentle usage to cure their angry and untractable tempers, rather than by cruelty and beating, much more should those who have the command of men try to bring them to order and discipline by the mildest and fairest means, and not treat them worse than gardeners do those wild plants, which, with care and attention, lose gradually the savageness of their nature, and bear excellent fruit.

At another time, some of his officers informed him that one of their men was very often absent from his place, and out at nights; he asked them what kind of man he was; they all answered, that the whole army had not a better man, that he was a native of Lucania, and proceeded to speak of several actions which they had seen him perform. Fabius made strict inquiry, and discovered at last that these frequent excursions which he ventured upon were to visit a young girl, with whom he was in love. Upon which he gave private order to some of his men to find out the woman and secretly convey her into his own tent; and then sent for the Lucanian, and, calling him aside, told him, that he very well knew how often he had been out away from the camp at night, which was a capital transgression against military discipline and the Roman laws, but he knew also how brave he was, and the good services he had done; therefore, in consideration of them, he was willing to forgive him his fault; but to keep him in good order, he was resolved to place one over him to be his keeper, who should be accountable for his good behaviour. Having said this, he produced the woman, and told the soldier, terrified and amazed at the adventure, "This is the person who must answer for you; and by your future behaviour we shall see whether your night rambles were on account of love, or for any other worse design."

Another passage there was, something of the same kind, which gained him possession of Tarentum. There was a young Tarentine in the army that had a sister in Tarentum, then in possession of the enemy, who entirely loved her brother, and wholly depended upon him. He, being informed that a certain Bruttian, whom Hannibal had made a commander of the garrison, was deeply in love with his sister, conceived hopes that he might possibly turn it to the advantage of the Romans. And having first communicated his design to Fabius, he left the army as a deserter in show, and went over to Tarentum. The first days passed, and the Bruttian abstained from visiting the sister; for neither of them knew that the brother had notice of the amour between them. The young Tarentine, however, took an occasion to tell his sister how he had heard that a man of station and authority had made his addresses to her, and desired her, therefore, to tell him who it was; "for," said he, "if he be a man that has bravery and reputation, it matters not what countryman he is, since at this time the sword mingles all nations, and makes them equal; compulsion makes all things honourable; and in a time when right is weak, we may be thankful if might assumes a form of gentleness." Upon this the woman sends for her friend, and makes the brother and him acquainted; and whereas she henceforth showed more countenance to her lover than formerly, in the same degrees that her kindness increased, his friendship, also, with the brother advanced. So that at last our Tarentine thought this Bruttian officer well enough prepared to receive the offers he had to make him, and that it would be easy for a mercenary man, who was in love, to accept, upon the terms proposed, the large rewards promised by Fabius. In conclusion, the bargain was struck, and the promise made of delivering the town. This is the common tradition, though some relate the story otherwise, and say, that this woman, by whom the Bruttian was inveigled to betray the town, was not a native of Tarentum, but a Bruttian born, and was kept by Fabius as his concubine; and being a country-woman and an acquaintance of the Bruttian governor, he privately sent her to him to corrupt him.

Whilst these matters were thus in process, to draw off Hannibal from scenting the design, Fabius sends orders to the garrison in Rhegium, that they should waste and spoil the Bruttian country, and should also lay siege to Caulonia, and storm the place with all their might. These were a body of eight thousand men, the worst of the Roman army, who had most of them been runaways, and had been brought home by Marcellus from Sicily, in dishonour, so that the loss of them would not be any great grief to the Romans. Fabius, therefore, threw out these men as a bait for Hannibal, to divert him from Tarentum; who instantly caught at it, and led his forces to Caulonia; in the meantime, Fabius sat down before Tarentum. On the sixth day of the siege, the young Tarentine slips by night out of the town, and, having carefully observed the place where the Bruttian commander, according to agreement, was to admit the Romans, gave an account of the whole matter to Fabius; who thought it not safe to rely wholly upon the plot, but, while proceeding with secrecy to the post, gave order for a general assault to be made on the other side of the town, both by land and sea. This being accordingly executed, while the Tarentines hurried to defend the town on the side attacked, Fabius received the signal from the Bruttian, scaled the walls, and entered the town unopposed.

Here, we must confess, ambition seems to have overcome him. To make it appear to the world that he had taken Tarentum by force and his own prowess, and not by treachery, he commanded his men to kill the Bruttians before all others; yet he did not succeed in establishing the impression he desired, but merely gained the character of perfidy and cruelty. Many of the Tarentines were also killed, and thirty thousand of them were sold for slaves; the army had the plunder of the town, and there was brought into the treasury three thousand talents. Whilst they were carrying off everything else as plunder, the officer who took the inventory asked what should be done with their gods, meaning the pictures and statues; Fabius answered, "Let us leave their angry gods to the Tarentines." Nevertheless, he removed the colossal statue of Hercules, and had it set up in the Capitol, with one of himself on horseback, in brass, near it; proceedings very different from those of Marcellus on a like occasion, and which, indeed, very much set off in the eyes of the world his clemency and humanity, as appears in the account of his life.

Hannibal, it is said, was within five miles of Tarentum, when he was informed that the town was taken. He said openly, "Rome then has also got a Hannibal; as we won Tarentum, so have we lost it." And, in private with some of his confidants, he told them, for the first time, that he always thought it difficult, but now he held it impossible, with the forces he then had, to master Italy.

Upon this success, Fabius had a triumph decreed him at Rome, much more splendid than his first; they looked upon him now as a champion who had learned to cope with his antagonist, and could now easily foil his arts and prove his best skill ineffectual. And, indeed, the army of Hannibal was at this time partly worn away with continual action, and partly weakened and become dissolute with overabundance and luxury. Marcus Livius, who was governor of Tarentum when it was betrayed to Hannibal, and then retired into the citadel, which he kept till the town was retaken, was annoyed at these honours and distinctions, and, on one occasion, openly declared in the senate, that by his resistance, more than by any action of Fabius, Tarentum had been recovered; on which Fabius laughingly replied: "You say very true, for if Marcus Livius had not lost Tarentum, Fabius Maximus had never recovered it." The people, amongst other marks of gratitude, gave his son the consulship of the next year; shortly after whose entrance upon his office, there being some business on foot about provision for the war, his father, either by reason of age and infirmity, or perhaps out of design to try his son, came up to him on horseback. While he was still at a distance, the young consul observed it, and bade one of his lictors command his father to alight, and tell him if he had any business with the consul, he should come on foot. The standers-by seemed offended at the imperiousness of the son towards a father so venerable for his age and his authority, and turned their eyes in silence towards Fabius. He, however, instantly alighted from his horse, and with open arms came up, almost running, and embraced his son, saying, "Yes, my son, you do well, and understand well what authority you have received, and over whom you are to use it. This was the way by which we and our forefathers advanced the dignity of Rome, preferring ever her honour and service to our own fathers and children."

And, in fact, it is told that the great-grandfather of our Fabius, who was undoubtedly the greatest man of Rome in his time, both in reputation and authority, who had been five times consul, and had been honoured with several triumphs for victories obtained by him, took pleasure in serving as lieutenant under his own son, when he went as consul to his command. And when afterwards his son had a triumph bestowed upon him for his good service, the old man followed, on horseback, his triumphant chariot, as one of his attendants; and made it his glory, that while he really was, and was acknowledged to be, the greatest man in Rome, and held a father's full power over his son, he yet submitted himself to the laws and the magistrate.

But the praises of our Fabius are not bounded here. He afterwards lost his son, and was remarkable for bearing the loss with the moderation becoming a pious father and a wise man, and as it was the custom amongst the Romans, upon the death of any illustrious person, to have a funeral oration recited by some of the nearest relations, he took upon himself that office, and delivered a speech in the forum, which he committed afterwards to writing.

After Cornelius Scipio, who was sent into Spain, had driven the Carthaginians, defeated by him in many battles, out of the country, and had gained over to Rome many towns and nations with large resources, he was received at his coming home with unexampled joy and acclamation of the people; who, to show their gratitude, elected him consul for the year ensuing. Knowing what high expectation they had of him, he thought the occupation of contesting Italy with Hannibal a mere old man's employment, and proposed no less a task to himself than to make Carthage the seat of the war, fill Africa with arms and devastation, and so oblige Hannibal, instead of invading the countries of others, to draw back and defend his own. And to this end he proceeded to exert all the influence he had with the people. Fabius, on the other side, opposed the undertaking with all his might, alarming the city, and telling them that nothing but the temerity of a hot young man could inspire them with such dangerous counsels, and sparing no means, by word or deed, to prevent it. He prevailed with the senate to espouse his sentiments; but the common people thought that he envied the fame of Scipio, and that he was afraid lest this young conqueror should achieve some great and noble exploit, and have the glory, perhaps, of driving Hannibal out of Italy, or even of ending the war, which had for so many years continued and been protracted under his management.

To say the truth, when Fabius first opposed this project of Scipio, he probably did it out of caution and prudence, in consideration only of the public safety, and of the danger which the commonwealth might incur; but when he found Scipio every day increasing in the esteem of the people, rivalry and ambition led him further, and made him violent and personal in his opposition. For he even applied to Crassus, the colleague of Scipio, and urged him not to yield the command to Scipio, but that, if his inclinations were for it, he should himself in person lead the army to Carthage. He also hindered the giving money to Scipio for the war; so that he was forced to raise it upon his own credit and interest from the cities of Etruria, which were extremely attached to him. On the other side, Crassus would not stir against him, nor remove out of Italy, being, in his own nature, averse to all contention, and also having, by his office of high priest, religious duties to retain him. Fabius, therefore, tried other ways to oppose the design; he impeded the levies, and he declaimed, both in the senate and to the people, that Scipio was not only himself flying from Hannibal, but was also endeavouring to drain Italy of all its forces, and to spirit away the youth of the country to a foreign war, leaving behind them their parents, wives, and children, and the city itself, a defenceless prey to the conquering and undefeated enemy at their doors. With this he so far alarmed the people, that at last they would only allow Scipio for the war the legions which were in Sicily, and three hundred, whom he particularly trusted, of those men who had served with him in Spain. In these transactions, Fabius seems to have followed the dictates of his own wary temper.

But, after that Scipio was gone over into Africa, when news almost immediately came to Rome of wonderful exploits and victories, of which the fame was confirmed by the spoils he sent home; of a Numidian king taken prisoner; of a vast slaughter of their men; of two camps of the enemy burnt and destroyed, and in them a great quantity of arms and horses; and when, hereupon, the Carthaginians were compelled to send envoys to Hannibal to call him home, and leave his idle hopes in Italy, to defend Carthage; when, for such eminent and transcending services, the whole people in Rome cried up and extolled the actions of Scipio; even then, Fabius contended that a successor should be sent in his place, alleging for it only the old reason of the mutability of fortune, as if she would be weary of long favouring the same person. With this language many did begin to feel offended; it seemed to be morosity and ill-will, the pusillanimity of old age, or a fear, that had now become exaggerated, of the skill of Hannibal. Nay, when Hannibal had put his army on shipboard, and taken his leave of Italy, Fabius still could not forbear to oppose and disturb the universal joy of Rome, expressing his fears and apprehensions, telling them that the commonwealth was never in more danger than now, and that Hannibal was a more formidable enemy under the walls

of Carthage than ever he had been in Italy; that it would
be fatal to Rome whenever Scipio should encounter his
victorious army, still warm with the blood of so many Roman generals, dictators, and consuls slain. And the people
were, in some degree, startled with these declamations, and
were brought to believe that the further off Hannibal was,
the nearer was their danger. Scipio, however, shortly afterwards fought Hannibal, and utterly defeated him, humbled
the pride of Carthage beneath his feet, gave his countrymen joy and exultation beyond all their hopes, and—

"Long shaken on the seas restored the state."

Fabius Maximus, however, did not live to see the prosperous end of this war, and the final overthrow of Hannibal, nor to rejoice in the re-established happiness and security of the commonwealth; for about the time that Hannibal
left Italy, he fell sick and died. At Thebes, Epaminondas died
so poor that he was buried at the public charge; one small
iron coin was all, it is said, that was found in his house.
Fabius did not need this, but the people, as a mark of their
affection, defrayed the expenses of his funeral by a private
contribution from each citizen of the smallest piece of coin;
thus owning him their common father, and making his end
no less honourable than his life.

✦

MARCELLUS

They say that Marcus Claudius, who was five times consul of the Romans, was the son of Marcus; and that he was the first of his family called Marcellus; that is, *martial,* as Posidonius affirms. He was, indeed, by long experience, skilful in the art of war, of a strong body, valiant of hand, and by natural inclinations addicted to war. This high temper and heat he showed conspicuously in battle; in other respects he was modest and obliging, and so far studious of Greek learning and discipline, as to honour and admire those that excelled in it, though he did not himself attain a proficiency in them equal to his desire, by reason of his employments. For if ever there were any men whom, as Homer says, Heaven

> "From their first youth unto their utmost age
> Appointed the laborious wars to wage,"

certainly they were the chief Romans of that time; who in their youth had war with the Carthaginians in Sicily, in their middle age with the Gauls in the defence of Italy itself; and at last, when now grown old, struggled again with Hannibal and the Carthaginians, and wanted in their latest years what is granted to most men, exemption from military toils; their rank and their great qualities still making them be called upon to undertake the command.

Marcellus, ignorant or unskilful of no kind of fighting, in single combat surpassed himself; he never declined a challenge, and never accepted without killing his challenger. In Sicily, he protected and saved his brother Otacilius when surrounded in battle, and slew the enemies that pressed upon him; for which act he was by the generals, while he was yet but young, presented with crowns and other honourable rewards; and, his good qualities more and more displaying themselves, he was created Curule Aedile by the people and by the high priests Augur; which is that priesthood to which chiefly the law assigns the observation of auguries.

After the end of the first Punic war, which lasted one-and-twenty years, the seed of Gallic tumults sprang up, and began again to trouble Rome. The Insubrians, a people inhabiting the subalpine region of Italy, strong in their own forces, raised from among the other Gauls aids of mercenary soldiers, called Gaesatae.

In the beginning of this war, in which the Romans sometimes obtained remarkable victories, sometimes were shamefully beaten, nothing was done toward the determination of the contest until Flaminius and Furius, being consuls, led large forces against the Insubrians. At the time of their departure, the river that runs through the country of Picenum was seen flowing with blood; there was a report that three moons had once been seen at Ariminum; and, in the consular assembly, the augurs declared that the consuls had been unduly and inauspiciously created. The senate, therefore, immediately sent letters to the camp, recalling the consuls to Rome with all possible speed, and commanding them to forbear from acting against the enemies, and to abdicate the consulship on the first opportunity. These letters being brought to Flaminius, he deferred to open them till, having defeated and put to flight the enemy's forces, he wasted and ravaged their borders. The people, therefore, did not go forth to meet him when he returned with huge spoils; nay, because he had not instantly obeyed the command in the letters, by which he was recalled, but slighted and contemned them, they were very near denying him the honour of a triumph. Nor was the triumph sooner passed than they deposed him, with his colleague, from the magistracy, and reduced them to the state of private citizens.

So soon as Flaminius with his colleague had resigned the

consulate, Marcellus was declared consul by the presiding officers called Interrexes; and, entering into the magistracy, chose Cnaeus Cornelius his colleague. There was a report that, the Gauls proposing a pacification, and the senate also inclining to peace, Marcellus inflamed the people to war; but a peace appears to have been agreed upon, which the Gaesatae broke; who, passing the Alps, stirred up the Insubrians (they being thirty thousand in number, and the Insubrians more numerous by far); and proud of their strength, marched directly to Acerrae, a city seated on the north of the river Po. From thence Britomartus, king of the Gaesatae, taking with him ten thousand soldiers, harassed the country round about. News of which being brought to Marcellus, leaving his colleague at Acerrae with the foot and all the heavy arms and a third part of the horse, and carrying with him the rest of the horse and six hundred light-armed foot, marching night and day without remission, he stayed not till he came up to these ten thousand near a Gaulish village called Clastidium, which not long before had been reduced under the Roman jurisdiction. Nor had he time to refresh his soldiers or to give them rest. For the barbarians, that were then present, immediately observed his approach, and contemned him, because he had very few foot with him. The Gauls were singularly skilful in horsemanship, and thought to excel in it; and as at present they also exceeded Marcellus in number, they made no account of him. They, therefore, with their king at their head, instantly charged upon him, as if they would trample him under their horses' feet, threatening all kinds of cruelties. Marcellus, because his men were few, that they might not be encompassed and charged on all sides by the enemy, extended his wings of horse, and, riding about, drew out his wings of foot in length, till he came near to the enemy. Just as he was in the act of turning round to face the enemy, it so happened that his horse, startled with their fierce look and their cries, gave back, and carried him forcibly aside. Fearing lest this accident, if converted into an omen, might discourage his soldiers, he quickly brought his horse round to confront the enemy, and made a gesture of adoration to the sun, as if he had wheeled about not by chance, but for a purpose of devotion. For it was customary to the Romans, when they offered worship to the gods, to turn round; and in this moment of meeting the enemy, he is said to have vowed the best of the arms to Jupiter Feretrius.

The king of the Gauls beholding Marcellus, and from the badges of his authority conjecturing him to be the general, advanced some way before his embattled army, and with a loud voice challenged him, and, brandishing his lance, fiercely ran in full career at him; exceeding the rest of the Gauls in stature, and with his armour, that was adorned with gold and silver and various colours, shining like lightning. These arms seeming to Marcellus, while he viewed the enemy's army drawn up in battalia, to be the best and fairest, and thinking them to be those he had vowed to Jupiter, he instantly ran upon the king, and pierced through his breastplate with his lance; then pressing upon him with the weight of his horse, threw him to the ground, and with two or three strokes more slew him. Immediately he leapt from his horse, laid his hand upon the dead king's arm and, looking up towards Heaven, thus spoke: "O Jupiter Feretrius, arbiter of the exploits of captains, and of the acts of commanders in war and battles, be thou witness that I, a general, have slain a general: I, a consul, have slain a king with my own hand, third of all the Romans; and that to thee I consecrate these first and most excellent of the spoils. Grant to us to despatch the relics of the war with the same course of fortune." Then the Roman horse joining battle not only with the enemy's horse, but also with the foot who attacked them, obtained a singular and unheard-of victory. For never before or since have so few horse defeated such numerous forces of horse and foot together. The enemies being to a great number slain, and the spoils collected, he returned to his colleague, who was conducting the war, with ill-success, against the enemies near the greatest and most populous of the Gallic cities, Milan. This was their capital, and, therefore, fighting valiantly in defence of it, they were not so much besieged by Cornelius, as they besieged him. But Marcellus having returned, and the Gaesatae retiring as soon as they were certified of the death of the king and the defeat of his army, Milan was taken. The rest of their towns, and all they had, the Gauls delivered up of their own accord to the Romans, and had peace upon equitable conditions granted to them.

When Hannibal invaded Italy, Marcellus was despatched with a fleet to Sicily. And when the army had been defeated at Cannae, and many thousands of them perished, and a few had saved themselves by flying to Canusium, and all feared lest Hannibal, who had destroyed the strength of the Roman army, should advance at once with his victorious troops to Rome, Marcellus first sent for the protection of the city fifteen hundred soldiers from the fleet. Then, by decree of the senate, going to Canusium, having heard that many of the soldiers had come together in that place, he led them out of the fortifications to prevent the enemy from ravaging the country. The chief Roman commanders had most of them fallen in battles; and the citizens complained that the extreme caution of Fabius Maximus, whose integrity and wisdom gave him the highest authority, verged upon timidity and inaction. They confided in him to keep them out of danger, but could not expect that he would enable them to retaliate. Fixing, therefore, their thoughts upon Marcellus, and hoping to combine his boldness, confidence, and promptitude with Fabius's caution and prudence, and to temper the one by the other, they sent, sometimes both with consular command, sometimes one as consul, the other as proconsul, against the enemy. Posidonius writes, that Fabius was called the buckler, Marcellus the sword of Rome. Certainly, Hannibal himself confessed that he feared Fabius as a schoolmaster, Marcellus as an adversary: the former, lest he should be hindered from doing mischief; the latter, lest he should receive harm himself.

He now was a third time created consul, and sailed over into Sicily. For the success of Hannibal had excited the Carthaginians to lay claim to that whole island; chiefly because, after the murder of the tyrant Hieronymus, all things had been in tumult and confusion at Syracuse. For which reason the Romans also had sent before to that city a force under the conduct of Appius, as praetor.

At this time Marcellus, first incensed by injuries done him by Hippocrates, commander of the Syracusans (who, to give proof of his good affection to the Carthaginians, and to acquire the tyranny to himself, had killed a number of Romans at Leontini), besieged and took by force the city of Leontini; yet violated none of the townsmen; only deserters, as many as he took, he subjected to the punishment of the rods and axe. But Hippocrates, sending a report to Syracuse, that Marcellus had put all the adult population to the sword, and then coming upon the Syracusans, who had risen in tumult upon that false report, made himself master of the city. Upon this Marcellus moved with his whole army to Syracuse, and encamping near the wall, sent ambassadors into the city to relate to the Syracusans the truth of what had been done in Leontini. When these could not prevail by treaty, the whole power being now in the hands of Hippocrates, he proceeded to attack the city both by land and by sea. The land forces were conducted by Appius: Marcellus, with sixty galleys, each with five rows of oars, furnished with all sorts of arms and missiles, and a huge bridge of planks laid upon eight ships chained together, upon which was carried the engine to cast stones and darts, assaulted the walls, relying on the abundance and magnificence of his preparations, and on his own previous glory; all which, however, were, it would seem, but trifles for Archimedes and his machines.

These machines he had designed and contrived, not as matters of any importance, but as mere amusements in geometry; in compliance with King Hiero's desire and request, some little time before, that he should reduce to practice some part of his admirable speculation in science, and by accommodating the theoretic truth to sensation and ordinary use, bring it more within the appreciation of the people in general. Eudoxus and Archytas had been the first originators of this far-famed and highly-prized art of mechanics, which they employed as an elegant illustration of geometrical truths, and as means of sustaining experimentally, to the satisfaction of the senses, conclusions too intricate for proof by words and diagrams. As, for example, to solve the problem, so often required in constructing geometrical figures, given the two extremes, to find the two mean lines of a proportion, both these mathematicians had recourse to the aid of instruments, adapting to their purpose certain curves and sections of lines. But what with Plato's indignation at it, and his invectives against it as the mere corruption and annihilation of the one good of geometry, which was thus shamefully turning its back upon the unembodied objects of pure intelligence to recur to sensation, and to ask help (not to be obtained without base supervisions and depravation) from matter; so it was that mechanics came to be separated from geometry, and, repudiated and neglected by philosophers, took its place as a military art. Archimedes, however, in writing to King Hiero, whose friend and near relation he was, had stated that given the force, any given weight might be moved, and even boasted, we are told, relying on the strength of demonstration, that if there were another earth, by going into it he could remove this. Hiero being struck with amazement at this, and entreating him to make good this problem by actual experiment, and show some great weight moved by a small engine, he fixed accordingly upon a ship of burden out of the king's arsenal, which could not be drawn out of the dock without great labour and many men; and, loading her with many passengers and a full freight, sitting himself the while far off, with no great endeavour, but only holding the head of the pulley in his hand and drawing the cords by degrees, he drew the ship in a straight line, as smoothly and evenly as if she had been in the sea. The king, astonished at this, and convinced of the power of the art, prevailed upon Archimedes to make him engines accommodated to all the purposes, offensive and defensive, of a siege. These the king himself never made use of, because he spent almost all his life in a profound quiet and the highest affluence. But the apparatus was, in most opportune time, ready at hand for the Syracusans, and with it also the engineer himself.

When, therefore, the Romans assaulted the walls in two places at once, fear and consternation stupefied the Syracusans, believing that nothing was able to resist that violence and those forces. But when Archimedes began to ply his engines, he at once shot against the land forces all sorts of missile weapons, and immense masses of stone that came down with incredible noise and violence; against which no man could stand; for they knocked down those upon whom they fell in heaps, breaking all their ranks and files. In the meantime huge poles thrust out from the walls over the ships sunk some by the great weights which they let down from on high upon them; others they lifted up into the air by an iron hand or beak like a crane's beak and, when they had drawn them up by the prow, and set them on end upon the poop, they plunged them to the bottom of the sea; or else the ships, drawn by engines within, and whirled about, were dashed against steep rocks that stood jutting out under the walls, with great destruction of the soldiers that were aboard them. A ship was frequently lifted up to a great height in the air (a dreadful thing to behold), and was rolled to and fro, and kept swinging, until the mariners were all thrown out, when at length it was dashed against the rocks, or let fall. At the engine that Marcellus brought upon the bridge of ships, which was called *Sambuca*, from some resemblance it had to an instrument of music, while it was as yet approaching the wall, there was discharged a piece of rock of ten talents weight, then a second and a third, which, striking upon it with immense force and a noise like thunder, broke all its foundation to pieces, shook out all its fastenings, and completely dislodged it from the bridge. So Marcellus, doubtful what counsel to pursue, drew off his ships to a safer distance, and sounded a retreat to his forces on land. They then took a resolution of coming up under the walls, if it were possible, in the night; thinking that as Archimedes used ropes stretched at length in playing his engines, the soldiers would now be under the shot, and the darts would, for want of sufficient distance to throw them, fly over their heads without effect. But he, it appeared, had long before framed for such occasions engines accommodated to any distance, and shorter weapons; and had made numerous small openings in the walls, through which, with engines of a shorter range, unexpected blows were inflicted on the assailants. Thus, when they who thought to deceive the defenders came close up to the walls, instantly a shower of darts and other missile weapons was again cast upon them. And when stones came tumbling down perpendicularly upon their heads, and, as it were, the whole wall shot out arrows at them, they retired. And now, again, as they were going off, arrows and darts of a longer range inflicted a great slaughter among them, and their ships were driven one against another; while they themselves were not able to retaliate in any way. For Archimedes had provided and fixed most of his engines immediately under the wall; whence the Romans, seeing that indefinite mischief overwhelmed them from no visible means, began to think they were fighting with the gods.

Yet Marcellus escaped unhurt, and deriding his own artificers and engineers, "What," said he, "must we give up fighting with this geometrical Briareus, who plays pitch-and-toss with our ships, and, with the multitude of darts which he showers at a single moment upon us, really outdoes the hundred-handed giants of mythology?" And, doubtless, the rest of the Syracusans were but the body of Archimedes's designs, one soul moving and governing all; for, laying aside all other arms, with this alone they infested the Romans and protected themselves. In fine, when such terror had seized upon the Romans, that, if they did but see a little rope or a piece of wood from the wall, instantly crying out, that there it was again, Archimedes was about to let fly some engine at them, they turned their backs and fled, Marcellus desisted from conflicts and assaults, putting all his hope in a long siege. Yet Archimedes possessed so high a spirit, so profound a soul, and such treasures of scientific knowledge, that though these inventions had now obtained him the renown of more than human sagacity, he yet would not deign to leave behind him any commentary or writing on such subjects; but, repudiating as sordid and ignoble the whole trade of engineering, and every sort of art that lends itself to mere use and profit, he placed his whole affection and ambition in those purer speculations where there can be no reference to the vulgar needs of life; studies, the superiority of which to all others is unquestioned, and in which the only doubt can be whether the beauty and grandeur of the subjects examined, or the precision and cogency of the methods and means of proof, must deserve our admiration. It is not possible to find in all geometry more difficult and intricate questions, or more simple and lucid explanations. Some ascribe this to his natural genius; while others think that incredible effort and toil produced these, to all appearances, easy and unlaboured results. No amount of investigation of yours would succeed in attaining the proof, and yet, once seen, you immediately believe you would have discovered it; by so smooth and so rapid a path he leads you to the conclusion required. And thus it ceases to be incredible that (as is commonly told of him) the charm of his familiar and domestic Siren made him forget his food and neglect his person, to that degree that when he was occasionally carried by absolute violence to bathe or have his body anointed, he used to trace geometrical figures in the ashes of the fire, and diagrams in the oil on his body, being in a state of entire preoccupation, and, in the truest sense, divine possession with his love and delight in science. His discoveries were numerous and admirable; but he is said to have requested his friends and relations that, when he was dead, they would place over his tomb a sphere containing a cylinder, inscribing it with the ratio which the containing solid bears to the contained.

Such was Archimedes, who now showed himself, and so far as lay in him the city also, invincible. While the siege continued, Marcellus took Megara, one of the earliest founded of the Greek cities in Sicily, and capturing also the camp of Hippocrates at Acilae, killed above eight thousand men, having attacked them whilst they were engaged in forming their fortifications. He overran a great part of Sicily; gained over many towns from the Carthaginians, and overcame all that dared to encounter him. As the siege went on, one Damippus, a Lacedaemonian, putting to sea in a ship from Syracuse, was taken. When the Syracusans much desired to redeem this man, and there were many meetings and treaties about the matter betwixt them and Marcellus, he had opportunity to notice a tower into which a body of men might be secretly introduced, as the wall near to it was not difficult to surmount, and it was itself carelessly guarded. Coming often thither, and entertaining conferences about the release of Damippus, he had pretty well calculated the height of the tower, and got ladders prepared. The Syracusans celebrated a feast to Diana; this juncture of time, when they were given up entirely to wine and sport, Marcellus laid hold of, and before the citizens perceived it, not only possessed himself of the tower, but, before the break of day, filled the wall around with soldiers, and made his way into the Hexapylum. The Syracusans now beginning to stir, and to be alarmed at the tumult, he ordered the trumpets everywhere to sound, and thus frightened them all into flight, as if all parts of the city were already won, though the most fortified, and the fairest, and most ample quarter was still ungained. It is called Acradina, and was divided by a wall from the outer city, one part of which they call Neapolis, the other Tycha. Possessing himself of these, Marcellus, about break of day, entered through the Hexapylum, all his officers congratulating him. But looking down from the higher places upon the beautiful and spacious city below, he is said to have wept much, commiserating the calamity that hung over it, when his thoughts represented to him how dismal and foul the face of the city would be in a few hours, when plundered and sacked by the soldiers. For among the officers of his army there was not one man that durst deny the plunder of the city to the soldiers' demands; nay, many were instant that it should be set on fire and laid level to the ground: but this Marcellus would not listen to. Yet he granted, but with great unwillingness and reluctance, that the money and slaves should be made prey; giving orders, at the same time, that none should violate any free person, nor kill, misuse, or make a slave of any of the Syracusans. Though he had used this moderation, he still esteemed the condition of that city to be pitiable, and, even amidst the congratulations and joy, showed his strong feelings of sympathy and commiseration at seeing all the riches accumulated during a long felicity now dissipated in an hour. For it is related that no less prey and plunder was taken here than afterward in Carthage. For not long after they obtained also the plunder of the other parts of the city, which were taken by treachery; leaving nothing untouched but the king's money, which was brought into the public treasury. But nothing afflicted Marcellus so much as the death of Archimedes, who was then, as fate would have it, intent upon working out some problem by a diagram, and having fixed his mind alike and his eyes upon the subject of his speculation, he never noticed the incursion of the Romans, nor that the city was taken. In this transport of study and contemplation, a soldier, unexpectedly coming up to him, commanded him to follow to Marcellus; which he declining to do before he had worked out his problem to a demonstration, the soldier, enraged, drew his sword and ran him through. Others write that a Roman soldier, running upon him with a drawn sword, offered to kill him; and that Archimedes, looking back, earnestly besought him to hold his hand a little while, that he might not leave what he was then at work upon inconclusive and imperfect; but the soldier, nothing moved by his entreaty, instantly killed him. Others again relate that, as Archimedes was carrying to Marcellus mathematical instruments, dials, spheres, and angles, by which the magnitude of the sun might be measured to the sight, some soldiers seeing him, and thinking that he carried gold in a vessel, slew him. Certain it is that his death was very afflicting to Marcellus; and that Marcellus ever after regarded him that killed him as a murderer; and that he sought for his kindred and honoured them with signal favours.

Indeed, foreign nations had held the Romans to be excellent soldiers and formidable in battle; but they had hitherto given no memorable example of gentleness, or humanity, or civil virtue; and Marcellus seems first to have shown to the Greeks that his countrymen were most illustrious for their justice. For such was his moderation to all with whom

he had anything to do, and such his benignity also to many
cities and private men, that, if anything hard or severe was
decreed concerning the people of Enna, Megara, or Syracuse, the blame was thought to belong rather to those upon
whom the storm fell, than to those who brought it upon
them. One example of many I will commemorate. In Sicily
there is a town called Engyum, not indeed great, but very
ancient and ennobled by the presence of the goddesses,
called the Mothers. The temple, they say, was built by the
Cretans; and they show some spears and brazen helmets,
inscribed with the names of Meriones, and (with the same
spelling as in Latin) of Ulysses, who consecrated them to
the goddesses. This city highly favouring the party of the
Carthaginians, Nicias, the most eminent of the citizens,
counselled them to go over to the Romans; to that end acting freely and openly in harangues to their assemblies,
arguing the imprudence and madness of the opposite course.
They, fearing his power and authority, resolved to deliver
him in bonds to the Carthaginians. Nicias, detecting the
design, and seeing that his person was secretly kept in
watch, proceeded to speak irreligiously to the vulgar of the
Mothers, and showed many signs of disrespect, as if he denied and contemned the received opinion of the presence of
those goddesses; his enemies the while rejoicing that he, of his
own accord, sought the destruction hanging over his head.
When they were just now about to lay hands upon him, an assembly was held, and here Nicias, making a speech to the
people concerning some affair then under deliberation, in the
midst of his address, cast himself upon the ground; and
soon after, while amazement (as usually happens on such
surprising occasions) held the assembly immovable, raising and turning his head round, he began in a trembling
and deep tone, but by degrees raised and sharpened his
voice. When he saw the whole theatre struck with horror
and silence, throwing off his mantle and rending his tunic
he leaps up half naked, and runs towards the door, crying
out aloud that he was driven by the wrath of the Mothers.
When no man durst, out of religious fear, lay hands upon
him or stop him, but all gave way before him, he ran out of

the gate, not omitting any shriek or gesture of men possessed and mad. His wife, conscious of his counterfeiting, and privy to his design, taking her children with her, first cast herself as a suppliant before the temple of the goddesses; then, pretending to seek her wandering husband, no man hindering her, went out of the town in safety; and by this means they all escaped to Marcellus at Syracuse. After many other such affronts offered him by the men of Engyum, Marcellus, having taken them all prisoners and cast them into bonds, was preparing to inflict upon them the last punishment; when Nicias, with tears in his eyes, addressed himself to him. In fine, casting himself at Marcellus's feet, and deprecating for his citizens, he begged most earnestly their lives, chiefly those of his enemies. Marcellus, relenting, set them all at liberty, and rewarded Nicias with ample lands and rich presents. This history is recorded by Posidonius the philosopher.

Marcellus, at length recalled by the people of Rome to the immediate war at home, to illustrate his triumph, and adorn the city, carried away with him a great number of the most beautiful ornaments of Syracuse. For, before that, Rome neither had, nor had seen, any of those fine and exquisite rarities; nor was any pleasure taken in graceful and elegant pieces of workmanship. Stuffed with barbarous arms and spoils stained with blood, and everywhere crowned with triumphal memorials and trophies, she was no pleasant or delightful spectacle for the eyes of peaceful or refined spectators; but, as Epaminondas named the fields of Boeotia the stage of Mars; and Xenophon called Ephesus the workhouse of war; so, in my judgment, may you call Rome, at that time (to use the words of Pindar), "the precinct of the peaceless Mars." Whence Marcellus was more popular with the people in general, because he had adorned the city with beautiful objects that had all the charms of Grecian grace and symmetry; but Fabius Maximus, who neither touched nor brought away anything of this kind from Tarentum, when he had taken it, was more approved of by the elder men. He carried off the money and valuables, but forbade the statues to be moved; adding, as it is commonly related,

"Let us leave to the Tarentines these offended gods." They blamed Marcellus, first for placing the city in an invidious position, as it seemed now to celebrate victories and lead processions of triumph, not only over men, but also over the gods as captives; then, that he had diverted to idleness, and vain talk about curious arts and artificers, the common people, which, bred up to wars and agriculture, had never tasted of luxury and sloth, and, as Euripides said of Hercules, had been—

"Rude, unrefined, only for great things good,"

so that now they misspent much of their time in examining and criticising trifles. And yet, notwithstanding this reprimand, Marcellus made it his glory to the Greeks themselves, that he had taught his ignorant countrymen to esteem and admire the elegant and wonderful productions of Greece.

Marcellus being the fourth time consul, moved against Hannibal. And whereas the other consuls and commanders, since the defeat received at Cannae, had all made use of the same policy against Hannibal, namely, to decline coming to a battle with him; and none had had the courage to encounter him in the field and put themselves to the decision by the sword; Marcellus entered upon the opposite course, thinking that Italy would be destroyed by the very delay by which they looked to wear out Hannibal; and that Fabius, who, adhering to his cautious policy, waited to see the war extinguished, while Rome itself meantime wasted away (like timid physicians, who, dreading to administer remedies, stay waiting, and believe that what is the decay of the patient's strength is the decline of the disease), was not taking a right course to heal the sickness of his country.

Having arranged with Fabius Maximus that, while he besieged Tarentum, he would, by following Hannibal and drawing him up and down, detain him from coming to the relief of the Tarentines, he overtook him at Canusium: and as Hannibal often shifted his camp, and still declined the combat, he everywhere sought to engage him. At last, pressing upon him while encamping, by light skirmishes he provoked him to a battle; but night again divided them in the very heat of the conflict. The next day Marcellus again showed himself in arms, and brought up his forces in array. Hannibal, in extreme grief, called his Carthaginians together to an harangue: and vehemently prayed them to fight to-day worthily of all their former success; "For you see," said he, "how, after such great victories, we have not liberty to respire, nor to repose ourselves, though victors; unless we drive this man back." Then the two armies, joining battle, fought fiercely; when the event of an untimely movement showed Marcellus to have been guilty of an error. The right wing being hard pressed upon, he commanded one of the legions to be brought up to the front. This change disturbing the array and posture of the legions gave the victory to the enemies; and there fell two thousand seven hundred Romans. Marcellus, after he had retreated into his camp, called his soldiers together. "I see," said he, "many Roman arms and bodies, but I see not so much as one Roman." To their entreaties for his pardon, he returned a refusal while they remained beaten, but promised to give it so soon as they should overcome; and he resolved to bring them into the field again the next day, that the fame of their victory might arrive at Rome before that of their flight. Dismissing the assembly, he commanded barley instead of wheat to be given to those companies that had turned their backs. These rebukes were so bitter to the soldiers, that though a great number of them were grievously wounded, yet they relate there was not one to whom the general's oration was not more painful and smarting than his wounds.

The day breaking, a scarlet toga, the sign of instant battle, was displayed. The companies marked with ignominy begged they might be posted in the foremost place, and obtained their request. Then the tribunes bring forth the rest of the forces, and draw them up. On news of which, "O strange!" said Hannibal, "what will you do with this man, who can bear neither good nor bad fortune? He is the only man who neither suffers us to rest when he is victor, nor rests himself when he is overcome. We shall have, it seems, perpetually to fight with him; as in good success his confidence, and in ill success his shame, still urges him to some further enterprise." Then the armies engaged. When the fight was doubtful, Hannibal commanded the elephants to be brought into the first battalion, and to be driven upon the van of the Romans. When the beasts, trampling upon many, soon caused disorder, Flavius, a tribune of soldiers, snatching an ensign, meets them, and wounding the first elephant with the spike at the bottom of the ensign staff, puts him to flight. The beast turned around upon the next, and drove back both him and the rest that followed. Marcellus, seeing this, pours in his horse with great force upon the elephants, and upon the enemy disordered by their flight. The horse, making a fierce impression, pursued the Carthaginians home to their camp, while the elephants, wounded and running upon their own party, caused a considerable slaughter. It is said more than eight thousand were slain; of the Roman army three thousand, and almost all wounded. This gave Hannibal opportunity to retire in the silence of the night, and to remove to greater distance from Marcellus; who was kept from pursuing by the number of his wounded men, and removed, by gentle marches, into Campania, and spent the summer at Sinuessa, engaged in restoring them.

No man was ever inflamed with so great desire of anything as was he to fight a battle with Hannibal. It was the subject of his dreams in the night, the topic of all his consultations with his friends and familiars, nor did he present to the gods any other wish, but that he might meet Hannibal in the field. And I think that he would most gladly have set upon him, with both armies environed within a single camp. Had he not been even loaded with honours, and had he not given proofs in many ways of his maturity of judgment and of prudence equal to that of any commander, you might have said that he was agitated by a youthful ambition, above what became a man of that age, for he had passed the sixtieth year of his life when he began his fifth consulship.

He tried all possible means to provoke Hannibal, who

at that time had a standing camp betwixt Bantia and Venusia. Hannibal declined an engagement, but having obtained intelligence that some troops were on their way to the town of Locri Epizephyrii, placing an ambush under the little hill of Petelia, he slew two thousand five hundred soldiers. This incensed Marcellus to revenge; and he therefore moved nearer Hannibal. Betwixt the two camps was a little hill, a tolerably secure post, covered with wood; it had steep descents on either side, and there were springs of water seen trickling down. This place was so fit and advantageous that the Romans wondered that Hannibal, who had come thither before them, had not seized upon it, but had left it to the enemies. But to him the place had seemed commodious indeed for a camp, but yet more commodious for an ambuscade; and to that use he chose to put it. So in the wood and the hollows he hid a number of archers and spearmen, confident that the commodiousness of the place would allure the Romans. Nor was he deceived in his expectation. For presently in the Roman camp they talked and disputed, as if they had all been captains, how the place ought to be seized, and what great advantage they should thereby gain upon the enemies, chiefly if they transferred their camp thither, at any rate, if they strengthened the place with a fort. Marcellus resolved to go, with a few horse, to view it. Having called a diviner he proceeded to sacrifice. In the first victim the aruspex showed him the liver without a head; in the second the head appeared of unusual size, and all the other indications highly promising. When these seemed sufficient to free them from the dread of the former, the diviners declared that they were all the more terrified by the latter; because entrails too fair and promising, when they appear after others that are maimed and monstrous, render the change doubtful and suspicious. But—

"Nor fire nor brazen wall can keep out fate;"

as Pindar observes. Marcellus, therefore, taking with him his colleague Crispinus, and his son, a tribune of soldiers, with two hundred and twenty horse at most (among whom there was not one Roman, but all were Etruscans, except forty Fregellans, of whose courage and fidelity he had on all occasions received full proof), goes to view the place. The hill was covered with woods all over; on the top of it sat a scout concealed from the sight of the enemy, but having the Roman camp exposed to his view. Upon signs received from him, the men that were placed in ambush stirred not till Marcellus came near; and then all starting up in an instant, and encompassing him from all sides, attacked him with darts, struck about and wounded the backs of those that fled, and pressed upon those who resisted. These were the forty Fregellans. For though the Etruscans fled in the very beginning of the fight, the Fregellans formed themselves into a ring, bravely defending the consuls, till Crispinus, struck with two darts, turned his horse to fly away; and Marcellus's side was run through with a lance with a broad head. Then the Fregellans, also, the few that remained alive, leaving the fallen consul, and rescuing young Marcellus, who also was wounded, got into the camp by flight. There were slain not much above forty; five lictors and eighteen horsemen came alive into the enemy's hands. Crispinus also died of his wounds a few days after. Such a disaster as the loss of both consuls in a single engagement was one that had never before befallen the Romans.

Hannibal, little valuing the other events, as soon as he was told of Marcellus's death, immediately hasted to the hill. Viewing the body, and continuing for some time to observe its strength and shape, he allowed not a word to fall from him expressive of the least pride or arrogancy, nor did he show in his countenance any sign of gladness, as another perhaps would have done, when his fierce and troublesome enemy had been taken away; but amazed by so sudden and unexpected an end, taking off nothing but his ring, gave order to have the body properly clad and adorned and honourably burned. The relics put into a silver urn, with a crown of gold to cover it, he sent back to his son. But some of the Numidians, setting upon these that were carrying the urn, took it from them by force, and cast away the bones; which being told to Hannibal, "It is impossible, it seems then," he said, "to do anything against the will of God!" He punished the Numidians; but took no further care of sending or re-collecting the bones; conceiving that Marcellus so fell, and so lay unburied, by a certain fate. So Cornelius Nepos and Valerius Maximus have left upon record: but Livy and Augustus Caesar affirm that the urn was brought to his son, and honoured with a magnificent funeral.

MARCUS CATO

Marcus Cato, we are told, was born at Tusculum, though (till he betook himself to civil and military affairs) he lived and was bred up in the country of the Sabines, where his father's estate lay. His ancestors seeming almost entirely unknown, he himself praises his father Marcus, as a worthy man and a brave soldier, and Cato, his great-grandfather, too, as one who had often obtained military prizes, and who, having lost five horses under him, received, on the account of his valour, the worth of them out of the public exchequer. Now it being the custom among the Romans to call those who, having no repute by birth, made themselves eminent by their own exertions, new men or upstarts, they called even Cato himself so, and so he confessed himself to be as to any public distinction or employment, but yet asserted that in the exploits and virtues of his ancestors he was very ancient. His third name originally was not Cato, but Priscus, though afterwards he had the surname of Cato, by reason of his abilities; for the Romans call a skilful or experienced man *Catus*. He was of a ruddy complexion and grey-eyed; as the writer, who, with no good-will, made the following epigram upon him lets us see:—

> "Porcius, who snarls at all in every place,
> With his grey eyes, and with his fiery face,
> Even after death will scarce admitted be
> Into the infernal realms by Hecate."

He gained, in early life, a good habit of body by working with his own hands, and living temperately, and serving in war; and seemed to have an equal proportion both of health and strength. And he exerted and practised his eloquence through all the neighbourhood and little villages; thinking it as requisite as a second body, and an all but necessary organ to one who looks forward to something above a mere humble and inactive life. He would never refuse to be counsel for those who needed him, and was, indeed, early reckoned a good lawyer, and, ere long, a capable orator.

Hence his solidity and depth of character showed itself gradually more and more to those with whom he was concerned, and claimed, as it were, employment in great affairs and places of public command. Nor did he merely abstain from taking fees for his counsel and pleading, but did not even seem to put any high price on the honour which proceeded from such kind of combats, seeming much more desirous to signalise himself in the camp and in real fights; and while yet but a youth, had his breast covered with scars he had received from the enemy: being (as he himself says) but seventeen years old when he made his first campaign; in the time when Hannibal, in the height of his success, was burning and pillaging all Italy. In engagements he would strike boldly, without flinching, stand firm to his ground, fix a bold countenance upon his enemies, and with a harsh threatening voice accost them, justly thinking himself and telling others that such a rugged kind of behaviour sometimes terrifies the enemy more than the sword itself. In his marches he bore his own arms on foot, whilst one servant only followed, to carry the provision for his table, with whom he is said never to have been angry or hasty whilst he made ready his dinner or supper, but would, for the most part, when he was free from military duty, assist and help himself to dress it. When he was with the army, he used to drink only water; unless, perhaps, when extremely thirsty, he might mingle it with a little vinegar, or if he found his strength fail him, take a little wine.

The little country house of Manius Curius, who had been thrice carried in triumph, happened to be near his farm; so that often going thither, and contemplating the small compass of the place, and plainness of the dwelling, he formed an idea of the mind of the person, who being one of the greatest of the Romans, and having subdued the most warlike nations, nay, had driven Pyrrhus out of Italy now, after three triumphs, was contented to dig in so small a piece of ground, and live in such a cottage. Here it was that the ambassadors of the Samnites, finding him boiling turnips in the chimney corner, offered him a present of gold; but he sent them away with this saying; that he, who was content with such a supper, had no need of gold; and that he thought it more honourable to conquer those who possessed the gold, than to possess the gold itself. Cato, after reflecting upon these things, used to return and, reviewing his own farm, his servants, and housekeeping, increase his labour and retrench all superfluous expenses.

When Fabius Maximus took Tarentum, Cato, being then but a youth, was a soldier under him; and being lodged with one Nearchus, a Pythagorean, desired to understand some of his doctrine, and hearing from him the language, which Plato also uses—that pleasure is evil's chief bait; the body the principal calamity of the soul; and that those thoughts which most separate and take it off from the affections of the body most enfranchise and purify it; he fell in love the more with frugality and temperance. With this exception, he is said not to have studied Greek until when he was pretty old; and in rhetoric to have then profited a little by Thucydides, but more by Demosthenes; his writings, however, are considerably embellished with Greek sayings and stories; nay, many of these, translated word for word, are placed with his own apothegms and sentences.

There was a man of the highest rank, and very influential among the Romans, called Valerius Flaccus, who was singularly skilful in discerning excellence yet in the bud, and also much disposed to nourish and advance it. He, it seems, had lands bordering upon Cato's; nor could he but admire when he understood from his servants the manner of his living, how he laboured with his own hands, went on foot betimes in the morning to the courts to assist those who wanted his counsel: how, returning home again, when it was winter, he would throw a loose frock over his shoulders, and in the summer time would work without anything on among his domestics, sit down with them, eat of the same bread, and drink of the same wine. When they spoke, also, of other good qualities, his fair dealing and moderation, mentioning also some of his wise sayings, he ordered that he should be invited to supper; and thus becoming personally assured of his fine temper and his superior character, which, like a plant, seemed only to require culture and a better situation, he urged and persuaded him to apply himself to state affairs at Rome. Thither, therefore, he went, and by his pleading soon gained many friends and admirers; but, Valerius chiefly assisting his promotion, he first of all got appointed tribune in the army, and afterwards was made quaestor, or treasurer. And now becoming eminent and noted, he passed, with Valerius himself, through the greatest commands, being first his colleague as consul, and then censor. But among all the ancient senators, he most attached himself to Fabius Maximus; not so much for the honour of his person, and the greatness of his power, as that he might have before him his habit and manner of life, as the best examples to follow; and so he did not hesitate to oppose Scipio the Great, who, being then but a young man, seemed to set himself against the power of Fabius, and to be envied by him. For being sent together with him as treasurer, when he saw him, according to his natural custom, make great expenses, and distribute among the soldiers without sparing, he freely told him that the expense in itself was not the greatest thing to be considered, but that he was corrupting the frugality of the soldiers, by giving them the means to abandon themselves to unnecessary pleasures and luxuries. Scipio answered, that he had no need for so accurate a treasurer (bearing on as he was, so to say, full sail to the war), and that he owed the people an account of his actions, and not of the money he spent. Hereupon Cato returned from Sicily and, together with Fabius, made loud complaints in the open senate of Scipio's lavishing unspeakable sums, and childishly loitering away his time in wrestling matches and comedies, as if he were not to make war, but holiday; and thus succeeded in getting some of the tribunes of the people sent to call him back to Rome, in case the accusations should prove true. But Scipio demonstrating, as it were, to them, by his preparations, the coming victory, and, being found merely to be living pleasantly with his friends, when there was nothing else to do, but in no respect because of that easiness and liberality at all the more negligent in things of consequence and moment, without impediment, set sail toward the war.

Cato grew more and more powerful by his eloquence, so that he was commonly called the Roman Demosthenes; but his manner of life was yet more famous and talked of. For oratorical skill was, as an accomplishment, commonly studied and sought after by all young men; but he was very rare who would cultivate the old habits of bodily labour, or prefer a light supper, and a breakfast which never saw the fire, or be in love with poor clothes and a homely lodging, or could set his ambition rather on doing without luxuries than on possessing them. For now the state, unable to keep its purity by reason of its greatness, and having so many affairs, and people from all parts under its government, was fain to admit many mixed customs and new examples of living. With reason, therefore, everybody admired Cato, when they saw others sink under labours and grow effeminate by pleasures; and yet beheld him unconquered by either, and that not only when he was young and desirous of honour, but also when old and grey-headed, after a consulship and triumph; like some famous victor in the games, persevering in his exercise and maintaining his character to the very last. He himself says that he never wore a suit of clothes which cost more than a hundred drachmas; and that, when he was general and consul, he

drank the same wine which his workmen did; and that the
meat or fish which was bought in the meat-market for his
dinner did not cost above thirty *asses*. All which was for the
sake of the commonwealth, that so his body might be the
hardier for the war. Having a piece of embroidered Baby-
lonian tapestry left him, he sold it; because none of his
farmhouses were so much as plastered. Nor did he ever buy
a slave for above fifteen hundred drachmas; as he did not
seek for effeminate and handsome ones, but able sturdy
workmen, horse-keepers and cow-herds: and these he
thought ought to be sold again, when they grew old, and no
useless servants fed in the house. In short, he reckoned
nothing a good bargain which was superfluous; but whatever it was, though sold for a farthing, he would think it
a great price, if you had no need of it; and was for the
purchase of lands for sowing and feeding, rather than
grounds for sweeping and watering.

Some imputed these things to petty avarice, but others
approved of him, as if he had only the more strictly denied
himself for the rectifying and amending of others. Yet certainly, in my judgment, it marks an over-rigid temper for
a man to take the work out of his servants as out of brute
beasts, turning them off and selling them in their old age,
and thinking there ought to be no further commerce between man and man than whilst there arises some profit by
it. We see that kindness or humanity has a larger field
than bare justice to exercise itself in; law and justice we
cannot, in the nature of things, employ on others than
men; but we may extend our goodness and charity even to
irrational creatures; and such acts flow from a gentle nature, as water from an abundant spring. It is doubtless the
part of a kind-natured man to keep even worn-out horses
and dogs, and not only take care of them when they are
foals and whelps, but also when they are grown old. The
Athenians, when they built their Hecatompedon, turned
those mules loose to feed freely which they had observed to
have done the hardest labour. One of these (they say)
came once of itself to offer its service, and ran along with,

nay, and went before, the teams which drew the waggons up to the acropolis, as if it would incite and encourage them to draw more stoutly; upon which there passed a vote that the creature should be kept at the public charge even till it died. The graves of Cimon's horses, which thrice won the Olympian races, are yet to be seen close by his own monument. Old Xanthippus, too (amongst many others who buried the dogs they had bred up), entombed his which swam after his galley to Salamis, when the people fled from Athens, on the top of a cliff, which they call the Dog's Tomb to this day. Nor are we to use living creatures like old shoes or dishes and throw them away when they are worn out or broken with service; but if it were for nothing else, but by way of study and practice in humanity, a man ought always to prehabituate himself in these things to be of a kind and sweet disposition. As to myself, I would not so much as sell my draught ox on the account of his age, much less for a small piece of money sell a poor old man, and so chase him, as it were, from his own country, by turning him not only out of the place where he has lived a long while, but also out of the manner of living he has been accustomed to, and that more especially when he would be as useless to the buyer as to the seller. Yet Cato for all this glories that he left that very horse in Spain which he used in the wars when he was consul, only because he would not put the public to the charge of his freight. Whether these acts are to be ascribed to the greatness or pettiness of his spirit, let every one argue as they please.

For his general temperance, however, and self-control he really deserves the highest admiration. For when he commanded the army, he never took for himself, and those that belonged to him, above three bushels of wheat for a month, and somewhat less than a bushel and a half a day of barley for his baggage-cattle. And when he entered upon the government of Sardinia, where his predecessors had been used to require tents, bedding and clothes upon the public account, and to charge the state heavily with the cost of provisions and entertainments for a great train

of servants and friends, the difference he showed in his
economy was something incredible. There was nothing of
any sort for which he put the public to expense; he would
walk without a carriage to visit the cities, with one only of
the common town officers, who carried his dress, and a
cup to offer libation with. Yet though he seemed thus easy
and sparing to all who were under his power, he, on the
other hand, showed most inflexible severity and strictness
in what related to public justice, and was rigorous and precise in what concerned the ordinances of the commonwealth; so that the Roman government never seemed more
terrible, nor yet more mild than under his administration.

His very manner of speaking seemed to have such a kind
of idea with it; for it was courteous, and yet forcible; pleasant, yet overwhelming; facetious, yet austere; sententious,
and yet vehement; like Socrates, in the description of Plato,
who seemed outwardly to those about him to be but a simple, talkative, blunt fellow; whilst at the bottom he was
full of such gravity and matter, as would even move tears
and touch the very hearts of his auditors. And, therefore, I
know not what has persuaded some to say that Cato's style
was chiefly like that of Lysias. However, let us leave those
to judge of these things who profess most to distinguish
between the several kinds of oratorical style in Latin; whilst
we write down some of his memorable sayings; being of
the opinion that a man's character appears much more by
his words than, as some think it does, by his looks.

Being once desirous to dissuade the common people of
Rome from their unseasonable and impetuous clamour for
largesses and distributions of corn, he began thus to harangue them: "It is a difficult task, O citizens, to make
speeches to the belly, which has no ears." Reproving, also,
their sumptuous habits, he said it was hard to preserve a
city where a fish sold for more than an ox. He had a saying, also, that the Roman people were like sheep; for they,
when single, do not obey, but when altogether in a flock,
they follow their leaders: "So you," said he, "when you
have got together in a body, let yourselves be guided by

those whom singly you would never think of being advised by." Discoursing of the power of women: "Men," said he, "usually command women; but we command all men, and the women command us." But this, indeed, is borrowed from the sayings of Themistocles, who, when his son was making many demands of him by means of the mother, said, "O woman, the Athenians govern the Greeks; I govern the Athenians, but you govern me, and your son governs you; so let him use his power sparingly since, simple as he is, he can do more than all the Greeks together." Another saying of Cato's was, that the Roman people did not only fix the value of such and such purple dyes, but also of such and such habits of life: "For," said he, "as dyers most of all dye such colours as they see to be most agreeable, so the young men learn, and zealously affect, what is most popular with you." He also exhorted them that, if they were grown great by their virtue and temperance, they should not change for the worse; but if intemperance and vice had made them great, they should change for the better; for by that means they were grown indeed quite great enough. He would say, likewise, of men who wanted to be continually in office, that apparently they did not know their road; since they could not do without beadles to guide them on it. He also reproved the citizens for choosing still the same men as their magistrates: "For you will seem," said he, "either not to esteem government worth much, or to think few worthy to hold it." Speaking, too, of a certain enemy of his, who lived a very base and discreditable life: "It is considered," he said, "rather as a curse than a blessing on him, that this fellow's mother prays that she may leave him behind her." Pointing at one who had sold the land which his father had left him, and which lay near the seaside, he pretended to express his wonder at his being stronger even than the sea itself; for what it washed away with a great deal of labour, he with a great deal of ease drank away. When the senate, with a great deal of splendour, received King Eumenes on his visit to Rome, and the chief citizens strove who should be most about him, Cato appeared to regard him with suspicion and apprehension; and when one that stood by, too, took occasion to say that he was a very good prince and a great lover of the Romans: "It may be so," said Cato; "but by nature this same animal of a king is a kind of man-eater"; nor, indeed, were there ever kings who deserved to be compared with Epaminondas, Pericles, Themistocles, Manius Curius, or Hamilcar, surnamed Barcas. He used to say, too, that his enemies envied him because he had to get up every day before light and neglect his own business to follow that of the public. He would also tell you that he had rather be deprived of the reward for doing well than not to suffer the punishment for doing ill; and that he could pardon all offenders but himself.

The Romans having sent three ambassadors to Bithynia, of whom one was gouty, another had his skull trepanned, and the other seemed little better than a fool, Cato, laughing, gave out that the Romans had sent an embassy which had neither feet, head, nor heart. His interest being entreated by Scipio, on account of Polybius, for the Achaean exiles, and there happening to be a great discussion in the senate about it, some being for, and some against their return, Cato, standing up, thus delivered himself: "Here do we sit all day long, as if we had nothing to do but beat our brains whether these old Greeks should be carried to their graves by the bearers here or by those in Achaea." The senate voting their return, it seems that a few days after Polybius's friends further wished that it should be further moved in the senate that the said banished persons should receive again the honours which they first had in Achaea; and to this purpose they sounded Cato for his opinion; but he, smiling, answered, that Polybius, Ulysses like, having escaped out of the Cyclops' den, wanted, it would seem, to go back again because he had left his cap and belt behind him. He used to assert, also, that wise men profited more by fools, than fools by wise men; for that wise men avoided the faults of fools, but that fools would not imitate the good examples of wise men. He would profess, too, that he was more taken with young men that blushed than with those who looked pale; and that he never desired to have a soldier that moved his hands too much in marching, and his feet too much in fighting; or snored louder than he shouted. Ridiculing a fat, overgrown man: "What use," said he, "can the state turn a man's body to, when all between the throat and groin is taken up by the belly?" When one who was much given to pleasures desired his acquaintance, begging his pardon, he said he could not live with a man whose palate was of a quicker sense than his heart. He would likewise say that the soul of a lover lived in the body of another: and that in his whole life he most repented of three things; one was, that he had trusted a secret to a woman; another, that he went by water when he might have gone by land; the third, that he had remained one whole day without doing any business of moment. Applying himself to an old man who was committing some vice: "Friend," said he, "old age has of itself blemishes enough; do not you add to it the deformity of vice." Speaking to a tribune, who was reputed a poisoner, and was very violent for the bringing in of a bill, in order to make a certain law: "Young man," cried he, "I know not which would be better, to drink, what you mix, or confirm what you would put up for a law." Being reviled by a fellow who lived a profligate and wicked life: "A contest," replied he, "is unequal between you and me: for you can hear ill words easily, and can as easily give them: but it is unpleasant to me to give such, and unusual to hear them." Such was his manner of expressing himself in his memorable sayings.

Being chosen consul, with his friend and familiar Valerius Flaccus, the government of that part of Spain which the Romans called the Hither Spain fell to his lot. Here, as he was engaged in reducing some of the tribes by force, and bringing over others by good words, a large army of barbarians fell upon him, so that there was danger of being disgracefully forced out again. He therefore called upon his neighbours, the Celtiberians, for help; and on their demanding two hundred talents for their assistance, everybody else thought it intolerable that even the Romans should promise barbarians a reward for their aid; but Cato said there was no discredit or harm in it; for, if they overcame, they would pay them out of the enemy's purse, and not out of their own; but if they were overcome, there would be nobody left either to demand the reward or to pay it. However, he won that battle completely, and, after that, all his other affairs succeeded splendidly. Polybius says that, by his command, the walls of all the cities on this side the river Baetis were in one day's time demolished, and yet there were a great many of them full of brave and warlike men. Cato himself says that he took more cities than he stayed days in Spain. Neither is this a mere rhodomontade, if it be true that the number was four hundred. And though the soldiers themselves had got much in the fights, yet he distributed a pound of silver to every man of them, saying, it was better that many of the Romans should return home with silver, rather than a few with gold. For himself, he affirms, that of all the things that were taken, nothing came to him beyond what he ate and drank. "Neither do I find fault," continued he, "with those that seek to profit by these spoils, but I had rather compete in valour with the best, than in wealth with the richest, or with the most covetous in love of money." Nor did he merely keep himself clear from taking anything, but even all those who more immediately belonged to him. He had five servants with him in the army; one of whom called Paccus, bought three boys out of those who were taken captive; which Cato coming to understand, the man, rather than venture into his presence, hanged himself. Cato sold the boys, and carried the price he got for them into the public exchequer.

Scipio the Great, being his enemy, and desiring, whilst he was carrying all things so successfully, to obstruct him, and take the affairs of Spain into his own hands, succeeded in getting himself appointed his successor in the government, and, making all possible haste, put a term to Cato's authority. But he, taking with him a convoy of five cohorts of foot and five hundred horse to attend him home, overthrew by the way the Lacetanians, and taking from them six hundred deserters, caused them all to be beheaded; upon which Scipio seemed to be in indignation, but Cato, in mock disparagment of himself, said, "Rome would become great indeed, if the most honourable and great men would not yield up the first place of valour to those who were more obscure, and when they who were of the commonalty (as he himself was) would contend in valour with those who were most eminent in birth and honour." The senate having voted to change nothing of what had been established by Cato, the government passed away under Scipio to no manner of purpose, in idleness and doing nothing; and so diminished his credit much more than Cato's. Nor did Cato, who now received a triumph, remit after this and slacken the reins of virtue, as many do, who strive not so much for virtue's sake, as for vainglory, and having attained the highest honours, as the consulship and triumphs, pass the rest of their life in pleasure and idleness, and quit all public affairs. But he, like those who are just entered upon public life for the first time, and thirst after gaining honour and glory in some new office, strained himself, as if he were but just setting out; and offering still publicly his service to his friends and citizens, would give up neither his pleadings nor his soldiery.

He accompanied and assisted Tiberius Sempronius, as his lieutenant, when he went into Thrace and to the Danube; and, in the quality of tribune, went with Manius Acilius into Greece, against Antiochus the Great, who, after Hannibal, more than any one struck terror into the Romans. For having reduced once more under a single command almost the whole of Asia, all, namely, that Seleucus Nicator had possessed, and having brought into obedience many warlike nations of the barbarians, he longed to fall upon the Greeks, as if they only were now worthy to fight with him. So across he came with his forces, pretending, as a specious cause of the war, that it was to free the Greeks, who had indeed no need of it, they having been but newly delivered from the power of king Philip and the Macedonians, and made independent, with the free use of their own laws, by the goodness of the Romans themselves: so that all Greece was in commotion and excitement, having been corrupted by the hopes of royal aid which the popular leaders in their cities put them into. Manius, therefore, sent ambassadors to the different cities; and Titus Flaminius (as is written in the account of him) suppressed and quieted most of the attempts of the innovators, without any trouble. Cato brought over the Corinthians, those of Patrea and Aegium, and spent a good deal of time at Athens. There is also an oration of his said to be extant which he spoke in Greek to the people; in which he expressed his admiration of the virtue of the ancient Athenians, and signified that he came with a great deal of pleasure to be a spectator of the beauty and greatness of their city. But this is a fiction; for he spoke to the Athenians by an interpreter, though he was able to have spoken himself; but he wished to observe the usage of his own country, and laughed at those who admired nothing but what was in Greek. Jesting upon Postumius Albinus, who had written an historical work in Greek, and requested that allowances might be made for his attempt, he said that allowance indeed might be made if he had done it under the express compulsion of an Amphictyonic decree. The Athenians, he says, admired the quickness and vehemence of his speech; for an interpreter would be very long in repeating what he expressed with a great deal of brevity; but on the whole he professed to believe that the words of the Greeks came only from their lips, whilst those of the Romans came from their hearts.

Now Antiochus, having occupied with his army the narrow passages about Thermopylae, and added palisades and walls to the natural fortifications of the place, sat down there, thinking he had done enough to divert the war; and the Romans, indeed, seemed wholly to despair of forcing the passage; but Cato, calling to mind the compass and circuit which the Persians had formerly made to come at this place, went forth in the night, taking along with him part of the army. Whilst they were climbing up, the guide, who was a prisoner, missed the way, and wandering up and down by impracticable and precipitous paths, filled the soldiers with fear and despondency. Cato, perceiving the danger, commanded all the rest to halt, and stay where they were, whilst he himself, taking along with him one Lucius Manlius, a most expert man at climbing mountains, went forward with a great deal of labour and danger, in the dark night, and without the least moonshine, among the wild olive-trees and steep craggy rocks, there being nothing but precipices and darkness before their eyes, till they struck into a little pass which they thought might lead down into the enemy's camp. There they put up marks upon some conspicuous peaks which surmount the hill called Callidromon, and, returning again, they led the army along with them to the said marks, till they got into their little path again, and there once made a halt; but when they began to go further, the path deserted them at a precipice, where they were in another strait and fear; nor did they perceive that they were all this while near the enemy. And now the day began to give some light, when they seemed to hear a noise, and presently after to see the Greek trenches and the guard at the foot of the rock. Here, therefore, Cato halted his forces, and commanded the troops from Firmum only, without the rest, to stick by him, as he had always found them faithful and ready. And when they came up and formed around him in close order, he thus spoke to them: "I desire," he said, "to take one of the enemy alive, that so I may understand what men these are who guard the passage; their number; and with what discipline, order, and preparation they expect us; but this feat," continued he, "must be an act of a great deal of quickness and boldness, such as that of lions, when they dart upon some timorous animal." Cato had no sooner thus expressed himself, but the Firmans forthwith rushed down the mountain, just as they were, upon the guard, and, falling unexpectedly upon them, affrighted and dispersed them all. One armed man they took, and brought to Cato,

who quickly learned from him that the rest of the forces
lay in the narrow passage about the king; that those who
kept the tops of the rocks were six hundred choice Aeto-
lians. Cato, therefore, despising the smallness of their number and carelessness, forthwith drawing his sword, fell
upon them with a great noise of trumpets and shouting.
The enemy, perceiving them thus tumbling, as it were,
upon them from the precipices, flew to the main body, and
put all things into disorder there.

In the meantime, whilst Manius was forcing the works
below, and pouring the thickest of his forces into the narrow passages, Antiochus was hit in the mouth with a stone,
so that his teeth being beaten out by it, he felt such excessive pain, that he was fain to turn away with his horse;
nor did any part of his army stand the shock of the Romans. Yet, though there seemed no reasonable hope of
flight, where all paths were so difficult, and where there
were deep marshes and steep rocks, which looked as if
they were ready to receive those who should stumble, the
fugitives, nevertheless, crowding and pressing together in
the narrow passages, destroyed even one another in their
terror of the swords and blows of the enemy. Cato (as it
plainly appears) was never oversparing of his own praises,
and seldom shunned boasting of any exploit; which quality, indeed, he seems to have thought the natural accom-
paniment of great actions; and with these particular exploits he was highly puffed up; he says that those who saw
him that day pursuing and slaying the enemies were ready
to assert that Cato owed not so much to the public as the
public did to Cato; nay, he adds, that Manius the consul,
coming hot from the fight, embraced him for a great while,
when both were all in a sweat; and then cried out with joy
that neither he himself, no, nor all the people together,
could make him a recompense equal to his actions. After
the fight he was sent to Rome, that he himself might be
the messenger of it: and so, with a favourable wind, he
sailed to Brundusium, and in one day got from thence to
Tarentum; and having travelled four days more, upon

the fifth, counting from the time of his landing, he arrived at Rome, and so brought the first news of the victory himself; and filled the whole city with joy and sacrifices, and the people with the belief that they were able to conquer every sea and every land.

These are pretty nearly all the eminent actions of Cato relating to military affairs: in civil policy, he was of opinion that one chief duty consisted in accusing and indicting criminals. He himself prosecuted many, and he would also assist others who prosecuted them, nay, would even procure such, as he did the Petilii against Scipio; but not being able to destroy him, by reason of the nobleness of his family, and the real greatness of his mind, which enabled him to trample all calumnies under foot, Cato at last would meddle no more with him; yet joining with the accusers against Scipio's brother Lucius, he succeeded in obtaining a sentence against him, which condemned him to the payment of a large sum of money to the state; and being insolvent, and in danger of being thrown into jail, he was, by the interposition of the tribunes of the people, with much ado dismissed. It is also said of Cato, that when he met a certain youth, who had effected the disgrace of one of his father's enemies, walking in the market-place, he shook him by the hand, telling him, that this was what we ought to sacrifice to our dead parents—not lambs and goats, but the tears and condemnations of their adversaries. But neither did he himself escape with impunity in his management of affairs; for if he gave his enemies but the least hold, he was still in danger, and exposed to be brought to justice. He is reported to have escaped at least fifty indictments; and one above the rest, which was the last, when he was eighty-six years old, about which time he uttered the well-known saying, that it was hard for him who had lived with one generation of men, to plead now before another. Neither did he make this the least of his lawsuits; for, four years after, when he was fourscore and ten, he accused Servilius Galba: so that his life and actions extended, we may say, as Nestor's did, over three ordinary ages of man. For, having had many contests, as we have related, with Scipio the Great, about affairs of state, he continued them down to Scipio the younger, who was the adopted grandson of the former, and the son of that Paulus who overthrew Perseus and the Macedonians.

Ten years after his consulship, Cato stood for the office of censor, which was indeed the summit of all honour, and in a manner the highest step in civil affairs; for besides all other power, it had also that of an inquisition into every one's life and manners. For the Romans thought that no marriage, or rearing of children, nay, no feast or drinking-bout, ought to be permitted according to every one's appetite or fancy, without being examined and inquired into; being indeed of opinion that a man's character was much sooner perceived in things of this sort than in what is done publicly and in open day. They chose, therefore, two persons, one out of the patricians, the other out of the commons, who were to watch, correct, and punish, if any one ran too much into voluptuousness, or transgressed the usual manner of life of his country; and these they called Censors. They had power to take away a horse, or expel out of the senate any one who lived intemperately and out of order. It was also their business to take an estimate of what every one was worth, and to put down in registers everybody's birth and quality; besides many other prerogatives. And therefore the chief nobility opposed his pretensions to it. Jealousy prompted the patricians, who thought that it would be a stain to everybody's nobility, if men of no original honour should rise to the highest dignity and power; while others, conscious of their own evil practices, and of the violation of the laws and customs of their country, were afraid of the austerity of the man; which, in an office of such great power, was likely to prove most uncompromising and severe. And so, consulting among themselves, they brought forward seven candidates in opposition to him, who sedulously set themselves to court the people's favour by fair promises, as though what they wished for was indulgent and easy government. Cato, on the contrary, promising no such mildness, but plainly threatening evil livers, from the very hustings openly declared himself, and exclaiming that the city needed a great and thorough purgation, called upon the people, if they were wise, not to choose the gentlest, but the roughest of physicians; such a one, he said, he was, and Valerius Flaccus, one of the patricians, another; together with him, he doubted not but he should do something worth the while, and that by cutting to pieces and burning like a hydra all luxury and voluptuousness. He added, too, that he saw all the rest endeavouring after the office with ill intent, because they were afraid of those who would exercise it justly, as they ought. And so truly great and so worthy of great men to be its leaders was, it would seem, the Roman people, that they did not fear the severity and grim countenance of Cato, but rejecting those smooth promisers who were ready to do all things to ingratiate themselves, they took him, together with Flaccus; obeying his recommendations not as though he were a candidate, but as if he had had the actual power of commanding and governing already.

Cato named, as chief of the senate, his friend and colleague Lucius Valerius Flaccus, and expelled, among many others, Lucius Quintius, who had been consul seven years before, and (which was greater honour to him than the consulship) brother to that Titus Flaminius who overthrew King Philip. The reason he had for his expulsion was this. Lucius, it seems, took along with him in all his commands a youth whom he had kept as his companion from the flower of his age, and to whom he gave as much power and respect as to the chiefest of his friends and relations.

Now it happened that Lucius being consular governor of one of the provinces, the youth setting himself down by him, as he used to do, among other flatteries with which he played upon him, when he was in his cups, told him he loved him so dearly that, "though there was a show of gladiators to be seen at Rome, and I," he said, "had never beheld one in my life; and though I, as it were, longed to see a man killed, yet I made all possible haste to come to

you." Upon this Lucius, returning his fondness, replied,
"Do not be melancholy on that account; I can remedy
that." Ordering therefore, forthwith, one of those condemned to die to be brought to the feast, together with
the headsman and axe, he asked the youth if he wished to
see him executed. The boy answering that he did, Lucius
commanded the executioner to cut off his neck; and this
several historians mention; and Cicero, indeed, in his dialogue *de Senectute*, introduces Cato relating it himself. But
Livy says that he that was killed was a Gaulish deserter,
and that Lucius did not execute him by the stroke of the
executioner, but with his own hand; and that it is so stated
in Cato's speech.

Lucius being thus expelled out of the senate by Cato, his
brother took it very ill, and appealing to the people, desired that Cato should declare his reasons; and when he
began to relate this transaction of the feast, Lucius endeavoured to deny it; but Cato challenging him to a formal
investigation, he fell off and refused it, so that he was then
acknowledged to suffer deservedly. Afterwards, however,
when there was some show at the theatre, he passed by the
seats where those who had been consuls used to be placed,
and taking his seat a great way off, excited the compassion of the common people, who presently with a great
noise made him go forward, and as much as they could
tried to set right and salve over what had happened. Manilius, also, who, according to the public expectation, would
have been next consul, he threw out of the senate, because,
in the presence of his daughter, and in open day, he had
kissed his wife. He said that, as for himself, his wife never
came into his arms except when there was great thunder;
so that it was for jest with him, that it was a pleasure for
him, when Jupiter thundered.

His treatment of Lucius, likewise the brother of Scipio,
and one who had been honoured with a triumph, occasioned some odium against Cato; for he took his horse
from him, and was thought to do it with a design of putting
an affront on Scipio Africanus, now dead. But he gave

most general annoyance by retrenching people's luxury; for though (most of the youth being thereby already corrupted) it seemed almost impossible to take it away with an open hand and directly, yet going, as it were, obliquely around, he caused all dress, carriages, women's ornaments, household furniture, whose price exceeded one thousand five hundred drachmas, to be rated at ten times as much as they were worth; intending by thus making the assessments greater, to increase the taxes paid upon them. He also ordained that upon every thousand *asses* of property of this kind, three should be paid, so that people, burdened with these extra charges and seeing others of as good estates, but more frugal and sparing, paying less into the public exchequer, might be tried out of their prodigality. And thus, on the one side, not only those were disgusted at Cato who bore the taxes for the sake of their luxury, but those, too, who on the other side laid by their luxury for fear of the taxes. For people in general reckon that an order not to display their riches is equivalent to the taking away of their riches, because riches are seen much more in superfluous than in necessary things. Indeed this was what excited the wonder of Ariston the philosopher; that we account those who possess superfluous things more happy than those who abound with what is necessary and useful. But when one of his friends asked Scopas, the rich Thessalian, to give him some article of no great utility, saying that it was not a thing that he had any great need or use for himself, "In truth," replied he, "it is just these useless and unnecessary things that make my wealth and happiness." Thus the desire of riches does not proceed from a natural passion within us, but arises rather from vulgar out-of-doors opinion of other people.

Cato, notwithstanding, being little solicitous as to those who exclaimed against him, increased his austerity. He caused the pipes, through which some persons brought the public water into their houses and gardens, to be cut, and threw down all buildings which jutted out into the common streets. He beat down also the price in contracts for

public works to the lowest, and raised it in contracts for
farming the taxes to the highest sum; by which proceedings he drew a great deal of hatred upon himself. Those
who were of Titus Flaminius's party cancelled in the senate all the bargains and contracts made by him for the repairing and carrying on of the sacred and public buildings
as unadvantageous to the commonwealth. They incited
also the boldest of the tribunes of the people to accuse
him and to fine him two talents. They likewise much opposed him in building the court or basilica, which he caused
to be erected at the common charge, just by the senate-
house, in the market-place, and called by his own name, the
Porcian. However, the people, it seems, liked his censor-
ship wondrously well; for, setting up a statue for him in
the temple of the goddess of Health, they put an inscription under it, not recording his commands in war or his
triumph, but to the effect that this was Cato the Censor,
who, by his good discipline and wise and temperate ordinances, reclaimed the Roman commonwealth when it was
declining and sinking down into vice. Before this honour
was done to himself, he used to laugh at those who loved
such kind of things, saying, that they did not see that
they were taking pride in the workmanship of brass-found-
ers and painters; whereas the citizens bore about his best
likeness in their breasts. And when any seemed to wonder
that he should have never a statue, while many ordinary
persons had one, "I would," said he, "much rather be
asked, why I have not one, than why I have one." In
short, he would not have any honest citizen endure to be
praised, except it might prove advantageous to the commonwealth. Yet still he had passed the highest commendation on himself; for he tells us that those who did anything wrong, and were found fault with, used to say it was
not worth while to blame them, for they were not Catos.
He also adds, that they who awkwardly mimicked some of
his actions were called left-handed Catos; and that the
senate in perilous times would cast their eyes on him, as
upon a pilot in a ship, and that often when he was not

present they put off affairs of greatest consequence. These things are indeed also testified of him by others; for he had a great authority in the city, alike for his life, his eloquence, and his age.

He was also a good father, an excellent husband to his wife, and an extraordinary economist; and as he did not manage his affairs of this kind carelessly, and as things of little moment, I think I ought to record a little further whatever was commendable in him in these points. He married a wife more noble than rich; being of opinion that the rich and the high-born are equally haughty and proud; but that those of noble blood would be more ashamed of base things, and consequently more obedient to their husbands in all that was fit and right. A man who beat his wife or child laid violent hands, he said, on what was most sacred; and a good husband he reckoned worthy of more praise than a great senator; and he admired the ancient Socrates for nothing so much as for having lived a temperate and contented life with a wife who was a scold, and children who were half-witted.

As soon as he had a son born, though he had never such urgent business upon his hands, unless it were some public matter, he would be by when his wife washed it and dressed it in its swaddling clothes. For she herself suckled it, nay, she often too gave her breast to her servants' children, to produce, by suckling the same milk, a kind of natural love in them to her son. When he began to come to years of discretion, Cato himself would teach him to read, although he had a servant, a very good grammarian, called Chilo, who taught many others; but he thought not fit, as he himself said, to have his son reprimanded by a slave, or pulled, it may be, by the ears when found tardy in his lesson: nor would he have him owe to a servant the obligation of so great a thing as his learning; he himself, therefore (as we were saying), taught him his grammar, law, and his gymnastic exercises. Nor did he only show him, too, how to throw a dart, to fight in armour, and to ride, but to box also and to endure both heat and cold, and to swim over the most rapid and rough rivers. He says, likewise, that he wrote histories, in large characters, with his own hand, that so his son, without stirring out of the house, might learn to know about his countrymen and forefathers; nor did he less abstain from speaking anything obscene before his son, than if it had been in the presence of the sacred virgins, called vestals. Nor would he ever go into the bath with him; which seems indeed to have been the common custom of the Romans. Sons-in-law used to avoid bathing with fathers-in-law, disliking to see one another naked; but having, in time, learned of the Greeks to strip before men, they have since taught the Greeks to do it even with the women themselves.

Thus, like an excellent work, Cato formed and fashioned his son to virtue; nor had he any occasion to find fault with his readiness and docility; but as he proved to be of too weak a constitution for hardships, he did not insist on requiring of him any very austere way of living. However, though delicate in health, he proved a stout man in the field, and behaved himself valiantly when Paulus Aemilius fought against Perseus; where when his sword was struck from him by a blow, or rather slipped out of his hand by reason of its moistness, he so keenly resented it, that he turned to some of his friends about him, and taking them along with him again fell upon the enemy; and having by a long fight and much force cleared the place, at length found it among great heaps of arms, and the dead bodies of friends as well as enemies piled one upon another. Upon which Paulus, his general, much commended the youth; and there is a letter of Cato's to his son, which highly praised his honourable eagerness for the recovery of his sword. Afterwards he married Tertia, Aemilius Paulus's daughter, and sister to Scipio; nor was he admitted into this family less for his own worth than his father's. So that Cato's care in his son's education came to a very fitting result.

He purchased a great many slaves out of the captives taken in war, but chiefly brought up the young ones, who were capable to be, as it were, broken and taught like whelps and colts. None of these ever entered another man's house, except sent either by Cato himself or his wife. If any one of them were asked what Cato did, they answered merely that they did not know. When a servant was at home, he was obliged either to do some work or sleep, for indeed Cato loved those most who used to lie down often to sleep, accounting them more docile than those who were wakeful, and more fit for anything when they were refreshed with a little slumber. Being also of opinion that the great cause of the laziness and misbehaviour of slaves was their running after their pleasures, he fixed a certain price for them to pay for permission amongst themselves, but would suffer no connections out of the house. At first, when he was but a poor soldier, he would not be difficult in anything which related to his eating, but looked upon it as a pitiful thing to quarrel with a servant for the belly's sake; but afterwards, when he grew richer, and made any feasts for his friends and colleagues in office, as soon as supper was over he used to go with a leather thong and scourge those who had waited or dressed the meat carelessly. He always contrived, too, that his servants should have some difference one among another, always suspecting and fearing a good understanding between them. Those who had committed anything worthy of death, he punished if they were found guilty by the verdict of their fellow-servants. But being after all much given to the desire of gain, he looked upon agriculture rather as a pleasure than profit; resolving, therefore, to lay out his money in safe and solid things, he purchased ponds, hot baths, grounds full of fuller's earth, remunerative lands, pastures, and woods; from all which he drew large returns, nor could Jupiter himself, he used to say, do him much damage. He was also given to the form of usury, which is considered most odious, in traffic by sea; and that thus:—he desired that those whom he put out his money to should have many partners; when the number of them and their ships came to be fifty, he himself took one share through Quintio his freedman, who therefore was to sail with the adventurers, and take a part in all their proceedings, so that thus there was no danger of losing his whole stock, but only a little part, and that with a prospect of great profit. He likewise lent money to those of his slaves who wished to borrow, with which they bought also other young ones, whom, when they had taught and bred up at his charges, they would sell again at the year's end; but some of them Cato would keep for himself, giving just as much for them as another had offered. To incline his son to be of his kind or temper, he used to tell him that it was not like a man, but rather like a widow woman, to lessen an estate. But the strongest indication of Cato's avaricious humour was when he took the boldness to affirm that he was a most wonderful, nay, a godlike man, who left more behind him than he had received.

He was now grown old, when Carneades the Academic, and Diogenes the Stoic, came as deputies from Athens to Rome, praying for release from a penalty of five hundred talents laid on the Athenians, in a suit, to which they did not appear, in which the Oropians were plaintiffs and Sicyonians judges. All the most studious youth immediately waited on these philosophers, and frequently, with admiration, heard them speak. But the gracefulness of Carneades's oratory, whose ability was really greatest, and his reputation equal to it, gathered large and favourable audiences, and ere long filled, like a wind, all the city with the sound of it. So that it soon began to be told that a Greek, famous even to admiration, winning and carrying all before him, had impressed so strange a love upon the young men, that quitting all their pleasures and pastimes, they ran mad, as it were, after philosophy; which indeed much pleased the Romans in general; nor could they but with much pleasure see the youth receive so welcomely the Greek literature, and frequent the company of learned men. But Cato, on the other side, seeing the passion for words flowing into the city, from the beginning took it ill, fearing lest the youth should be diverted that way, and so should prefer the glory of speaking well before that of arms and doing well. And when the fame of the philosophers increased in the city, and Caius Acilius, a person of distinction, at his own request, became their interpreter to the senate at their first audience, Cato resolved, under some specious pretence, to have all philosophers cleared out of the city; and, coming into the senate, blamed the magistrates for letting these deputies stay so long a time without being despatched, though they were persons that could easily persuade the people to what they pleased; that therefore in all haste something should be determined about their petition, that so they might go home again to their own schools, and declaim to the Greek children, and leave the Roman youth to be obedient, as hitherto, to their own laws and governors.

Yet he did this not out of any anger, as some think, to Carneades; but because he wholly despised philosophy, and out of a kind of pride scoffed at the Greek studies and literature; as, for example, he would say, that Socrates was a prating, seditious fellow, who did his best to tyrannise over his country, to undermine the ancient customs, and to entice and withdraw the citizens to opinions contrary to the laws. Ridiculing the school of Isocrates, he would add, that his scholars grew old men before they had done learning with him, as if they were to use their art and plead causes in the court of Minos in the next world. And to frighten his son from anything that was Greek, in a more vehement tone than became one of his age, he pronounced, as it were, with the voice of an oracle, that the Romans would certainly be destroyed when they began once to be infected with Greek literature; though time indeed has shown the vanity of this his prophecy; as, in truth, the city of Rome has risen to its highest fortune while entertaining Grecian learning. Nor had he an aversion only against the Greek philosophers, but the physicians also; for having, it seems, heard how Hippocrates, when the king of Persia sent for him, with offers of a fee of several talents, said, that he would never assist barbarians who were enemies to the Greeks; he affirmed, that this was now become a common oath taken by all physicians, and enjoined his son to have a care and avoid them; for that he himself had written a little book of prescriptions for curing those who were sick in his family; he never enjoined fasting to any one, but ordered them either vegetables, or the meat of a duck, pigeon, or leveret; such kind of diet being of light digestion and fit for sick folks, only it made those who ate it dream a little too much; and by the use of this kind of physic, he said, he not only made himself and those about him well, but kept them so.

However, for this his presumption he seemed not to have escaped unpunished; for he lost both his wife and his son; though he himself, being of a strong, robust constitution, held out longer; so that he would often, even in his old days, address himself to women, and when he was past a lover's age, married a young woman, upon the following pretence: Having lost his own wife, he married his son to the daughter of Paulus Aemilius, who was sister to Scipio; so that being now a widower himself, he had a young girl who came privately to visit him, but the house being very small, and a daughter-in-law also in it, this practice was quickly discovered; for the young woman seeming once to pass through it a little too boldly, the youth, his son, though he said nothing, seemed to look somewhat indignantly upon her. The old man perceiving and understanding that what he did was disliked, without finding any fault or saying a word, went away, as his custom was, with his usual companions to the market: and among the rest, he called aloud to one Salonius, who had been a clerk under him, and asked him whether he had married his daughter? He answered no, nor would he, till he had consulted him. Said Cato, "Then I have found out a fit son-in-law for you, if he should not displease by reason of his age; for in all other points there is no fault to be found in him; but he is indeed, as I said, extremely old." However, Salonius desired him to undertake the business, and to give the young girl to whom he pleased, she being a humble servant of his, who stood in need of his care and patronage. Upon this Cato, without any more ado, told him he desired to have the damsel himself. These words, as may well be imagined, at first astonished the man, conceiving that Cato was as far off from marrying, as he from a likelihood of being allied to the family of one who had been consul and had triumphed; but perceiving him in earnest, he consented willingly; and going onwards to the forum, they quickly completed the bargain.

Whilst the marriage was in hand, Cato's son, taking some of his friends along with him, went and asked his father if it were for any offence he brought in a step-mother upon him? But Cato cried out, "Far from it, my son, I have no fault to find with you or anything of yours; only I desire to have many children, and to leave the commonwealth more such citizens as you are." Pisistratus, the tyrant of Athens, made, they say, this answer to his sons, when they were grown men, when he married his second wife, Timonassa of Argos, by whom he had, it is said, Iophon and Thessalus. Cato had a son by this second wife, to whom, from his mother, he gave the surname of Salonius. In the meantime, his eldest died in his praetor-ship; of whom Cato often makes mention in his books, as having been a good man. He is said, however, to have borne the loss moderately and like a philosopher, and was nothing the more remiss in attending to affairs of state; so that he did not, as Lucius Lucullus and Metellus Pius did, grow languid in his old age, as though public business were a duty once to be discharged, and then quitted; nor did he, like Scipio Africanus, because envy had struck at his glory, turn from the public, and change and pass away the rest of his life without doing anything; but as one persuaded Dionysius, that the most honourable tomb he could have would be to die in the exercise of his dominion; so Cato thought that old age to be the most honourable which was busied in public affairs; though he would, now and then, when he had leisure, recreate himself with husbandry and writing.

And, indeed, he composed various books and histories; and in his youth he addicted himself to agriculture for profit's sake; for he used to say he had but two ways of getting—agriculture and parsimony; and now, in his old age, the first of these gave him both occupation and a subject of study. He wrote one book on country matters, in which he treated particularly even of making cakes and preserving fruit; it being his ambition to be curious and singular in all things. His suppers, at his country house, used also to be plentiful; he daily invited his friends and neighbours about him, and passed the time merrily with them; so that his company was not only agreeable to those of the same age, but even to younger men; for he had had experience in many things, and had been concerned in much, both by word and deed, that was worth the hearing. He looked upon a good table as the best place for making friends; where the commendations of brave and good citizens were usually introduced, and little said of base and unworthy ones; as Cato would not give leave in his company to have anything, either good or ill, said about them.

Some will have the overthrow of Carthage to have been one of his last acts of state; when, indeed, Scipio the younger did by his valour give it the last blow, but the war, chiefly by the counsel and advice of Cato, was undertaken on the following occasion. Cato was sent to the Carthaginians and Masinissa, King of Numidia, who were at war with one another, to know the cause of their difference. He, it seems, had been a friend of the Romans from the beginning; and they, too, since they were conquered by Scipio, were of the Roman confederacy, having been shorn of their power by loss of territory and a heavy tax. Finding Carthage, not (as the Romans thought) low and in an ill condition, but well manned, full of riches and all sorts of arms and ammunition, and perceiving the Carthaginians carry it high, he conceived that it was not a time for the Romans to adjust affairs between them and Masinissa; but rather that they themselves would fall into danger, unless they should find means to check this rapid new growth of Rome's ancient irreconcilable enemy. Therefore, returning quickly to Rome, he acquainted the senate that the former defeats and blows given to the Carthaginians had not so much diminished their strength, as it had abated their imprudence and folly; that they were not become weaker, but more experienced in war, and did only skirmish with the Numidians to exercise themselves the better to cope with the Romans: that the peace and league they had made was but a kind of suspension of war which awaited a fairer opportunity to break out again.

Moreover, they say that, shaking his gown, he took occasion to let drop some African figs before the senate. And on their admiring the size and beauty of them, he presently added, that the place that bore them was but three days' sail from Rome. Nay, he never after this gave his opinion, but at the end he would be sure to come out with this sentence, "ALSO, CARTHAGE, METHINKS, OUGHT UTTERLY TO BE DESTROYED." But Publius Scipio Nasica would always declare his opinion to the contrary, in these words, "It seems requisite to me that Carthage should still stand." For seeing his countrymen to be grown wanton and insolent, and the people made, by their prosperity, obstinate and disobedient to the senate, and drawing the whole city, whither they would, after them, he would have had the fear of Carthage to serve as a bit to hold the contumacy of the multitude; and he looked upon the Carthaginians as too weak to overcome the Romans, and too great to be despised by them. On the other side, it seemed a perilous thing to Cato that a city which had been always great, and was now grown sober and wise, by reason of its former calamities, should still lie, as it were, in wait for the follies and dangerous excesses of the over-powerful Roman people; so that he thought it the wisest course to have all outward dangers removed, when they had so many inward ones among themselves.

Thus Cato, they say, stirred up the third and last war against the Carthaginians: but no sooner was the said war begun, than he died, prophesying of the person that should put an end to it who was then only a young man; but, being tribune in the army, he in several fights gave proof of his courage and conduct. The news of which being brought to Cato's ears at Rome, he thus expressed himself:—

"The only wise man of them all is he,
    The others e'en as shadows flit and flee."

This prophecy Scipio soon confirmed by his actions.

Cato left no posterity, except one son by his second wife, who was named, as we said, Cato Salonius; and a grandson by his eldest son, who died. Cato Salonius died when he was praetor, but his son Marcus was afterwards consul, and he was grandfather of Cato the philosopher, who for virtue and renown was one of the most eminent personages of his time.

CRASSUS

Marcus Crassus, whose father had borne the office of a censor, and received the honour of a triumph, was educated in a little house together with his two brothers, who both married in their parents' lifetime; they kept but one table amongst them; all which, perhaps, was not the least reason of his own temperance and moderation in diet. One of his brothers dying, he married his widow, by whom he had his children; neither was there in these respects any of the Romans who lived a more orderly life than he did, though later in life he was suspected to have been too familiar with one of the vestal virgins, named Licinia, who was, nevertheless, acquitted, upon an impeachment brought against her by one Plotinus. Licinia stood possessed of a beautiful property in the suburbs, which Crassus desiring to purchase at a low price, for this reason was frequent in his attentions to her, which gave occasion to the scandal, and his avarice, so to say, serving to clear him of the crime, he was acquitted. Nor did he leave the lady till he had got the estate.

People were wont to say that the many virtues of Crassus were darkened by the one vice of avarice, and indeed he seemed to have no other but that; for it being the most predominant, obscured others to which he was inclined. The arguments in proof of his avarice were the vastness of his estate, and the manner of raising it; for whereas at first he was not worth above three hundred talents, yet, though in the course of his political life he dedicated the tenth of all he had to Hercules, and feasted the people, and gave to every citizen corn enough to serve him three months, upon casting up his accounts, before he went upon his Parthian expedition, he found his possessions to amount to seven thousand one hundred talents; most of which, if we may scandal him with a truth, he got by fire and rapine, making his advantages of the public calamities. For when Sylla seized the city, and exposed to sale the goods of those that he had caused to be slain, accounting them booty and spoils, and, indeed, calling them so too, and was desirous of making as many, and as eminent men as he could, partakers in the crime, Crassus never was the man that refused to accept, or give money for them. Moreover, observing how extremely subject the city was to fire and falling down of houses, by reason of their height and their standing so near together, he bought slaves that were builders and architects, and when he had collected these to the number of more than five hundred, he made it his practice to buy houses that were on fire, and those in the neighbourhood, which, in the immediate danger and uncertainty the proprietors were willing to part with for little or nothing, so that the greatest part of Rome, at one time or other, came into his hands. Yet for all he had so many workmen, he never built anything but his own house, and used to say that those that were addicted to building would undo themselves soon enough without the help of other enemies. And though he had many silver mines, and much valuable land, and labourers to work in it, yet all this was nothing in comparison of his slaves, such a number and variety did he possess of excellent readers, amanuenses, silversmiths, stewards and table-waiters, whose instruction he always attended to himself, superintending in person, while they learned, and teaching them himself, accounting it the main duty of a master to look over the servants that are, indeed, the living tools of housekeeping; and in this, indeed, he was in the right, in thinking, that is, as he used to say, that servants ought to look after all other things, and the master after them. For economy, which in things inanimate is but money-making, when exercised over men becomes policy. But it was surely a mistaken judgment, when he said no man was to be accounted rich that could not maintain an army at his own cost and charges, for war, as Archidamus well observed, is not fed at a fixed allowance, so that there is no saying what wealth suffices for it, and certainly it was one very far removed from that of Marius; for when he had distributed fourteen acres of land a man, and understood that some desired more, "God forbid," said he, "that any Roman should think that too little which is enough to keep him alive and well."

Crassus, however, was very eager to be hospitable to strangers; he kept open house, and to his friends he would lend money without interest, but called it in precisely at the time; so that his kindness was often thought worse than the paying the interest would have been. His entertainments were, for the most part, plain and citizenlike, the company general and popular; good taste and kindness made them pleasanter than sumptuosity would have done. As for learning he chiefly cared for rhetoric, and what would be serviceable with large numbers; he became one of the best speakers at Rome, and by his pains and industry outdid the best natural orators. For there was no trial how mean and contemptible soever that he came to unprepared; nay, several times he undertook and concluded a cause when Pompey and Caesar and Cicero refused to stand up, upon which account particularly he got the love of the people, who looked upon him as a diligent and careful man, ready to help and succour his fellow citizens. Besides, the people were pleased with his courteous and unpretending salutations and greetings, for he never met any citizen however humble and low, but he returned him his salute by name. He was looked upon as a man well-read in history, and pretty well versed in Aristotle's philosophy, in which one Alexander instructed him, a man whose intercourse with Crassus gave a sufficient proof of his good nature and gentle disposition; for it is hard to say whether he was poorer when he entered into his service, or while he continued in it; for being his only friend that used to accompany him when travelling, he used to receive from him a cloak for the journey, and when he came home had it demanded from him again; poor, patient sufferer, when even the philosophy he professed did not look upon poverty as a thing indifferent. But of this hereafter.

When Cinna and Marius got the power in their hands it was soon perceived that they had not come back for any good they intended to their country, but to effect the ruin and utter destruction of the nobility. And as many as they could lay their hands on they slew, amongst whom were Crassus's father and brother; he himself, being very young, for the moment escaped the danger; but understanding that he was every way beset and hunted after by the tyrants, taking with him three friends and ten servants, with all possible speed he fled into Spain, having formerly been there and secured a great number of friends, while his father was praetor of that country.

After Crassus had lain concealed there eight months, on hearing that Cinna was dead, he appeared abroad, and a great number of people flocking to him, out of whom he selected a body of two thousand five hundred, he visited many cities, and, as some write, sacked Malaca, which he himself, however, always denied, and contradicted all who said so. Afterwards, getting together some ships, he passed into Africa, and joined with Metellus Pius, an eminent person that had raised a very considerable force; but upon some difference between him and Metellus, he stayed not long there, but went over to Sylla, by whom he was very much esteemed. When Sylla passed over into Italy, he was anxious to put all the young men that were with him in employment; and as he despatched some one way, and some another, Crassus, on its falling to his share to raise men among the Marsians, demanded a guard, being to pass through the enemy's country, upon which Sylla replied sharply, "I give you for guard your father, your brother, your friends and kindred, whose unjust and cruel murder I am now going to revenge"; and Crassus, being nettled, went his way, broke boldly through the enemy, collected a considerable force, and in all Sylla's wars acted with great zeal and courage. And in these times and occasions, they say, began the emulation and rivalry for glory between him and Pompey; for though Pompey was the younger man,

and had the disadvantage to be descended of a father that
was disesteemed by the citizens, and hated as much as ever
man was, yet in these actions he shone out and was proved
so great that Sylla always used, when he came in, to stand
up and uncover his head, an honour which he seldom
showed to older men and his own equals, and always
saluted him *Imperator*. This fired and stung Crassus,
though, indeed, he could not with any fairness claim to
be preferred; for he both wanted experience, and his two
innate vices, sordidness and avarice, tarnished all the lustre of his actions. For when he had taken Tudertia, a town
of the Umbrians, he converted, it was said, all the spoils to
his own use, for which he was complained of to Sylla. But
in the last and greatest battle before Rome itself when
Sylla was worsted, some of his battalions giving ground,
and others being quite broken, Crassus got the victory on
the right wing, which he commanded, and pursued the
enemy till night, and then sent to Sylla to acquaint him
with his success, and demand provision for his soldiers. In
the time, however, of the proscriptions and sequestrations,
he lost his repute again, by making great purchases for
little or nothing, and asking for grants. Nay, they say he
proscribed one of the Bruttians without Sylla's order, only
for his own profit, and that, on discovering this, Sylla never
after trusted him in any public affairs. As no man was more
cunning than Crassus to ensnare others by flattery, so no
man lay more open to it, or swallowed it more greedily
than himself. And this particularly was observed of him,
that though he was the most covetous man in the world,
yet he habitually disliked and cried out against others who
were so.

It troubled him to see Pompey so successful in all his
undertakings; that he had had a triumph before he was
capable to sit in the senate, and that the people had surnamed him Magnus, or the great. When somebody was
saying Pompey the Great was coming, he smiled, and
asked him, "How big is he?" Despairing to equal him by
feats of arms, he betook himself to civil life, where by doing
kindnesses, pleading, lending money, by speaking and

canvassing among the people for those who had objects to obtain from them, he gradually gained as great honour and power as Pompey had from his many famous expeditions. And it was a curious thing in their rivalry, that Pompey's name and interests in the city was greatest when he was absent, for his renown in war, but when present he was often less successful than Crassus, by reason of his superciliousness and haughty way of living, shunning crowds of people, and appearing rarely in the forum, and assisting only some few, and that not readily, that his interests might be the stronger when he came to use it for himself. Whereas Crassus, being a friend always at hand, ready to be had and easy of access, and always with his hands full of other people's business, with his freedom and courtesy, got the better of Pompey's formality. In point of dignity of person, eloquence of language, and attractiveness of countenance, they were pretty equally excellent. But, however, this emulation never transported Crassus so far as to make him bear enmity or any ill-will; for though he was vexed to see Pompey and Caesar preferred to him, yet he never mingled any hostility or malice with his jealousy; though Caesar, when he was taken captive by the corsairs in Asia, cried out, "O Crassus, how glad you will be at the news of my captivity!" Afterwards they lived together on friendly terms, for when Caesar was going praetor into Spain, and his creditors, he being then in want of money, came upon him and seized his equipage, Crassus then stood by him and relieved him, and was his security for eight hundred and thirty talents. And in general, Rome being divided into three great interests, those of Pompey, Caesar, and Crassus (for as for Cato, [the younger], his fame was greater than his power, and he was rather admired than followed), the sober and quiet part were for Pompey, the restless and hot-headed followed Caesar's ambition, but Crassus trimmed between them, making advantages of both, and changed sides continually, being neither a trusty friend nor an implacable enemy, and easily abandoned both his attachments and his animosities, as he found it for his advantage, so that in short spaces of time the same men and the same measures had him both as their supporter and as their opponent. He was much liked, but was feared as much or even more. At any rate, when Sicinius, who was the greatest troubler of the magistrates and ministers of his time, was asked how it was he let Crassus alone, "Oh," said he, "he carries hay on his horns," alluding to the custom of tying hay to the horns of the bull that used to butt, that people might keep out of his way.

The insurrection of the gladiators and the devastation of Italy, commonly called the war of Spartacus, began upon this occasion. One Lentulus Batiates trained up a great many gladiators in Capua, most of them Gauls and Thracians, who, not for any fault by them committed, but simply through the cruelty of their master, were kept in confinement for this object of fighting one with another. Two hundred of these formed a plan to escape, but being discovered, those of them who became aware of it in time to anticipate their master, being seventy-eight, got out of a cook's shop chopping-knives and spits, and made their way through the city, and lighting by the way on several waggons that were carrying gladiators' arms to another city, they seized upon them and armed themselves. And seizing upon a defensible place, they chose three captains, of whom Spartacus was chief, a Thracian of one of the nomad tribes, and a man not only of high spirit and valiant, but in understanding, also, and in gentleness superior to his condition, and more of a Grecian than the people of his country usually are. When he first came to be sold at Rome, they say a snake coiled itself upon his face as he lay asleep, and his wife, who at this latter time also accompanied him in his flight, his countrywoman, a kind of prophetess, and one of those possessed with the bacchanal frenzy, declared that it was a sign portending great and formidable power to him with no happy event.

First, then, routing those that came out of Capua against them, and thus procuring a quantity of proper soldiers' arms, they gladly threw away their own as barbarous and dishonourable. Afterwards Clodius, the praetor, took the command against them with a body of three thousand men from Rome, and besieged them within a mountain, accessible only by one narrow and difficult passage, which Clodius kept guarded, encompassed on all other sides with steep and slippery precipices. Upon the top, however, grew a great many wild vines, and cutting down as many of their boughs as they had need of, they twisted them into strong ladders long enough to reach from thence to the bottom, by which, without any danger, they got down all but one, who stayed there to throw them down their arms, and after this succeeded in saving himself. The Romans were ignorant of all this, and, therefore, coming upon them in the rear, they assaulted them unawares and took their camp. Several, also, of the shepherds and herdsmen that were there, stout and nimble fellows, revolted over to them, to some of whom they gave complete arms, and made use of others as scouts and light-armed soldiers. Publius Varinus, the praetor, was now sent against them, whose lieutenant, Furius, with two thousand men, they fought and routed. Then Cossinius was sent with considerable forces, to give his assistance and advice, and him Spartacus missed but very little of capturing in person, as he was bathing at Salinae; for he with great difficulty made his escape, while Spartacus possessed himself of his baggage, and following the chase with a great slaughter, stormed his camp and took it, where Cossinius himself was slain. After many successful skirmishes with the praetor himself, in one of which he took his lictors and his own horse, he began to be great and terrible; but wisely considering that he was not to expect to match the force of the empire, he marched his army towards the Alps, intending, when he had passed them, that every man should go to his own home, some to Thrace, some to Gaul. But they, grown confident in their numbers, and puffed up with their success, would give no obedience to him, but went about and ravaged Italy; so that now the senate was not only moved at the indignity and baseness, both of the enemy and of the insurrection, but, looking upon it as a matter of alarm and of dangerous consequence, sent out both the consuls to it, as to a

great and difficult enterprise. The consul Gellius, falling
suddenly upon a party of Germans, who through contempt and confidence had straggled from Spartacus, cut
them all to pieces. But when Lentulus with a large army
besieged Spartacus, he sallied out upon him, and, joining
battle, defeated his chief officers, and captured all his baggage. As he made toward the Alps, Cassius, who was praetor of that part of Gaul that lies about the Po, met him with
ten thousand men, but being overcome in the battle, he
had much ado to escape himself, with the loss of a great
many of his men.

When the senate understood this, they were displeased at
the consuls, and ordering them to meddle no further, they
appointed Crassus general of the war, and a great many
of the nobility went volunteers with him, partly out of
friendship, and partly to get honour. He stayed himself
on the borders of Picenum, expecting Spartacus would
come that way, and sent his lieutenant, Mummius, with
two legions, to wheel about and observe the enemy's motions, but upon no account to engage or skirmish. But he,
upon the first opportunity, joined battle, and was routed,
having a great many of his men slain, and a great many
only saving their lives with the loss of their arms. Crassus
rebuked Mummius severely, and arming the soldiers again,
he made them find sureties for their arms, that they would
part with them no more, and five hundred that were the
beginners of the flight he divided into fifty tens, and one
of each was to die by lot, thus reviving the ancient Roman
punishment of decimation, where ignominy is added to the
penalty of death, with a variety of appalling and terrible
circumstances, presented before the eyes of the whole
army, assembled as spectators. When he had thus reclaimed
his men, he led them against the enemy; but Spartacus retreated through Lucania toward the sea, and in the straits
meeting with some Cilician pirate ships, he had thoughts
of attempting Sicily, where, by landing two thousand men,
he hoped to new kindle the war of the slaves, which was
but lately extinguished, and seemed to need but little fuel
to set it burning again. But after the pirates had struck a

bargain with him, and received his earnest, they deceived him and sailed away. He thereupon retired again from the sea, and established his army in the peninsula of Rhegium; there Crassus came upon him, and considering the nature of the place, which of itself suggested the undertaking, he set to work to build a wall across the isthmus; thus keeping his soldiers at once from idleness and his foes from forage. This great and difficult work he perfected in a space of time short beyond all expectation, making a ditch from one sea to the other, over the neck of land, three hundred furlongs long, fifteen feet broad, and as much in depth, and above it built a wonderfully high and strong wall. All which Spartacus at first slighted and despised, but when provisions began to fail, and on his proposing to pass further, he found he was walled in, and no more was to be had in the peninsula, taking the opportunity of a snowy, stormy night, he filled up part of the ditch with earth and boughs of trees, and so passed the third part of his army over.

Crassus was afraid lest he should march directly to Rome, but was soon eased of that fear when he saw many of his men break out in a mutiny and quit him, and encamped by themselves upon the Lucanian lake. This lake they say changes at intervals of time, and is sometimes sweet, and sometimes so salt that it cannot be drunk. Crassus falling upon these beat them from the lake, but he could not pursue the slaughter, because of Spartacus suddenly coming up and checking the flight. Now he began to repent that he had previously written to the senate to call Lucullus out of Thrace, and Pompey out of Spain; so that he did all he could to finish the war before they came, knowing that the honour of the action would redound to him that came to his assistance. Resolving, therefore, first to set upon those that had mutinied and encamped apart, whom Caius Cannicius and Castus commanded, he sent six thousand men before to secure a little eminence, and to do it as privately as possible, which that they might do they covered their helmets, but being discovered by two women that were sacrificing for the enemy, they had been in great hazard, had not Crassus immediately appeared, and en-

gaged in a battle which proved a most bloody one. Of
twelve thousand three hundred whom he killed, two only
were found wounded in their backs, the rest all having
died standing in their ranks and fighting bravely. Spartacus,
after this discomfiture, retired to the mountains of Petelia,
but Quintius, one of Crassus's officers, and Scrofa, the
quaestor, pursued and overtook him. But when Spartacus
rallied and faced them, they were utterly routed and fled,
and had much ado to carry off their quaestor, who was
wounded. This success, however, ruined Spartacus, because
it encouraged the slaves, who now disdained any longer
to avoid fighting, or to obey their officers, but as they were
upon the march, they came to them with their swords in
their hands, and compelled them to lead them back again
through Lucania, against the Romans, the very thing which
Crassus was eager for. For news was already brought that
Pompey was at hand; and people began to talk openly
that the honour of this war was reserved to him, who
would come and at once oblige the enemy to fight and put
an end to the war. Crassus, therefore, eager to fight a decisive battle, encamped very near the enemy, and began to
make lines of circumvallation; but the slaves made a sally
and attacked the pioneers. As fresh supplies came in on
either side, Spartacus, seeing there was no avoiding it, set
all his army in array, and when his horse was brought him,
he drew out his sword and killed him, saying, if he got the
day he should have a great many better horses of the enemies', and if he lost it he should have no need of this. And
so making directly towards Crassus himself, through the
midst of arms and wounds, he missed him, but slew two
centurions that fell upon him together. At last being deserted by those that were about him, he himself stood his
ground, and, surrounded by the enemy, bravely defending
himself, was cut in pieces. But though Crassus had good
fortune, and not only did the part of a good general, but
gallantly exposed his person, yet Pompey had much of the
credit of the action. For he met with many of the fugitives,
and slew them, and wrote to the senate that Crassus indeed
had vanquished the slaves in a pitched battle, but that he

had put an end to the war, Pompey was honoured with a magnificent triumph for his conquest over Sertorius and Spain, while Crassus could not himself so much as desire a triumph in its full form, and indeed it was thought to look but meanly in him to accept of the lesser honour, called the ovation, for a servile war, and perform a procession on foot.

And Pompey being immediately invited to the consulship, Crassus, who had hoped to be joined with him, did not scruple to request his assistance. Pompey most readily seized the opportunity, as he desired by all means to lay some obligation upon Crassus, and zealously promoted his interest; and at last he declared in one of his speeches to the people that he should be not less beholden to them for his colleague than for the honour of his own appointment. But once entered upon the employment, this amity continued not long; but differing almost in everything, disagreeing, quarrelling, and contending, they spent the time of their consulship without effecting any measure of consequence, except that Crassus made a great sacrifice to Hercules, and feasted the people at ten thousand tables, and measured them out corn for three months. When their command was now ready to expire, and they were, as it happened, addressing the people, a Roman knight, one Onatius Aurelius, an ordinary private person, living in the country, mounted the hustings, and declared a vision he had in his sleep. "Jupiter," said he, "appeared to me, and commanded me to tell you, that you should not suffer your consuls to lay down their charge before they are made friends." When he had spoken, the people cried out that they should be reconciled. Pompey stood still and said nothing, but Crassus, first offering him his hand, said, "I cannot think, my countrymen, that I do anything humiliating or unworthy of myself, if I make the first offers of accommodation and friendship with Pompey, whom you yourselves styled the Great before he was of man's estate, and decreed him a triumph before he was capable of sitting in the senate."

Caesar now returning from his command, and designing

to get the consulship, and seeing that Crassus and Pompey were again at variance, was unwilling to disoblige one by making application to the other, and despaired of success without the help of one of them; he therefore made it his business to reconcile them, making it appear that by weakening each other's influence they were promoting the interest of the Ciceros, the Catuli, and the Catos, who would really be of no account if they would join their interests and their factions, and act together in public with one policy and one united power. And so reconciling them by his persuasions, out of the three parties he set up one irresistible power, which utterly subverted the government both of senate and people. When Caesar came out of Gaul to Lucca, a great many went thither from Rome to meet him. Pompey and Crassus had various conferences with him in secret, in which they came to the resolution to proceed to still more decisive steps, and to get the whole management of affairs into their hands, Caesar to keep his army, and Pompey and Crassus to obtain new ones and new provinces. To effect all which there was but one way, the getting the consulate a second time, which they were to stand for, and Caesar to assist them by writing to his friends and sending many of his soldiers to vote.

But when they returned to Rome, their design was presently suspected, and a report was soon spread that this interview had been for no good. When Marcellinus and Domitius asked Pompey in the senate if he intended to stand for the consulship, he answered, perhaps he would, perhaps not; and being urged again, replied, he would ask it of the honest citizens, but not of the dishonest. Which answer appearing too haughty and arrogant, Crassus said, more modestly, that he would desire it if it might be for the advantage of the public, otherwise he would decline it. Upon this some others took confidence and came forward as candidates, among them Domitius. But when Pompey and Crassus now openly appeared for it, the rest were afraid and drew back; only Cato encouraged Domitius, who was his friend and relation, to proceed, exciting him to persist, as though he was now defending the public liberty, as these men, he said, did not so much aim at the consulate as at arbitrary government, and it was not a petition for office, but a seizure of provinces and armies. Thus spoke and thought Cato, and almost forcibly compelled Domitius to appear in the forum, where many sided with them. For there was, indeed, much wonder and question among the people, "Why should Pompey and Crassus want another consulship? and why they two together, and not with some third person? We have a great many men not unworthy to be fellow-consuls with either the one or the other." Pompey's party, being apprehensive of this, committed all manner of indecencies and violences, and amongst other things lay in wait for Domitius, as he was coming thither before daybreak with his friends; his torch-bearer they killed, and wounded several others, of whom Cato was one. And these being beaten back and driven into a house, Pompey and Crassus were proclaimed consuls. Not long after, they surrounded the house with armed men, thrust Cato out of the forum, killed some that made resistance, and decreed Caesar his command for five years longer, and provinces for themselves, Syria and both the Spains, which being divided by lots, Syria fell to Crassus, and the Spains to Pompey.

Crassus was so transported with his fortune, that it was manifest he thought he had never had such good luck befall him as now, so that he had much to do to contain himself before company and strangers; but amongst his private friends he let fall many vain and childish words, which were unworthy of his age, and contrary to his usual character, for he had been very little given to boasting hitherto. But then being strangely puffed up, his head heated, he would not limit his fortune with Parthia and Syria; but looking on the actions of Lucullus against Tigranes and the exploits of Pompey against Mithridates as but child's play, he proposed to himself in his hopes to pass as far as Bactria and India, and the utmost ocean. Not that he was called upon by the decree which appointed him to his office to undertake any expedition against the Parthians, but it was well known that he was eager for it, and Caesar wrote to him out of Gaul commending his resolution, and inciting him to the war. And when Ateius, the tribune of the people, designed to stop his journey, and many others murmured that one man should undertake a war against a people that had done them no injury, and were at amity with them, he desired Pompey to stand by him and accompany him out of the town, as he had a great name amongst the common people. And when several were ready prepared to interfere and raise an outcry, Pompey appeared with a pleasing countenance, and so mollified the people, that they let Crassus pass quietly. Ateius, however, met him, and first by word of mouth warned and conjured him not to proceed, and then commanded his attendant officer to seize him and detain him; but the other tribunes not permitting it, the officer released Crassus. Ateius, therefore, running to the gate, when Crassus was come thither, set down a chafing-dish with lighted fire in it, and burning incense and pouring libations on it, cursed him with dreadful imprecations, calling upon and naming several strange and horrible deities. In the Roman belief there is so much virtue in these sacred and ancient rites, that no man can escape the effects of them, and that the utterer himself seldom prospers; so that they are not often made use of, and but upon a great occasion. And Ateius was blamed at the time for resorting to them, as the city itself, in whose cause he used them, would be the first to feel the ill effects of these curses and supernatural terrors.

Crassus arrived at Brundusium, and though the sea was very rough, he had not patience to wait, but went on board, and lost many of his ships. With the remnant of his army he marched rapidly through Galatia, where meeting with King Deiotarus, who, though he was very old, was about building a new city, Crassus scoffingly told him, "Your majesty begins to build at the twelfth hour." "Neither do you," said he, "O general, undertake your Parthian expedition very early." For Crassus was then sixty years old, and he seemed older than he was. At his first coming, things went as he would have them, for he made a bridge over the Euphrates, without much difficulty, and passed

over his army in safety, and occupied many cities of Mesopotamia, which yielded voluntarily. But a hundred of his
men were killed in one, in which Apollonius was tyrant;
therefore, bringing his forces against it, he took it by storm,
plundered the goods, and sold the inhabitants. The Greeks
call this city Zenodotia, upon the taking of which he permitted the army to salute him Imperator, but this was
very ill thought of, and it looked as if he despaired a nobler
achievement, that he made so much of this little success.
Putting garrisons of seven thousand foot and one thousand horse in the new conquests, he returned to take up
his winter quarters in Syria, where his son was to meet
him coming from Caesar out of Gaul, decorated with rewards for his valour, and bring with him one thousand select horse. Here Crassus seemed to commit his first error,
and except, indeed, the whole expedition, his greatest; for,
whereas he ought to have gone forward and seized Babylon
and Seleucia, cities that were ever at enmity with the Parthians, he gave the enemy time to provide against him. Besides, he spent his time in Syria more like an usurer than
a general, not in taking an account of the arms, and in
improving the skill and discipline of his soldiers, but in
computing the revenue of the cities, wasting many days in
weighing by scale and balance the treasure that was in
the temple of Hierapolis, issuing requisitions for levies of
soldiers upon particular towns and kingdoms, and then
again withdrawing them on payment of sums of money,
by which he lost his credit and became despised. Here, too,
he met with the first ill-omen from that goddess, whom
some call Venus, others Juno, others Nature, or the Cause
that produces out of moisture the first principles and seeds
of all things, and gives mankind their earliest knowledge
of all that is good for them. For as they were going out
of the temple young Crassus stumbled and his father fell
upon him.

When he drew his army out of winter quarters, ambassadors came to him from Arsaces, with this short speech: If
the army was sent by the people of Rome, he denounced
mortal war, but if, as he understood was the case, against

the consent of his country, Crassus for his own private
profit had invaded his territory, then their king would be
more merciful, and taking pity upon Crassus's dotage,
would send those soldiers back who had been left not so
truly to keep guard on him as to be his prisoners. Crassus
boastfully told them he would return his answer at Seleucia,
upon which Vagises, the eldest of them, laughed and
showed the palm of his hand, saying, "Hair will grow
here before you will see Seleucia"; so they returned to their
king, Hyrodes, telling him it was war. Several of the Romans that were in garrison in Mesopotamia with great
hazard made their escape, and brought word that the danger was worth consideration, urging their own eye-witness
of the numbers of the enemy, and the manner of their
fighting, when they assaulted their towns; and, as men's
manner is, made all seem greater than really it was. By
flight it was impossible to escape them, and as impossible
to overtake them when they fled, and they had a new and
strange sort of darts, as swift as sight, for they pierced
whatever they met with, before you could see who threw
them; their men-at-arms were so provided that their weapons would cut through anything, and their armour give
way to nothing. All which when the soldiers heard their
hearts failed them; for till now they thought there was no
difference between the Parthians and the Armenians or Cap-
padocians, whom Lucullus grew weary with plundering,
and had been persuaded that the main difficulty of the war
consisted only in the tediousness of the march and the trouble of chasing men that durst not come to blows, so that
the danger of a battle was beyond their expectation; accordingly, some of the officers advised Crassus to proceed
no further at present, but reconsider the whole enterprise,
amongst whom in particular was Cassius, the quaestor. The
soothsayers, also, told him privately the signs found in
the sacrifices were continually adverse and unfavourable.
But he paid no heed to them, or to anybody who gave any
other advice than to proceed. Nor did Artabazes, King of
Armenia, confirm him a little, who came to his aid with
six thousand horse; who, however, were said to be only

the king's life-guard and suit, for he promised ten thousand cuirassiers more, and thirty thousand foot, at his own charge. He urged Crassus to invade Parthia by the way of Armenia, for not only would he be able there to supply his army with abundant provision, which he would give him, but his passage would be more secure in the mountains and hills, with which the whole country was covered, making it almost impassable to horse, in which the main strength of the Parthians consisted. Crassus returned him but cold thanks for his readiness to serve him, and for the splendour of his assistance, and told him he was resolved to pass through Mesopotamia, where he had left a great many brave Roman soldiers; whereupon the Armenian went his way. As Crassus was taking the army over the river at Zeugma, he encountered preternaturally violent thunder, and the lightning flashed in the faces of the troops, and during the storm a hurricane broke upon the bridge, and carried part of it away; two thunderbolts fell upon the very place where the army was going to encamp; and one of the general's horses, magnificently caparisoned, dragged away the groom into the river and was drowned. It is said, too, that when they went to take up the first standard, the eagle of itself turned its head backward; and after he had passed over his army, as they were distributing provisions, the first thing they gave was lentils and salt, which with the Romans are the food proper to funerals, and are offered to the dead. And as Crassus was haranguing his soldiers, he let fall a word which was thought very ominous in the army; for "I am going," he said, "to break down the bridge, that none of you may return"; and whereas he ought, when he had perceived his blunder, to have corrected himself, and explained his meaning, seeing the men alarmed at the expression, he would not do it out of mere stubbornness. And when at the last general sacrifice the priest gave him the entrails, they slipt out of his hand, and when he saw the standers-by concerned at it, he laughed and said, "See what it is to be an old man; but I shall hold my sword fast enough."

So he marched his army along the river with seven legions, little less than four thousand horse, and as many light-armed soldiers, and the scouts returning declared that not one man appeared, but that they saw the footing of a great many horses which seemed to be retiring in flight, whereupon Crassus conceived great hopes, and the Romans began to despise the Parthians, as men that would not come to combat, hand to hand. But Cassius spoke with him again, and advised him to refresh his army in some of the garrison towns, and remain there till they could get some certain intelligence of the enemy, or at least to make toward Selucia, and keep by the river, that so they might have the convenience of having provision constantly supplied by the boats, which might always accompany the army, and the river would secure them from being environed, and, if they should fight, it might be upon equal terms.

While Crassus was still considering, and as yet undetermined, there came to the camp an Arab chief named Ariamnes, a cunning and wily fellow, who, of all the evil chances which combined to lead them on to destruction, was the chief and the most fatal. Some of Pompey's old soldiers knew him, and remembered him to have received some kindnesses of Pompey, and to have been looked upon as a friend to the Romans, but he was now suborned by the king's generals, and sent to Crassus to entice him if possible from the river and hills into the wide open plain, where he might be surrounded. For the Parthians desired anything rather than to be obliged to meet the Romans face to face. He, therefore, coming to Crassus (and he had a persuasive tongue), highly commended Pompey as his benefactor, and admired the forces that Crassus had with him, but seemed to wonder why he delayed and made preparations, as if he should not use his feet more than any arms, against men that, taking with them their best goods and chattels, had designed long ago to fly for refuge to the Scythians or Hyrcanians. "If you meant to fight, you should have made all possible haste, before the king should recover courage, and collect his forces together; at present you see Surena and Sillaces opposed to you, to draw you off in pursuit of them, while the king himself keeps out of the way." But this was all a lie, for Hyrodes had divided his army in two parts; with one he in person wasted Armenia, revenging himself upon Artavasdes, and sent Surena against the Romans, not out of contempt, as some pretend, for there is no likelihood that he should despise Crassus, one of the chiefest men of Rome, to go and fight with Artavasdes, and invade Armenia; but much more probably he really apprehended the danger, and therefore waited to see the event, intending that Surena should first run the hazard of a battle, and draw the enemy on. Nor was this Surena an ordinary person, but in wealth, family, and reputation, the second man in the kingdom, and in courage and prowess the first, and for bodily stature and beauty no man like him. Whenever he travelled privately, he had one thousand camels to carry his baggage, two hundred chariots for his concubines, one thousand completely armed men for lifeguards, and a great many more light-armed; and he had at least ten thousand horsemen altogether, of his servants and retinue. The honour had long belonged to his family, that at the king's coronation he put the crown upon his head, and when this very king Hyrodes had been exiled, he brought him in; it was he, also, that took the great city of Selucia, was the first man that scaled the walls, and with his own hand beat off the defenders. And though at this time he was not above thirty years old, he had a great name for wisdom and sagacity, and, indeed, by these qualities chiefly, he overthrew Crassus, who first through his overweening confidence, and afterwards because he was cowed by his calamities, fell a ready victim to his subtlety. When Ariamnes had thus worked upon him, he drew him from the river into vast plains, by a way that at first was pleasant and easy but afterwards very troublesome by reason of the depth of the sand; no tree, nor any water, and no end of this to be seen; so that they were not only spent with thirst, and the difficulty of the passage, but were dismayed with the uncomfortable prospect of not a bough, not a stream, not a hillock, not a green herb, but in fact a sea of sand, which encompassed the army with its waves.

he should endeavour to fall in upon them before he wa
quite surrounded; for the enemy advanced most upon tha
quarter, and seemed to be trying to ride around and com
upon the rear. Therefore the young man, taking with hin
thirteen hundred horse, one thousand of which he hac
from Caesar, five hundred archers, and eight cohorts o
the full-armed soldiers that stood next him, led them up
with design to charge the Parthians. Whether it was that they
found themselves in a piece of marshy ground, as some
think, or else designing to entice young Crassus as far as
they could from his father, they turned and began to fly
whereupon he crying out that they durst not stand, pursued
them, and with him Censorinus and Megabacchus, both
famous, the latter for his courage and prowess, the other
for being of a senator's family, and an excellent orator
both intimates of Crassus, and of about the same age. The
horse thus pushing on, the infantry stayed a little behind
being exalted with hopes and joy, for they supposed they
ad already conquered, and now were only pursuing; till
when they were gone too far, they perceived the deceit, for
they that seemed to fly now turned again, and a great
many fresh ones came on. Upon this they made a halt, for
they doubted not but now the enemy would attack them,
because they were so few. But they merely placed their
cuirassiers to face the Romans, and with the rest of their
horse rode about scouring the field, and thus stirring up
the sand, they raised such a dust that the Romans could
neither see nor speak to one another, and being driven in
upon one another in one close body, they were thus hit
and killed, dying, not by a quick and easy death, but with
miserable pains and convulsions; for writhing upon the
darts in their bodies, they broke them in their wounds, and
when they would by force pluck out the barbed points,
they caught the nerves and veins, so that they tore and
tortured themselves. Many of them died thus, and those
that survived were disabled for any service, and when
Publius exhorted them to charge the cuirassiers, they
showed him their hands nailed to their shields, and their
feet stuck to the ground, so that they could neither fly nor

They began to suspect some treachery, and privately railed
at the barbarian, "What evil genius, O thou worst of men,
brought thee to our camp, and with what charms and potions hast thou bewitched Crassus, that he should march
his army through a vast and deep desert, through ways
which are rather fit for a captain of Arabian robbers, than
for the general of a Roman army?" But the barbarian, being a wily fellow, very submissively exhorted them, and
encouraged them to sustain it a little further, and ran
about the camp, and professing to cheer up the soldiers,
asked them, jokingly, "What, do you think you march
through Campania, expecting everywhere to find springs, and
shady trees, and baths, and inns of entertainment? Consider
you now travel through the confines of Arabia and Assyria."
Thus he managed them like children, and before the cheat
was discovered, he rode away; not but that Crassus was
aware of his going, but he had persuaded him that he
would go and contrive how to disorder the affairs of the
enemy.

It is related that Crassus came abroad that day not in
his scarlet robe, which Roman generals usually wear, but in
a black one, which, as soon as he perceived, he changed.
And the standard-bearers had much ado to take up their
eagles, which seemed to be fixed to the place. Crassus
laughed at it, and hastened their march, and compelled his
infantry to keep pace with his cavalry, till some few of the
scouts returned and told them that their fellows were slain
and they hardly escaped, that the enemy was at hand in
full force, and resolved to give them battle. On this all
was in an uproar; Crassus was struck with amazement, and
for haste could scarcely put his army in good order. First,
as Cassius advised, he opened their ranks and files that
they might take up as much space as could be, to prevent
their being surrounded, and distributed the horse upon the
wings, but afterwards changing his mind, he drew up his
army in a square, and made a front every way, each of
which consisted of twelve cohorts, to every one of which
he allotted a troop of horse, that no part might be destitute of the assistance that the horse might give, and that

they might be ready to assist everywhere, as need should require. Cassius commanded one of the wings, young Crassus the other, and he himself was in the middle. Thus they marched on till they came to a little river named Balissus, a very inconsiderable one in itself, but very grateful to the soldiers, who had suffered so much by drouth and heat all along their march. Most of the commanders were of the opinion that they ought to remain there that night, and to inform themselves as much as possible of the number of the enemies, and their order, and so march against them at break of day; but Crassus was so carried away by the eagerness of his son, and the horsemen that were with him, who desired and urged him to lead them on and engage, that he commanded those that had a mind to it to eat and drink as they stood in their ranks, and before they had all well done, he led them on, not leisurely and with halts to take breath, as if he was going to battle, but kept on his pace as if he had been in haste, till they saw the enemy, contrary to their expectation, neither so many nor so magnificently armed as the Romans expected. For Surena had hid his main force behind the first ranks and ordered them to hide the glittering of their armour with coats and skins. But when they approached and the general gave the signal, immediately all the field rung with a hideous noise and terrible clamour. For the Parthians do not encourage themselves to war with cornets and trumpets, but with a kind of kettledrum, which they strike all at once in various quarters. With these they make a dead, hollow noise, like the bellowing of beasts, mixed with sounds resembling thunder, having, it would seem, very correctly observed that of all our senses hearing most confounds and disorders us, and that the feelings excited through it most quickly disturb and most entirely overpower the understanding.

When they had sufficiently terrified the Romans with their noise, they threw off the covering of their armour, and shone like lightning in their breastplates and helmets of polished Margianian steel, and with their horses covered with brass and steel trappings. Surena was the tallest and finest looking man himself, but the delicacy of his looks

and effeminacy of his dress did not promise so much hood as he really was master of; for his face was pa and his hair parted after the fashion of the Medes, whe the other Parthians made a more terrible appearance, their shaggy hair gathered in a mass upon their forehe after the Scythian mode. Their first design was with th lances to beat down and force back the first ranks of t Romans, but when they perceived the depth of their battle and that the soldiers firmly kept their ground, they made a retreat, and pretending to break their order and disperse, they encompassed the Roman square before they were aware of it. Crassus commanded his light-armed soldiers to charge, but they had not gone far before they were received with such a shower of arrows that they were glad to retire amongst the heavy-armed, with whom this was the first occasion of disorder and terror, when they perceived the strength and force of their darts, which pierced their arms, and passed through every kind of covering hard and soft alike. The Parthians now placing themselve at distances began to shoot from all sides, not aiming at ar particular mark (for, indeed, the order of the Romans was so close, that they could not miss if they would), but simply sent their arrows with great force out of strong bent bows, the strokes from which came with extreme violence. The position of the Romans was a very bad one from the first; for if they kept their ranks, they were wounded, and if they tried to charge, they hurt the enemy none the more, and themselves suffered none the less. For the Parthians threw their darts as they fled, an art in which none but the Scythians excel them, and it is, indeed, a cunning practice for while they thus fight to make their escape, they avoi the dishonour of a flight.

However, the Romans had some comfort to think th when they had spent all their arrows, they would eith give over or come to blows; but when they presently unde stood that there were numerous camels loaded with rows, and that when the first ranks had discharged th they had, they wheeled off and took more, Crassus see no end of it, was out of all heart, and sent to his son t they might be ready to assist everywhere, as need should require. Cassius commanded one of the wings, young Crassus the other, and he himself was in the middle. Thus they marched on till they came to a little river named Balissus, a very inconsiderable one in itself, but very grateful to the soldiers, who had suffered so much by drouth and heat all along their march. Most of the commanders were of the opinion that they ought to remain there that night, and to inform themselves as much as possible of the number of the enemies, and their order, and so march against them at break of day; but Crassus was so carried away by the eagerness of his son, and the horsemen that were with him, who desired and urged him to lead them on and engage, that he commanded those that had a mind to it to eat and drink as they stood in their ranks, and before they had all well done, he led them on, not leisurely and with halts to take breath, as if he was going to battle, but kept on his pace as if he had been in haste, till they saw the enemy, contrary to their expectation, neither so many nor so magnificently armed as the Romans expected. For Surena had hid his main force behind the first ranks and ordered them to hide the glittering of their armour with coats and skins. But when they approached and the general gave the signal, immediately all the field rung with a hideous noise and terrible clamour. For the Parthians do not encourage themselves to war with cornets and trumpets, but with a kind of kettle-drum, which they strike all at once in various quarters. With these they make a dead, hollow noise, like the bellowing of beasts, mixed with sounds resembling thunder, having, it would seem, very correctly observed that of all our senses hearing most confounds and disorders us, and that the feelings excited through it most quickly disturb and most entirely overpower the understanding.

When they had sufficiently terrified the Romans with their noise, they threw off the covering of their armour, and shone like lightning in their breastplates and helmets of polished Margianian steel, and with their horses covered with brass and steel trappings. Surena was the tallest and finest looking man himself, but the delicacy of his looks

They began to suspect some treachery, and privately railed at the barbarian, "What evil genius, O thou worst of men, brought thee to our camp, and with what charms and potions hast thou bewitched Crassus, that he should march his army through a vast and deep desert, through ways which are rather fit for a captain of Arabian robbers, than for the general of a Roman army?" But the barbarian, being a wily fellow, very submissively exhorted them, and encouraged them to sustain it a little further, and ran about the camp, and professing to cheer up the soldiers, asked them, jokingly, "What, do you think you march through Campania, expecting everywhere to find springs, and shady trees, and baths, and inns of entertainment? Consider you now travel through the confines of Arabia and Assyria." Thus he managed them like children, and before the cheat was discovered, he rode away; not but that Crassus was aware of his going, but he had persuaded him that he would go and contrive how to disorder the affairs of the enemy.

It is related that Crassus came abroad that day not in his scarlet robe, which Roman generals usually wear, but in a black one, which, as soon as he perceived, he changed. And the standard-bearers had much ado to take up their eagles, which seemed to be fixed to the place. Crassus laughed at it, and hastened their march, and compelled his infantry to keep pace with his cavalry, till some few of the scouts returned and told them that their fellows were slain and they hardly escaped, that the enemy was at hand in full force, and resolved to give them battle. On this all was in an uproar; Crassus was struck with amazement, and for haste could scarcely put his army in good order. First, as Cassius advised, he opened their ranks and files that they might take up as much space as could be, to prevent their being surrounded, and distributed the horse upon the wings, but afterwards changing his mind, he drew up his army in a square, and made a front every way, each of which consisted of twelve cohorts, to every one of which he allotted a troop of horse, that no part might be destitute of the assistance that the horse might give, and that fight. He charged in himself boldly, however, with his horse, and came to close quarters with them, but was very unequal, whether as to the offensive or defensive part; for with his weak and little javelins, he struck against targets that were of tough raw hides and iron, whereas, the lightly-clad bodies of his Gaulish horsemen were exposed to the strong spears of the enemy. For upon these he mostly depended, and with them he wrought wonders; for they would catch hold of the great spears, and close upon the enemy, and so pull them off from their horses, where they could scarce stir by reason of the heaviness of their armour, and many of the Gauls quitting their own horses, would creep under those of the enemy, and stick them in the belly; which, growing unruly with the pain, trampled upon their riders and upon the enemies promiscuously. The Gauls were chiefly tormented by the heat and drouth, being not accustomed to either, and most of their horses were slain by being spurred on against the spears, so that they were forced to retire among the foot, bearing off Publius grievously wounded. Observing a sandy hillock not far off, they made to it, and tying their horses to one another, and placing them in the midst, and joining all their shields together before them, they thought they might make some defence against the barbarians. But it fell out quite contrary, for when they were drawn up in a plain, the front in some measure secured those that were behind; but when they were upon the hill, one being of necessity higher up than another, none were in shelter, but all alike stood equally exposed, bewailing their inglorious and useless fate. There were with Publius two Greeks that lived near there at Carrhae, Hieronymus and Nicomachus; these men urged him to retire with them and fly to Ichnae, a town not far from thence, and friendly to the Romans. "No," said he, "there is no death so terrible, for the fear of which Publius would leave his friends that die upon his account"; and bidding them to take care of themselves, he embraced them and sent them away, and, because he could not use his arm, for he was run through with a dart, he opened his side to his armour-bearer, and commanded him to run him through. It is said Censorinus fell in the same manner. Megabacchus slew himself, as did also the rest of best note. The Parthians coming upon the rest with their lances, killed them fighting, nor were there above five hundred taken prisoners. Cutting off the head of Publius, they rode off directly towards Crassus.

His condition was thus. When he had commanded his son to fall upon the enemy, and word was brought him that they fled and that there was a distant pursuit, and perceiving also that the enemy did not press upon him so hard as formerly, for they were mostly gone to fall upon Publius, he began to take heart a little; and drawing his army towards some sloping ground, expected when his son would return from the pursuit. Of the messengers whom Publius sent to him (as soon as he saw his danger), the first were intercepted by the enemy, and slain; the last, hardly escaping, came and declared that Publius was lost, unless he had speedy succours. Crassus was terribly distracted, not knowing what counsel to take, and indeed no longer capable of taking any; overpowered now by fear for the whole army, now by desire to help his son. At last he resolved to move with his forces. Just upon this, up came the enemy with their shouts and noises more terrible than before, their drums sounding again in the ears of the Romans, who now feared a fresh engagement. And they who brought Publius's head upon the point of a spear, riding up near enough that it could be known, scoffingly inquired where were his parents, and what family he was of, for it was impossible that so brave and gallant a warrior should be the son of so pitiful a coward as Crassus. This sight above all the rest dismayed the Romans, for it did not incite them to anger as it might have done, but to horror and trembling, though they say Crassus outdid himself in this calamity, for he passed through the ranks and cried out to them, "This, O my countrymen, is my own peculiar loss, but the fortune and the glory of Rome is safe and untainted so long as you are safe. But if any one be concerned for my loss of the best of sons, let him show it in revenging him upon the enemy. Take away their joy, revenge their cruelty, nor be dismayed at what is past; for whoever tries for great objects must suffer something. Neither did Lucullus overthrow Tigranes without bloodshed, nor Scipio Antiochus; our ancestors lost one thousand ships about Sicily, and how many generals and captains in Italy? no one of which losses hindered them from overthrowing their conquerors; for the State of Rome did not arrive to this height by fortune, but by perseverance and virtue in confronting danger."

While Crassus thus spoke exhorting them, he saw but few that gave much heed to him, and when he ordered them to shout for battle, he could no longer mistake the despondency of his army, which made but a faint and unsteady noise, while the shout of the enemy was clear and bold. And when they came to the business, the Parthian servants and dependents riding about shot their arrows, and the horsemen in the foremost ranks with their spears drove the Romans close together, except those who rushed upon them for fear of being killed by their arrows. Neither did these do much execution, being quickly despatched; for the strong, thick spears made large and mortal wounds, and often ran through two men at once. As they were thus fighting, the night coming on parted them, the Parthians boasting that they would indulge Crassus with one night to mourn his son, unless upon better consideration he would rather go to Arsaces than be carried to him. These, therefore, took up their quarters near them, being flushed with their victory. But the Romans had a sad night of it; for neither taking care for the burial of their dead, nor the cure of the wounded, nor the groans of the expiring, every one bewailed his own fate. For there was no means of escaping, whether they should stay for the light, or venture to retreat into the vast desert in the dark. And now the wounded men gave them new trouble, since to take them with them would retard their flight, and if they should leave them, they might serve as guides to the enemy by their cries. However, they were all desirous to see and hear Crassus, though they were sensible that he was the cause of all their mischief. But he wrapped his cloak around him, and hid himself, where he lay as an example, to ordinary minds, of the caprice of fortune, but to the wise, of inconsiderateness and ambition; who, not content to be superior to so many millions of men, being inferior to two, esteemed himself as the lowest of all. Then came Octavius, his lieutenant, and Cassius, to comfort him, but he being altogether past helping, they themselves called together the centurions and tribunes, and agreeing that the best way was to fly, they ordered the army out, without sound of trumpet, and at first with silence. But before long, when the disabled men found they were left behind, strange confusion and disorder, with an outcry and lamentation, seized the camp, and a trembling and dread presently fell upon them, as if the enemy were at their heels. By which means, now and then turning out of their way, now and then standing to their ranks, sometimes taking up the wounded that followed, sometimes laying them down, they wasted the time, except three hundred horse, whom Egnatius brought safe to Carrhae about midnight; where calling, in the Roman tongue, to the watch, as soon as they heard him, he bade them tell Coponius, the governor, that Crassus had fought a very great battle with the Parthians; and having said but this, and not so much as telling his name, he rode away at full speed to Zeugma. And by this means he saved himself and his men, but lost his reputation by deserting his general. However, his message to Coponius was for the advantage of Crassus; for he, suspecting by this hasty and confused delivery of the message that all was not well, immediately ordered the garrison to be in arms, and as soon as he understood that Crassus was upon the way towards him, he went out to meet him, and received him with his army into the town.

Soon after a false report was brought to Surena, that Crassus, with his principal officers, had escaped, and that those who were got into Carrhae were but a confused rout of insignificant people, not worth further pursuit. Supposing, therefore, that he had lost the very crown and glory of his victory, and yet being uncertain whether it were so or not, and anxious to ascertain the fact, that so he should either stay and besiege Carrhae or follow Crassus, he sent

one of his interpreters to the walls, commanding him in
Latin to call for Crassus or Cassius, for that the general,
Surena, desired a conference. As soon as Crassus heard
this, he embraced the proposal, and soon after there came
up a band of Arabians, who very well knew the faces of
Crassus and Cassius, as having been frequently in the Roman camp before the battle. They having espied Cassius
from the wall, told him that Surena desired a peace, and
would give them safe convoy, if they would make a treaty
with the king his master and withdraw all their troops out
of Mesopotamia; and this he thought most advisable for
them both, before things came to the last extremity; Cassius, embracing the proposal, desired that a time and place
might be appointed where Crassus and Surena might have
an interview. The Arabians, having charged themselves with
the message, went back to Surena, who was not a little rejoiced that Crassus was there to be besieged.

Next day, therefore, he came up with his army, insulting
over the Romans, and haughtily demanded of them Crassus and Cassius, bound, if they expected any mercy. The
Romans, seeing themselves deluded and mocked, were
much troubled at it, but advising Crassus to lay aside his
distant and empty hopes of aid from the Armenians, resolved to fly for it; and this design ought to have been kept
private, till they were upon their way, and not have been
told to any of the people of Carrhae. But Crassus let this
also be known to Andromachus, the most faithless of men,
nay, he was so infatuated as to choose him for his guide.
The Parthians then, to be sure, had punctual intelligence
of all that passed; but it being contrary to their usage, and
also difficult for them to fight by night, and Crassus having
chosen that time to set out, Andromachus, lest he should
get the start too far of his pursuers, led him hither and
thither, and at last conveyed him into the midst of morasses
and places full of ditches, so that the Romans had a troublesome and perplexing journey of it, and some were who,
supposing by these windings and turnings of Andromachus
that no good was intended, resolved to follow him no further. And at last Cassius himself returned to Carrhae, and

his guides, the Arabians, advising him to tarry there till the moon was got out of Scorpio, he told them that he was most afraid of Sagittarius, and so with five hundred horse went off to Syria. Others there were who, having got honest guides, took their way by the mountains called Sinnaca, and got into places of security by daybreak; these were five thousand under the command of Octavius, a very gallant man. But Crassus fared worse; day overtook him still deceived by Andromachus, and entangled in the fens and the difficult country. There were with him four cohorts of legionary soldiers, a very few horsemen, and five lictors, with whom having with great difficulty got into the way, and not being a mile and a half from Octavius, instead of going to join him, although the enemy were already upon him, he retreated to another hill, neither so defensible nor impassable for the horse, but lying under the hills at Sinnaca, and continued so as to join them in a long ridge through the plain. Octavius could see in what danger the general was, and himself, at first but slenderly followed, hurried to the rescue. Soon after, the rest, upbraiding one another with baseness in forsaking their officers, marched down, and falling upon the Parthians, drove them from the hill, and compassing Crassus about, and fencing him with their shields, declared proudly, that no arrow in Parthia should ever touch their general, so long as there was a man of them left alive to protect him.

Surena, therefore, perceiving his soldiers less inclined to expose themselves, and knowing that if the Romans should prolong the battle till night, they might then gain the mountains and be out of his reach, betook himself to his usual craft. Some of the prisoners were set free, who had, as it was contrived, been in hearing, while some of the barbarians spoke a set purpose in the camp to the effect that the king did not design the war to be pursued to extremity against the Romans, but rather desired, by his generous treatment of Crassus, to make a step towards reconciliation. And the barbarians desisted from fighting, and Surena himself, with his chief officers, riding gently to the hill, unbent his bow and held out his hand, inviting Crassus to an agreement, and saying that it was beside the king's intentions, that they had thus had experience of the courage and the strength of his soldiers; that now he desired no other contention but that of kindness and friendship, by making a truce, and permitting them to go away in safety. These words of Surena the rest received joyfully, and were eager to accept the offer; but Crassus, who had sufficient experience of their perfidiousness, and was unable to see any reason for the sudden change, would give no ear to them, and only took time to consider. But the soldiers cried out and advised him to treat, and then went on to upbraid and affront him, saying that it was very unreasonable that he should bring them to fight with such men armed, whom himself, without their arms, durst not look in the face. He tried first to prevail with them by entreaties, and told them that if they would have patience till evening, they might get into the mountains and passes, inaccessible for horse, and be out of danger, and withal he pointed out the way with his hand, entreating them not to abandon their preservation, now close before them. But when they mutinied and clashed their targets in a threatening manner, he was overpowered and forced to go, and only turning about at parting, said, "You, Octavius and Petronius, and the rest of the officers who are present, see the necessity of going which I lie under, and cannot but be sensible of the indignities and violence offered to me. Tell all men when you have escaped, that Crassus perished rather by the subtlety of his enemies, than by the disobedience of his countrymen."

Octavius, however, would not stay there, but with Petronius went down from the hill; as for the lictors, Crassus bade them be gone. The first that met him were two half-blood Greeks, who, leaping from their horses, made a profound reverence to Crassus, and desired him, in Greek, to send some before him, who might see that Surena himself was coming towards them, his retinue disarmed, and not having so much as their wearing swords along with them. But Crassus answered, that if he had the least concern for his life, he would never have intrusted himself in their hands, but sent two brothers of the name of Roscius to inquire on what terms and in what numbers they should meet. These Surena ordered immediately to be seized, and himself with his principal officers came up on horseback, and greeting him, said, "How is this, then? A Roman commander is on foot, whilst I and my train are mounted." But Crassus replied, that there was no error committed on either side, for they both met according to the custom of their own country. Surena told him that from that time there was a league between the king his master and the Romans, but that Crassus must go with him to the river to·sign it, "for you Romans," said he, "have not good memories for conditions," and so saying, reached out his hand to him. Crassus, therefore, gave order that one of his horses should be brought; but Surena told him there was no need, "the king, my master, presents you with this"; and immediately a horse with a golden bit was brought up to him, and himself was forcibly put into the saddle by the grooms, who ran by the side and struck the horse to make the more haste. But Octavius running up, got hold of the bridle, and soon after one of the officers, Petronius, and the rest of the company came up, striving to stop the horse, and pulling back those who on both sides of him forced Crassus forward. Thus from pulling and thrusting one another, they came to a tumult, and soon after to blows. Octavius, drawing his sword, killed a groom of one of the barbarians, and one of them, getting behind Octavius, killed him. Petronius was not armed, but being struck on the breastplate, fell down from his horse, though without hurt. Crassus was killed by a Parthian, called Pomaxathres; others say by a different man, and that Pomaxathres only cut off his head and right hand after he had fallen.

Surena sent the head and hand of Crassus to Hyrodes the king, into Armenia. Whilst these things were doing, Hyrodes had struck up a peace with the King of Armenia, and made a match between his son Pacorus and the King of Armenia's sister. Their feastings and entertainments in consequence were very sumptuous, and various Grecian compositions, suitable to the occasion, were recited before them. For Hyrodes was not ignorant of the Greek language and literature, and Artavasdes was so expert in it, that he wrote tragedies and orations and histories, some of which are still extant. When the head of Crassus was brought to the door, the tables were just taken away, and one Jason, a tragic actor, of the town of Tralles, was singing the scene in the Bacchae of Euripides concerning Agave. He was receiving much applause, when Sillaces, coming to the room, and having made obeisance to the king, threw down the head of Crassus into the midst of the company. The Parthians receiving it with joy and acclamations, Sillaces, by the king's command, was made to sit down, while Jason handed over the costume of Pentheus to one of the dancers in the chorus, and taking up the head of Crassus, and acting the part of a bacchante in her frenzy, in a rapturous impassioned manner, sang the lyric passages—

"We've hunted down a mighty chase to-day,
    And from the mountain bring the noble prey,"

to the great delight of all the company; but when the verses of the dialogue followed—

"What happy hand the glorious victim slew?
    I claim that honour to my courage due,"

Pomaxathres, who happened to be there at the supper, started up and would have got the head into his own hands, "for it is my due," said he, "and no man's else." The king was greatly pleased, and gave presents according to the custom of the Parthians, to them, and to Jason, the actor, a talent. Such was the burlesque that was played, they tell us, as the afterpiece to the tragedy of Crassus's expedition. But divine justice failed not to punish both Hyrodes for his cruelty and Surena for his perjury; for Surena not long after was put to death by Hyrodes, out of mere envy to his glory; and Hyrodes himself, having lost his son Pacorus, who was beaten in battle with the Romans, falling into a disease which turned to a dropsy, had aconite given him by his second son, Phraates; but the poison working only upon the disease, and carrying away the dropsical matter with itself, the king began suddenly to recover, so that Phraates at length was forced to take the shortest course, and strangled him.

⚜

CAESAR

After Sylla became master of Rome, he wished to make Caesar put away his wife Cornelia, daughter of Cinna, the late sole ruler of the commonwealth, but was unable to effect it either by promises or intimidation, and so contented himself with confiscating her dowry. The ground of Sylla's hostility to Caesar was the relationship between him and Marius; for Marius, the elder, married Julia, the sister of Caesar's father, and had by her the younger Marius, who consequently was Caesar's first cousin. And though at the beginning, while so many were to be put to death, and there was so much to do, Caesar was overlooked by Sylla, yet he would not keep quiet, but presented himself to the people as a candidate for the priesthood, though he was yet a mere boy. Sylla, without any open opposition, took measures to have him rejected, and in consultation whether he should be put to death, when it was urged by some that it was not worth his while to contrive the death of a boy, he answered, that they knew little who did not see more than one Marius in that boy. Caesar, on being informed of this saying, concealed himself, and for a considerable time kept out of the way in the country of the Sabines, often changing his quarters, till one night, as he was removing from one house to another on account of his health, he fell into the hands of Sylla's soldiers, who were searching those parts in order to apprehend any who had absconded. Caesar, by a bribe of two talents, prevailed with Cornelius, their captain, to let him go, and was no sooner dismissed but he put to sea and made for Bithynia. After a short stay there with Nicomedes, the king, in his passage back he was taken near the island of Pharmacusa by some of the pirates, who, at that time, with large fleets of ships and innumerable smaller vessels, infested the seas everywhere.

When these men at first demanded of him twenty talents for his ransom, he laughed at them for not understanding the value of their prisoner, and voluntarily engaged to give them fifty. He presently despatched those about him to several places to raise the money, till at last he was left among a set of the most bloodthirsty people in the world, the Cilicians, only with one friend and two attendants. Yet he made so little of them, that when he had a mind to sleep, he would send to them, and order them to make no noise. For thirty-eight days, with all the freedom in the world he amused himself with joining in their exercises and games, as if they had not been his keepers, but his guards. He wrote verses and speeches, and made them his auditors, and those who did not admire them, he called to their faces illiterate and barbarous, and would often, in raillery, threaten to hang them. They were greatly taken with this, and attributed his free talking to a kind of simplicity and boyish playfulness. As soon as his ransom was come from Miletus, he paid it, and was discharged, and proceeded at once to man some ships at the port of Miletus, and went in pursuit of the pirates, whom he surprised with their ships still stationed at the island, and took most of them. Their money he made his prize, and the men he secured in prison at Pergamus, and he made application to Junius, who was then governor of Asia, to whose office it belonged, as praetor, to determine their punishment. Junius, having his eye upon the money, for the sum was considerable, said he would think at his leisure what to do with the prisoners, upon which Caesar took his leave of him, and went off to Pergamus, where he ordered the pirates to be brought forth and crucified; the the punishment he had often threatened them with whilst he was in their hands, and they little dreamt he was in earnest.

In the meantime Sylla's power being now on the decline, Caesar's friends advised him to return to Rome, but he went to Rhodes, and entered himself in the school of Apollonius, Molon's son, a famous rhetorician, one who had the reputation of a worthy man, and had Cicero for one of his scholars. Caesar is said to have been admirably fitted by nature to make a great statesman and orator, and to have taken such pains to improve his genius this way that without dispute he might challenge the second place. More he did not aim at, as choosing to be first rather amongst men of arms and power, and, therefore, never rose to that height of eloquence to which nature would have carried him, his attention being diverted to those expeditions and designs which at length gained him the empire. And he himself, in his answer to Cicero's panegyric on Cato, desires his reader not to compare the plain discourse of a soldier with the harangues of an orator who had not only fine parts, but had employed his life in this study.

When he was returned to Rome, he accused Dolabella of mal-administration, and many cities of Greece came in to attest it. Dolabella was acquitted, and Caesar, in return for the support he had received from the Greeks, assisted them in their prosecution of Publius Antonius for corrupt practices, before Marcus Lucullus, praetor of Macedonia. In this course he so far succeeded, that Antonius was forced to appeal to the tribunes at Rome, alleging that in Greece he could not have fair play against Grecians. In his pleadings at Rome, his eloquence soon obtained him great credit and favour, and he won no less upon the affections of the people by the affability of his manners and address, in which he showed a tact and consideration beyond what could have been expected at his age; and the open house he kept, the entertainments he gave, and the general splendour of his manner of life contributed little by little to create and increase his political influence. His enemies slighted the growth of it at first, presuming it would soon fail when his money was gone; whilst in the meantime it was growing up and flourishing among the common people. When his power at last was established and not to be overthrown, and now openly tended to the altering of the whole constitution, they were aware too late that there is no beginning so mean, which continued application will not make considerable, and that despising a danger at first will make it at last irresistible. Cicero was the first who had any suspicions of his designs upon the government, and as a good pilot is apprehensive of a storm when the sea is most smiling, saw the designing temper of the man through this disguise of good humour and affability, and said that, in general, in all he did and undertook, he detected the ambition for absolute power, "but when I see his hair so carefully arranged, and observe him adjusting it with one finger, I cannot imagine it should enter into such a man's thoughts to subvert the Roman state." But of this more hereafter.

The first proof he had of the people's good-will to him was when he received by their suffrages a tribuneship in the army, and came out on the list with a higher place than Caius Popilius. A second and clearer instance of their favour appeared upon his making a magnificent oration in praise of his aunt Julia, wife to Marius, publicly in the forum, at whose funeral he was so bold as to bring forth the images of Marius, which nobody had dared to produce since the government came into Sylla's hands, Marius's party having from that time been declared enemies of the state. When some who were present had begun to raise a cry against Caesar, the people answered with loud shouts and clapping in his favour, expressing their joyful surprise and satisfaction at his having, as it were, brought up again from the grave those honours of Marius, which for so long a time had been lost to the city. It had always been the custom at Rome to make funeral orations in praise of elderly matrons, but there was no precedent of any upon young women till Caesar first made one upon the death of his own wife. This also procured him favour, and by this show of affection he won upon the feelings of the people, who looked upon him as a man of great tenderness and kindness of heart. After he had buried his wife, he went as quaestor into Spain under one of the praetors, named Vetus, whom he honoured ever after, and made his son his own quaestor, when he himself came to be praetor. After this employment was ended, he married Pompeia, his third wife, having then a daughter by Cornelia, his first wife, whom he afterwards married to Pompey the Great. He was so profuse in his ex-

penses that, before he had any public employment, he was
in debt thirteen hundred talents, and many thought that by
incurring such expense to be popular he changed a solid
good for what would prove but a short and uncertain return; but in truth he was purchasing what was of the
greatest value at an inconsiderable rate. When he was made
surveyor of the Appian Way, he disbursed, besides the public money, a great sum out of his private purse; and when
he was aedile, he provided such a number of gladiators,
that he entertained the people with three hundred and
twenty single combats, and by his great liberality and magnificence in theatrical shows, in processions, and public
feastings, he threw into the shade all the attempts that had
been made before him, and gained so much upon the people, that every one was eager to find out new offices and
new honours for him in return for his munificence.

There being two factions in the city, one that of Sylla,
which was very powerful, the other that of Marius, which
was then broken and in a low condition, he undertook to
revive this and to make it his own. And to this end, whilst
he was in the height of his repute with the people for the
magnificent shows he gave as aedile, he ordered images of
Marius and figures of Victory, with trophies in their hands,
to be carried privately in the night and placed in the capitol. Next morning when some saw them bright with gold
and beautifully made, with inscriptions upon them, referring them to Marius's exploits over the Cimbrians, they
were surprised at the boldness of him who had set them
up, nor was it difficult to guess who it was. The fame of
this soon spread and brought together a great concourse
of people. Some cried out that it was an open attempt
against the established government thus to revive those
honours which had been buried by the laws and decrees of
the senate; that Caesar had done it to sound the temper
of the people whom he had prepared before, and to try
whether they were tame enough to bear his humour, and
would quietly give way to his innovations. On the other
hand, Marius's party took courage, and it was incredible
how numerous they were suddenly seen to be, and what

a multitude of them appeared and came shouting into the capitol. Many, when they saw Marius's likeness, cried for joy, and Caesar was highly extolled as the one man, in the place of all others, who was a relation worthy of Marius. Upon this the senate met, and Catulus Lutatius, one of the most eminent Romans of that time, stood up and inveighed against Caesar, closing his speech with the remarkable saying that Caesar was now not working mines, but planting batteries to overthrow the state. But when Caesar had made an apology for himself, and satisfied the senate, his admirers were very much animated, and advised him not to depart from his own thoughts for any one, since with the people's good favour he would ere long get the better of them all, and be the first man in the commonwealth.

At this time, Metellus, the high priest, died, and Catulus and Isauricus, persons of the highest reputation, and who had great influence in the senate, were competitors for the office, yet Caesar would not give way to them, but presented himself to the people as a candidate against them. The several parties seeming very equal, Catulus, who, because he had the most honour to lose, was the most apprehensive of the event, sent to Caesar to buy him off, with offers of a great sum of money. But his answer was, that he was ready to borrow a larger sum than that to carry on the contest. Upon the day of election, as his mother conducted him out of doors with tears, after embracing her, "My mother," he said, "to-day you will see me either high priest or an exile." When the votes were taken, after a great struggle, he carried it, and excited among the senate and nobility great alarm lest he might now urge on the people to every kind of insolence. And Piso and Catulus found fault with Cicero for having let Caesar escape, when in the conspiracy of Catiline he had given the government such advantage against him. For Catiline, who had designed not only to change the present state of affairs, but to subvert the whole empire and confound all, had himself taken to flight, while the evidence was yet incomplete against him, before his ultimate purposes had been properly discovered. But he had left Lentulus and Cethegus in the city to supply his place in the conspiracy, and whether they received any secret encouragement and assistance from Caesar is uncertain; all that is certain is, that they were fully convicted in the senate, and when Cicero, the consul, asked the several opinions of the senators, how they would have them punished, all who spoke before Caesar sentenced them to death; but Caesar stood up and made a set speech, in which he told them that he thought it without precedent and not just to take away the lives of persons of their birth and distinction before they were fairly tried, unless there was an absolute necessity for it; but that if they were kept confined in any towns of Italy Cicero himself should choose till Catiline was defeated, then the senate might in peace and at their leisure determine what was best to be done.

This sentence of his carried so much appearance of humanity, and he gave it such advantage by the eloquence with which he urged it, that not only those who spoke after him closed with it, but even they who had before given a contrary opinion now came over to his, till it came about to Catulus's and Cato's turn to speak. They warmly opposed it, and Cato intimated in his speech the suspicion of Caesar himself, and pressed the matter so strongly that the criminals were given up to suffer execution. As Caesar was going out of the senate, many of the young men who at that time acted as guards to Cicero ran in with their naked swords to assault him. But Curio, it is said, threw his gown over him, and conveyed him away, and Cicero himself, when the young men looked up to see his wishes, gave a sign not to kill him, either for fear of the people or because he thought the murder unjust and illegal. If this be true, I wonder how Cicero came to omit all mention of it in his book about his consulship. He was blamed, however, afterwards, for not having made use of so fortunate an opportunity against Caesar, as if he had let it escape him out of fear of the populace, who, indeed, showed remarkable solicitude about Caesar, and some time after, when he went into the senate to clear himself of the suspicions he lay under, and found great clamours raised against him, upon the senate in consequence sitting longer than ordinary, they went up to the house in a tumult, and beset it, demanding Caesar, and requiring them to dismiss him. Upon this, Cato, much fearing some movement among the poor citizens, who were always the first to kindle the flame among the people, and placed all their hopes in Caesar, persuaded the senate to give them a monthly allowance of corn, an expedient which put the commonwealth to the extraordinary charge of seven million five hundred thousand drachmas in the year, but quite succeeded in removing the great cause of terror for the present, and very much weakened Caesar's power, who at that time was just going to be made praetor, and consequently would have been more formidable by his office.

But there was no disturbance during his praetorship, only what misfortune he met with in his own domestic affairs. Publius Clodius was a patrician by descent, eminent both for his riches and eloquence, but in licentiousness of life and audacity exceeded the most noted profligates of the day. He was in love with Pompeia, Caesar's wife, and she had no aversion to him. But there was strict watch kept on her apartment, and Caesar's mother, Aurelia, who was a discreet woman, being continually about her, made any interview very dangerous and difficult. The Romans have a goddess whom they call Bona, the same whom the Greeks call Gynaecea. The Phrygians, who claim a peculiar title to her, say she was mother to Midas. The Romans profess she was one of the Dryads, and married to Faunus. The Grecians affirm that she is that mother of Bacchus whose name is not to be uttered, and, for this reason, the women who celebrate her festival cover the tents with vine-branches, and, in accordance with the fable, a consecrated serpent is placed by the goddess. It is not lawful for a man to be by, nor so much as in the house, whilst the rites are celebrated, but the women by themselves perform the sacred offices, which are said to be much the same with those used in the solemnities of Orpheus. When the festival comes, the husband, who is either consul or praetor, and with him every male creature, quits the house. The wife then taking it under her care sets it in order, and the principal ceremonies are performed during the night, the women playing together amongst themselves as they keep watch, and music of various kinds going on.

As Pompeia was at that time celebrating this feast, Clodius, who as yet had no beard, and so thought to pass undiscovered, took upon him the dress and ornaments of a singing woman, and so came thither, having the air of a young girl. Finding the doors open, he was without any stop introduced by the maid, who was in the intrigue. She presently ran to tell Pompeia, but as she was away a long time, he grew uneasy in waiting for her, and left his post and traversed the house from one room to another, still taking care to avoid the lights, till at last Aurelia's woman met him, and invited him to play with her, as the women did among themselves. He refused to comply, and she presently pulled him forward, and asked him who he was and whence he came. Clodius told her he was waiting for Pompeia's own maid, Abra, being in fact her own name also, and as he said so, betrayed himself by his voice. Upon which the woman shrieking, ran into the company where there were lights, and cried out she had discovered a man. The women were all in a fright. Aurelia covered up the sacred things and stopped the proceedings, and having ordered the doors to be shut, went about with lights to find Clodius, who was got into the maid's room that he had come in with, and was seized there. The women knew him, and drove him out of doors, and at once, that same night, went home and told their husbands the story. In the morning, it was all about the town, what an impious attempt Clodius had made, and how he ought to be punished as an offender, not only against those whom he had offended, but also against the public and the gods. Upon which one of the tribunes impeached him for profaning the holy rites, and some of the principal senators combined together and gave evidence against him, that besides many other horrible crimes, he had been guilty of incest with his own sister, who was married to Lucullus. But the people set themselves against this combination of the nobility, and defended Clodius, which was of great service to him with the judges, who took alarm and were afraid to provoke the multitude. Caesar at once dismissed Pompeia, but being summoned as a witness against Clodius, said he had nothing to charge him with. This looking like a paradox, the accuser asked him why he parted with his wife. Caesar replied, "I wished my wife to be not so much as suspected." Some say that Caesar spoke this as his real thought, others, that he did it to gratify the people, who were very earnest to save Clodius. Clodius, at any rate, escaped; most of the judges giving their opinions so written as to be illegible that they might not be in danger from the people by condemning him, nor in disgrace with the nobility by acquitting him.

Caesar, in the meantime, being out of his praetorship, had got the province of Spain, but was in great embarrassment with his creditors, who, as he was going off, came upon him, and were very pressing and importunate. This led him to apply himself to Crassus, who was the richest man in Rome, but wanted Caesar's youthful vigour and heat to sustain the opposition against Pompey. Crassus took upon him to satisfy those creditors who were most uneasy to him, and would not be put off any longer, and engaged himself to the amount of eight hundred and thirty talents, upon which Caesar was now at liberty to go to his province. In his journey, as he was crossing the Alps, and passing by a small village of the barbarians with but few inhabitants, and those wretchedly poor, his companions asked the question among themselves by way of mockery, if there were any canvassing for offices there; any contention which should be uppermost, or feuds of great men one against another. To which Caesar made answer seriously, "For my part, I had rather be the first man among these fellows, than the second man in Rome." It is said that another time, when free from business in Spain, after reading some part of the history of Alexander, he sat a great while very thoughtful, and at last burst out into tears. His friends were surprised, and asked him the reason of it. "Do you think," said he, "I have not just cause to weep, when I consider that Alexander at my age had conquered so many nations, and I have all this time done nothing that is memorable." As soon as he came into Spain he was very active, and in a few days had got together ten new cohorts of foot in addition to the twenty which were there before. With these he marched against the Calaici and Lusitani and conquered them, and advancing as far as the ocean, subdued the tribes which never before had been subject to the Romans. Having managed his military affairs with good success, he was equally happy in the course of his civil government. He took pains to establish a good understanding amongst the several states, and no less care to heal the differences between debtors and creditors. He ordered that the creditor should receive two parts of the debtor's yearly income, and that the other part should be managed by the debtor himself, till by this method the whole debt was at last discharged. This conduct made him leave his province with a fair reputation; being rich himself, and having enriched his soldiers, and having received from them the honourable name of Imperator.

There is a law among the Romans, that whoever desires the honour of a triumph must stay without the city and expect his answer. And another, that those who stand for the consulship shall appear personally upon the place. Caesar was come home at the very time of choosing consuls, and being in a difficulty between these two opposite laws, sent to the senate to desire that, since he was obliged to be absent, he might sue for the consulship by his friends. Cato, being backed by the law, at first opposed his request; afterwards perceiving that Caesar had prevailed with a great part of the senate to comply with it, he made it his business to gain time and went on wasting the whole day in speaking. Upon which Caesar thought fit to let the triumph fall, and pursued the consulship. Entering the town and coming forward immediately, he had recourse to a piece of state policy by which everybody was deceived but Cato. This was the reconciling of Crassus and Pompey, the two men who then were most powerful in Rome. There had been a quarrel between them, which he now succeeded in making up, and by this means strengthened himself by the united power of both, and so under the cover of an action which carried all the appearance of a piece of kindness and good-nature, caused what was in effect a revolution in the government. For it was not the quarrel between Pompey and Caesar, as most men imagine, which was the origin of the civil wars, but their union, their conspiring together at first to subvert the aristocracy, and so quarrelling afterwards between themselves. Cato, who often foretold what the consequence of this alliance would be, had then the character of a sullen, interfering man, but in the end the reputation of a wise but unsuccessful counsellor.

Thus Caesar, being doubly supported by the interests of Crassus and Pompey, was promoted to the consulship, and triumphantly proclaimed with Calpurnius Bibulus. When he entered on his office he brought in bills which would have been preferred with better grace by the most audacious of the tribunes than by a consul, in which he proposed the plantation of colonies and the division of lands, simply to please the commonalty. The best and most honourable of the senators opposed it, upon which, as he had long wished for nothing more than for such a colourable pretext, he loudly protested how much it was against his will to be driven to seek support from the people, and how the senate's insulting and harsh conduct left no other course possible for him than to devote himself henceforth to the popular cause and interest. And so he hurried out of the senate, and presenting himself to the people, and there placing Crassus and Pompey, one on each side of him, he asked them whether they consented to the bills he had proposed. They owned their assent, upon which he desired them to assist him against those who had threatened to oppose him with their swords. They engaged they would, and Pompey added further, that he would meet their swords with a sword and buckler too. These words the nobles much resented, as neither suitable to his own dignity, nor becoming the reverence due to the senate, but resembling rather the vehemence of a boy or the fury of a madman. But the people were pleased with it. In order to get a yet firmer hold upon Pompey, Caesar having a daughter, Julia, who had been

before contracted to Servilius Caepio, now betrothed her to
Pompey, and told Servilius he should have Pompey's daughter, who was not unengaged either, but promised to Sylla's
son, Faustus. A little time after, Caesar married Calpurnia,
the daughter of Piso, and got Piso made consul for the year
following. Cato exclaimed loudly against this, and protested, with a great deal of warmth, that it was intolerable
the government should be prostituted by marriages, and that
they should advance one another to the commands of armies, provinces, and other great posts, by means of women.
Bibulus, Caesar's colleague, finding it was to no purpose
to oppose his bills, but that he was in danger of being murdered in the forum, as also was Cato, confined himself to
his house, and there let the remaining part of his consulship expire. Pompey, when he was married, at once filled
the forum with soldiers, and gave the people his help in
passing the new laws, and secured Caesar the government
of all Gaul, both on this and the other side of the Alps,
together with Illyricum, and the command of four legions
for five years. Cato made some attempts against these proceedings, but was seized and led off on the way to prison
by Caesar, who expected that he would appeal to the tribunes. But when he saw that Cato went along without
speaking a word, and not only the nobility were indignant,
but the people also, out of respect for Cato's virtue, were
following in silence, and with dejected looks, he himself
privately desired one of the tribunes to rescue Cato. As
for the other senators, some few of them attended the
house, the rest, being disgusted, absented themselves. Hence
Considius, a very old man, took occasion one day to tell
Caesar that the senators did not meet because they were
afraid of his soldiers. Caesar asked, "Why don't you, then,
out of the same fear, keep at home?" To which Considius
replied, that age was his guard against fear, and that the
small remains of his life were not worth much caution.
But the most disgraceful thing that was done in Caesar's
consulship was his assisting to gain the tribuneship for
the same Clodius who had made the attempt on his wife's
chastity and intruded upon the secret vigils. He was elected

on purpose to effect Cicero's downfall; nor did Caesar leave the city to join his army till they two had overpowered Cicero and driven him out of Italy.

Thus far have we followed Caesar's actions before the wars of Gaul. After this, he seems to begin his course afresh, and to enter upon a new life and scene of action. And the period of those wars which he now fought, and those many expeditions in which he subdued Gaul, showed him to be a soldier and general not in the least inferior to any of the greatest and most admired commanders who had ever appeared at the head of armies. For if we compare him with the Fabii, the Metelli, the Scipios, and with those who were his contemporaries, or not long before him, Sylla, Marius, the Luculli, or even Pompey himself, whose glory, it may be said, went up at that time to heaven for every excellence in war, we shall find Caesar's actions to have surpassed them all. One he may be held to have outdone in consideration of the difficulty of the country in which he fought, another in the extent of territory which he conquered; some, in the number and strength of the enemy whom he defeated; one man, because of the wildness and perfidiousness of the tribes whose good-will he conciliated, another in his humanity and clemency to those he overpowered; others, again, in his gifts and kindnesses to his soldiers; all alike in the number of the battles which he fought and the enemies whom he killed. For he had not pursued the wars in Gaul full ten years when he had taken by storm above eight hundred towns, subdued three hundred states, and of the three millions of men, who made up the gross sum of those with whom at several times he engaged, he had killed one million and taken captive a second.

He was so much master of the good-will and hearty service of his soldiers that those who in other expeditions were but ordinary men displayed a courage past defeating or withstanding when they went upon any danger where Caesar's glory was concerned. Such a one was Acilius, who, in the sea-fight before Marseilles, had his right hand struck off with a sword, yet did not quit his buckler out of his left, but struck the enemies in the face with it, till he drove them off and made himself master of the vessel. Such another was Cassius Scaeva, who, in a battle near Dyrrhachium, had one of his eyes shot out with an arrow, his shoulder pierced with one javelin, and his thigh with another; and having received one hundred and thirty darts upon his target, called to the enemy, as though he would surrender himself. But when two of them came up to him, he cut off the shoulder of one with a sword, and by a blow over the face forced the other to retire, and so with the assistance of his friends, who now came up, made his escape. Again, in Britain, when some of the foremost officers had accidentally got into a morass full of water, and there were assaulted by the enemy, a common soldier, whilst Caesar stood and looked on, threw himself in the midst of them, and after many signal demonstrations of his valour, rescued the officers and beat off the barbarians. He himself, in the end, took to the water, and with much difficulty, partly by swimming, partly by wading, passed it, but in the passage lost his shield. Caesar and his officers saw it and admired, and went to meet him with joy and acclamation. But the soldier, much dejected and in tears, threw himself down at Caesar's feet and begged his pardon for having let go his buckler. Another time in Africa, Scipio having taken a ship of Caesar's in which Granius Petro, lately appointed quaestor, was sailing, gave the other passengers as free prize to his soldiers, but thought fit to offer the quaestor his life. But he said it was not usual for Caesar's soldiers to take but give mercy, and having said so, fell upon his sword and killed himself.

This love of honour and passion for distinction were inspired into them and cherished in them by Caesar himself, who, by his unsparing distribution of money and honours, showed them that he did not heap up wealth from the wars for his own luxury, or the gratifying his private pleasures, but that all he received was but a public fund laid by the reward and encouragement of valour, and that he looked upon all he gave to deserving soldiers as so much increase to his own riches. Added to this also, there was no danger to which he did not willingly expose himself, no labour from which he pleaded an exemption. His contempt of danger was not so much wondered at by his soldiers because they knew how much he coveted honour. But his enduring so much hardship, which he did to all appearance beyond his natural strength, very much astonished them. For he was a spare man, had a soft and white skin, was distempered in the head and subject to an epilepsy, which, it is said, first seized him at Corduba. But he did not make the weakness of his constitution a pretext for his ease, but rather used war as the best physic against his indispositions; whilst, by indefatigable journeys, coarse diet, frequent lodging in the field, and continual laborious exercise, he struggled with his diseases and fortified his body against all attacks. He slept generally in his chariots or litters, employing even his rest in pursuit of action. In the day he was thus carried to the forts, garrisons, and camps, one servant sitting with him, who used to write down what he dictated as he went, and a soldier attending behind him with his sword drawn. He drove so rapidly that when he first left Rome he arrived at the river Rhone within eight days. He had been an expert rider from his childhood; for it was usual with him to sit with his hands joined together behind his back, and so to put his horse to its full speed. And in this way he disciplined himself so far as to be able to dictate letters from on horseback, and to give directions to two who took notes at the same time or, as Oppius says, to more. And it is thought that he was the first who contrived means for communicating with friends by cipher, when either press of business, or the large extent of the city, left him no time for a personal conference about matters that required despatch. How little nice he was in his diet may be seen in the following instance. When at the table of Valerius Leo, who entertained him at supper at Milan, a dish of asparagus was put before him on which his host instead of oil had poured sweet ointment, Caesar partook of it without any disgust, and reprimanded his friends for finding fault with it. "For it was enough," said he, "not to eat what you did not like; but he who reflects on another man's want of breeding, shows he wants it as much himself." Another time upon the road he was driven by a storm into a poor man's cottage, where he found but one room, and that such as would afford but a mean reception to a single person, and therefore told his companions places of honour should be given up to the greater men, and necessary accommodations to the weaker, and accordingly ordered that Oppius, who was in bad health, should lodge within, whilst he and the rest slept under a shed at the door.

His first war in Gaul was against the Helvetians and Tigurini, who having burnt their own towns, twelve in number, and four hundred villages, would have marched forward through that part of Gaul which was included in the Roman province, as the Cimbrians and Teutons formerly had done. Nor were they inferior to these in courage; and in numbers they were equal, being in all three hundred thousand, of which one hundred and ninety thousand were fighting men. Caesar did not engage the Tigurini in person, but Labienus, under his directions, routed them near the river Arar. The Helvetians surprised Caesar, and unexpectedly set upon him as he was conducting his army to a confederate town. He succeeded, however, in making his retreat into a strong position, where, when he had mustered and marshalled his men, his horse was brought to him; upon which he said, "When I have won the battle, I will use my horse for the chase, but at present let us go against the enemy," and accordingly charged them on foot. After a long and severe combat, he drove the main army out of the field, but found the hardest work at their carriages and ramparts, where not only the men stood and fought, but the women also and children defended themselves till they were cut to pieces; insomuch that the fight was scarcely ended till midnight. This action, glorious in itself, Caesar crowned with another yet more noble, by gathering in a body all the barbarians that had escaped out of the battle, above one hundred thousand in number, and obliging them to re-occupy the country which they had

deserted and the cities which they had burnt. This he did
for fear the Germans should pass it and possess themselves
of the land whilst it lay uninhabited.

His second war was in defence of the Gauls against the
Germans, though some time before he had made Ariovistus, their king, recognised at Rome as an ally. But they
were very insufferable neighbours to those under his government; and it was probable, when occasion offered, they
would renounce the present arrangements, and march on
to occupy Gaul. But finding his officers timorous, and especially those of the young nobility who came along with him
in hopes of turning their campaigns with him into a means
for their own pleasure or profit, he called them together,
and advised them to march off, and not run the hazard of
a battle against their inclinations, since they had such weak
unmanly feelings; telling them that he would take only
the tenth legion and march against the barbarians, whom
he did not expect to find an enemy more formidable than
the Cimbri, nor, he added, should they find him a general
inferior to Marius. Upon this, the tenth legion deputed
some of their body to pay him their acknowledgments and
thanks, and the other legions blamed their officers, and all,
with great vigour and zeal, followed him many days' journey, till they encamped within two hundred furlongs of the
enemy. Ariovistus's courage to some extent was cooled
upon their very approach; for never expecting the Romans would attack the Germans whom he had thought it
more likely they would not venture to withstand even in
defence of their own subjects, he was the more surprised
at Caesar's conduct, and saw his army to be in consternation. They were still more discouraged by the prophecies of
their holy women, who foretell the future by observing the
eddies of rivers, and taking signs from the windings and
noise of streams, and who now warned them not to engage
before the next new moon appeared. Caesar having had
intimation of this, and seeing the Germans lie still, thought
it expedient to attack them whilst they were under these
apprehensions, rather than sit still and wait their time. Accordingly he made his approaches to the strongholds and

hills on which they lay encamped, and so galled and fretted them that at last they came down with great fury to engage. But he gained a signal victory, and pursued them for four hundred furlongs, as far as the Rhine; all which space was covered with spoils and bodies of the slain. Ariovistus made shift to pass the Rhine with the small remains of an army, for it is said the number of the slain amounted to eighty thousand.

After this action, Caesar left his army at their winter quarters in the country of the Sequani, and, in order to attend to affairs at Rome, went into that part of Gaul which lies on the Po, and was part of his province; for the river Rubicon divides Gaul, which is on this side the Alps, from the rest of Italy. There he sat down and employed himself in courting people's favour; great numbers coming to him continually, and always finding their requests answered; for he never failed to dismiss all with present pledges of his kindness in hand, and further hopes for the future. And during all this time of the war in Gaul, Pompey never observed how Caesar was on the one hand using the arms of Rome to effect his conquests, and on the other was gaining over and securing to himself the favour of the Romans with the wealth which those conquests obtained him. But when he heard that the Belgae, who were the most powerful of all the Gauls, and inhabited a third part of the country, were revolted, and had got together a great many thousand men in arms, he immediately set out and took his way hither with great expedition, and falling upon the enemy as they were ravaging the Gauls, his allies, he soon defeated and put to flight the largest and least scattered division of them. For though their numbers were great, yet they made but a slender defence, and the marshes and deep rivers were made passable to the Roman foot by the vast quantity of dead bodies. Of those who revolted, all the tribes that lived near the ocean came over without fighting, and he, therefore, led his army against the Nervii, the fiercest and most warlike people of all in those parts. These live in a country covered with continuous woods, and having lodged their children and property out of the way in the

depth of the forest, fell upon Caesar with a body of sixty
thousand men, before he was prepared for them, while he
was making his encampment. They soon routed his cavalry,
and having surrounded the twelfth and seventh legions,
killed all the officers, and had not Caesar himself snatched
up a buckler and forced his way through his own men to
come up to the barbarians, or had not the tenth legion,
when they saw him in danger, run in from the tops of the
hills, where they lay, and broken through the enemy's
ranks to rescue him, in all probability not a Roman would
have been saved. But now, under the influence of Caesar's
bold example, they fought a battle, as the phrase is, of more
than human courage, and yet with their utmost efforts they
were not able to drive the enemy out of the field, but cut
them down fighting in their defence. For out of sixty thousand men, it is stated that not above five hundred survived
the battle, and of four hundred of their senators not above
three.

When the Roman senate had received news of this, they
voted sacrifices and festivals to the gods, to be strictly observed for the space of fifteen days, a longer space than
ever was observed for any victory before. The danger to
which they had been exposed by the joint outbreak of such
a number of nations was felt to have been great; and the
people's fondness for Caesar gave additional lustre to successes achieved by him. He now, after settling everything
in Gaul, came back again, and spent the winter by the Po,
in order to carry on the designs he had in hand at Rome.
All who were candidates for offices used his assistance, and
were supplied with money from him to corrupt the people
and buy their votes, in return of which, when they were
chosen, they did all things to advance his power. But what
was more considerable, the most eminent and powerful
men in Rome in great numbers came to visit him at Lucca,
Pompey, and Crassus, and Appius, the governor of Sardinia, and Nepos, the pro-consul of Spain, so that there
were in the place at one time one hundred and twenty lictors and more than two hundred senators. In deliberation
here held, it was determined that Pompey and Crassus

should be consuls again for the following year; that Caesar
should have a fresh supply of money, and that his command should be renewed to him for five years more. It
seemed very extravagant to all thinking men that those
very persons who had received so much money from Caesar should persuade the senate to grant him more, as if
he were in want. Though in truth it was not so much
upon persuasion as compulsion that, with sorrow and
groans for their own acts, they passed the measure. Cato
was not present, for they had sent him seasonably out of
the way into Cyprus; but Favonius, who was a zealous
imitator of Cato, when he found he could do no good by
opposing it, broke out of the house, and loudly declaimed
against these proceedings to the people, but none gave him
any hearing; some slighting him out of respect to Crassus
and Pompey, and the greater part to gratify Caesar, on
whom depended their hopes.

After this, Caesar returned again to his forces in Gaul,
when he found that country involved in a dangerous war,
two strong nations of the Germans having lately passed
the Rhine to conquer it; one of them called the Usipes, the
other the Tenteritae. Of the war with the people, Caesar
himself has given this account in his commentaries, that
the barbarians, having sent ambassadors to treat with him,
did, during the treaty, set upon him in his march, by which
means with eight hundred men they routed five thousand
of his horse, who did not suspect their coming; that afterwards they sent other ambassadors to renew the same fraud-
ulent practices, whom he kept in custody, and led on his
army against the barbarians, as judging it mere simplicity
to keep faith with those who had so faithlessly broken the
terms they had agreed to. But Tanusius states that when
the senate decreed festivals and sacrifices for this victory,
Cato declared it to be his opinion that Caesar ought to be
given into the hands of the barbarians, that so the guilt
which this breach of faith might otherwise bring upon the
state might be expiated by transferring the curse on him,
who was the occasion of it. Of those who passed the Rhine,
there were four hundred thousand cut off; those few who

escaped were sheltered by the Sugambri, a people of Germany. Caesar took hold of this pretence to invade the Germans, being at the same time ambitious of the honour of being the first man that should pass the Rhine with an army. He carried a bridge across it, though it was very wide, and the current at that particular point very full, strong, and violent, bringing down with its waters trunks of trees, and other lumber, which much shook and weakened the foundations of his bridge. But he drove great piles of wood into the bottom of the river above the passage, to catch and stop these as they floated down, and thus fixing his bridle upon the stream, successfully finished his bridge, which no one who saw could believe to be the work but of ten days.

In the passage of his army over it he met with no opposition: the Suevi themselves, who are the most warlike people of all Germany, flying with their effects into the deepest and most densely wooded valleys. When he had burnt all the enemy's country, and encouraged those who embraced the Roman interest, he went back into Gaul, after eighteen days' stay in Germany. But his expedition into Britain was the most famous testimony of his courage. For he was the first who brought a navy into the western ocean, or who sailed into the Atlantic with an army to make war; and by invading an island, the reported extent of which had made its existence a matter of controversy among historians, many of whom questioned whether it were not a mere name and fiction, not a real place, he might be said to have carried the Roman empire beyond the limits of the known world. He passed thither twice from that part of Gaul which lies over against it, and in several battles which he fought did more hurt to the enemy than service to himself, for the islanders were so miserably poor that they had nothing worth being plundered of. When he found himself unable to put such an end to the war as he wished, he was content to take hostages from the king, and to impose a tribute, and then quitted the island. At his arrival in Gaul, he found letters which lay ready to be conveyed over the water to him from his friends at Rome, announcing his daughter's death, who died in labour of a child by Pompey. Caesar and Pompey both were much afflicted with her death, nor were their friends less disturbed, believing that the alliance was now broken which had hitherto kept the sickly commonwealth in peace, for the child also died within a few days after the mother. The people took the body of Julia, in spite of the opposition of the tribunes, and carried it into the field of Mars, and there her funeral rites were performed, and her remains are laid.

Caesar's army was now grown very numerous, so that he was forced to disperse them into various camps for their winter quarters, and he having gone himself to Italy as he used to do, in his absence a general outbreak throughout the whole of Gaul commenced, and large armies marched about the country, and attacked the Roman quarters, and attempted to make themselves masters of the forts where they lay. The greatest and strongest party of the rebels, under the command of Abriorix, cut off Cotta and Titurius with all their men, while a force sixty thousand strong besieged the legion under the command of Cicero, and had almost taken it by storm, the Roman soldiers being all wounded, and having quite spent themselves by a defence beyond their natural strength. But Caesar, who was at a great distance, having received the news, quickly got together seven thousand men, and hastened to relieve Cicero. The besiegers were aware of it, and went to meet him, with great confidence that they should easily overpower such a handful of men. Caesar, to increase their presumption, seemed to avoid fighting, and still marched off till he found a place conveniently situated for a few to engage against many, where he encamped. He kept his soldiers from making any attack upon the enemy, and commanded them to raise the ramparts higher and barricade the gates, that by show of fear they might heighten the enemy's contempt of them. Till at last they came without any order in great security to make an assault, when he issued forth and put them in flight with the loss of many men.

This quieted the greater part of the commotions in these parts of Gaul, and Caesar, in the course of the winter, visited every part of the country, and with great vigilance took precautions against all innovations. For there were three legions now come to him to supply the place of the men he had lost, of which Pompey furnished him with two out of those under his command; the other was newly raised in the part of Gaul by the Po. But in a while the seeds of war, which had long since been secretly sown and scattered by the most powerful men in those warlike nations, broke forth into the greatest and most dangerous war that was in those parts, both as regards the number of men in the vigour of their youth who were gathered and armed from all quarters, the vast funds of money collected to maintain it, the strength of the towns, and the difficulty of the country where it was carried on. It being winter, the rivers were frozen, the woods covered with snow, and the level country flooded, so that in some places the ways were lost through the depth of the snow; in others, the overflowing of marshes and streams made every kind of passage uncertain. All which difficulties made it seem impracticable for Caesar to make any attempt upon the insurgents. Many tribes had revolted together, the chief of them being the Arveni and Carnutini; the general who had the supreme command in war was Vergentorix, whose father the Gauls had put to death on suspicion of his aiming at absolute government.

He having disposed his army in several bodies, and set officers over them, drew over to him all the country round about as far as those that lie upon the Arar, and having intelligence of the opposition which Caesar now experienced at Rome, thought to engage all Gaul in the war. Which if he had done a little later, when Caesar was taken up with the civil wars, Italy had been put into as great a terror as before it was by the Cimbri. But Caesar, who above all men was gifted with the faculty of making the right use of everything in war, and most especially of seizing the right moment, as soon as he heard of the revolt, returned immediately the same way he went, and showed the barbarians,

by the quickness of his march in such a severe season, that
an army was advancing against them which was invincible.
For in the time that one would have thought it scarce
credible that a courier or express should have come with
a message from him, he himself appeared with all his army,
ravaging the country, reducing their posts, subduing their
towns, receiving into his protection those who declared for
him. Till at last the Edui, who hitherto had styled themselves brethren to the Romans, and had been much honoured by them, declared against him, and joined the rebels,
to the great discouragement of his army. Accordingly he
removed thence, and passed the country of the Ligones, desiring to reach the territories of the Sequani, who were his
friends, and who lay like a bulwark in front of Italy against
the other tribes of Gaul. There the enemy came upon him,
and surrounded him with many myriads, whom he also was
eager to engage; and at last, after some time and with
much slaughter, gained on the whole a complete victory;
though at first he appears to have met with some reverse,
and the Aruveni show you a small sword hanging up in a
temple, which they say was taken from Caesar. Caesar saw
this afterwards himself, and smiled, and when his friends
advised it should be taken down, would not permit it, because he looked upon it as consecrated.

After the defeat, a great part of those who had escaped
fled with their king into a town called Alesia, which Caesar
besieged, though the height of the walls, and number of
those who defended them, made it appear impregnable;
and meantime, from without the walls, he was assailed by a
greater danger than can be expressed. For the choice men
of Gaul, picked out of each nation, and well armed, came
to relieve Alesia, to the number of three hundred thousand;
nor were there in the town less than one hundred and seventy thousand. So that Caesar being shut up betwixt two
such forces, was compelled to protect himself by two walls,
one towards the town, the other against the relieving army,
as knowing if these forces should join, his affairs would
be entirely ruined. The danger that he underwent before
Alesia justly gained him great honour on many accounts,

and gave him an opportunity of showing greater instances of his valour and conduct than any other contest had done. One wonders much how he should be able to engage and defeat so many thousands of men without the town, and not be perceived by those within, but yet more, that the Romans themselves, who guarded their wall which was next to the town, should be strangers to it. For even they knew nothing of the victory, till they heard the cries of the men and lamentations of the women who were in the town, and had from thence seen the Romans at a distance carrying into their camp a great quantity of bucklers, adorned with gold and silver, many breastplates stained with blood, besides cups and tents made in the Gallic fashion. So soon did so vast an army dissolve and vanish like a ghost or dream, the greatest part of them being killed upon the spot. Those who were in Alesia, having given themselves and Caesar much trouble, surrendered at last; and Vergentorix, who was the chief spring of all the war, putting his best armour on, and adorning his horse, rode out of the gates, and made a turn about Caesar as he was sitting, then quitting his horse, threw off his armour, and remained quietly sitting at Caesar's feet until he was led away to be reserved for the triumph.

Caesar had long ago resolved upon the overthrow of Pompey, as had Pompey, for that matter, upon his. For Crassus, the fear of whom had hitherto kept them in peace, having now been killed in Parthia, if the one of them wished to make himself the greatest man in Rome, he had only to overthrow the other; and if he again wished to prevent his own fall, he had nothing for it but to be beforehand with him whom he feared. Pompey had not been long under any such apprehensions, having till lately despised Caesar, as thinking it no difficult matter to put down him whom he himself had advanced. But Caesar had entertained this design from the beginning against his rivals, and had retired, like an expert wrestler, to prepare himself apart for the combat. Making the Gallic wars his exercise-ground, he had at once improved the strength of his soldiery, and had heightened his own glory by his great actions, so that he was looked on as one who might challenge comparison with Pompey. Nor did he let go any of those advantages which were now given him both by Pompey himself and the times, and the ill-government of Rome, where all who were candidates for offices publicly gave money, and without any shame bribed the people, who, having received their pay, did not contend for their benefactors with their bare suffrages, but with bows, swords, and slings. So that after having many times stained the place of election with blood of men killed upon the spot, they left the city at last without a government at all, to be carried about like a ship without a pilot to steer her; while all who had any wisdom could only be thankful if a course of such wild and stormy disorder and madness might end no worse than in a monarchy. Some were so bold as to declare openly that the government was incurable but by a monarchy, and that they ought to take that remedy from the hands of the gentlest physician, meaning Pompey, who, though in words he pretended to decline it, yet in reality made his utmost efforts to be declared dictator. Cato, perceiving his design, prevailed with the senate to make him sole consul, that with the offer of a more legal sort of monarchy he might be withheld from demanding the dictatorship. They over and above voted him the continuance of his provinces, for he had two, Spain and all Africa, which he governed by his lieutenants, and maintained armies under him, at the yearly charge of a thousand talents out of the public treasury.

Upon this Caesar also sent and petitioned for the consulship and the continuance of his provinces. Pompey at first did not stir in it, but Marcellus and Lentulus opposed it, who had always hated Caesar, and now did everything, whether fit or unfit, which might disgrace and affront him. For they took away the privilege of Roman citizens from the people of New Comum, who were a colony that Caesar had lately planted in Gaul, and Marcellus, who was then consul, ordered one of the senators of that town, then at Rome, to be whipped, and told him he laid that mark upon him to signify he was no citizen of Rome, bidding him, when he went back again, to show it to Caesar. After Marcellus's consulship, Caesar began to lavish gifts upon all the public men out of the riches he had taken from the Gauls; discharged Curio, the tribune, from his great debts; gave Paulus, then consul, fifteen hundred talents, with which he built the noble court of justice adjoining the forum, to supply the place of that called the Fulvian. Pompey, alarmed at these preparations, now openly took steps, both by himself and his friends, to have a successor appointed in Caesar's room, and sent to demand back the soldiers whom he had lent him to carry on the wars in Gaul. Caesar returned them, and made each soldier a present of two hundred and fifty drachmas. The officer who brought them home to Pompey spread amongst the people no very fair or favourable report of Caesar, and flattered Pompey himself with false suggestions that he was wished for by Caesar's army; and though his affairs here were in some embarrassment through the envy of some, and the ill state of the government, yet there the army was at his command, and if they once crossed into Italy would presently declare for him; so weary were they of Caesar's endless expeditions, and so suspicious of his designs for a monarchy. Upon this Pompey grew presumptuous, and neglected all warlike preparations as fearing no danger, and used no other means against him than mere speeches and votes, for which Caesar cared nothing. And one of his captains, it is said, who was sent by him to Rome, standing before the senate house one day, and being told that the senate would not give Caesar longer time in his government, clapped his hand on the hilt of his sword and said, "But this shall."

Yet the demands which Caesar made had the fairest colours of equity imaginable. For he proposed to lay down his arms, and that Pompey should do the same, and both together should become private men, and each expect a reward of his services from the public. For that those who proposed to disarm him, and at the same time to confirm Pompey in all the power he held, were simply establishing the one in the tyranny which they accused the other of aiming at. When Curio made these proposals to the people in Caesar's name, he was loudly applauded, and some threw garlands towards him, and dismissed him as they do successful wrestlers, crowned with flowers. Antony, being tribune, produced a letter sent from Caesar on this occasion, and read it though the consuls did what they could to oppose it. But Scipio, Pompey's father-in-law, proposed in the senate, that if Caesar did not lay down his arms within such a time he should be voted an enemy; and the consuls putting it to the question, whether Pompey should dismiss his soldiers, and again, whether Caesar should disband his, very few assented to the first, but almost all to the latter. But Antony proposing again, that both should lay down their commissions, all but a very few agreed to it. Scipio was upon this very violent, and Lentulus, the consul, cried aloud, that they had need of arms, and not of suffrages, against a robber; so that the senators for the present adjourned, and appeared in mourning as a mark of their grief for the dissension.

Afterwards there came other letters from Caesar, which seemed yet more moderate, for he proposed to quit everything else, and only to retain Gaul within the Alps, Illyricum, and two legions, till he should stand a second time for consul. Cicero, the orator, who was lately returned from Cilicia, endeavoured to reconcile differences, and softened Pompey, who was willing to comply in other things, but not to allow him the soldiers. At last Cicero used his persuasions with Caesar's friends to accept of the provinces and six thousand soldiers only, and so to make up the quarrel. And Pompey was inclined to give way to this, but Lentulus, the consul, would not hearken to it, but drove Antony and Curio out of the senate-house with insults, by which he afforded Caesar the most plausible pretence that could be, and one which he could readily use to inflame the soldiers, by showing them two persons of such repute and authority who were forced to escape in a hired carriage in the dress of slaves. For so they were glad to disguise themselves when they fled out of Rome.

There were not about him at that time above three hundred horse and five thousand foot; for the rest of his army, which was left behind the Alps, was to be brought after him by officers who had received orders for that purpose. But he thought the first motion towards the design which he had on foot did not require large forces at present, and that what was wanted was to make this first step suddenly, and so to astound his enemies with the boldness of it; as it would be easier, he thought, to throw them into consternation by doing what they never anticipated than fairly to conquer them, if he had alarmed them by his preparations. And therefore he commanded his captains and other officers to go only with their swords in their hands, without any other arms, and make themselves masters of Ariminum, a large city of Gaul, with as little disturbance and bloodshed as possible. He committed the care of these forces to Hortensius, and himself spent the day in public as a stander-by and spectator of the gladiators, who exercised before him. A little before night he attended to his person, and then went into the hall, and conversed for some time with those he had invited to supper, till it began to grow dusk, when he rose from table and made his excuses to the company, begging them to stay till he came back, having already given private directions to a few immediate friends that they should follow him, not all the same way, but some one way, some another. He himself got into one of the hired carriages, and drove at first another way, but presently turned towards Ariminum. When he came to the river Rubicon, which parts Gaul within the Alps from the rest of Italy, his thoughts began to work, now he was just entering upon the danger, and he wavered much in his mind when he considered the greatness of the enterprise into which he was throwing himself. He checked his course and ordered a halt, while he revolved with himself, and often changed his opinion one way and the other, without speaking a word. This was when his purposes fluctuated most; presently he also discussed the matter with his friends who were about him (of which number Asinius Pollio was one), computing how many calamities his passing that river would bring upon mankind, and what a relation of it would be transmitted to posterity. At last, in a sort of passion, casting aside calculation, and abandoning himself to what might come, and using the proverb frequently in their mouths who enter upon dangerous and bold attempts, "The die is cast," with these words he took the river. Once over, he used all expedition possible, and before it was day reached Ariminum and took it. It is said that the night before he passed the river he had an impious dream, that he was unnaturally familiar with his own mother.

As soon as Ariminum was taken, wide gates, so to say, were thrown open, to let in war upon every land alike and sea, and with the limits of the province, the boundaries of the laws were transgressed. Nor would one have thought that, as at other times, the mere men and women fled from one town of Italy to another in their consternation, but that the very towns themselves left their sites and fled for succour to each other. The city of Rome was overrun, as it were, with a deluge, by the conflux of people flying in from all the neighbouring places. Magistrates could not longer govern, nor the eloquence of any orator quiet it; it was all but suffering shipwreck by the violence of its own tempestuous agitation. The most vehement contrary passions and impulses were at work everywhere. Nor did those who rejoiced at the prospect of the change altogether conceal their feelings, but when they met, as in so great a city they frequently must, with the alarmed and dejected of the other party, they provoked quarrels by their bold expressions of confidence in the event. Pompey, sufficiently disturbed of himself, was yet more perplexed by the clamours of others; some telling him that he justly suffered for having armed Caesar against himself and the government; others blaming him for permitting Caesar to be insolently used by Lentulus, when he made such ample concessions, and offered such reasonable proposals towards an accommodation. Favonius bade him now stamp upon the ground; for once talking big in the senate, he desired them not to trouble themselves about making any preparations for the war, for that he himself, with one stamp of his foot, would fill all Italy with soldiers. Yet still Pompey at that time had more forces than Caesar; but he was not permitted to pursue his own thoughts, but, being continually disturbed with false reports and alarms, as if the enemy was close upon him and carrying all before him, he gave way and let himself be borne down by the general cry. He put forth an edict declaring the city to be in a state of anarchy, and left it with orders that the senate should follow him, and that no one should stay behind who did not prefer tyranny to their country and liberty.

The consuls at once fled, without making even the usual sacrifices; so did most of the senators, carrying off their own goods in as much haste as if they had been robbing their neighbours. Some, who had formerly much favoured Caesar's cause, in the prevailing alarm quitted their own sentiments, and without any prospect of good to themselves, were carried along by the common stream. It was a melancholy thing to see the city tossed in these tumults, like a ship given up by her pilots, and left to run, as chance guides her, upon any rock in her way. Yet, in spite of their sad condition people still esteemed the place of their exile to be their country for Pompey's sake, and fled from Rome, as if it had been Caesar's camp. Labienus even, who had been one of Caesar's nearest friends, and his lieutenant, and who had fought by him zealously in the Gallic wars, now deserted him, and went over to Pompey. Caesar sent all his money and equipage after him, and then sat down before Corfinium, which was garrisoned with thirty cohorts under the command of Domitius. He, in despair of maintaining the defence, requested a physician, whom he had among his attendants, to give him poison; and taking the dose, drank it, in hopes of being despatched by it. But soon after, when he was told that Caesar showed the utmost clemency towards those he took prisoners, he lamented his misfortune, and blamed the hastiness of his resolution. His physician consoled him by informing him that he had taken a sleeping draught, not a poison; upon which, much rejoiced, and rising from his bed, he went presently to Caesar and gave him the pledge of his hand, yet afterwards again went over to Pompey. The report of these actions at Rome quieted those who were there, and some who had fled thence returned.

Caesar took into his army Domitius's soldiers, as he did all those whom he found in any town enlisted for Pompey's service. Being now strong and formidable enough, he advanced against Pompey himself, who did not stay to receive him, but fled to Brundusium, having sent the consuls before with a body of troops to Dyrrhachium. Soon after, upon Caesar's approach, he set to sea, as shall be more particularly related in his Life. Caesar would have immediately pursued him, but wanted shipping, and therefore went back to Rome, having made himself master of all Italy without bloodshed in the space of sixty days. When he came thither, he found the city more quiet than he expected, and many senators present, to whom he addressed himself with courtesy and deference, desiring them to send to Pompey about any reasonable accommodation towards a peace. But nobody complied with this proposal; whether out of fear of Pompey, whom they had deserted, or that they thought Caesar did not mean what he said, but thought it his interest to talk plausibly. Afterwards, when Metellus, the tribune, would have hindered him from taking money out of the public treasure, and adduced some laws against it, Caesar replied that arms and laws had each their own time; "If what I do displeases you, leave the place; war allows no free talking. When I have laid down my arms, and made peace, come back and make what speeches you please. And this," he added, "I tell you in diminution of my own just right, as indeed you and all others who have appeared against me and are now in my power may be treated as I please." Having said this to Metellus, he went to the doors of the treasury, and the keys being not to be found, sent for smiths to force them open. Metellus again making resistance and some encouraging him in it, Caesar, in a louder tone, told him he would put him to death if he gave him any further disturbance. "And this," said he, "you know, young man, is more disagreeable for me to say than to do." These words made Metellus withdraw for fear, and obtained speedy execution henceforth for all orders that Caesar gave for procuring necessaries for the war.

He was now proceeding to Spain, with the determination of first crushing Afranius and Varro, Pompey's lieutenants, and making himself master of the armies and provinces under them, that he might then more securely advance against Pompey, when he had no enemy left behind him. In this expedition his person was often in danger from ambuscades, and his army by want of provisions, yet he did not desist from pursuing the enemy, provoking them to fight, and hemming them with his fortifications, till by main force he made himself master of their camps and their forces. Only the generals got off, and fled to Pompey.

When Caesar came back to Rome, Piso, his father-in-law, advised him to send men to Pompey to treat of a peace; but Isauricus, to ingratiate himself with Caesar, spoke against it. After this, being created dictator by the senate, he called home the exiles, and gave back their rights as citizens to the children of those who had suffered under Sylla; he relieved the debtors by an act remitting some part of the interest on their debts, and passed some other measures of the same sort, but not many. For within eleven days he resigned his dictatorship, and having declared himself consul, with Servilius Isauricus, hastened again to the war. He marched so fast that he left all his army behind him, except six hundred chosen horse and five legions, with which he put to sea in the very middle of winter, about the beginning of the month of January (which corresponds pretty nearly with the Athenian month Posideon), and having passed the Ionian Sea, took Oricum and Apollonia, and then sent back the ships to Brundusium, to bring over the soldiers who were left behind in the march. They, while yet on the march, their bodies now no longer in the full vigour, and they themselves weary with such a multitude of wars, could not but exclaim against Caesar, "When at last, and where, will this Caesar let us be quiet? He carries us from place to place, and uses us as if we were not to be worn out, and had no sense of labour. Even our iron it-

self is spent by blows, and he ought to have some pity on
our bucklers, and breastplates, which have been used so
long. Our wounds, if nothing else, should make him see
that we are mortal men whom he commands, subject to the
same pains and sufferings as other human beings. The very
gods themselves cannot force the winter season, or hinder
the storms in their time; yet he pushes forward, as if he
were not pursuing, but flying from an enemy." So they
talked as they marched leisurely towards Brundusium. But
when they came thither, and found Caesar gone off before
them, their feelings changed, and they blamed themselves
as traitors to their general. They now railed at their officers
for marching so slowly, and placing themselves on the
heights overlooking the sea towards Epirus, they kept watch
to see if they could espy the vessels which were to transport them to Caesar.

He in the meantime was posted in Apollonia, but had
not an army with him able to fight the enemy, the forces
from Brundusium being so long in coming, which put
him to great suspense and embarrassment what to do. At
last he resolved upon a most hazardous experiment, and
embarked, without any one's knowledge, in a boat of
twelve oars, to cross over to Brundusium, though the sea
was at that time covered with a vast fleet of the enemies. He
got on board in the night-time, in the dress of a slave, and
throwing himself down like a person of no consequence lay
along at the bottom of the vessel. The river Anius was to
carry them down to sea, and there used to blow a gentle
gale every morning from the land, which made it calm at
the mouth of the river, by driving the waves forward; but
this night there had blown a strong wind from the sea,
which overpowered that from the land, so that where the
river met the influx of the seawater and the opposition of
the waves it was extremely rough and angry; and the
current was beaten back with such a violent swell that the
master of the boat could not make good his passage, but
ordered his sailors to tack about and return. Caesar, upon
this, discovers himself, and taking the man by the hand,
who was surprised to see him there, said, "Go on, my

friend, and fear nothing; you carry Caesar and his fortune in your boat." The mariners, when they heard that, forgot the storm, and laying all their strength to their oars, did what they could to force their way down the river. But when it was to no purpose, and the vessel now took in much water, Caesar finding himself in such danger in the very mouth of the river, much against his will permitted the master to turn back. When he was come to land, his soldiers ran to him in a multitude, reproaching him for what he had done, and indignant that he should think himself not strong enough to get a victory by their sole assistance, but must disturb himself, and expose his life for those who were absent, as if he could not trust those who were with him.

After this, Antony came over with the forces from Brundusium, which encouraged Caesar to give Pompey battle, though he was encamped very advantageously, and furnished with plenty of provisions both by sea and land, whilst he himself was at the beginning but ill supplied, and before the end was extremely pinched for want of necessaries, so that his soldiers were forced to dig up a kind of root which grew there, and tempering it with milk, to feed on it. Sometimes they made a kind of bread of it, and advancing up to the enemy's outposts, would throw in these loaves, telling them, that as long as the earth produced such roots they would not give up blockading Pompey. But Pompey took what care he could that neither the loaves nor the words should reach his men, who were out of heart and despondent through terror at the fierceness and hardihood of their enemies whom they looked upon as a sort of wild beasts. There were continual skirmishes about Pompey's outworks, in all which Caesar had the better, except one, when his men were forced to fly in such a manner that he had like to have lost his camp. For Pompey made such a vigorous sally on them that not a man stood his ground; the trenches were filled with the slaughter, many fell upon their own ramparts and bulwarks, whither they were driven in flight by the enemy. Caesar met them and would have turned them back, but could not. When he

went to lay hold of the ensigns, those who carried them
threw them down, so that the enemy took thirty-two of
them. He himself narrowly escaped; for taking hold of one
of his soldiers, a big and strong man, that was flying by
him, he bade him stand and face about; but the fellow, full
of apprehensions from the danger he was in, laid hold of
his sword, as if he would strike Caesar, but Caesar's armour-bearer cut off his arm. Caesar's affairs were so desperate at that time that when Pompey, either through over-
cautiousness or his ill fortune, did not give the finishing
stroke to that great success, but retreated after he had
driven the routed enemy within their camp, Caesar, upon
seeing his withdrawal, said to his friends, "The victory
to-day had been on the enemies' side if they had had a general who knew how to gain it." When he was retired into
his tent, he laid himself down to sleep, but spent that night
as miserable as ever he did any, in perplexity and consideration with himself, coming to the conclusion that he had
conducted the war amiss. For when he had a fertile country before him, and all the wealthy cities of Macedonia and
Thessaly, he had neglected to carry the war thither, and
had sat down by the seaside, where his enemies had such
a powerful fleet, so that he was in fact rather besieged by
the want of necessaries, than besieging others with his
arms. Being thus distracted in his thoughts with the view
of the difficulty and distress he was in, he raised his camp,
with the intention of advancing towards Scipio, who lay
in Macedonia; hoping either to entice Pompey into a country where he should fight without the advantage he now
had of supplies from the sea, or to overpower Scipio if not
assisted.

This set all Pompey's army and officers on fire to hasten
and pursue Caesar, whom they concluded to be beaten and
flying. But Pompey was afraid to hazard a battle on which
so much depended, and being himself provided with all
necessaries for any length of time, thought to tire out and
waste the vigour of Caesar's army, which could not last
long. For the best part of his men, though they had great
experience, and showed an irresistible courage in all en-

gagements, yet by their frequent marches, changing their camps, attacking fortifications, and keeping long night-watches, were getting worn out and broken; they being now old, their bodies less fit for labour, and their courage, also, beginning to give way with the failure of their strength. Besides, it was said that an infectious disease, occasioned by their irregular diet, was prevailing in Caesar's army, and what was of greatest moment, he was neither furnished with money nor provisions, so that in a little time he must needs fall of himself.

For these reasons Pompey had no mind to fight him, but was thanked for it by none but Cato, who rejoiced at the prospect of sparing his fellow-citizens. For he, when he saw the dead bodies of those who had fallen in the last battle on Caesar's side, to the number of a thousand, turned away, covered his face, and shed tears. But every one else upbraided Pompey for being reluctant to fight, and tried to goad him on by such nicknames as Agamemnon, and king of kings, as if he were in no hurry to lay down his sovreign authority, but was pleased to see so many commanders attending on him, and paying their attendance at his tent. Favonius, who affected Cato's free way of speaking his mind, complained bitterly that they should eat no figs even this year at Tusculum, because of Pompey's love of command. Afranius, who was lately returned out of Spain, and, on account of his ill success there, laboured under the suspicion of having been bribed to betray the army, asked why they did not fight this purchaser of provinces. Pompey was driven, against his own will, by this kind of language, into offering battle, and proceeded to follow Caesar. Caesar had found great difficulties in his march, for no country would supply him with provisions, his reputation being very much fallen since his late defeat. But after he took Gomphi, a town of Thessaly, he not only found provisions for his army, but physic too. For there they met with plenty of wine, which they took very freely, and heated with this, sporting and revelling on their march in bacchanalian fashion, they shook off the disease, and their whole constitution was relieved and changed into another habit.

When the two armies were come into Pharsalia, and both encamped there, Pompey's thoughts ran the same way as they had done before, against fighting, and the more because of some unlucky presages, and a vision he had in a dream. But those who were about him were so confident of success, that Domitius, and Spinther, and Scipio, as if they had already conquered, quarrelled which should succeed Caesar in the pontificate. And many sent to Rome to take houses fit to accommodate consuls and praetors, as being sure of entering upon those offices as soon as the battle was over. The cavalry especially were obstinate for fighting, being splendidly armed and bravely mounted, and valuing themselves upon the fine horses they kept, and upon their own handsome persons; as also upon the advantage of their numbers, for they were five thousand against one thousand of Caesar's. Nor were the numbers of the infantry less disproportionate, there being forty-five thousand of Pompey's against twenty-two thousand of the enemy.

Caesar, collecting his soldiers together, told them that Corfinius was coming up to them with two legions, and that fifteen cohorts more under Calenus were posted at Megara and Athens; he then asked them whether they would stay till these joined them, or would hazard the battle by themselves. They all cried out to him not to wait, but on the contrary to do whatever he could to bring about an engagement as soon as possible. When he sacrificed to the gods for the lustration of his army, upon the death of the first victim, the augur told him, within three days he should come to a decisive action. Caesar asked him whether he saw anything in the entrails which promised a happy event. "That," said the priest, "you can best answer yourself; for the gods signify a great alteration from the present posture of affairs. If, therefore, you think yourself well off now, expect worse fortune; if unhappy, hope for better." The night before the battle, as he walked the rounds about midnight, there was a light seen in the heavens, very bright and flaming, which seemed to pass over Caesar's camp and fall into Pompey's. And when Caesar's soldiers came to relieve the watch in the morning, they perceived a panic disorder among the enemies. However, he did not expect to fight that day, but set about raising his camp with the intention of marching towards Scotussa.

But when the tents were now taken down, his scouts rode up to him, and told him the enemy would give him battle. With this news he was extremely pleased, and having performed his devotions to the gods, set his army in battle array, dividing them into three bodies. Over the middlemost he placed Domitius Calvinus; Antony commanded the left wing, and he himself the right, being resolved to fight at the head of the tenth legion. But when he saw the enemy's cavalry taking position against him, being struck with their fine appearance and their number, he gave private orders that six cohorts from the rear of the army should come and join him, whom he posted behind the right wing, and instructed them what they should do when the enemy's horse came to charge. On the other side, Pompey commanded the right wing, Domitius the left, and Scipio, Pompey's father-in-law, the centre. The whole weight of the cavalry was collected on the left wing, with the intent that they should outflank the right wing of the enemy, and rout that part where the general himself commanded. For they thought no phalanx of infantry could be solid enough to sustain such a shock, but that they must necessarily be broken and shattered all to pieces upon the onset of so immense a force of cavalry. When they were ready on both sides to give the signal for battle, Pompey commanded his foot, who were in the front, to stand their ground, and without breaking their order, receive, quietly, the enemy's first attack, till they came within javelin's cast. Caesar, in this respect, also, blames Pompey's generalship, as if he had not been aware how the first encounter, when made with an impetus and upon the run, gives weight and force to the strokes, and fires the men's spirits into a flame, which the general concurrence fans to full heat. He himself was just putting the troops into motion and advancing to the action, when he found one of his captains, a trusty and experienced soldier, encouraging his men to exert their utmost. Caesar called him by his name, and said, "What hopes, Caius Crassinius, and what grounds for encouragement?" Crassinius stretched out his hand, and cried in a loud voice, "We shall conquer nobly, Caesar; and I this day will deserve your praises, either alive or dead." So he said, and was the first man to run in upon the enemy, followed by the hundred and twenty soldiers about him, and breaking through the first rank, still pressed on forwards with much slaughter of the enemy, till at last he was struck back by the wound of a sword, which went in at his mouth with such force that it came out at his neck behind.

Whilst the foot was thus sharply engaged in the main battle, on the flank Pompey's horse rode up confidently, and opened their ranks very wide, that they might surround the right wing of Caesar. But before they engaged, Caesar's cohorts rushed out and attacked them, and did not dart their javelins at a distance, nor strike at the thighs and legs, as they usually did in close battle, but aimed at their faces. For thus Caesar had instructed them, in hopes that young gentlemen, who had not known much of battles and wounds, but came wearing their hair long, in the flower of their age and height of their beauty, would be more apprehensive of such blows, and not care for hazarding both a danger at present and a blemish for the future. And so it proved, for they were so far from bearing the stroke of the javelins, that they could not stand the sight of them, but turned about, and covered their faces to secure them. Once in disorder, presently they turned about to fly; and so most shamefully ruined all. For those who had beat them back at once outflanked the infantry, and falling on their rear, cut them to pieces. Pompey, who commanded the other wing of the army, when he saw his cavalry thus broken and flying, was no longer himself, nor did he now remember that he was Pompey the Great, but, like one whom some god had deprived of his senses, retired to his tent without speaking a word, and there sat to expect the event, till the whole army was routed and the enemy appeared upon the works which were thrown up before the camp, where they closely engaged with his men who were posted there to defend it. Then first he seemed to have recovered his senses, and uttering, it is said, only these words, "What, into the camp too?" he laid aside his general's habit, and putting on such clothes as might best favour his flight, stole off. What fortune he met with afterwards, how he took shelter in Egypt, and was murdered there, we tell you in his Life.

Caesar, when he came to view Pompey's camp, and saw some of his opponents dead upon the ground, others dying, said, with a groan, "This they would have; they brought me to this necessity. I, Caius Caesar, after succeeding in so many wars, had been condemned had I dismissed my army." These words, Pollio says, Caesar spoke in Latin at that time, and that he himself wrote them in Greek; adding, that those who were killed at the taking of the camp were most of them servants; and that not above six thousand soldiers fell. Caesar incorporated most of the foot whom he took prisoners with his own legions, and gave a free pardon to many of the distinguished persons, and amongst the rest to Brutus, who afterwards killed him. He did not immediately appear after the battle was over, which put Caesar, it is said, into great anxiety for him; nor was his pleasure less when he saw him present himself alive.

There were many prodigies that foreshadowed this victory, but the most remarkable that we are told of was that at Tralles. In the temple of Victory stood Caesar's statue. The ground on which it stood was naturally hard and solid, and the stone with which it was paved still harder; yet it is said that a palm-tree shot itself up near the pedestal of this statue. In the city of Padua, one Caius Cornelius, who had the character of a good augur, the fellow-citizen and acquaintance of Livy, the historian, happened to be making some augural observations that very day when the battle was fought. And first, as Livy tells us, he pointed out the time of the fight, and said to those who were by him that just then the battle was begun and the men engaged. When he looked a second time, and observed the omens, he much displeased with all these. But Caesar, for the prosecution of his own scheme of government, though he knew their characters and disapproved them, was forced to make use of those who would serve him.

After the battle of Pharsalia, Cato and Scipio fled into Africa, and there, with the assistance of King Juba, got together a considerable force, which Caesar resolved to engage. He accordingly passed into Sicily about the winter solstice, and to remove from his officers' minds all hopes of delay there, encamped by the seashore, and as soon as ever he had a fair wind, put to sea with three thousand foot and a few horse. When he had landed them, he went back secretly, under some apprehensions for the larger part of his army, but met them upon the sea, and brought them all to the same camp. There he was informed that the enemies relied much upon an ancient oracle, that the family of the Scipios should be always victorious in Africa. There was in his army a man, otherwise mean and contemptible, but of the house of the Africani, and his name Scipio Sallutio. This man Caesar (whether in raillery to ridicule Scipio, who commanded the enemy, or seriously to bring over the omen to his side, it were hard to say), put at the head of his troops, as if he were general, in all the frequent battles which he was compelled to fight. For he was in such want both of victualling for his men and forage for his horses, that he was forced to feed the horses with seaweed, which he washed thoroughly to take off its saltness, and mixed with a little grass to give it a more agreeable taste. The Numidians, in great numbers, and well horsed, whenever he went, came up and commanded the country. Caesar's cavalry, being one day unemployed, diverted themselves with seeing an African, who entertained them with dancing and at the same time played upon the pipe to admiration. They were so taken with this, that they alighted, and gave their horses to some boys, when on a sudden the enemy surrounded them, killed some, pursued the rest and fell in with them into their camp; and had not Caesar himself and Asinius Pollio come to their assistance, and put a stop to their flight, the war had been then at an end. In another

leaped up as if he had been inspired, and cried out, "Caesar, you are victorious." This much surprised the standersby, but he took the garland which he had on from his head, and swore he would never wear it again till the event should give authority to his art. This Livy positively states for a truth.

Caesar, as a memorial of his victory, gave the Thessalians their freedom, and then went in pursuit of Pompey. When he was come into Asia, to gratify Theopompus, the author of the collection of fables, he enfranchised the Cnidians, and remitted one-third of their tribute to all the people of the province of Asia. When he came to Alexandria, where Pompey was already murdered, he would not look upon Theodotus, who presented him with his head, but taking only his signet, shed tears. Those of Pompey's friends who had been arrested by the King of Egypt, as they were wandering in those parts, he relieved, and offered them his own friendship. In his letter to his friends at Rome, he told them that the greatest and most signal pleasure his victory had given him was to be able continually to save the lives of fellow-citizens who had fought against him. As to the war in Egypt, some say it was at once dangerous and dishonourable, and noways necessary, but occasioned only by his passion for Cleopatra. Others blame the ministers of the king, and especially the eunuch Pothinus, who was the chief favourite and had lately killed Pompey, who had banished Cleopatra, and was now secretly plotting Caesar's destruction (to prevent which, Caesar from that time began to sit up whole nights, under pretence of drinking, for the security of his person), while openly he was intolerable in his affronts to Caesar, both by his words and actions. For when Caesar's soldiers had musty and unwholesome corn measured out to them, Pothinus told them they must be content with it, since they were fed at another's cost. He ordered that his table should be served with wooden and earthen dishes, and said Caesar had carried off all the gold and silver plate, under pretence of arrears of debt. For the present king's father owed Caesar one thousand seven hundred and fifty myriads of money. Caesar had

formerly remitted to his children the rest, but thought fit
to demand the thousand myriads at that time to maintain
his army. Pothinus told him that he had better go now and
attend to his other affairs of greater consequence, and that
he should receive his money at another time with thanks.
Caesar replied that he did not want Egyptians to be his
counsellors, and soon after privately sent for Cleopatra
from her retirement.

She took a small boat, and one only of her confidants,
Apollodorus, the Sicilian, along with her, and in the dusk
of the evening landed near the palace. She was at a loss
how to get in undiscovered, till she thought of putting herself into the coverlet of a bed and lying at length, whilst
Apollodorus tied up the bedding and carried it on his back
through the gates to Caesar's apartment. Caesar was first
captivated by this proof of Cleopatra's bold wit, and was
afterwards so overcome by the charm of her society that
he made a reconciliation between her and her brother, on
the condition that she should rule as his colleague in the
kingdom. A festival was kept to celebrate this reconciliation, where Caesar's barber, a busy listening fellow, whose
excessive timidity made him inquisitive into everything,
discovered that there was a plot carrying on against Caesar
by Achillas, general of the king's forces, and Pothinus,
the eunuch. Caesar, upon the first intelligence of it, set a
guard upon the hall where the feast was kept and killed
Pothinus. Achillas escaped to the army, and raised a troublesome and embarrassing war against Caesar, which it was
not easy for him to manage with his few soldiers against
so powerful a city and so large an army. The first difficulty
he met with was want of water, for the enemies had turned
the canals. Another was, when the enemy endeavoured to
cut off his communication by sea, he was forced to divert
that danger by setting fire to his own ships, which, after
burning the docks, thence spread on and destroyed the
great library. A third was, when in an engagement near
Pharos, he leaped from the mole into a small boat to assist
his soldiers who were in danger, and when the Egyptians
pressed him on every side, he threw himself into the sea,

and with much difficulty swam off. This was the time w
according to the story, he had a number of manuscrip
his hand, which, though he was continually darted at,
forced to keep his head often under water, yet he did
let go, but held them up safe from wetting in one ha
whilst he swam with the other. His boat in the meanti
was quickly sunk. At last, the king having gone off
Achillas and his party, Caesar engaged and conque
them. Many fell in that battle, and the king himself v
never seen after. Upon this, he left Cleopatra queen
Egypt, who soon after had a son by him, whom the Ale
andrians called Caesarion, and then departed for Syria.

Thence he passed to Asia, where he heard that Domiti
was beaten by Pharnaces, son of Mithridates, and had fl
out of Pontus with a handful of men; and that Pharnace
pursued the victory so eagerly, that though he was alread
master of Bithynia and Cappadocia, he had a further desig
of attempting the Lesser Armenia, and was inviting all th
kings and tetrarchs there to rise. Caesar immediately
marched against him with three legions, fought him near
Zela, drove him out of Pontus, and totally defeated his
army. When he gave Amantius, a friend of his at Rome, an
account of this action, to express the promptness and rapidity of it he used three words, I came, saw, and conquered
[Veni, vidi, vici], which in Latin, having all the same ca-
dence, carry with them a very suitable air of brevity.

Hence he crossed into Italy, and came to Rome at the
end of that year, for which he had been a second time
chosen dictator, though that office had never before lasted a
whole year, and was elected consul for the next. He was ill
spoken of, because upon a mutiny of some soldiers, who
killed Cosconius and Galba, who had been praetors, he gave
them only the slight reprimand of calling them *Citizens* instead of *Fellow-Soldiers*, and afterwards assigned to each
man a thousand drachmas, besides a share of lands in Italy.
He was also reflected on for Dolabella's extravagance,
Amantius's covetousness, Antony's debauchery, and Corfinius's profuseness, who pulled down Pompey's house, and
rebuilt it, as not magnificent enough; for the Romans were

engagement, also, the enemy had again the better, when Caesar, it is said, seized a standard-bearer, who was running away, by the neck, and forcing him to face about, said, "Look, that is the way to the enemy."

Scipio, flushed with this success at first, had a mind to come to one decisive action. He therefore left Afranius and Juba in two distinct bodies not far distant and marched himself towards Thapsus, where he proceeded to build a fortified camp above a lake, to serve as a centre-point for their operations, and also as a place of refuge. Whilst Scipio was thus employed, Caesar with incredible despatch made his way through thick woods, and a country supposed to be impassable, cut off one part of the enemy and attacked another in the front. Having routed these, he followed up his opportunity and the current of his good fortune, and on the first onset carried Afranius's camp, and ravaged that of the Numidians, Juba, their king, being glad to save himself by flight; so that in a small part of a single day he made himself master of three camps, and killed fifty thousand of the enemy, with the loss only of fifty of his own men. This is the account some give of that fight. Others say he was not in the action, but that he was taken with his usual distemper just as he was setting his army in order. He perceived the approaches of it, and before it had too far disordered his senses, when he was already beginning to shake under its influence, withdrew into a neighbouring fort where he reposed himself. Of the men of consular and praetorian dignity that were taken after the fight, several Caesar put to death, others anticipated him by killing themselves.

Cato had undertaken to defend Utica, and for that reason was not in the battle. The desire which Caesar had to take him alive made him hasten thither; and upon the intelligence that he had despatched himself, he was much discomposed, for what reason is not so well agreed. He certainly said, "Cato, I must grudge you your death, as you grudged me the honour of saving your life." Yet the discourse he wrote against Cato after his death is no great sign of his kindness, or that he was inclined to be reconciled to him. For how is it probable that he would have been tender of his life when he was so bitter against his memory? But from his clemency to Cicero, Brutus, and many others who fought against him, it may be divined that Caesar's book was not written so much out of animosity to Cato, as in his own vindication. Cicero had written an encomium upon Cato, and called it by his name. A composition by so great a master upon so excellent a subject was sure to be in every one's hands. This touched Caesar, who looked upon a panegyric on his enemies as no better than an invective against himself; and therefore he made in his Anti-Cato a collection of whatever could be said in his derogation. The two compositions, like Cato and Caesar themselves, have each of them their several admirers.

Caesar, upon his return to Rome, did not omit to pronounce before the people a magnificent account of his victory, telling them that he had subdued a country which would supply the public every year with two hundred thousand attic bushels of corn and three million pounds' weight of oil. He then led three triumphs for Egypt, Pontus, and Africa, the last for the victory over, not Scipio, but King Juba, as it was professed, whose little son was then carried in the triumph, the happiest captive that ever was, who, of a barbarian Numidian, came by this means to obtain a place among the most learned historians of Greece. After the triumphs, he distributed rewards to his soldiers, and treated the people with feasting and shows. He entertained the whole people together at one feast, where twenty-two thousand dining couches were laid out; and he made a display of gladiators, and of battles by sea, in honour, as he said, of his daughter Julia, though she had been long since dead. When these shows were over, an account was taken of the people who, from three hundred and twenty thousand, were now reduced to one hundred and fifty thousand. So great a waste had the civil war made in Rome alone, not to mention what the other parts of Italy and the provinces suffered.

He was now chosen a fourth time consul, and went into Spain against Pompey's sons. They were but young, yet had gathered together a very numerous army, and showed they had courage and conduct to command it, so that Caesar was in extreme danger. The great battle was near the town of Munda, in which Caesar, seeing his men hard pressed, and making but a weak resistance, ran through the ranks among the soldiers, and crying out, asked them whether they were not ashamed to deliver him into the hands of boys? At last, with great difficulty, and the best efforts he could make, he forced back the enemy, killing thirty thousand of them, though with the loss of one thousand of his best men. When he came back from the fight, he told his friends that he had often fought for victory, but this was the first time he had ever fought for life. This battle was won on the feast of Bacchus, the very day in which Pompey, four years before, had set out for the war. The younger of Pompey's sons escaped; but Didius, some days after the fight, brought the head of the elder to Caesar. This was the last war he was engaged in. The triumph which he celebrated for this victory displeased the Romans beyond anything, for he had not defeated foreign generals or barbarian kings, but had destroyed the children and family of one of the greatest men of Rome, though unfortunate; and it did not look well to lead a procession in celebration of the calamities of his country, and to rejoice in those things for which no other apology could be made either to gods or men than their being absolutely necessary. Besides that, hitherto he had never sent letters or messengers to announce any victory over his fellow-citizens, but had seemed rather to be ashamed of the action than to expect honour from it.

Nevertheless his countrymen, conceding all to his fortune, and accepting the bit, in the hope that the government of a single person would give them time to breathe after so many civil wars and calamities, made him dictator for life. This was indeed a tyranny avowed, since his power now was not only absolute, but perpetual too. Cicero made the first proposals to the senate for conferring honours upon him, which might in some sort be said not to exceed the limits of ordinary human moderation. But others, striving which should deserve most, carried them so excessively high, that they made Caesar odious to the most indifferent and moderate sort of men, by the pretentions and extravagance of the titles which they decreed him. His enemies, too, are thought to have had some share in this, as well as his flatterers. It gave them advantage against him, and would be their justification for any attempt they should make upon him; for since the civil wars were ended, he had nothing else that he could be charged with. And they had good reason to decree a temple to Clemency, in token of their thanks for the mild use he made of his victory. For he not only pardoned many of those who fought against him, but, further, to some gave honours and offices; as particularly to Brutus and Cassius, who both of them were praetors. Pompey's images that were thrown down he set up again, upon which Cicero also said that by raising Pompey's statues he had fixed his own. When his friends advised him to have a guard, and several offered their services, he would not hear of it; but said it was better to suffer death once than always to live in fear of it. He looked upon the affections of the people to be the best and surest guard, and entertained them again with public feasting and general distributions of corn; and to gratify his army, he sent out colonies to several places, of which the most remarkable were Carthage and Corinth; which as before they had been ruined at the same time, so now were restored and repeopled together.

As for the men of high rank, he promised to some of them future consulships and praetorships, some he consoled with other offices and honours, and to all held out hopes of favour by the solicitude he showed to rule with the general good-will, insomuch that upon the death of Maximus one day before his consulship was ended, he made Caninius Revilius consul for that day. And when many went to pay the usual compliments and attentions to the new consul, "Let us make haste," said Cicero, "lest the man be gone out of his office before we come."

Caesar was born to do great things, and had a passion after honour, and the many noble exploits he had done did not now serve as an inducement to him to sit still and reap the fruit of his past labours, but were incentives and encouragements to go on, and raised in him ideas of still greater actions, and a desire of new glory, as if the present were all spent. It was in fact a sort of emulous struggle with himself, as it had been with another, how he might outdo his past actions by his future. In pursuit of these thoughts, he resolved to make war upon the Parthians, and when he had subdued them, to pass through Hyrcania; thence to march along by the Caspian Sea to Mount Caucasus, and so on about Pontus, till he came into Scythia; then to overrun all the countries bordering upon Germany, and Germany itself; and so to return through Gaul into Italy, after completing the whole circle of his intended empire, and bounding it on every side by the ocean. While preparations were making for this expedition, he proposed to dig through the isthmus on which Corinth stands; and appointed Anienus to superintend the work. He had also a design of diverting the Tiber, and carrying it by a deep channel directly from Rome to Circeii, and so into the sea near Tarracina, that there might be a safe and easy passage for all merchants who traded to Rome. Besides this, he intended to drain all the marshes by Pomentium and Setia, and gain ground enough from the water to employ many thousands of men in tillage. He proposed further to make great mounds on the shore nearest Rome, to hinder the sea from breaking in upon the land, to clear the coast at Ostia of all the hidden rocks and shoals that made it unsafe for shipping and to form ports and harbours fit to receive the large number of vessels that would frequent them.

These things were designed without being carried into effect; but his reformation of the calendar in order to rectify the irregularity of time was not only projected with great scientific ingenuity, but was brought to its completion, and proved of very great use. For it was not only in ancient time that the Romans had wanted a certain rule to make the revolutions of their months fall in with the course of the year, so that their festivals and solemn days for sacrifice were removed by little and little, till at last they came to be kept at seasons quite the contrary to what was at first intended, but even at this time the people had no way of computing the solar year; only the priests could say the time, and they, at their pleasure, without giving any notice,

slipped in the intercalary month, which they called Merce-
donius. Numa was the first who put in this month, but his
expedient was but a poor one and quite inadequate to correct all the errors that arose in the returns of the annual
cycles, as we have shown in his life. Caesar called in the best
philosophers and mathematicians of his time to settle the
point, and out of the systems he had before him formed a
new and more exact method of correcting the calendar,
which the Romans use to this day, and seem to succeed better than any nation in avoiding the errors occasioned by the
inequality of the cycles. Yet even this gave offence to those
who looked with an evil eye on his position, and felt oppressed by his power. Cicero the orator, when some one in
his company chanced to say the next morning Lyra would
rise, replied, "Yes, in accordance with the edict," as if even
this were a matter of compulsion.

But that which brought upon him the most apparent and
mortal hatred was his desire of being king; which gave the
common people the first occasion to quarrel with him, and
proved the most specious pretence to those who had been
his secret enemies all along. Those who would have procured him that title gave it out that it was foretold in the
Sibyls' books that the Romans should conquer the Parthians when they fought against them under the conduct of a
king, but not before. And one day, as Caesar was coming
down from Alba to Rome, some were so bold as to salute
him by the name of king; but he, finding the people disrelish
it, seemed to resent it himself, and said his name was
Caesar, not king. Upon this there was a general silence, and
he passed on looking not very well pleased or contented.
Another time, when the senate had conferred on him some
extravagant honours, he chanced to receive the message as
he was sitting on the rostra, where, though the consuls and
praetors themselves waited on him, attended by the whole
body of the senate, he did not rise, but behaved himself to
them as if they had been private men, and told them his
honours wanted rather to be retrenched than increased. This
treatment offended not only the senate, but the commonalty
too, as if they thought the affront upon the senate equally

reflected upon the whole republic; so that all who could decently leave him went off, looking much discomposed. Caesar, perceiving the false step he had made, immediately retired home; and laying his throat bare, told his friends that he was ready to offer this to any one who would give the stroke. But afterwards he made the malady from which he suffered the excuse for his sitting, saying that those who are attacked by it lose their presence of mind if they talk much standing; that they presently grow giddy, fall into convulsions, and quite lose their reason. But this was not the reality, for he would willingly have stood up to the senate, had not Cornelius Balbus, one of his friends, or rather flatterers, hindered him. "Will you not remember," said he, "you are Caesar, and claim the honour which is due to your merit?"

He gave a fresh occasion of resentment by his affront to the tribunes. The Lupercalia were then celebrated, a feast at the first institution belonging, as some writers say, to the shepherds, and having some connection with the Arcadian Lycae. Many young noblemen and magistrates run up and down the city with their upper garments off, striking all they meet with thongs of hide, by way of sport; and many women, even of the highest rank, place themselves in the way, and hold out their hands to the lash, as boys in a school do to the master, out of a belief that it procures an easy labour to those who are with child, and makes those conceive who are barren. Caesar, dressed in a triumphal robe, seated himself in a golden chair at the rostra to view this ceremony. Antony, as consul, was one of those who ran this course, and when he came into the forum, and the people made way for him, he went up and reached to Caesar a diadem wreathed with laurel. Upon this there was a shout, but only a slight one, made by the few who were planted there for that purpose; but when Caesar refused it, there was universal applause. Upon the second offer, very few, and upon the second refusal, all again applauded. Caesar finding it would not take, rose up, and ordered the crown to be carried into the capitol. Caesar's statues were afterwards found with royal diadems on their heads. Flavius and Marullus, two tribunes of the people, went presently and pulled them off, and having apprehended those who first saluted Caesar as king committed them to prison. The people followed them with acclamations, and called them by the name of Brutus, because Brutus was the first who ended the succession of kings, and transferred the power which before was lodged in one man into the hands of the senate and people. Caesar so far resented this, that he displaced Marullus and Flavius; and in urging his charges against them, at the same time ridiculed the people by himself giving the men more than once the names of Bruti and Cumaei.

This made the multitude turn their thoughts to Marcus Brutus, who, by his father's side, was thought to be descended from that first Brutus, and by his mother's side from the Servilii, another noble family, being besides nephew and son-in-law to Cato. But the honours and favours he had received from Caesar took off the edge from the desires he might himself have felt for overthrowing the new monarchy. For he had not only been pardoned himself after Pompey's defeat at Pharsalia, and had procured the same grace for many of his friends, but was one in whom Caesar had a particular confidence. He had at that time the most honourable praetorship for the year, and was named for the consulship four years after, being preferred before Cassius, his competitor. Upon the question as to the choice, Caesar, it is related, said that Cassius had the fairer pretensions, but that he could not pass by Brutus. Nor would he afterwards listen to some who spoke against Brutus, when the conspiracy against him was already afoot, but laying his hand on his body, said to the informers, "Brutus will wait for this skin of mine," intimating that he was worthy to bear rule on account of his virtue, but would not be base and ungrateful to gain it. Those who desired a change, and looked on him as the only, or at least the most proper, person to effect it, did not venture to speak with him; but in the night-time laid papers about his chair of state, where he used to sit and determine causes, with such sentences in them as, "You are asleep, Brutus," "You are no longer

Brutus." Cassius, when he perceived his ambition a little raised upon this, was more instant than before to work him yet further, having himself a private grudge against Caesar for some reasons that we have mentioned in the Life of Brutus. Nor was Caesar without suspicions of him, and said once to his friends, "What do you think Cassius is aiming at? I don't like him, he looks so pale." And when it was told him that Antony and Dolabella were in a plot against him, he said he did not fear such fat, luxurious men, but rather the pale, lean fellows, meaning Cassius and Brutus.

Fate, however, is to all appearances more unavoidable than unexpected. For many strange prodigies and apparitions are said to have been observed shortly before this event. As to the lights in the heavens, the noises heard in the night, and the wild birds which perched in the forum, these are not perhaps worth taking notice of in so great a case as this. Strabo, the philosopher, tells us that a number of men were seen, looking as if they were heated through with fire, contending with each other; that a quantity of flame issued from the hand of a soldier's servant, so that they who saw it thought he must be burnt, but that after all he had no hurt. As Caesar was sacrificing, the victim's heart was missing, a very bad omen, because no living creature can subsist without a heart. One finds it also related by many that a soothsayer bade him prepare for some great danger on the Ides of March. When this day was come, Caesar, as he went to the senate, met this soothsayer, and said to him by way of raillery, "The Ides of March are come," who answered him calmly, "Yes, they are come, but they are not past." The day before his assassination he supped with Marcus Lepidus; and as he was signing some letters according to his custom, as he reclined at table, there arose a question what sort of death was the best. At which he immediately, before any one could speak, said, "A sudden one."

After this, as he was in bed with his wife, all the doors and windows of the house flew open together; he was startled at the noise, and the light which broke into the room, and sat up in his bed, where by the moonshine he perceived

Calpurnia fast asleep, but heard her utter in her dream some indistinct words and inarticulate groans. She fancied at that time she was weeping over Caesar, and holding him butchered in her arms. Others say this was not her dream, but that she dreamed that a pinnacle, which the senate, as Livy relates, had ordered to be raised on Caesar's house by way of ornament and grandeur, was tumbling down, which was the occasion of her tears and ejaculations. When it was day, she begged of Caesar, if it were possible, not to stir out, but to adjourn the senate to another time; and if he slighted her dreams, that she would be pleased to consult his fate by sacrifices and other kinds of divination. Nor was he himself without some suspicion and fears; for he never before discovered any womanish superstition in Calpurnia, whom he now saw in such great alarm. Upon the report which the priest made to him, that they had killed several sacrifices, and still found them inauspicious, he resolved to send Antony to dismiss the senate.

In this juncture, Decimus Brutus, surnamed Albinus, one whom Caesar had such confidence in that he made him his second heir, who nevertheless was engaged in the conspiracy with the other Brutus and Cassius, fearing lest if Caesar should put off the senate to another day, the business might get wind, spoke scoffingly and in mockery of the diviners, and blamed Caesar for giving the senate so fair an occasion of saying he had put a slight upon them, for that they were met upon his summons, and were ready to vote unanimously that he should be declared king of all the provinces out of Italy, and might wear a diadem in any other place but Italy, by sea or land. If any one should be sent to tell them they might break up for the present, and meet again when Calpurnia should chance to have better dreams, what would his enemies say? Or who would with any patience hear his friends, if they should presume to defend his government as not arbitrary and tyrannical? But if he was possessed so far as to think this day unfortunate, yet it were more decent to go himself to the senate, and to adjourn it in his own person. Brutus, as he spoke these words, took Caesar by the hand, and conducted him forth. He was not gone far from the door, when a servant of some other person's made towards him, but not being able to come up to him, on account of the crowd of those who pressed about him, he made his way into the house, and committed himself to Calpurnia, begging of her to secure him till Caesar returned, because he had matters of great importance to communicate to him.

Artemidorus, a Cnidian, a teacher of Greek logic, and by that means so far acquainted with Brutus and his friends as to have got into the secret, brought Caesar in a small written memorial the heads of what he had to depose. He had observed that Caesar, as he received any papers, presently gave them to the servants who attended on him; and therefore came as near to him as he could, and said, "Read this, Caesar, alone, and quickly, for it contains matter of great importance which nearly concerns you." Caesar received it, and tried several times to read it, but was still hindered by the crowd of those who came to speak to him. However, he kept it in his hand by itself till he came into the senate. Some say it was another who gave Caesar this note, and that Artemidorus could not get to him, being all along kept off by the crowd.

All these things might happen by chance. But the place which was destined for the scene of this murder, in which the senate met that day, was the same in which Pompey's statue stood, and was one of the edifices which Pompey had raised and dedicated with his theatre to the use of the public, plainly showing that there was something of a supernatural influence which guided the action and ordered it to that particular place. Cassius, just before the act, is said to have looked towards Pompey's statue, and silently implored his assistance, though he had been inclined to the doctrines of Epicurus. But this occasion, and the instant danger, carried him away out of all his reasonings, and filled him for the time with a sort of inspiration. As for Antony, who was firm to Caesar, and a strong man, Brutus Albinus kept him outside the house, and delayed him with a long conversation contrived on purpose. When Caesar entered, the senate stood up to show their respect to him, and of Brutus's con-

federates, some came about his chair and stood behind it,
others met him, pretending to add their petitions to those
of Tillius Cimber, in behalf of his brother, who was in
exile; and they followed him with their joint applications till
he came to his seat. When he was sat down, he refused to
comply with their requests, and upon their urging him
further began to reproach them severely for their impor-
tunities, when Tillius, laying hold of his robe with both his
hands, pulled it down from his neck, which was the signal
for the assault. Casca gave him the first cut in the neck,
which was not mortal nor dangerous, as coming from one
who at the beginning of such a bold action was probably
very much disturbed; Caesar immediately turned about, and
laid his hand upon the dagger and kept hold of it. And both
of them at the same time cried out, he that received the
blow, in Latin, "Vile Casca, what does this mean?" and he
that gave it, in Greek to his brother, "Brother, help!" Upon
this first onset, those who were not privy to the design were
astonished, and their horror and amazement at what they
saw were so great that they durst not fly nor assist Caesar,
nor so much as speak a word. But those who came prepared
for the business enclosed him on every side, with their
naked daggers in their hands. Which way soever he turned
he met with blows, and saw their swords levelled at his face
and eyes, and was encompassed like a wild beast in the toils
on every side. For it had been agreed they should each of
them make a thrust at him, and flesh themselves with his
blood: for which reason Brutus also gave him one stab in
the groin. Some say that he fought and resisted all the rest,
shifting his body to avoid the blows, and calling out for
help, but that when he saw Brutus's sword drawn, he covered his face with his robe and submitted, letting himself
fall, whether it were by chance or that he was pushed in
that direction by his murderers, at the foot of the pedestal
on which Pompey's statue stood, and which was thus wetted
with his blood. So that Pompey himself seemed to have presided, as it were, over the revenge upon his adversary, who
lay here at his feet, and breathed out his soul through his

multitude of wounds, for they say he received three-and-twenty. And the conspirators themselves were many of them wounded by each other, whilst they all levelled their blows at the same person.

When Caesar was despatched, Brutus stood forth to give a reason for what they had done, but the senate would not hear him, but flew out of doors in all haste, and filled the people with so much alarm and distraction, that some shut up their houses, others left their counters and shops. All ran one way or the other, some to the place to see the sad spectacle, others back again after they had seen it. Antony and Lepidus, Caesar's most faithful friends, got off privately, and hid themselves in some friends' houses. Brutus and his followers, being yet hot from the deed, marched in a body from the senate-house to the capitol with their drawn swords, not like persons who thought of escaping, but with an air of confidence and assurance, and as they went along, called to the people to resume their liberty, and invited the company of any more distinguished people whom they met. And some of these joined the procession and went up along with them, as if they also had been of the conspiracy, and could claim a share in the honour of what had been done. As, for example, Caius Octavius and Lentulus Spinther, who suffered afterwards for their vanity, being taken off by Antony and the young Caesar, and lost the honour they desired, as well as their lives, which it cost them, since no one believed they had any share in the action. For neither did those who punished them profess to revenge the fact, but the ill-will. The day after, Brutus with the rest came down from the capitol and made a speech to the people, who listened without expressing either any pleasure or resentment, but showed by their silence that they pitied Caesar and respected Brutus. The senate passed acts of oblivion for what was past, and took measures to reconcile all parties. They ordered that Caesar should be worshipped as a divinity, and nothing, even of the slightest consequence, should be revoked which he had enacted during his government. At the same time they gave Brutus and his followers the command of provinces, and other considerable posts. So that all the people now thought things were well settled, and brought to the happiest adjustment.

But when Caesar's will was opened, and it was found that he had left a considerable legacy to each one of the Roman citizens, and when his body was seen carried through the market-place all mangled with wounds, the multitude could no longer contain themselves within the bounds of tranquillity and order, but heaped together a pile of benches, bars, and tables, which they placed the corpse on, and setting fire to it, burnt it on them. Then they took brands from the pile and ran some to fire the houses of the conspirators, others up and down the city, to find out the men and tear them to pieces, but met, however, with none of them, they having taken effectual care to secure themselves.

One Cinna, a friend of Caesar's, chanced the night before to have an odd dream. He fancied that Caesar invited him to supper, and that upon his refusal to go with him, Caesar took him by the hand and forced him, though he hung back. Upon hearing the report that Caesar's body was burning in the market-place, he got up and went thither, out of respect to his memory, though his dream gave him some ill apprehensions, and though he was suffering from a fever. One of the crowd who saw him there asked another who that was, and having learned his name, told it to his neighbour. It presently passed for a certainty that he was one of Caesar's murderers, as, indeed, there was another Cinna, a conspirator, and they, taking this to be the man, immediately seized him and tore him limb from limb upon the spot.

Brutus and Cassius, frightened at this, within a few days retired out of the city. What they afterwards did and suffered, and how they died, is written in the Life of Brutus. Caesar died in his fifty-sixth year, not having survived Pompey above four years. That empire and power which he had pursued through the whole course of his life with so much hazard, he did at last with much difficulty compass, but reaped no other fruits from it than the empty name and invidious glory. But the great genius which attended him through his lifetime even after his death remained as the avenger of his murder, pursuing through every sea and land all those who were concerned in it, and suffering none to escape, but reaching all who in any sort or kind were either actually engaged in the fact, or by their counsels any way promoted it.

The most remarkable of mere human coincidences was that which befell Cassius, who, when he was defeated at Philippi, killed himself with the same dagger which he had made use of against Caesar. The most signal preternatural appearances were the great comet, which shone very bright for seven nights after Caesar's death, and then disappeared, and the dimness of the sun, whose orb continued pale and dull for the whole of that year, never showing its ordinary radiance at its rising, and giving but a weak and feeble heat. The air consequently was damp and gross for want of stronger rays to open and rarefy it. The fruits, for that reason, never properly ripened, and began to wither and fall off for want of heat before they were fully formed. But above all, the phantom which appeared to Brutus showed the murder was not pleasing to the gods. The story of it is this.

Brutus, being to pass his army from Abydos to the continent on the other side, laid himself down one night, as he used to do, in his tent, and was not asleep, but thinking of his affairs, and what events he might expect. For he is related to have been the least inclined to sleep of all men who have commanded armies, and to have had the greatest natural capacity for continuing awake, and employing himself without need of rest. He thought he heard a noise at the door of his tent, and looking that way, by the light of his lamp, which was almost out, saw a terrible figure, like that of a man, but of unusual stature and severe countenance. He was somewhat frightened at first, but seeing it neither did nor spoke anything to him, only stood silently by his bedside, he asked who it was. The spectre answered him, "Thy evil genius, Brutus, thou shalt see me at Philippi." Brutus answered courageously, "Well, I shall see you," and immediately the appearance vanished. When the time was come, he drew up his army near Philippi against Antony and Caesar, and in the first battle won the day, routed the enemy, and plundered Caesar's camp. The night before the second battle, the same phantom appeared to him again, but spoke not a word. He presently understood his destiny was at hand, and exposed himself to all the danger of the battle. Yet he did not die in the fight, but seeing his men defeated, got up to the top of a rock, and there presenting his sword to his naked breast, and assisted, as they say, by a friend, who helped him to give the thrust, met his death.

POMPEY

The people of Rome seem to have entertained for Pompey from his childhood the same affection that Prometheus, in the tragedy of Aeschylus, expresses for Hercules, speaking of him as the author of his deliverance, in these words:—

> "Ah cruel Sire! how dear thy son to me!
> The generous offspring of my enemy!"

For on the one hand, never did the Romans give such demonstrations of a vehement and fierce hatred against any of their generals as they did against Strabo, the father of Pompey; during whose lifetime, it is true, they stood in awe of his military power, as indeed he was a formidable warrior, but immediately upon his death, which happened by a stroke of thunder, they treated him with the utmost contumely, dragging his corpse from the bier, as it was carried to his funeral. On the other side, never had any Roman the people's good-will and devotion more zealous throughout all the changes of fortune, more early in its first springing up, or more steadily rising with his prosperity, or more constant in his adversity than Pompey had. In Strabo, there was one great cause of their hatred, his insatiable covetousness; in Pompey, there were many that helped to make him the object of their love; his temperance, his skill and exercise in war, his eloquence of speech, integrity of mind, and affability in conversation and address; insomuch that no man ever asked a favour with less offence, or conferred one with a better grace. When he gave, it was without assumption; when he received, it was with dignity and honour.

In his youth, his countenance pleaded for him, seeming to anticipate his eloquence, and win upon the affections of the people before he spoke. His beauty even in his bloom of youth had something in it at once of gentleness and dignity; and when his prime of manhood came, the majesty and kingliness of his character at once became visible in it. His hair sat somewhat hollow or rising a little; and this, with the languishing motion of his eyes, seemed to form a resemblance in his face, though perhaps more talked of than really apparent, to the statues of the King Alexander. And because many applied that name to him in his youth, Pompey himself did not decline it, insomuch that some called him so in derision. And Lucius Philippus, a man of consular dignity, when he was pleading in favour of him, thought it not unfit to say, that people could not be surprised if Philip was a lover of Alexander.

It is related of Flora, the courtesan, that when she was now pretty old, she took great delight in speaking of her early familiarity with Pompey, and was wont to say that she could never part after being with him without a bite. She would further tell, that Geminius, a companion of Pompey's, fell in love with her, and made his court with great importunity; and on her refusing, and telling him, however her inclinations were, yet she could not gratify his desires for Pompey's sake, he therefore made his request to Pompey, and Pompey frankly gave his consent, but never afterwards would have any converse with her, notwithstanding that he seemed to have a great passion for her; and Flora, on this occasion, showed none of the levity that might have been expected of her, but languished for some time after under a sickness brought on by grief and desire.

Immediately upon the death of Strabo, there was an action commenced against Pompey, as his heir, for that his father had embezzled the public treasure. But Pompey, having traced the principal thefts, charged them upon one Alexander, a freed slave of his father's, and proved before the judges that he had been the appropriator. But he himself was accused of having in his possession some hunting tackle, and books, that were taken at Asculum. To this he confessed thus far, that he received them from his father when he took Asculum, but pleaded further, that he had lost them since, upon Cinna's return to Rome, when his house was broken open and plundered by Cinna's guards. In this cause he had a great many preparatory pleadings against his accuser, in which he showed an activity and steadfastness beyond his years, and gained great reputation and favour, insomuch that Antistius, the praetor and judge of the cause, took a great liking to him, and offered him his daughter in marriage, having had some communications with his friends about it. Pompey accepted the proposal, and they were privately contracted; however, the secret was not so closely kept as to escape the multitude, but it was discernible enough, from the favour shown him by Antistius in his cause. And at last, when Antistius pronounced the absolutory sentence of the judges, the people, as if it had been upon a signal given, made the acclamation used according to ancient custom at marriages, *Talasio*. And some few days after this judgment, Pompey married Antistia.

After this he went to Cinna's camp, where finding some false suggestions and calumnies prevailing against him, he began to be afraid, and presently withdrew himself secretly; which sudden disappearance occasioned great suspicion. And there went a rumour and speech through all the camp that Cinna had murdered the young man; upon which all that had been anyways disobliged, and bore any malice to him, resolved to make an assault upon him. He, endeavouring to make his escape, was seized by a centurion, who pursued him with his naked sword. Cinna, in this distress, fell upon his knees, and offered him his seal-ring, of great value, for his ransom; but the centurion repulsed him insolently, saying, "I did not come to seal a covenant, but to be revenged upon a lawless and wicked tyrant"; and so despatched him immediately.

Thus Cinna being slain, Carbo, a tyrant yet more sense-

less than he, took the command and exercised it, while
Sylla meantime was approaching, much to the joy and satisfaction of most people, who in their present evils were ready
to find some comfort if it were but in the exchange of a
master. For the city was brought to that pass by oppression
and calamities that, being utterly in despair of liberty, men
were only anxious for the mildest and most tolerable bon-
dage. At that time Pompey was in Picenum in Italy, where
he spent some time amusing himself, as he had estates in
the country there, though the chief motive of his stay was
the liking he felt for the towns of that district, which all regarded him with hereditary feelings of kindness and attach-
ment. But when he now saw that the noblest and best of the
city began to forsake their homes and property, and fly
from all quarters to Sylla's camp, as to their haven, he likewise was desirous to go; not, however, as a fugitive, alone
and with nothing to offer, but as a friend rather than a suppliant, in a way that would gain him honour, bringing help
along with him, and at the head of a body of troops. Accordingly he solicited the Picentines for their assistance,
who as cordially embraced his motion, and rejected the
messengers sent from Carbo; insomuch that a certain Vindius taking upon him to say that Pompey was come from
the school-room to put himself at the head of the people,
they were so incensed that they fell forthwith upon this
Vindius and killed him.

From henceforward Pompey, finding a spirit of government upon him, though not above twenty-three years of
age, nor deriving an authority by a commission from any
man, took the privilege to grant himself full power, and,
causing a tribunal to be erected in the market-place of
Auximum, a populous city, expelled two of their principal
men, brothers, of the name of Ventidius, who were acting
against him in Carbo's interest, commanding them by a public edict to depart the city; and then proceeding to levy soldiers, issuing out commissions to centurions and other officers, according to the form of military discipline. And in
this manner he went round all the rest of the cities in the

district. So that those of Carbo's faction flying, and all others cheerfully submitting to his command, in a little time he mustered three entire legions, having supplied himself besides with all manner of provisions, beasts of burden, carriages, and other necessaries of war. And with this equipage he set forward on his march toward Sylla, not as if he were in haste, or desirous of escaping observation, but by small journeys, making several halts upon the road, to distress and annoy the enemy, and exerting himself to detach from Carbo's interest every part of Italy that he passed through.

Three commanders of the enemy encountered him at once, Carinna, Cloelius, and Brutus, and drew up their forces, not all in the front, nor yet together on any one part, but encamping three several armies in a circle about him, they resolved to encompass and overpower him. Pompey was noway alarmed at this, but collecting all his troops into one body, and placing his horse in the front of the battle, where he himself was in person, he singled out and bent all his forces against Brutus, and when the Celtic horsemen from the enemy's side rode out to meet him, Pompey himself encountering hand to hand with the foremost and stoutest among them, killed him with his spear. The rest seeing this turned their backs and fled, and breaking the ranks of their own foot, presently caused a general rout; whereupon the commanders fell out among themselves, and marched off, some one way, some another, as their fortunes led them, and the towns round about came in and surrendered themselves to Pompey, concluding that the enemy was dispersed for fear. Next after these, Scipio, the consul, came to attack him, and with as little success; for before the armies could join, or be within the throw of their javelins, Scipio's soldiers saluted Pompey's, and came over to them, while Scipio made his escape by flight. Last of all, Carbo himself sent down several troops of horse against him by the river Arsis, which Pompey assailed with the same courage and success as before; and having routed and put them to flight, he forced them in the pursuit into difficult ground, unpassable for horse, where, seeing no hopes of escape, they yielded themselves with their horses and armour, all to his mercy.

Sylla was hitherto unacquainted with all these actions; and on the first intelligence he received of his movements was in great anxiety about him, fearing lest he should be cut off among so many and such experienced commanders of the enemy, and marched therefore with all speed to his aid. Now Pompey, having advice of his approach, sent out orders to his officers to marshal and draw up all his forces in full array, that they might make the finest and noblest appearance before the commander-in-chief; for he expected indeed great honours from him, but met with even greater. For as soon as Sylla saw him thus advancing, his army so well appointed, his men so young and strong, and their spirits so high and hopeful with their successes, he alighted from his horse, and being first, as was his due, saluted by them with the title of Imperator, he returned the salutation upon Pompey, in the same term and style of Imperator, which might well cause surprise, as none could have ever anticipated that he would have imparted, to one so young in years and not yet a senator, a title which was the object of contention between him and the Scipios and Marii. And indeed all the rest of his deportment was agreeable to this first compliment; whenever Pompey came into his presence, he paid some sort of respect to him, either in rising and being uncovered, or the like, which he was rarely seen to do with any one else, notwithstanding that there were many about him of great rank and honour. Yet Pompey was not puffed up at all, or exalted with these favours. And when Sylla would have sent him with all expedition into Gaul, a province in which it was thought Metellus, who commanded in it, had done nothing worthy of the large forces at his disposal, Pompey urged that it could not be fair or honourable for him to take a province out of the hands of his senior in command and his superior in reputation; however, if Metellus were willing, and should request his service, he should be very ready to accompany and assist him in the war, which when Metellus came to understand, he approved of the proposal, and invited him over by letter. On this Pompey fell immediately into Gaul, where he not only achieved wonderful exploits of himself, but also fired up and kindled again that bold and warlike spirit, which old age had in a manner extinguished in Metellus, into a new heat; just as molten copper, they say, when poured upon that which is cold and solid, will dissolve and melt it faster than fire itself.

About this time news came to Sylla that Perpenna was fortifying himself in Sicily, that the island was now become a refuge and receptacle for the relics of the adverse party, that Carbo was hovering about those seas with a navy, that Domitius had fallen in upon Africa, and that many of the exiled men of note who had escaped from the proscriptions were daily flocking into those parts. Against these, therefore, Pompey was sent with a large force; and no sooner was he arrived in Sicily, but Perpenna immediately departed, leaving the whole island to him. Pompey received the distressed cities into favour, and treated all with great humanity, except the Mamertines in Messena; for when they protested against his court and jurisdiction, alleging their privilege and exemption founded upon an ancient charter or grant of the Romans, he replied sharply, "What! will you never cease prating of laws to us that have swords by our sides?" It was thought, likewise, that he showed some inhumanity to Carbo, seeming rather to insult over his misfortunes than to chastise his crimes. For if there had been a necessity, as perhaps there was, that he should be taken off, that might have been done at first, as soon as he was taken prisoner, for then it would have been the act of him that commanded it. But here Pompey commanded a man that had been thrice consul of Rome to be brought in fetters to stand at the bar, he himself sitting upon the bench in judgment, examining the cause with the formalities of law, to the offence and indignation of all that were present, and afterwards ordered him to be taken away and put to death.

This is certain, that there lay a necessity upon Pompey to be severe upon many of Sylla's enemies, those at least that were eminent persons in themselves, and notoriously known to be taken; but for the rest, he acted with all the clemency possible for him, conniving at the concealment of some, and himself being the instrument in the escape of others. So in the case of the Himeraeans; for when Pompey had determined on severely punishing their city, as they had been abettors of the enemy, Sthenis, the leader of the people there, craving liberty of speech, told him that what he was about to do was not at all consistent with justice, for that he would pass by the guilty and destroy the innocent; and on Pompey demanding who that guilty person was that would assume the offences of them all, Sthenis replied it was himself, who had engaged his friends by persuasion to what they had done, and his enemies by force; whereupon Pompey, being much taken with the frank speech and noble spirit of the man, first forgave his crime, and then pardoned all the rest of the Himeraeans. Hearing, likewise, that his soldiers were very disorderly in their march, doing violence upon the roads, he ordered their swords to be sealed up in their scabbards, and whosoever kept them not so were severely punished.

Whilst Pompey was thus busy in the affairs and government of Sicily, he received a decree of the senate, and a commission from Sylla, commanding him forthwith to sail into Africa, and make war upon Domitius with all his forces: for Domitius had rallied up a far greater army than Marius had had not long since, when he sailed out of Africa into Italy, and caused a revolution in Rome, and himself, of a fugitive outlaw, became a tyrant. Pompey, therefore, having prepared everything with the utmost speed, left Memmius, his sister's husband, governor of Sicily, and set sail with one hundred and twenty galleys, and eight hundred other vessels laden with provisions, money, ammunition, and engines of battery.

Domitius had prepared himself and drawn out his army in array against Pompey; but there was a watercourse betwixt them, craggy, and difficult to pass over; and this, together with a great storm of wind and rain pouring down even from break of day, seemed to leave but little possibility of their coming together; so that Domitius, not expecting any engagement that day, commanded his forces to draw off and retire to the camp. Now Pompey, who was watchful upon every occasion, making use of the opportunity, ordered a march forthwith, and having passed over the torrent, fell in immediately upon their quarters. The enemy was in great disorder and tumult, and in that confusion attempted a resistance; but they neither were all there, nor supported one another; besides, the wind having veered about beat the rain full in their faces. Neither indeed was the storm less troublesome to the Romans, for that they could not clearly discern one another, insomuch that even Pompey himself, being unknown, escaped narrowly; for when one of his soldiers demanded of him the word of battle, it happened that he was somewhat slow in his answer, which might have cost him his life.

The enemy being routed with a great slaughter (for it is said that of twenty thousand there escaped but three thousand), the army saluted Pompey by the name of Imperator; but he declined it, telling them that he could not by any means accept of that title as long as he saw the camp of the enemy standing; but if they designed to make him worthy of the honour, they must first demolish that. The soldiers on hearing this went at once and made an assault upon the works and trenches, and there Pompey fought without his helmet, in memory of his former danger, and to avoid the like. The camp was thus taken by storm, and among the rest Domitius was slain.

Pompey could not rest here, but being ambitious to follow the good fortune and use the valour of his army, entered Numidia; and marching forward many days' journey up into the country, he conquered all wherever he came. And having revived the terror of the Roman power, which was now almost obliterated among the barbarous nations, he said likewise, that the wild beasts of Africa ought not to be left without some experience of the courage and success of the Romans, and therefore he bestowed some few days in hunting lions and elephants. And it is said that it was not above the space of forty days at the utmost in which he gave a total overthrow to the enemy, reduced Africa, and established the affairs of the kings and kingdoms of all that country, being then in the twenty-fourth year of his age.

When Pompey returned back to the city of Utica, there were presented to him letters and orders from Sylla, commanding him to disband the rest of his army, and himself with one legion only to wait there the coming of another general, to succeed him in the government. This, inwardly, was extremely grievous to Pompey, though he made no show of it. But the army resented it openly, and when Pompey besought them to depart and go home before him, they began to revile Sylla, and declared broadly that they were resolved not to forsake him, neither did they think it safe for him to trust the tyrant. Pompey at first endeavoured to appease and pacify them by fair speeches; but when he saw that his persuasions were vain, he left the bench, and retired to his tent with tears in his eyes. But the soldiers followed him, and seizing upon him, by force brought him again, and placed him in his tribunal; where great part of that day was spent in dispute, they on their part persuading him to stay and command them, he, on the other side, pressing upon them obedience and the danger of mutiny. At last, when they grew yet more importunate and clamorous, he swore that he would kill himself if they attempted to force him; and scarcely even thus appeased them. Nevertheless, the first tidings brought to Sylla were that Pompey was up in rebellion; on which he remarked to some of his friends, "I see, then, it is my destiny to contend with children in my old age"; alluding at the same time to Marius, who, being but a mere youth, had given him great trouble, and brought him into extreme danger. But being undeceived afterwards by better intelligence, and finding the whole city prepared to meet Pompey, and receive him with every display of kindness and honour, he resolved to exceed them all. And, therefore, going out foremost to meet him and embracing him with great cordiality, he gave him his welcome aloud in the title of Magnus, or the Great, and bade all that were present call him by that name. Others say that he had this title first given him by a general acclamation of all the army in Africa, but that it was fixed upon him by this ratification of Sylla. It is certain that he himself was the last that owned the title; for it was a long time after, when he was sent pro-consul into Spain against Sertorius, that he began to write himself in his letters and commissions by the name of Pompeius Magnus; common and familiar use having then worn off the invidiousness of the title. And one cannot but accord respect and admiration to the ancient Romans, who did not reward the successes of action and conduct in war alone with such honourable titles, but adorned likewise the virtue and services of eminent men in civil government with the same distinctions and marks of honour. Two persons received from the people the name of Maximus, or the Greatest, Valerius for reconciling the senate and people, and Fabius Rullus, because he put out of the senate certain sons of freed slaves who had been admitted into it because of their wealth.

Pompey now desired the honour of a triumph, which Sylla opposed, alleging that the law allowed that honour to none but consuls and praetors, and therefore Scipio the elder, who subdued the Carthaginians in Spain in far greater and nobler conflicts, never petitioned for a triumph, because he had never been consul or praetor; and if Pompey, who had scarcely yet fully grown a beard, and was not of age to be a senator, should enter the city in triumph, what a weight of envy would it bring, he said, at once upon his government and Pompey's honour. This was his language to Pompey, intimating that he could not by any means yield to his request, but if he would persist in his ambition, that he was resolved to interpose his power to humble him. Pompey, however, was not daunted; but bade Sylla recollect that more worshipped the rising than the setting sun; as if to tell him that his power was increasing and Sylla's in the wane. Sylla did not perfectly hear the words, but observing a sort of amazement and wonder in the looks and gestures of those that did hear them, he asked what it was that he said. When it was told him, he seemed astounded at Pompey's boldness, and cried out twice together, "Let him triumph," and when others began to show their disapprobation and offence at it, Pompey, it is said, to gall and vex them the more, designed to have his triumphant chariot drawn with four elephants (having brought over several which belonged to the African kings), but the gates of the city being too narrow, he was forced to desist from that project, and be content with horses. And when his soldiers, who had not received as large rewards as they had expected, began to clamour, and interrupt the triumph, Pompey regarded these as little as the rest, and plainly told them that he had rather lose the honour of his triumph than flatter them. Upon which Servilius, a man of great distinction, and at first one of the chief opposers of Pompey's triumph, said, he now perceived that Pompey was truly great and worthy of a triumph. It is clear that he might easily have been a senator, also, if he had wished, but he did not sue for that, being ambitious, it seems, only of unusual honours. For what wonder had it been for Pompey to sit in the senate before his time? But to triumph before he was in the senate was really an excess of glory.

And, moreover, it did not a little ingratiate him with the people, who were much pleased to see him after his triumph take his place again among the Roman knights. On the other side, it was no less distasteful to Sylla to see how fast he came on, and to what a height of glory and power he was advancing; yet being ashamed to hinder him, he kept quiet. But when, against his direct wishes, Pompey got Lepidus made consul, having openly joined in the canvass and, by the good-will the people felt for himself, conciliated their favour for Lepidus, Sylla could forbear no longer, but when he saw him coming away from the election through the forum with a great train after him, cried out to him, "Well, young man, I see you rejoice in your victory. And, indeed, is it not a most generous and worthy act, that the

untry. For Perpenna, having in his custody all Ser-
papers, offered to produce several letters from the
men in Rome, who, desirous of a change and sub-
of the government, had invited Sertorius into Italy.
mpey, fearing that these might be the occasion of
wars than those which were now ended, thought it
le to put Perpenna to death, and burnt the letters
t reading them.

mpey continued in Spain after this so long a time as
ecessary for the suppression of all the greatest dis-
s in the province; and after moderating and allaying
more violent heats of affairs there, returned with his
into Italy, where he arrived, as chance would have it,
e height of the servile war. Accordingly, upon his ar-
l, Crassus, the commander in that war, at some hazard,
ipitated a battle, in which he had great success, and
v upon the place twelve thousand three hundred of the
urgents. Nor yet was he so quick, but that fortune re-
ved to Pompey some share of honour in the success of
is war, for five thousand of those that had escaped out of
e battle fell into his hands; and when he had totally cut
hem off, he wrote to the senate, that Crassus had over-
hrown the slaves in battle, but that he had plucked up the
whole war by the roots.

Though a second triumph was decreed him, and he was
declared consul, yet all these honours did not seem so great
an evidence of his power and glory as the ascendant which
he had over Crassus; for he, the wealthiest among all the
statesmen of his time, and the most eloquent and greatest
too, who had looked down on Pompey himself and on all
others beneath him, durst not appear a candidate for the
consulship before he had applied to Pompey. The request
was made accordingly, and was eagerly embraced by Pompey, who had long sought an occasion to oblige him in some
friendly office; so that he solicited for Crassus, and entreated the people heartily, declaring that their favour
would be no less to him in choosing Crassus his colleague,
than in making himself consul. Yet for all this, when they

consulship should be given to Lepidus, the vilest of men, in
preference to Catulus, the best and most deserving in the
city, and all by your influence with the people? It will be
well, however, for you to be wakeful and look to your interests; as you have been making your enemy stronger than
yourself."

Shortly after the death of Sylla, his prophetic words were
fulfilled; and Lepidus proposing to be the successor to all his
power and authority, without any ambiguities or pretences,
immediately appeared in arms, rousing once more and gathering about him all the long dangerous remains of the old
factions, which had escaped the hand of Sylla. Pompey,
therefore, was not long in suspense which way to dispose of
himself, but joining with the nobility, was presently appointed general of the army against Lepidus. Lepidus, being
driven out of Italy, fled to Sardinia, where he fell sick and
died of sorrow, not for his public misfortunes, as they say,
but upon the discovery of a letter proving his wife to have
been unfaithful to him.

There yet remained Sertorius, a very different general
from Lepidus, in possession of Spain, and making himself
formidable to Rome; the final disease, as it were, in which
the scattered evils of the civil wars had now collected. He
had already cut off various inferior commanders, and was
at this time coping with Metellus Pius, a man of repute and
a good soldier, though perhaps he might now seem too slow,
by reason of his age, to second and improve the happier
moments of war, and might be sometimes wanting to those
advantages which Sertorius, by his quickness and dexterity,
would wrest out of his hands. Pompey, therefore, keeping
his army in readiness, made it his object to be sent in aid to
Metellus.

When Pompey was arrived in Spain, as is usual upon the
fame of a new leader, men began to be inspired with new
hopes, and those nations that had not entered into a very
strict alliance with Sertorius began to waver and revolt. The
fortune of the war was very various; nothing, however, annoyed Pompey so much as the taking of the town of Lauron

by Sertorius. For when Pompey thought he had him safe enclosed, and had boasted somewhat largely of raising the siege, he found himself all of a sudden encompassed; insomuch that he durst not move out of his camp; but was forced to sit still whilst the city was taken and burnt before his face. However, afterwards, in a battle near Valentia, he gave a great defeat to Herennius and Perpenna, two commanders among the refugees who had fled to Sertorius, and now lieutenants under him, in which he slew above ten thousand men.

Pompey, being elated and filled with confidence by this victory, made all haste to engage Sertorius himself, and the rather lest Metellus should come in for a share in the honour of the victory. Late in the day towards sunset they joined battle near the river Sucro, both being in fear lest Metellus should come: Pompey, that he might engage alone, Sertorius, that he might have one alone to engage with. The issue of the battle proved doubtful, for a wing of each side had the better, but of the generals Sertorius had the greater honour, for that he maintained his post, having put to flight the entire division that was opposed to him, whereas Pompey was himself almost made a prisoner; for being set upon by a strong man-at-arms that fought on foot (he being on horseback), as they were closely engaged hand to hand the strokes of their swords chanced to light upon their hands, but with a different success; for Pompey's was a slight wound only, whereas he cut off the other's hand. However, it happened so, that many now falling upon Pompey together, and his own forces there being put to the rout, he made his escape beyond expectation, by quitting his horse, and turning him out among the enemy. For the horse being richly adorned with golden trappings, and having a caparison of great value, the soldiers quarrelled among themselves for the booty, so that while they were fighting with one another, and dividing the spoil, Pompey made his escape. By break of day the next morning each drew out his forces into the field to claim the victory; but Metellus coming up, Sertorius vanished, having broken up and dispersed his army.

For this was the way in which he his armies, so that sometimes he and down all alone, and at other ti pouring into the field at the head dred and fifty thousand fighting me like a winter torrent.

Pompey, having made use of and part of his own private revenues upon manded moneys of the senate, adding not furnish him speedily, he should be f Italy with his army. Lucullus being co though at variance with Pompey, yet in he himself was a candidate for the comman dates, procured and hastened these supp there should be any pretence or occasion g of returning home, who of himself was no leaving Sertorius and of undertaking the war dates, as an enterprise which by all appearanc much more honourable and not so dangerous. time Sertorius died, being treacherously murde of his own party; and Perpenna, the chief an took the command and attempted to carry on th terprises with Sertorius, having indeed the same the same means, only wanting the same skill and c the use of them. Pompey therefore marched directl Perpenna, and finding him acting merely at randon affairs, had a decoy ready for him, and sent out a ment of ten cohorts into the level country with ord range up and down and disperse themselves abroad. bait took accordingly, and no sooner had Perpenna tu upon the prey and had them in chase, but Pompey appe suddenly with all his army, and joining battle, gave hin total overthrow. Most of his officers were slain in the fie and he himself being brought prisoner to Pompey, was b his order put to death. Neither was Pompey guilty in this o ingratitude or unmindfulness of what had occurred in Sicily, which some have laid to his charge, but was guided by a high-minded policy and a deliberate counsel for the security

were created consuls, they were always at variance, and opposing one another. Crassus prevailed most in the senate, and Pompey's power was no less with the people, he having restored to them the office of tribune, and having allowed the courts of judicature to be transferred back to the knights by a new law. He himself in person, too, afforded them a most grateful spectacle, when he appeared and craved his discharge from the military service. For it is an ancient custom among the Romans that the knights, when they had served out their legal time in the wars, should lead their horses into the market-place before the two officers, called censors, and having given an account of the commanders and generals under whom they served, as also of the places and actions of their service, should be discharged, every man with honour or disgrace, according to his deserts. There were then sitting in state upon the bench two censors, Gellius and Lentulus, inspecting the knights, who were passing by in muster before them, when Pompey was seen coming down into the forum, with all the ensigns of a consul, but leading his horse in his hand. When he came up, he bade his lictors make way for him, and so he led his horse to the bench; the people being all this while in a sort of a maze, and all in silence, and the censors themselves regarding the sight with a mixture of respect and gratification. Then the senior censor examined him: "Pompeius Magnus, I demand of you whether you have served the full time in the wars that is prescribed by the law?" "Yes," replied Pompey, with a loud voice, "I have served all, and all under myself as general." The people hearing this gave a great shout, and made such an outcry for delight, that there was no appeasing it; and the censors rising from their judgment-seat accompanied him home to gratify the multitude who followed after, clapping their hands and shouting.

Pompey's consulship was now expiring, and yet his difference with Crassus increasing, when one Caius Aurelius, a knight, a man who had declined public business all his lifetime, mounted the hustings, and addressed himself in an oration to the assembly, declaring that Jupiter had appeared to him in a dream, commanding him to tell the consuls that they should not give up office until they were friends. After this was said, Pompey stood silent, but Crassus took him by the hand, and spoke in this manner: "I do not think, fellow-citizens, that I shall do anything mean or dishonourable in yielding first to Pompey, whom you were pleased to ennoble with the title of Great, when as yet he scarce had a hair on his face; and granted the honour of two triumphs before he had a place in the senate." Hereupon they were reconciled and laid down their office.

The power of the pirates first commenced in Cilicia, having in truth but a precarious and obscure beginning, but gained life and boldness afterwards in the wars of Mithridates, where they hired themselves out and took employment in the king's service. Afterwards, whilst the Romans were embroiled in their civil wars, being engaged against one another even before the very gates of Rome, the seas lay waste and unguarded, and by degrees enticed and drew them on not only to seize upon and spoil the merchants and ships upon the seas, but also to lay waste the islands and seaport towns. So that now there embarked with these pirates men of wealth and noble birth and superior abilities, as if it had been a natural occupation to gain distinction in. They had divers arsenals, or piratic harbours, as likewise watch-towers and beacons, all along the sea-coast; and fleets were here received that were well manned with the finest mariners, and well served with the expertest pilots, and composed of swift-sailing and light-built vessels adapted for their special purpose. Nor was it merely their being thus formidable that excited indignation; they were even more odious for their ostentation than they were feared for their force. Their ships had gilded masts at their stems; the sails woven of purple, and the oars plated with silver, as if their delight were to glory in their iniquity. There was nothing but music and dancing, banqueting and revels, all along the shore. Officers in command were taken prisoners, and cities put under contribution, to the reproach and dishonour of the Roman supremacy.

There were of these corsairs above one thousand sail, and they had taken no less than four hundred cities, committing sacrilege upon the temples of the gods, and enriching themselves with the spoils of many never violated before. Once they seized upon two Roman praetors, Sextilius and Bellinus, in their purple-edged robes, and carried them off together with their officers and lictors. The daughter also of Antonius, a man that had had the honour of a triumph, taking a journey into the country, was seized, and redeemed upon payment of a large ransom. But it was most abusive of all that, when any of the captives declared himself to be a Roman, and told his name, they affected to be surprised, and feigning fear, smote their thighs and fell down at his feet, humbly beseeching him to be gracious and forgive them.

The captives, seeing them so humble and suppliant, believed them to be in earnest; and some of them now would proceed to put Roman shoes on his feet, and to dress him in a Roman gown, to prevent, they said, his being mistaken another time. After all this pageantry, when they had thus deluded and mocked him long enough, at last putting out a ship's ladder, when they were in the midst of the sea, they told him he was free to go, and wished him a pleasant journey; and if he resisted they themselves threw him overboard and drowned him.

This piratic power having got the dominion and control of all the Mediterranean, there was left no place for navigation or commerce. And this it was which most of all made the Romans, finding themselves to be extremely straitened in their markets, and considering that if it should continue, there would be a dearth and famine in the land, determined at last to send out Pompey to recover the seas from the pirates. Gabinius, one of Pompey's friends, preferred a law, whereby there was granted to him, not only the government of the seas as admiral, but, in direct words, sole and irresponsible sovereignty over all men. For the decree gave him absolute power and authority in all the seas within the pillars of Hercules, and in the adjacent mainland for the space of four hundred furlongs from the sea. Now there were but few regions in the Roman empire out of that compass; and the greatest of the nations and most powerful of the kings were included in the limit. Moreover, by this decree he had a power of selecting fifteen lieutenants out of the senate, and of assigning to each his province in charge; then he might take likewise out of the treasury and out of the hands of the revenue-farmers what moneys he pleased; as also two hundred sail of ships, with a power to press and levy what soldiers and seamen he thought fit.

Five hundred ships were manned for him, and an army raised of one hundred and twenty thousand foot and five thousand horse. Twenty-four senators that had been generals of armies were appointed to serve as lieutenants under him, and to these were added two quaestors. Now it happened within this time that the prices of provisions were much reduced which gave an occasion to the joyful people of saying that the very name of Pompey had ended the war. However, Pompey, in pursuance of his charge, divided all the seas and the whole Mediterranean into thirteen parts, allotting, a squadron to each, under the command of his officers; and having thus dispersed his power into all quarters, and encompassed the pirates everywhere, they began to fall into his hands by whole shoals, which he seized and brought into his harbours. As for those that withdrew themselves betimes, or otherwise escaped his general chase, they all made to Cilicia, where they hid themselves as in their hives; against whom Pompey now proceeded in person with sixty of his best ships, not, however, until he had first scoured and cleared all the seas near Rome, the Tyrrhenian, and the African, and all the waters of Sardinia, Corsica, and Sicily; all which he performed in the space of forty days by his own indefatigable industry and the zeal of his lieutenants.

Thus was this war ended, and the whole power of the pirates at sea dissolved everywhere in the space of three months, wherein, besides a great number of other vessels, he took ninety men-of-war with brazen beaks; and likewise prisoners of war to the number of no less than twenty thousand.

When the news came to Rome that the war with the pirates was at an end, and that Pompey was unoccupied, diverting himself in visits to the cities for want of employment, one Manlius, a tribune of the people, preferred a law that Pompey should have all the forces of Lucullus, and the provinces under his government, together with Bithynia, which was under the command of Glabrio; and that he should forthwith conduct the war against the two kings, Mithridates and Tigranes, retaining still the same naval forces and the sovereignty of the seas as before. But this was nothing less than to constitute one absolute monarch of all the Roman empire. For the provinces which seemed to be exempt from his commission by the former decree, such as were Phrygia, Lycaonia, Galatia, Cappadocia, Cilicia, the upper Colchis, and Armenia, were all added in by this latter law, together with all the troops and forces with which Lucullus had defeated Mithridates and Tigranes. And though Lucullus was thus simply robbed of the glory of his achievements in having a successor assigned him, rather to the honour of his triumph than the danger of the war; yet this was of less moment in the eyes of the aristocratical party, though they could not but admit the injustice and ingratitude to Lucullus. But their great grievance was that the power of Pompey should be converted into a manifest tyranny; and they therefore exhorted and encouraged one another privately to bend all their forces in opposition to this law, and not tamely to cast away their liberty; yet when the day came on which it was to pass into a decree, their hearts failed them for fear of the people, and all were silent except Catulus, who boldly inveighed against the law and its proposer, and when he found that he could do nothing with the people, turned to the senate, crying out and bidding them seek out some mountain as their forefathers had done, and fly to the rocks where they might preserve their liberty. The law passed into a decree, as it is said, by the suffrages of all the tribes. And Pompey, in his absence, was made lord of almost all that power which Sylla only obtained by force of arms, after a conquest of the very city itself.

When Pompey had advice by letters of the decree, it is said, that in the presence of his friends, who came to give him joy of his honour, he seemed displeased, frowning and smiting his thigh, and exclaimed as one overburdened and weary of government, "Alas, what a series of labours upon labours! If I am never to end my service as a soldier, nor to escape from this invidious greatness and live at home in the country with my wife, I had better have been an unknown man." But all this was looked upon as mere trifling, neither indeed could the best of his friends call it anything else, well knowing that his enmity with Lucullus, setting a flame just now to his natural passion for glory and empire, made him feel more than usually gratified.

As indeed appeared not long afterwards by his àctions, which clearly unmasked him; for, in the first place, he sent out his proclamations into all quarters, commanding the soldiers to join him, and summoned all the tributary kings and princes within his charge; and in short, as soon as he had entered upon his province, he left nothing unaltered that had been done and established by Lucullus. To some he remitted their penalties, and deprived others of their rewards, and acted in all respects as if with the express design that the admirers of Lucullus might know that all his authority was at an end.

Lucullus expostulated by friends, and it was thought fitting that there should be a meeting betwixt them; and accordingly they met in the country of Galatia. As they were both great and successful generals, their officers bore their rods before them all wreathed with branches of laurel; Lucullus came through a country full of green trees and shady woods, but Pompey's march was through a cold and barren district. Therefore the lictors of Lucullus, perceiving that Pompey's laurels were withered and dry, helped him to some of their own, and adorned and crowned his rods with fresh laurels. This was thought ominous, and looked as if Pompey came to take away the reward and honour of Lucullus's victories. Lucullus had the priority in the order of consulships, and also in age; but Pompey's two

triumphs made him the greater man. Their first addresses
in this interview were dignified and friendly, each magnifying the other's actions, and offering congratulations upon
his success. But when they came to the matter of their conference or treaty, they could agree on no fair or equitable
terms of any kind, but even came to harsh words against
each other, Pompey upbraiding Lucullus with avarice, and
Lucullus retorting ambition upon Pompey, so that their
friends could hardly part them. Lucullus remaining in Galatia, made a distribution of the lands within his conquests,
and gave presents to whom he pleased; and Pompey encamping not far distant from him, sent out his prohibi-
tions, forbidding the execution of any of the orders of Lucullus, and commanded away all his soldiers, except sixteen hundred, whom he thought likely to be unserviceable
to himself, being disorderly and mutinous, and whom he
knew to be hostile to Lucullus; and to these acts he added
satirical speeches, detracting openly from the glory of his
actions, and giving out that the battles of Lucullus had been
but with the mere stage-shows and idle pictures of royal
pomp, whereas the real war against a genuine army, disciplined by defeat, was reserved to him, Mithridates having
now begun to be in earnest, and having betaken himself
to his shields, swords, and horses. Lucullus, on the other
side, to be even with him, replied, that Pompey came to
fight with the mere image and shadow of war, it being
his usual practice, like a lazy bird of prey, to come upon
the carcass when others had slain the dead, and to tear in
pieces the relics of a war.

Thus he had appropriated to himself the victories over
Sertorius, over Lepidus, and over the insurgents under Spartacus; whereas this last had been achieved by Crassus, that
obtained by Catulus, and the first won by Metellus. And
therefore it was no great wonder that the glory of the Pon-
tic and Armenian war should be usurped by a man who had
condescended to any artifices to work himself into the
honour of a triumph over a few runaway slaves.

After this Lucullus went away, and Pompey having

placed his whole navy in guard upon the seas betwixt Phoenicia and Bosphorus, himself marched against Mithridates, who had a phalanx of thirty thousand foot, with two thousand horse, yet durst not bid him battle. He had encamped upon a strong mountain where it would have been hard to attack him, but abandoned it in no long time as destitute of water. No sooner was he gone but Pompey occupied it, and observing the plants that were thriving there, together with the hollows which he found in several places, conjectured that such a plot could not be without springs, and therefore ordered his men to sink wells in every corner. After which there was, in a little time, great plenty of water throughout all the camp, insomuch that he wondered how it was possible for Mithridates to be ignorant of this, during all that time of his encampment there. After this Pompey followed him to his next camp, and there drawing lines round about him, shut him in. But he, after having endured a siege of forty-five days, made his escape secretly, and fled away with all the best part of his army, having first put to death all the sick and unserviceable. Not long after Pompey overtook him again near the banks of the river Euphrates, and encamped close by him; but fearing lest he should pass over the river and give him the slip there too, he drew up his army to attack him at midnight. And at that very time Mithridates, it is said, saw a vision in his dream foreshowing what should come to pass. For he seemed to be under sail in the Euxine Sea with a prosperous gale, and just in view of Bosphorus, discoursing pleasantly with the ship's company, as one overjoyed for his past danger and present security, when on a sudden he found himself deserted of all, and floating upon a broken plank of the ship at the mercy of the sea. Whilst he was thus labouring under these passions and phantasms, his friends came and awaked him with the news of Pompey's approach; who was now indeed so near at hand that the fight must be for the camp itself, and the commanders accordingly drew up the forces in battle array.

Pompey perceiving how ready they were and well pre-

pared for defence began to doubt with himself whether he
should put it to the hazard of a fight in the dark, judging
it more prudent to encompass them only at present, lest
they should fly, and to give them battle with the advantage
of numbers the next day. But his oldest officers were of
another opinion, and by entreaties and encouragements
obtained permission that they might charge them immediately. Neither was the night so very dark, but that,
though the moon was going down, it yet gave light enough
to discern a body, and indeed this was one especial disadvantage to the king's army. For the Romans coming upon
them with the moon on their backs, the moon, being very
low, and just upon setting, cast the shadows a long way
before their bodies, reaching almost to the enemy, whose
eyes were thus so much deceived that not exactly discerning the distance, but imagining them to be near at hand,
they threw their darts at the shadows without the least execution. The Romans therefore, perceiving this, ran in
upon them with a great shout; but the barbarians, all in a
panic, unable to endure the charge, turned and fled, and
were put to great slaughter, above ten thousand being
slain; the camp also was taken. As for Mithridates himself,
he at the beginning of the onset, with a body of eight hundred horse, charged through the Roman army, and made
his escape. But before long all the rest dispersed, some one
way, some another, and he was left only with three persons,
among whom was his concubine, Hypsicratia, a girl always of a manly and daring spirit, and the king called her
on that account Hypsicrates. She being attired and mounted
like a Persian horseman, accompanied the king in all his
flight, never weary even in the longest journey, nor even
failing to attend the king in person, and look after his horse
too, until they came to Inora, a castle of the king's, well
stored with gold and treasure. From thence Mithridates
took his richest apparel, and gave it among those that had
resorted to him in their flight; and so to every one of his
friends he gave a deadly poison, that they might not fall
into the power of the enemy against their wills. From

thence he designed to have gone to Tigranes in Armenia, but being prohibited by Tigranes who put out a proclamation with a reward of one hundred talents to any one that should apprehend him, he passed by the headwaters of the river Euphrates and fled through the country of Colchis.

Pompey went himself in chase of Mithridates; to do which he was forced of necessity to march through several nations inhabiting about Mount Caucasus. Of these the Albanians and Iberians were the two chiefest. The Iberians stretch out as far as the Moschian mountains and the Pontus; the Albanians lie more eastwardly, and towards the Caspian Sea. These Albanians at first permitted Pompey, upon his request, to pass through the country; but when winter had stolen upon the Romans whilst they were still in the country, and they were busy celebrating the festival of Saturn, they mustered a body of no less than forty thousand fighting men, and set upon them, having passed over the river Cyrnus, which rising from the mountains of Iberia, and receiving the river Araxes in its course from Armenia, discharges itself by twelve mouths into the Caspian. Or, according to others, the Araxes does not fall into it, but they flow near one another, and so discharge themselves as neighbours into the same sea. It was in the power of Pompey to have obstructed the enemy's passage over the river, but he suffered them to pass over quietly; and then leading on his forces and giving battle he routed them and slew great numbers of them in the field. The king sent ambassadors with his submission, and Pompey upon his supplication pardoned the offence, and making a treaty with him, he marched directly against the Iberians, a nation no less in number than the other, but much more warlike, and extremely desirous of gratifying Mithridates and driving out Pompey.

These Iberians were never subject to the Medes or Persians, and they happened likewise to escape the dominion of the Macedonians, because Alexander was so quick in his march through Hyrcania. But these also Pompey subdued in a great battle, where there were slain nine thousand upon the spot, and more than ten thousand taken prisoners. From thence he entered into the country of Colchis, where Servilius met him by the river Phasis, bringing the fleet with which he was guarding the Pontus.

The pursuit of Mithridates, who had thrown himself among the tribes inhabiting Bosphorus and the shores of the Maeotian Sea, presented great difficulties. News was also brought to Pompey that the Albanians had again revolted. This made him turn back, out of anger and determination not to be beaten by them, and with difficulty and great danger passed back over the Cyrnus, which the barbarous people had fortified a great way down the banks with palisadoes. And after this, having a tedious march to make through a waterless and difficult country, he ordered ten thousand skins to be filled with water, and so advanced towards the enemy, whom he found drawn up in order of battle near the river Abas, to the number of sixty thousand horse and twelve thousand foot, ill-armed generally, and most of them covered only with the skins of wild beasts. Their general was Cosis, the king's brother, who, as soon as the battle was begun, singled out Pompey, and rushing in upon him darted his javelin into the joints of his breastplate; while Pompey, in return, struck him through the body with his lance and slew him. It is related that in this battle there were Amazons fighting as auxiliaries with the barbarians, and that they came down from the mountains by the river Thermodon. For that after the battle, when the Romans were taking the spoils and plunder of the field, they met with several targets and buskins of the Amazons; but no woman's body was found among the dead. They inhabit the parts of Mount Caucasus that reach down to the Hyrcanian Sea, not immediately bordering upon the Albanians, for the Gelae and the Leges lie betwixt; and they keep company with these people yearly, for two months only, near the river Thermodon; after which they retire to their own habitations, and live alone all the rest of the year.

Of the concubines of King Mithridates that were brought

before Pompey, he took none to himself, but sent them all away to their parents and relations; most of them being either the daughters or wives of princes and great commanders. Stratonice, however, who had the greatest power and influence with him, and to whom he had committed the custody of his best and richest fortress, had been, it seems, the daughter of a musician, an old man, and of no great fortune, and happening to sing one night before Mithridates at a banquet, she struck his fancy so that immediately he took her with him, and sent away the old man much dissatisfied, the king having not so much as said one kind word to himself. But when he rose in the morning, and saw tables in his house richly covered with gold and silver plate, a great retinue of servants, eunuchs, and pages bringing him rich garments, and a horse standing before the door richly caparisoned, in all respects as was usual with the king's favourites, he looked upon it all as a piece of mockery, and thinking himself trifled with, attempted to make off and run away. But the servants laying hold upon him, and informing him really that the king had bestowed on him the house and furniture of a rich man lately deceased, and that these were but the first fruits or earnests of greater riches and possessions that were to come, he was persuaded at last with much difficulty to believe them. And so putting on his purple robes, and mounting his horse, he rode through the city, crying out, "All this is mine"; and to those that laughed at him, he said, there was no such wonder in this, but it was a wonder rather that he did not throw stones at all he met, he was so transported with joy. Such was the parentage and blood of Stratonice. She now delivered up this castle into the hands of Pompey, and offered him many presents of great value, of which he accepted only such as he thought might serve to adorn the temples of the gods and add to the splendour of his triumph: the rest he left to Stratonice's disposal, bidding her please herself in the enjoyment of them.

And in the same manner he dealt with the presents offered him by the King of Iberia, who sent him a bedstead, table, and a chair of state, all of gold, desiring him to accept of them; but he delivered them all into the custody of the public treasurers, for the use of the commonwealth.

In another castle called Caenum, Pompey found and read with pleasure several secret writings of Mithridates, containing much that threw light on his character. For there were memoirs by which it appeared that, besides others, he had made away with his son Ariarathes by poison, as also with Alcaeus the Sardian, for having robbed him of the first honours in a horse-race. There were several judgments upon the interpretation of dreams, which either he himself or some of his mistresses had had; and besides these, there was a series of wanton letters to and from his concubine Monime. Theophanes tells us that there was found also an address by Rutilius, in which he attempted to exasperate him to the slaughter of all the Romans in Asia; though most men justly conjecture this to be a malicious invention of Theophanes, who probably hated Rutilius because he was a man in nothing like himself; or perhaps it might be to gratify Pompey, whose father is described by Rutilius in his history as the vilest man alive.

From thence Pompey came to the city of Amisus, where his passion for glory put him into a position which might be called a punishment on himself. For whereas he had often sharply reproached Lucullus, in that while the enemy was still living he had taken upon him to issue decrees, and distribute rewards and honours, as conquerors usually do only when the war is brought to an end, yet now was he himself, while Mithridates was paramount in the kingdom of Bosphorus, and at the head of a powerful army, as if all were ended, just doing the same thing, regulating the provinces, and distributing rewards, many great commanders and princes having flocked to him, together with no less than twelve barbarian kings; insomuch that to gratify these other kings, when he wrote to the King of Parthia, he would not condescend, as others used to do, in the superscription of his letter, to give him his title of king of kings.

Moreover, he had a great desire and emulation to occupy

Syria, and to march through Arabia to the Red Sea, that
he might thus extend his conquests every way to the great
ocean that encompasses the habitable earth; as in Africa
he was the first Roman that advanced his victories to the
ocean; and again in Spain he made the Atlantic Sea the
limit of the empire; and then thirdly, in his late pursuit of
the Albanians, he had wanted but little of reaching the Hyrcanian Sea. Accordingly he raised his camp designing to
bring the Red Sea within the circuit of his expedition; especially as he saw how difficult it was to hunt after Mithridates with an army, and that he would prove a worse enemy
flying than fighting. But yet he declared that he would
leave a sharper enemy behind him than himself, namely,
famine; and therefore he appointed a guard of ships to
lie in wait for the merchants that sailed to Bosphorus, death
being the penalty for any who should attempt to carry provisions thither.

Pompey having now by his forces under the command
of Afranius subdued the Arabians about the mountain
Amanus, himself entered Syria, and finding it destitute of
any natural and lawful prince, reduced it into the form of
a province, as a possession of the people of Rome. He conquered also Judaea, and took its king, Aristobulus, captive.
Some cities he built anew, and to others he gave their liberty, chastising their tyrants. Most part of the time that he
spent there was employed in the administration of justice,
in deciding controversies of kings and states; and where
he himself could not be present in person, he gave commissions to his friends, and sent them. Thus when there
arose a difference betwixt the Armenians and Parthians
about some territory, and the judgment was referred to
him, he gave a power by commission to three judges and
arbiters to hear and determine the controversy. For the reputation of his power was great; nor was the fame of his
justice and clemency inferior to that of his power, and
served indeed as a veil for a multitude of faults committed
by his friends and familiars. For although it was not in
his nature to check or chastise wrongdoers, yet he himself

always treated those that had to do with him in such a manner that they submitted to endure with patience the acts of covetousness and oppression done by others.

The king of the Arabs near Petra, who had hitherto despised the power of the Romans, now began to be in great alarm at it, and sent letters to him promising to be at his commands, and to do whatever he should see fit to order. However, Pompey having a desire to confirm and keep him in the same mind, marched forwards for Petra, an expedition not altogether irreprehensible in the opinion of many; who thought it a mere running away from their proper duty, the pursuit of Mithridates, Rome's ancient and inveterate enemy, who was now rekindling the war once more, and taking preparations, it was reported, to lead his army through Scythia and Paeonia into Italy. Pompey, on the other side, judging it easier to destroy his forces in battle than to seize his person in flight, resolved not to tire himself out in a vain pursuit, but rather to spend his leisure upon another enemy, as a sort of digression in the meanwhile. But fortune resolved the doubt, for when he was now not far from Petra, and had pitched his tents and encamped for that day, as he was taking exercise with his horse outside the camp, couriers came riding up from Pontus, bringing good news, as was known at once by the heads of their javelins, which it is the custom to carry crowned with branches of laurel. The soldiers, as soon as they saw them, flocked immediately to Pompey, who, notwithstanding, was minded to finish his exercise; but when they began to be clamorous and importunate, he alighted from his horse, and taking the letters went before them into the camp.

Now there being no tribunal erected there, not even that military substitute for one which they make by cutting up thick turfs of earth, and piling them one upon another, they, through eagerness and impatience, heaped up a pile of pack-saddles, and Pompey standing upon that, told them the news of Mithridates's death, how that he had himself put an end to his life upon the revolt of his son Pharnaces, and that Pharnaces had taken all things there into his hands and possession, which he did, his letters said, in right of himself and the Romans. Upon this news the whole army, expressing their joy, as was to be expected, fell to sacrificing to the gods, and feasting as if in the person of Mithridates alone there had died many thousands of their enemies.

Pompey by this event having brought this war to its completion, with much more ease than was expected, departed forthwith out of Arabia, and passing rapidly through the intermediate provinces, he came at length to the city Amisus. There he received many presents brought from Pharnaces, with several dead bodies of the royal blood, and the corpse of Mithridates himself, which was not easy to be known by the face, for the physicians that embalmed him had not dried up his brain, but those who were curious to see him knew him by the scars there. Pompey himself would not endure to see him, but to deprecate the divine jealousy sent it away to the city of Sinope. He admired the richness of his robes no less than the size and splendour of his armour. His sword-belt, however, which had cost four hundred talents, was stolen by Publius, and sold to Ariarathes; his tiara also, a piece of admirable workmanship, Gaius, the foster-brother of Mithridates, gave secretly to Faustus, the son of Sylla, at his request. All which Pompey was ignorant of, but afterwards, when Pharnaces came to understand it, he severely punished those that embezzled them.

Pompey now having ordered all things, and established that province, took his journey homewards in greater pomp and with more festivity. For when he came to Mitylene, he gave the city their freedom upon the intercession of Theophanes, and was present at the contest, there periodically held, of the poets, who took at that time no other theme or subject than the actions of Pompey. He was extremely pleased with the theatre itself, and had a model of it taken, intending to erect one in Rome on the same design, but larger and more magnificent. When he came to Rhodes, he attended the lectures of all the philosophers there, and gave to every one of them a talent. Posidonius has published the disputation which he held before him against Hermagoras the rhetorician, upon the subject of Invention in general. At Athens, also, he showed similar munificence to the philosophers, and gave fifty talents towards the repairing and beautifying the city. So that now by all these acts he well hoped to return into Italy in the greatest splendour and glory possible to man, and find his family as desirous to see him as he felt himself to come home to them. But that supernatural agency, whose province and charge it is always to mix some ingredient of evil with the greatest and most glorious goods of fortune, had for some time back been busy in his household, preparing him a sad welcome. For Mucia during his absence had dishonoured his bed. Whilst he was abroad at a distance he had refused all credence to the report; but when he drew nearer to Italy, where his thoughts were more at leisure to give consideration to the charge, he sent her a bill of divorce; but neither then in writing, nor afterwards by word of mouth, did he ever give a reason why he discharged her; the cause of it is mentioned in Cicero's epistles.

Rumours of every kind were scattered abroad about Pompey, and were carried to Rome before him, so that there was a great tumult and stir, as if he designed forthwith to march with his army into the city and establish himself securely as sole ruler. Crassus withdrew himself, together with his children and property, out of the city, either that he was really afraid, or that he counterfeited rather, as is most probable, to give credit to the calumny and exasperate the jealousy of the people. Pompey, therefore, as soon as he entered Italy, called a general muster of the army; and having made a suitable address and exchanged a kind farewell with his soldiers, he commanded them to depart every man to his country and place of habitation, only taking care that they should not fail to meet again at his triumph. Thus the army being disbanded, and the news commonly reported, a wonderful result ensued. For when the cities saw Pompey the Great passing through the country unarmed, and with a small train of familiar friends only, as if he was returning from a journey of pleasure, not from his conquests, they came pouring out to display their affection for him, attending and conducting him to Rome with far greater forces than he disbanded; insomuch that if he had designed any movement or innovation in the state, he might have done it without his army.

Now, because the law permitted no commander to enter into the city before his triumph, he sent to the senate, entreating them as a favour to him to prorogue the election of consuls, that thus he might be able to attend and give countenance to Piso, one of the candidates. The request was resisted by Cato, [the younger], and met with a refusal. However, Pompey could not but admire the liberty and boldness of speech which Cato alone had dared to use in the maintenance of law and justice. He therefore had a great desire to win him over, and purchase his friendship at any rate; and to that end, Cato having two nieces, Pompey asked for one in marriage for himself, the other for his son. But Cato looked unfavourably on the proposal, regarding it as a design for undermining his honesty, and in a manner bribing him by a family alliance; much to the displeasure of his wife and sister, who were indignant that he should reject a connection with Pompey the Great. About that time Pompey having a design of setting up Afranius for the consulship, gave a sum of money among the tribes for their votes, and people came and received it in his own gardens, a proceeding which, when it came to be generally known, excited great disapprobation, that he should thus, for the sake of men who could not obtain the honour by their own merits, make merchandise of an office which had been given to himself as the highest reward of his services. "Now," said Cato, to his wife and sister, "had we contracted an alliance with Pompey, we had been allied to this dishonour too"; and this they could not but acknowledge, and allow his judgment of what was right and fitting to have been wiser and better than theirs.

The splendour and magnificence of Pompey's triumph was such that though it took up the space of two days, yet they were extremely straitened in time, so that of what was prepared for that pageantry, there was as much withdrawn as would have set out and adorned another triumph. In the first place, there were tables carried, inscribed with the names and titles of the nations over whom he triumphed, Pontus, Armenia, Cappadocia, Paphlagonia, Media, Colchis, the Iberians, the Albanians, Syria, Cilicia, and Mesopotamia, together with Phoenicia and Palestine, Judaea, Arabia, and all the power of the pirates subdued by sea and land. And in these different countries there appeared the capture of no less than one thousand fortified places, nor much less than nine hundred cities, together with eight hundred ships of the pirates, and the foundation of thirty-nine towns. Besides, there was set forth in these tables an account of all the tributes throughout the empire, and how that before these conquests the revenue amounted but to fifty millions, whereas from his acquisitions they had a revenue of eighty-five millions; and that in present payment he was bringing into the common treasury ready money, and gold and silver plate, and ornaments, to the value of twenty thousand talents, over and above what had been distributed among the soldiers, of whom he that had least had fifteen hundred drachmas for his share. The prisoners of war that were led in triumph, besides the chief pirates, were the son of Tigranes, King of Armenia, with his wife and daughter; as also Zosime, wife of King Tigranes himself, and Aristobulus, King of Judaea, the sister of King Mithridates, and her five sons, and some Scythian women. There were likewise the hostages of the Albanians and Iberians, and of the King of Commagene, besides a vast number of trophies, one for every battle in which he was conqueror, either himself in person or by his lieutenants. But that which seemed to be his greatest glory, being one which no other Roman ever attained to, was this, that he made his third triumph over the third division of the world. For others among the Romans had the honour of triumphing thrice, but his first triumph was over Africa, his second over Europe, and this last over Asia; so that he seemed in these three triumphs to have led the whole world captive.

As for his age, those who affect to make the parallel exact in all things betwixt him and Alexander the Great, do not allow him to have been quite thirty-four, whereas in truth at that time he was near forty. And well had it been for him had he terminated his life at this date, while he still enjoyed Alexander's fortune, since all his after-time served only either to bring him prosperity that made him odious, or calamities too great to be retrieved. For that great authority which he had gained in the city by his merits he made use of only in patronising the iniquities of others, so that by advancing their fortunes he detracted from his own glory, till at last he was overthrown even by the force and greatness of his own power. And as the strongest citidel or fort in a town, when it is taken by an enemy, does then afford the same strength to the foe as it had done to friends before, so Caesar, after Pompey's aid had made him strong enough to defy his country, ruined and overthrew at last the power which had availed him against the rest.

[*The events of Caesar's rise to dominance, his advance upon Rome, the internal disorders of the city, and the civil war, have been related fully in the life of Caesar, preceding. Accordingly, to avoid this duplication of material, we move directly to the figure of the ruined Pompey, in the closing action of the decisive battle of Pharsalia. Thence we shall follow him the brief and melancholy way to the conclusion of his tragedy.* E. F.]

When Pompey, by the dust flying in the air, conjectured the fate of his horse, it were very hard to say what his thoughts or intentions were, but looking like one distracted and beside himself, and without any recollection or reflection that he was Pompey the Great, he retired slowly towards his camp, without speaking a word to any man, exactly according to the description in the verses—

"But Jove from heaven struck Ajax with a fear;
Ajax the bold then stood astonished there,
Flung o'er his back the mighty sevenfold shield,
And trembling gazed and spied about the field."

In this state and condition he went into his own tent and sat down, speechless still, until some of the enemy fell in together with his men that were flying into the camp, and then he let fall only this one word, "What! into the very camp?" and said no more, but rose up, and putting on a dress suitable to his present fortune, made his way secretly out.

By this time the rest of the army was put to flight, and there was a great slaughter in the camp among the servants and those that guarded the tents, but of the soldiers themselves there were not above six thousand slain, as is stated by Asinius Pollio, who himself fought in this battle on Caesar's side. When Caesar's soldiers had taken the camp, they saw clearly the folly and vanity of the enemy; for all their tents and pavilions were richly set out with garlands of myrtle, embroidered carpets and hangings, and tables laid and covered with goblets. There were large bowls of wine ready, and everything prepared and put in array, in the manner rather of people who had offered sacrifice and were going to celebrate a holiday, than of soldiers who had armed themselves to go out to battle, so possessed with the expectation of success and so full of empty confidence had they gone out that morning.

When Pompey had got a little way from the camp, he dismounted and forsook his horse, having but a small retinue with him; and finding that no man pursued him, walked on softly afoot, taken up altogether with thoughts, such as probably might possess a man that for the space of thirty-four years together had been accustomed to conquest and victory, and was then at last, in his old age, learning for the first time what defeat and flight were. And it was no small affliction to consider that he had lost in one hour all that glory and power which he had been getting in so many wars and bloody battles; and that he who but a little before was guarded with such an army of foot, so many squadrons of horse, and such a mighty fleet, was now flying in so mean a condition, and with such a slender retinue, that his very enemies who fought him could not know him. Thus, when he had passed by the city of Larissa, and came into the pass of Tempe, being very thirsty, he kneeled down and drank out of the river; then rising up again, he passed through Tempe, until he came to the seaside, and there he betook himself to a poor fisherman's cottage, where he rested the remainder of the night. The next morning about break of day he went into one of the river boats, and taking none of those that followed him except such as were free, dismissed his servants, advising them to go boldly to Caesar and not be afraid. As he was rowing up and down near the shore, he chanced to spy a large merchant ship, lying off, just ready to set sail; the master of which was a Roman citizen, named Peticius, who, though he was not familiarly acquainted with Pompey, yet knew him well by sight. Now it happened that this Peticius dreamed, the night before, that he saw Pompey, not like the man he had often seen him, but in a humble and dejected condition, and in that posture discoursing with him. He was then telling his dream to the people on board, as men do when at leisure, and especially dreams of that consequence, when of a sudden one of the mariners told him he saw a river boat with oars putting off from shore, and that some of the men there shook their garments, and held out their hands, with signs to take them in; thereupon Peticius, looking attentively, at once recognised Pompey, just as he appeared in his dream, and smiting his hand on his head, ordered the mariners to let down the ship's boat, he himself waving his hand, and calling to him by his name, already assured of his change and the change of his fortune by that of his garb. So that without waiting for any further entreaty or discourse he took him into his ship, together with as many of his company as he thought fit, and hoisted sail. There were with him the two Lentuli and Favonius; and a little after they spied King Deiotarus, making up towards them from the shore; so they stayed and took him in along with them. At supper time, the master of the ship having made ready such provisions as he had aboard, Pompey, for want of his servants, began to undo his shoes himself, which Favonius noticing, ran to him and undid them, and helped him to anoint himself, and always after continued to wait upon, and attended him in all things, as servants do their masters, even to the washing of his feet and preparing his supper. Insomuch that any one there present, observing the free and unaffected courtesy of these services, might have well exclaimed—

> "O heavens, in those that noble are,
> Whate'er they do is fit and fair."

Pompey, sailing by the city of Amphipolis, crossed over from thence to Mitylene, with a design to take in Cornelia * and his son; and as soon as he arrived at the port in that island, he despatched a messenger into the city with news very different from Cornelia's expectation. For she, by all the former messages and letters sent to please her, had been put in hopes that the war was ended at Dyrrhachium, and that there was nothing more remaining for Pompey but the pursuit of Caesar. The messenger, finding her in the same hopes still, was not able to salute or speak to her, but declaring the greatness of her misfortune by his tears rather than his words, desired her to make haste if she would see Pompey, with one ship only, and that not of his own. The young lady hearing this, fell down in a swoon, and continued a long time senseless and speechless. And when with some trouble she was brought to her senses again, being conscious to herself that this was no time for lamentation

---

* Cornelia, whom Pompey had married, was the young widow of Publius, son of Crassus, slain in Parthia. E. F.

and tears, she started up and ran through the city towards the seaside, where Pompey meeting and embracing her, as she sank down, supported by his arms, "This, sir," she exclaimed, "is the effect of my fortune, not of yours, that I see you thus reduced to one poor vessel, who before your marriage with Cornelia were wont to sail in these seas with a fleet of five hundred ships. Why therefore should you come to see me, or why not rather have left to her evil genius one who has brought upon you her own ill fortune? How happy a woman had I been if I had breathed out my last before the news came from Parthia of the death of Publius, the huband of my youth, and how prudent if I had followed his destiny, as I designed! But I was reserved for a greater mischief, even the ruin of Pompey the Great."

Thus, they say, Cornelia spoke to him, and this was Pompey's reply: "You have had, Cornelia, but one season of a better fortune, which, it may be, gave you unfounded hopes, by attending me a longer time than is usual. It behooves us, who are mortals born, to endure these events, and to try fortune yet again; neither is it any less possible to recover our former state than it was to fall from that into this." Thereupon Cornelia sent for her servants and baggage out of the city. The citizens also of Mitylene came out to salute and invite Pompey into the city, but he refused, advising them to be obedient to the conqueror and fear not, for that Caesar was a man of great goodness and clemency. Then turning to Cratippus, the philosopher, who came among the rest out of the city to visit him, he began to find some fault, and briefly argued with him upon Providence, but Cratippus modestly declined the dispute, putting him in better hopes only, lest by opposing he might seem too austere or unseasonable. For he might have put Pompey a question in his turn in defence of Providence; and might have demonstrated the necessity there was that the commonwealth should be turned into a monarchy, because of their ill government in the state; and could have asked, "How, O Pompey, and by what token or assurance can we ascertain, that if the victory had been yours, you would have used your fortune better than Caesar? We must leave the divine power to act as we find it do."

Pompey having taken his wife and friends aboard, set sail, making no port, or touching anywhere, but when he was necessitated to take in provisions or fresh water. The first city he entered was Attalia, in Pamphylia, and whilst he was there, there came some galleys thither to him out of Cilicia, together with a small body of soldiers, and he had almost sixty senators with him again; then hearing that his navy was safe too, and that Cato had allied a considerable body of soldiers after their overthrow, and was crossing with them over into Africa, he began to complain and blame himself to his friends that he had allowed himself to be driven into engaging by land, without making use of his other forces, in which he was irresistibly the stronger, and had not kept near enough to his fleet, that failing by land, he might have reinforced himself from the sea, and would have been again at the head of a power quite sufficient to encounter the enemy on equal terms. And, in truth, neither did Pompey during all the war commit a greater oversight, nor Caesar use a more subtle stratagem, than in drawing the fight so far off from the naval forces.

As it now was, however, since he must come to some decision and try some plan within his present ability, he despatched his agents to the neighbouring cities, and himself sailed about in person to others, requiring their aid in money and men for his ships. But, fearing lest the rapid approach of the enemy might cut off all his preparations, he began to consider what place would yield him the safest refuge and retreat at present. A consultation was held, and it was generally agreed that no province of the Romans was secure enough. As for foreign kingdoms, he himself was of opinion that Parthia would be the fittest to receive and defend them in their present weakness, and best able to furnish them with new means, and send them out again with large forces. Others of the council were for going into Africa, and to King Juba. But Theophanes the Lesbian thought it madness to leave Egypt, that was but at a distance of three days' sailing, and make no use of Ptolemy, who was still a boy, and was highly indebted to Pompey for the friendship and favour he had shown to his father, only to put himself under the Parthian, and trust the most treacherous nation in the world; and rather than make any trial of the clemency of a Roman, and his own near connection, to whom if he would but yield to be second he might be the first and chief over all the rest, to go and place himself at the mercy of Arsaces, which even Crassus had not submitted to while alive; and, moreover, to expose his young wife, of the family of the Scipios, among a barbarous people, who govern by their lusts, and measure their greatness by their power to commit affronts and insolences; from whom, though she suffered no dishonour, yet it might be thought she did, being in the hands of those who had the power to do it. This argument alone, they say, was persuasive enough to divert his course, that was designed towards Euphrates, if it were so indeed that any counsel of Pompey's, and not some superior power, made him take this other way.

As soon, therefore, as it was resolved upon that he should fly into Egypt, setting sail from Cyprus in a galley of Seleucia, together with Cornelia, while the rest of his company sailed along near him, some in ships of war, and others in merchant vessels, he passed over sea without danger. But on hearing that King Ptolemy was posted with his army at the city of Pelusium, making war against his sister, he steered his course that way, and sent a messenger before to acquaint the king with his arrival, and to crave his protection. Ptolemy himself was quite young, and therefore Pothinus, who had the principal administration of affairs, called a council of the chief men, those being the greatest whom he pleased to make so, and commanded them every man to deliver his opinion touching the reception of Pompey. It was, indeed, a miserable thing that the fate of the great Pompey should be left to the determinations of Pothinus the eunuch, Theodotus of Chios, the paid rhetoric master, and Achillas the Egyptian. For these, among the

chamberlains and menial domestics that made up the rest
of the council, were the chief and leading men. Pompey,
who thought it dishonourable for him to owe his safety to
Caesar, riding at anchor at a distance from shore, was
forced to wait the sentence of this tribunal. It seems they
were so far different in their opinions that some were for
sending the man away, and others, again, for inviting and
receiving him; but Theodotus, to show his cleverness and
the cogency of his rhetoric, undertook to demonstrate that
neither the one nor the other was safe in that juncture of
affairs. For if they entertained him, they would be sure to
make Caesar their enemy and Pompey their master; or if
they dismissed him, they might render themselves hereafter
obnoxious to Pompey, for that inhospitable expulsion, and
to Caesar, for the escape; so that the most expedient course
would be to send for him and take away his life, for by
that means they would ingratiate themselves with the one,
and have no reason to fear the other; adding, it is related,
with a smile, that "a dead man cannot bite."

This advice being approved of, they committed the execution of it to Achillas. He, therefore, taking with him as
his accomplices one Septimius, a man that had formerly
held a command under Pompey, and Salvius, another centurion, with three or four attendants, made up towards
Pompey's galley. In the meantime, all the chiefest of those
who accompanied Pompey in this voyage were come into
his ship to learn the event of their embassy. But when they
saw the manner of their reception, that in appearance it
was neither princely nor honourable, nor indeed in any way
answerable to the hopes of Theophanes, or their expectation (for there came but a few men in a fisherman's boat
to meet them), they began to suspect the meanness of their
entertainment, and gave warning to Pompey that he should
row back his galley, whilst he was out of their reach, and
make for the sea. By this time the Egyptian boat drew
near, and Septimius standing up first, saluted Pompey, in
the Latin tongue, by the title of Imperator. Then Achillas,
saluting him in the Greek language, desired him to come

aboard his vessel, telling him that the sea was very shallow towards the shore, and that a galley of that burden could not avoid striking upon the sands. At the same time they saw several of the king's galleys getting their men on board, and all the shore covered with soldiers; so that even if they changed their minds, it seemed impossible for them to escape, and besides, their distrust would have given the assassins a pretence for their cruelty. Pompey, therefore, taking his leave of Cornelia, who was already lamenting his death before it came, bade two centurions, with Philip, one of his freedmen, and a slave called Scythes, go on board the boat before him. And as some of the crew with Achillas were reaching out their hands to help him, he turned about towards his wife and son, and repeated those iambics of Sophocles—

> "He that once enters at a tyrant's door
> Becomes a slave, though he were free before."

These were the last words he spoke to his friends, and so he went aboard. Observing presently that notwithstanding there was a considerable distance betwixt his galley and the shore, yet none of the company addressed any words of friendliness or welcome to him all the way, he looked earnestly upon Septimius, and said, "I am not mistaken, surely, in believing you to have been formerly my fellow-soldier." But he only nodded with his head, making no reply at all, nor showing any other courtesy. Since, therefore, they continued silent, Pompey took a little book in his hand, in which was written out an address in Greek, which he intended to make to King Ptolemy, and began to read it. When they drew near to the shore, Cornelia, together with the rest of his friends in the galley, was very impatient to see the event, and began to take courage at last when she saw several of the royal escort coming to meet him, apparently to give him a more honourable reception; but in the meantime, as Pompey took Philip by the hand to rise up more easily, Septimius first stabbed him from be-

hind with his sword, and after him likewise Salvius and
Achillas drew out their swords. He, therefore, taking up
his gown with both hands, drew it over his face, and neither
saying nor doing anything unworthy of himself, only groaning a little, endured the wounds they gave him, and so
ended his life, in the fifty-ninth year of his age, the very
next day after the day of his birth.

Cornelia, with her company from the galley, seeing him
murdered, gave such a cry that it was heard on the shore,
and weighing anchor with all speed, they hoisted sail, and
fled. A strong breeze from the shore assisted their flight into
the open sea, so that the Egyptians, though desirous to overtake them, desisted from the pursuit. But they cut off Pompey's head, and threw the rest of his body overboard, leaving it naked upon the shore, to be viewed by any that had
the curiosity to see so sad a spectacle. Philip stayed by and
watched till they had glutted their eyes in viewing it; and
then washing it with sea-water, having nothing else, he
wrapped it up in a shirt of his own for a winding-sheet.
Then seeking up and down about the sands, at last he found
some rotten planks of a little fisher-boat, not much, but
yet enough to make up a funeral pile for a naked body,
and that not quite entire. As Philip was busy in gathering
and putting these old planks together, an old Roman citizen, who in his youth had served in the wars under Pompey, came up to him and demanded who he was that was
preparing the funeral of Pompey the Great. And Philip
making answer that he was his freedman, "Nay, then," said
he, "you shall not have this honour alone; let even me, too,
I pray you, have my share in such a pious office, that I
may not altogether repent me of this pilgrimage in a
strange land, but in compensation of many misfortunes may
obtain this happiness at last, even with mine own hands
to touch the body of Pompey, and do the last duties to the
greatest general among the Romans." And in this manner
were the obsequies of Pompey performed. The next day
Lucius Lentulus, not knowing what had passed, came sailing from Cyprus along the shore of that coast, and seeing

a funeral pile, and Philip standing by, exclaimed, before
he was yet seen by any one, "Who is this that has found
his end here?" adding after a short pause, with a sigh,
"Possibly even thou Pompeius Magnus" and so going
ashore, he was presently apprehended and slain. This was
the end of Pompey.

Not long after, Caesar arrived in the country that was
polluted with this foul act, and when one of the Egyptians
was sent to present him with Pompey's head, he turned
away from him with abhorrence as from a murderer; and
on receiving his seal, on which was engraved a lion holding a sword in his paw, he burst into tears. Achillas and
Pothinus he put to death; and King Ptolemy himself, being
overthrown in battle upon the banks of the Nile, fled away
and was never heard of afterwards. Theodotus, the rhetorician, flying out of Egypt, escaped the hands of Caesar's
justice, but lived a vagabond in banishment, wandering up
and down, despised and hated of all men, till at last Marcus
Brutus, after he had killed Caesar, finding him in his province of Asia, put him to death with every kind of ignominy.
The ashes of Pompey were carried to his wife Cornelia,
who deposited them at his country-house near Alba.

✤

CICERO

It is generally said, that Helvia, the mother of Cicero, was both well-born and lived a fair life; but of his father nothing is reported but in extremes. For whilst some would have him the son of a fuller, and educated in that trade, others carry back the origin of his family to Tullus Attius, an illustrious king of the Volscians, who waged war not without honour against the Romans. However, he who first of that house was surnamed Cicero seems to have been a person worthy to be remembered; since those who succeeded him not only did not reject, but were fond of that name, though vulgarly made a matter of reproach. For the Latins call a vetch *Cicer*, and a nick or dent at the tip of his nose, which resembled the opening in a vetch, gave him the surname of *Cicero*.

Cicero, whose story I am writing, is said to have replied with spirit to some of his friends, who recommended him to lay aside or change the name when he first stood for office and engaged in politics, that he would make it his endeavour to render the name of Cicero more glorious than that of the Scauri and Catuli. And when he was quaestor in Sicily, and was making an offering of silver plate to the gods, and had inscribed his two names, Marcus and Tullius, instead of the third, he jestingly told the artificer to engrave the figure of a vetch by them. Thus much is told us about his name.

Of his birth it is reported that his mother was delivered, without pain or labour, on the third of the new Calends, the same day on which now the magistrates of Rome pray

and sacrifice for the emperor. It is said, also, that a vision
appeared to his nurse, and foretold the child she then
suckled should afterwards become a great benefit to the
Roman state. To such presages, which might in general
be thought mere fancies and idle talk, he himself ere long
gave the credit of true phophecies. For as soon as he was
of an age to begin to have lessons, he became so distinguished for his talent, and got such a name and reputation
among the boys, that their fathers would often visit the
school that they might see young Cicero, and might be
able to say that they themselves had witnessed the quickness and readiness in learning for which he was renowned.
And the more rude among them used to be angry with their
children, to see them, as they walked together, receiving
Cicero with respect into the middle place. And being, as
Plato would have the scholar-like and philosophical temper,
eager for every kind of learning, and indisposed to no description of knowledge or instruction, he showed, however,
a more peculiar propensity to poetry; and there is a poem
now extant made by him when a boy, in tetrameter verse,
called Pontius Glaucus. And afterwards, when he applied
himself more curiously to these accomplishments, he had
the name of being not only the best orator, but also the best
poet of Rome. And the glory of his rhetoric still remains,
notwithstanding the many new modes in speaking since his
time; but his verses are forgotten and out of all repute, so
many ingenious poets have followed him.

Leaving his juvenile studies, he became an auditor of
Philo the Academic, whom the Romans, above all the other
scholars of Clitomachus, admired for his eloquence and
loved for his character. He also sought the company of the
Mucii, who were eminent statesmen and leaders in the senate, and acquired from them a knowledge of the laws. For
some short time he served in arms under Sylla, in the Marsian war. But perceiving the commonwealth running into
factions, and from faction all things tending to an absolute
monarchy, he betook himself to a retired and contemplative
life, and conversing with the learned Greeks, devoted him-

self to study, till Sylla had obtained the government, and the commonwealth was in some kind of settlement.

At this time, Chrysogonus, Sylla's emancipated slave, having laid an information about an estate belonging to one who was said to have been put to death by proscription, had bought it himself for two thousand drachmas. And when Roscius, the son and heir of the dead, complained, and demonstrated the estate to be worth two hundred and fifty talents, Sylla took it angrily to have his actions questioned, and preferred a process against Roscius for the murder of his father, Chrysogonus managing the evidence. None of the advocates durst assist him, but, fearing the cruelty of Sylla, avoided the cause. The young man, being thus deserted, came for refuge to Cicero. Cicero's friends encouraged him, saying he was not likely ever to have a fairer and more honourable introduction to public life; he therefore undertook the defence, carried the cause, and got much renown for it.

But fearing Sylla, he travelled into Greece, and gave it out that he did so for the benefit of his health. And indeed he was lean and meagre, and had such a weakness in his stomach that he could take nothing but a spare and thin diet, and that not till late in the evening. His voice was loud and good, but so harsh and unmanaged that in vehemence and heat of speaking he always raised it to so high a tone that there seemed to be reason to fear about his health.

When he came to Athens he was a hearer of Antiochus of Ascalon, with whose fluency and elegance of diction he was much taken, although he did not approve of his innovations in doctrine. For Antiochus had now fallen off from the New Academy, as they call it, and forsaken the sect of Carneades, whether that he was moved by the argument of manifestness and the senses, or, as some say, had been led by feelings of rivalry and opposition to the followers of Clitomachus and Philo to change his opinions, and in most things to embrace the doctrine of the Stoics. But Cicero rather affected and adhered to the doctrines of the

New Academy; and purposed with himself, if he should be disappointed of any employment in the commonwealth, to retire hither from pleading and political affairs, and to pass his life with quiet in the study of philosophy.

But after he had received the news of Sylla's death, and his body, strengthened again by exercise, was come to a vigorous habit, his voice managed and rendered sweet and full to the ear and pretty well brought into keeping with his general constitution, his friends at Rome earnestly soliciting him by letters, and Antiochus also urging him to return to public affairs, he again prepared for use his orator's instrument of rhetoric, and summoned into action his political faculties, diligently exercising himself in declamations and attending the most celebrated rhetoricians of the time. He sailed from Athens for Asia and Rhodes. Amongst the Asian masters, he conversed with Xenocles of Adramyttium, Dionysius of Magnesia, and Menippus of Caria; at Rhodes, he studied oratory with Apollonius, the son of Molon, and philosophy with Posidonius. Apollonius, we are told, not understanding Latin, requested Cicero to declaim in Greek. He complied willingly, thinking that his faults would thus be better pointed out to him. And after he finished, all his other hearers were astonished, and contended who should praise him most, but Apollonius, who had shown no signs of excitement whilst he was hearing him, so also now, when it was over, sate musing for some considerable time, without any remark. And when Cicero was discomposed at this, he said, "You have my praise and admiration, Cicero, and Greece my pity and commiseration, since those arts and that eloquence which are the only glories that remain to her, will now be transferred by you to Rome."

And now when Cicero, full of expectation, was again bent upon political affairs, a certain oracle blunted the edge of his inclination; for consulting the god of Delphi how he should attain most glory, the Pythoness answered, by making his own genius and not the opinion of the people the guide of his life; and therefore at first he passed his time in Rome cautiously, and was very backward in pre-

tending to public offices, so that he was at that time in little esteem, and had got the names, so readily given by low
and ignorant people in Rome, of Greek and Scholar. But
when his own desire of fame and the eagerness of his
father and relations had made him take in earnest to pleading, he made no slow or gentle advance to the first place,
but shone out in full lustre at once, and far surpassed all
the advocates of the bar. At first, it is said, he, as well as
Demosthenes, was defective in his delivery, and on that
account paid much attention to the instructions, sometimes
of Roscius the comedian, and sometimes of Aesop the
tragedian. They tell of this Aesop, that whilst he was representing on the theatre Atreus deliberating the revenge
of Thyestes, he was so transported beyond himself in the
heat of action, that he struck with his sceptre one of the
servants, who was running across the stage, so violently
that he laid him dead upon the place. And such afterwards
was Cicero's delivery that it did not a little contribute to
render his eloquence persuasive. He used to ridicule loud
speakers, saying that they shouted because they could not
speak, like lame men who get on horseback because they
cannot walk. And his readiness and address in sarcasm,
and generally in witty sayings, was thought to suit a pleader
very well, and to be highly attractive, but his using it to
excess offended many, and gave him the repute of ill-
nature.

He was appointed quaestor in a great scarcity of corn
and had Sicily for his province, where though at first he
displeased many, by compelling them to send in their provisions to Rome, yet after they had had experience of his
care, justice, and clemency, they honoured him more than
ever they did any of their governors before. It happened,
also, that some young Romans of good and noble families,
charged with neglect of discipline and misconduct in military service, were brought before the praetor in Sicily.
Cicero undertook their defence, which he conducted admirably, and got them acquitted. So returning to Rome
with a great opinion of himself for these things, a ludicrous
incident befell him, as he tells us himself. Meeting an emi-

nent citizen in Campania, whom he accounted his friend, he asked him what the Romans said and thought of his actions, as if the whole city had been filled with the glory of what he had done. His friend asked him in reply, "Where is it you have been, Cicero?" This for the time utterly mortified and cast him down to perceive that the report of his actions had sunk into the city of Rome as into an immense ocean, without any visible effect or result in reputation. And afterwards considering with himself that the glory he contended for was an infinite thing, and that there was no fixed end nor measure in its pursuit, he abated much of his ambitious thoughts. Nevertheless, he was always excessively pleased with his own praise, and continued to the very last to be passionately fond of glory; which often interfered with the prosecution of his wisest resolutions.

On beginning to apply himself more resolutely to public business, he remarked it as an unreasonable and absurd thing that artificers, using vessels and instruments inanimate, should know the name, place, and use of every one of them, and yet the statesman, whose instruments for carrying out public measures are men, should be negligent and careless in the knowledge of persons. And so he not only acquainted himself with the names, but also knew the particular place where every one of the more eminent citizens dwelt, what lands he possessed, the friends he made use of, and those that were of his neighbourhood, and when he travelled on any road in Italy, he could readily name and show the estates and seats of his friends and acquaintance. Having so small an estate, though a sufficient competency for his own expenses, it was much wondered at that he took neither fees nor gifts from his clients, and more especially that he did not do so when he undertook the prosecution of Verres. This Verres, who had been praetor of Sicily, and stood charged by the Sicilians of many evil practices during his government there, Cicero succeeded in getting condemned, not by speaking, but in a manner by holding his tongue. For the praetors, favouring Verres, had deferred the trial by several adjournments to the last day, in which it was evident there could not be sufficient time for the advocates to be heard, and the cause brought to an issue. Cicero, therefore, came forward, and said there was no need of speeches; and after producing and examining witnesses, he required the judges to proceed to sentence. However, many witty sayings are on record, as having been used by Cicero on the occasion. When a man named Caecilius, one of the freed slaves, who was said to be given to Jewish practices, would have put by the Sicilians, and undertaken the prosecution of Verres himself, Cicero asked, "What has a Jew to do with swine?" *verres* being the Roman word for a boar. And when Verres began to reproach Cicero with effeminate living, "You ought," replied he, "to use this language at home, to your sons"; Verres having a son who had fallen into disgraceful courses. Hortensius the orator, not daring directly to undertake the defence of Verres, was yet persuaded to appear for him at the laying on of the fine, and received an ivory sphinx for his reward; and when Cicero in some passage of the speech, obliquely reflected on him, and Hortensius told him he was not skilful in solving riddles, "No," said Cicero, "and yet you have the sphinx in your house!"

Verres was thus convicted; though Cicero, who set the fine at seventy-five myriads, lay under the suspicion of being corrupted by bribery to lessen the sum. But the Sicilians, in testimony of their gratitude, came and brought him all sorts of presents from the island, when he was aedile; of which he made no private profit himself, but used their generosity only to reduce the public price of provisions.

He had a very pleasant seat at Arpi, he had also a farm near Naples, and another about Pompeii, but neither of any great value. The portion of his wife, Terentia, amounted to ten myriads, and he had a bequest valued at nine myriads of denarii; upon these he lived in a liberal but temperate style with the learned Greeks and Romans that were his familiars. He rarely, if at any time, sat down to meat till sunset, and that not so much on account of business, as for his health and the weakness of his stomach. He was otherwise in the care of his body nice and delicate, appointing himself, for example, a set number of walks and rubbings. And after this manner managing the habit of his body, he brought it in time to be healthful, and capable of supporting many great fatigues and trials. His father's house he made over to his brother, living himself near the Palatine hill, that he might not give the trouble of long journeys to those that made suit to him. And, indeed, there were not fewer daily appearing at his door, to do their court to him, than there were that came to Crassus for his riches, or to Pompey for his power amongst the soldiers, these being at that time the two men of the greatest repute and influence in Rome. Nay, even Pompey himself used to pay court to Cicero, and Cicero's public actions did much to establish Pompey's authority and reputation in the state.

Numerous distinguished competitors stood with him for the praetor's office; but he was chosen before them all, and managed the decision of causes with justice and integrity. It is related that Licinius Macer, a man himself of great power in the city, and supported also by the assistance of Crassus, was accused before him of extortion, and that, in confidence on his own interest and the diligence of his friends, whilst the judges were debating about the sentence, he went to his house, where hastily trimming his hair and putting on a clean gown as already acquitted, he was setting off again to go to the Forum; but at his hall door meeting Crassus, who told him that he was condemned by all the votes, he went in again, threw himself upon his bed, and died immediately. This verdict was considered very creditable to Cicero, as showing his careful management of the courts of justice. On another occasion, Vatinius, a man of rude manners and often insolent in court to the magistrates, who had large swellings on his neck, came before his tribunal and made some request, and on Cicero's desiring further time to consider it, told him that he himself would have made no question about it had he been praetor. Cicero, turning quickly upon him, answered, "But I, you see, have not the neck that you have."

When there were but two or three days remaining in his office, Manilius was brought before him, and charged with peculation. Manilius had the good opinion and favour of the common people, and was thought to be prosecuted only for Pompey's sake, whose particular friend he was. And therefore, when he asked a space of time before his trial, and Cicero allowed him but one day, and that the next only, the common people grew highly offended, because it had been the custom of the praetors to allow ten days at least to the accused; and the tribunes of the people, having called him before the people and accused him, he, desiring to be heard, said, that as he had always treated the accused with equity and humanity, as far as the law allowed, so he thought it hard to deny the same to Manilius, and that he had studiously appointed that day of which alone, as praetor, he was master, and that it was not the part of those that were desirous to help him to cast the judgment of his cause upon another praetor. These things being said made a wonderful change in the people, and commending him much for it they desired that he himself would undertake the defence of Manilius; which he willingly consented to, and that principally for the sake of Pompey, who was absent. And, accordingly, taking his place before the people again, he delivered a bold invective upon the oligarchical party and on those who were jealous of Pompey.

Yet he was preferred to the consulship no less by the nobles than the common people, for the good of the city; and both parties jointly assisted his promotion, upon the following reasons. The change of government made by Sylla, which at first seemed a senseless one, by time and usage had now come to be considered by the people no unsatisfactory settlement. But there were some that endeavoured to alter and subvert the whole present state of affairs, not from any good motives, but for their own private gain; and Pompey being at this time employed in the wars with the kings of Pontus and Armenia, there was no sufficient force at Rome to suppress any attempts at a revolution. These people had for their head a man of bold, daring, and restless character, Lucius Catiline, who was accused, besides other great offences, of deflowering his virgin daughter, and killing his own brother; for which latter crime, fearing to be prosecuted at law, he persuaded Sylla to set him down, as though he were yet alive, amongst those that were to be put to death by proscription. This man the profligate citizens choosing for their captain, gave faith to one another, amongst other pledges, by sacrificing a man, and eating of his flesh; and a great part of the young men of the city were corrupted by him, he providing for every one pleasures, drink, and women, and profusely supplying the expense of these debauches. Etruria, moreover, had all been excited to revolt, as well as a great part of Gaul within the Alps. But Rome itself was in the most dangerous inclination to change on account of the unequal distribution of wealth and property, those of highest rank and greatest spirit having impoverished themselves by shows, entertainments, ambition of offices, and sumptuous buildings, and the riches of the city having thus fallen into the hands of mean and low-born persons. So that there wanted but a slight impetus to set all in motion, it being in the power of every daring man to overturn a sickly commonwealth.

Catiline, however, being desirous of procuring a strong position to carry out his designs, stood for the consulship, and had great hopes of success, thinking he should be appointed with Caius Antonius as his colleague, who was a man fit to lead neither in a good cause nor in a bad one, but might be a valuable accession to another's power. These things the greatest part of the good and honest citizens apprehending, put Cicero upon standing for the consulship; whom the people readily receiving, Catiline was put by, so that he and Caius Antonius were chosen, although amongst the competitors he was the only man descended from a father of the equestrian and not of the senatorial order.

Though the designs of Catiline were not yet publicly known, yet considerable preliminary troubles immediately followed upon Cicero's entrance upon the consulship. For, on the one side, those who were disqualified by the laws of Sylla from holding any public offices, being neither inconsiderable in power nor in number, came forward as candidates and caressed the people for them; speaking many things truly and justly against the tyranny of Sylla, only that they disturbed the government at an improper and unseasonable time; on the other hand, the tribunes of the people proposed laws to the same purpose, constituting a commission of ten persons, with unlimited powers, in whom as supreme governors should be vested the right of selling the public lands of all Italy and Syria and Pompey's new conquest, of judging and banishing whom they pleased, of planting colonies, of taking moneys out of the treasury, and of levying and paying what soldiers should be thought needful. And several of the nobility favoured this law, but especially Caius Antonius, Cicero's colleague, in hopes of being one of the ten. But what gave the greatest fear to the nobles was, that he was thought privy to the conspiracy of Catiline, and not to dislike it because of his great debts.

Cicero, endeavouring in the first place to provide a remedy against this danger, procured a decree assigning to him the province of Macedonia, he himself declining that of Gaul, which was offered to him. And this piece of favour so completely won over Antonius, that he was ready to second and respond to, like a hired player, whatever Cicero said for the good of the country. And now, having made his colleague thus tame and tractable, he could with greater courage attack the conspirators. And, therefore, in the senate, making an oration against the law of the ten commissioners, he so confounded those who proposed it, that they had nothing to reply. And when they again endeavoured, and, having prepared things beforehand, had called the consuls before the assembly of the people, Cicero, fearing nothing, went first out, and commanded the senate to follow him, and not only succeeded in throwing out the law, but so entirely overpowered the tribunes by his oratory, that they abandoned all thought of their other projects.

For Cicero, it may be said, was the one man, above all others who made the Romans feel how great a charm eloquence lends to what is good, and how invincible justice is, if it be well spoken; and that it is necessary for him who would dexterously govern a commonwealth, in action, always to prefer that which is honest before that which is popular, and in speaking, to free the right and useful measure from everything that may occasion offence. An incident occurred in the theatre, during his consulship, which showed what his speaking could do. For whereas formerly the knights of Rome were mingled in the theatre, with the common people, and took their places among them as it happened, Marcus Otho, when he was praetor, was the first who distinguished them from the other citizens and appointed them a proper seat, which they still enjoy as their special place in the theatre. This the common people took as an indignity done to them, and, therefore, when Otho appeared in the theatre they hissed him; the knights, on the contrary, received him with loud clapping. The people repeated and increased their hissing; the knights continued their clapping. Upon this, turning upon one another, they broke out into insulting words, so that the theatre was in great disorder. Cicero being informed of it, came himself to the theatre, and, summoning the people into the temple of Bellona, he so effectually chid and chastised them for it, that again returning into the theatre they received Otho with great applause, contending with the knights who should give him the greatest demonstrations of honour and respect.

The conspirators with Catiline, at first cowed and disheartened, began presently to take courage again. And assembling themselves together, they exhorted one another boldly to undertake the design before Pompey's return, who, as it was said, was now on his march with his forces for Rome. But the old soldiers of Sylla were Catiline's chief stimulus to action. They had been disbanded all about Italy, but the greatest number and the fiercest of them lay scattered among the cities of Etruria entertaining themselves with dreams of new plunder and rapine amongst the hoarded riches of Italy. These, having for their leader Manlius, who had served with distinction in the wars under Sylla, joined themselves to Catiline, and came to Rome to assist him with their suffrages at the election. For he again pretended to the consulship, having resolved to kill Cicero in a tumult at the elections. Also, the divine powers seemed to give intimation of the coming troubles, by earthquakes, thunderbolts, and strange appearances. Nor was human evidence wanting certain enough in itself, though not sufficient for the conviction of the noble and powerful Catiline. Therefore Cicero, deferring the day of election, summoned Catiline into the senate, and questioned him as to the charges made against him. Catiline, believing there were many in the senate desirous of change, and to give a specimen of himself to the conspirators present, returned an audacious answer, "What harm," said he, "when I see two bodies, the one lean and consumptive with a head, the other great and strong without one, if I put a head to that body which wants one?" This covert representation of the senate and the people excited yet greater apprehensions in Cicero. He put on armour, and was attended from his house by the noble citizens in a body; and a number of the young men went with him into the Plain. Here, designedly letting his tunic slip partly off from his shoulders, he showed his armour underneath, and discovered his danger to the spectators; who, being much moved at it, gathered round about him for his defence. At length, Catiline was by a general suffrage again put by, and Silanus and Murena chosen consuls.

Not long after this, Catiline's soldiers got together in a body in Etruria, and began to form themselves into companies, the day appointed for the design being near at hand. About midnight, some of the principal and most powerful citizens of Rome, Marcus Crassus, Marcus Marcellus, and Scipio Metellus went to Cicero's house, where, knocking at the gate, and calling up the porter, they commanded him to awake Cicero, and tell him they were there. The business was this: Crassus's porter after supper had de-

livered to him letters brought by an unknown person. Some
of them were directed to others, but one to Crassus, without a name; this only Crassus read, which informed him
that there was a great slaughter intended by Catiline, and
advised him to leave the city. The others he did not open,
but went with them immediately to Cicero, being affrighted
at the danger, and to free himself of the suspicion he lay
under for his familiarity with Catiline. Cicero, considering
the matter, summoned the senate at break of day. The letters he brought with him, and delivered them to those to
whom they were directed, commanding them to read them
publicly; they all alike contained an account of the conspiracy. And when Quintus Arrius a man of praetorian dignity, recounted to them how soldiers were collecting in
companies in Etruria, and Manlius stated to be in motion
with a large force, hovering about those cities, in expectation of intelligence from Rome, the senate made a decree
to place all in the hands of the consuls who should undertake the conduct of everything, and do their best to save
the state. This was not a common thing, but only done
by the senate in case of imminent danger.

After Cicero had received this power, he committed all
affairs outside to Quintus Metellus, but the management
of the city he kept in his own hands. Such a numerous attendance guarded him every day when he went abroad, that
the greatest part of the market-place was filled with his
train when he entered it. Catiline, impatient of further delay, resolved himself to break forth and go to Manlius, but
he commanded Marcius and Cethegus to take their swords,
and go early in the morning to Cicero's gates, as if only
intending to salute him, and then to fall upon him and slay
him. This a noble lady, Fulvia, coming by night, discovered
to Cicero, bidding him beware of Cethegus and Marcius.
They came by break of day and being denied entrance,
made an outcry and disturbance at the gates, which excited
all the more suspicion. But Cicero, going forth, summoned
the senate into the temple of Jupiter Stator, which stands
at the end of the Sacred Street, going up to the Palatine.
And when Catiline with others of his party also came, as

intending to make his defence, none of the senators would
sit by him, but all of them left the bench where he had
placed himself. And when he began to speak, they interrupted him with outcries. At length Cicero, standing up,
commanded him to leave the city, for since one governed
the commonwealth with words, the other with arms, it was
necessary there should be a wall betwixt them. Catiline,
therefore, immediately left the town, and three hundred
armed men; and assuming, as if he had been a magistrate,
the rods, axes, and military ensigns, he went to Manlius,
and having got together a body of near twenty thousand
men, with these he marched to the several cities, endeavouring to persuade or force them to revolt. So it being now
come to open war, Antonius was sent forth to fight him.

The remainder of those in the city whom he had corrupted, Cornelius Lentulus kept together and encouraged.
He had the surname Sura, and was a man of a noble family, but a dissolute liver, who for his debauchery was formerly turned out of the senate, and was now holding the office
of praetor for the second time, as the custom is with those
who desire to regain the dignity of senator. It is said that
he got the surname Sura upon this occasion; being quaestor
in the time of Sylla, he had lavished away and consumed a
great quantity of the public moneys, at which Sylla being
provoked, called him to give an account in the senate;
he appeared with great coolness and contempt, and said
he had no account to give, but they might take this, holding up the calf of his leg, as boys do at ball, when they
have missed. Upon which he was surnamed *Sura, sura* being
the Roman word for the calf of the leg. Being at another
time prosecuted at law, and having bribed some of the
judges, he escaped only by two votes and complained of
the needless expense he had gone to in paying for a second,
as one would have sufficed to acquit him. This man, such
in his own nature, and now inflamed by Catiline, false
prophets and fortune-tellers had also corrupted with vain
hopes, quoting to him fictitious verses and oracles, and
proving from the Sibylline prophecies that there were three
of the name Cornelius designed by fate to be monarchs of

Rome; two of whom, Cinna and Sylla, had already fulfilled the decree, and that divine fortune was now advancing with the gift of monarchy for the remaining third Cornelius; and that therefore he ought by all means to accept it, and not lose opportunity by delay, as Catiline had done.

Lentulus, therefore, designed no mean or trivial matter, for he had resolved to kill the whole senate, and as many other citizens as he could, to fire the city, and spare nobody, except only Pompey's children, intending to seize and keep them as pledges of his reconciliation with Pompey. For there was then a common and strong report that Pompey was on his way homeward from his great expedition. The night appointed for the design was one of the Saturnalia; swords, flax, and sulphur they carried and hid in the house of Cethegus; and providing one hundred men, and dividing the city into as many parts, they had allotted to every one singly his proper place, so that in a moment, many kindling the fire, the city might be in a flame all together. Others were appointed to stop up the aqueducts, and to kill those who should endeavour to carry water to put it out. Whilst these plans were preparing, it happened there were two ambassadors from the Allobroges staying in Rome; a nation at that time in a distressed condition, and very uneasy under the Roman government. These Lentulus and his party judging useful instruments to move and seduce Gaul to revolt, admitted into the conspiracy and they gave them letters to their own magistrates, and letters to Catiline; in those they promised liberty, in these they exhorted Catiline to set all slaves free, and to bring them along with him to Rome. They sent also to accompany them to Catiline, one Titus, a native of Croton, who was to carry those letters to him.

These counsels of inconsidering men, who conversed over wine and with women, Cicero watched with sober industry and forethought, and with most admirable sagacity, having several emissaries abroad, who observed and traced with him all that was done, and keeping also a secret correspondence with many who pretended to join in the conspiracy. He thus knew all the discourse which passed betwixt them and the strangers; and lying in wait for them by night, he took the Crotonian with his letters, the ambassadors of the Allobroges acting secretly in concert with him.

By break of day, he summoned the senate into the temple of Concord, where he read the letters and examined the informers. Junius Silanus further stated that several persons had heard Cethegus say that three consuls and four praetors were to be slain. Piso, also, a person of consular dignity, testified other matters of the like nature; and Caius Sulpicius, one of the praetors, being sent to Cethegus's house, found there a quantity of darts and of armour, and a still greater number of swords and daggers, all recently whetted. At length, the senate decreeing indemnity to the Crotonian upon his confession of the whole matter, Lentulus was convicted, abjured his office (for he was then praetor), and put off his robe edged with purple in the senate, changing it for another garment more agreeable to his present circumstances. He thereupon, with the rest of his confederates present, was committed to the charge of the praetors in free custody.

It being evening, and the common people in crowds expecting without, Cicero went forth to them, and told them what was done, and then, attended by them, went to the house of a friend and near neighbour; for his own was taken up by the women who were celebrating with secret rites the feast of the goddess whom the Romans call the Good, and the Greeks the Women's goddess. For a sacrifice is annually performed to her in the consul's house, either by his wife or mother, in the presence of the vestal virgins. And having got into his friend's house privately, a few only being present, he began to deliberate how he should treat these men. The severest, and the only punishment fit for such heinous crimes, he was somewhat shy and fearful of inflicting, as well from the clemency of his nature, as also lest he should be thought to exercise his authority too insolently, and to treat too harshly men of the noblest birth and most powerful friendships in the city; and yet, if he should use them more mildly, he had a dread-

ful prospect of danger from them. For there was no likelihood, if they suffered less than death, they would be reconciled, but rather, adding new rage to their former wickedness, they would rush into every kind of audacity, while
he himself, whose character for courage already did not
stand very high with the multitude, would be thought guilty
of the greatest cowardice and want of manliness.

Whilst Cicero was doubting what course to take, a por-
tent happened to the women in their sacrificing. For on the
altar, where the fire seemed wholly extinguished, a great
and bright flame issued forth from the ashes of the burnt
wood; at which others were affrighted, but the holy virgins
called to Terentia, Cicero's wife, and bade her haste to her
husband, and command him to execute what he had resolved for the good of his country, for the goddess had sent
a great light to the increase of his safety and glory. Terentia, therefore, as she was otherwise in her own nature
neither tender-hearted nor timorous, but a woman eager for
distinction (who, as Cicero himself says, would rather
thrust herself into his public affairs, than communicate her
domestic matters to him), told him these things, and excited him against the conspirators. So also did Quintus
his brother, and Publius Nigidius, one of his philosophical
friends, whom he often made use of in his greatest and
most weighty affairs of state.

The next day, a debate arising in the senate about the
punishment of the men, Silanus, being the first who was
asked his opinion, said it was fit they should be all sent to
the prison, and there suffer the utmost penalty. To him
all consented in order till it came to Caius Caesar, who was
afterwards dictator. He was then but a young man, and
only at the outset of his career, but had already directed
his hopes and policy to that course by which he afterwards
changed the Roman state into a monarchy. Of this others
foresaw nothing; but Cicero had seen reason for strong
suspicion, though without obtaining any sufficient means of
proof. And there were some indeed that said that he was
very near being discovered, and only just escaped him;
others are of opinion that Cicero voluntarily overlooked

and neglected the evidence against him, for fear of his friends and power; for it was very evident to everybody that if Caesar was to be accused with the conspirators, they were more likely to be saved with him, than he to be punished with them.

When, therefore, it came to Caesar's turn to give his opinion, he stood up and proposed that the conspirators should not be put to death, but their estates confiscated, and their persons confined in such cities in Italy as Cicero should approve, there to be kept in custody till Catiline was conquered. To this sentence, as it was the most moderate, and he that delivered it a most powerful speaker, Cicero himself gave no small weight, for he stood up and, turning the scale on either side, spoke in favour partly of the former, partly of Caesar's sentence. And all Cicero's friends, judging Caesar's sentence most expedient for Cicero, because he would incur the less blame if the conspirators were not put to death, chose rather the latter; so that Silanus, also changing his mind, retracted his opinion, and said he had not declared for capital, but only the utmost punishment, which to a Roman senator is imprisonment. The first man who spoke against Caesar's motion was Catulus Lutatius. Cato followed, and so vehemently urged in his speech the strong suspicion against Caesar himself, and so filled the senate with anger and resolution, that a decree was passed for the execution of the conspirators. But Caesar opposed the confiscation of their goods, not thinking it fair that those who rejected the mildest part of his sentence should avail themselves of the severest. And when many insisted upon it, he appealed to the tribunes, but they would do nothing; till Cicero himself yielding, remitted that part of the sentence.

After this, Cicero went out with the senate to the conspirators; they were not all together in one place, but the several praetors had them, some one, some another, in custody. And first he took Lentulus from the Palatine, and brought him by the Sacred Street, through the middle of the marketplace, a circle of the most eminent citizens encompassing and protecting him. The people, affrighted at what was doing, passed along in silence, especially the young men; as if, with fear and trembling, they were undergoing a rite of initiation into some ancient sacred mysteries of aristocratic power. Thus passing from the market-place, and coming to the gaol, he delivered Lentulus to the officer, and commanded him to execute him; and after him Cethegus, and so all the rest in order, he brought and delivered up to execution. And when he saw many of the conspirators in the market-place, still standing together in companies, ignorant of what was done, and waiting for the night, supposing the men were still alive and in a possibility of being rescued, he called out in a loud voice, and said, *"They did live";* for so the Romans, to avoid inauspicious language, name those that are dead.

It was now evening, when he returned from the market-place to his own house, the citizens no longer attending him with silence, nor in order, but receiving him, as he passed, with acclamations and applauses, and saluting him as the saviour and founder of his country. A bright light shone through the streets from the lamps and torches set up at the doors, and the women showed lights from the tops of the houses, to honour Cicero, and to behold him returning home with a splendid train of the most principal citizens; amongst whom were many who had conducted great wars, celebrated triumphs, and added to the possessions of the Roman empire, both by sea and land. These, as they passed along with him, acknowledged to one another, that though the Roman people were indebted to several officers and commanders of that age for riches, spoils, and power, yet to Cicero alone they owed the safety and security of all these, for delivering them from so great and imminent a danger. For though it might seem no wonderful thing to present the design, and punish the conspirators, yet to defeat the greatest of all conspiracies with so little disturbance, trouble, and commotion, was very extraordinary. For the greater part of those who had flocked in to Catiline, as soon as they heard the fate of Lentulus and Cethegus, left and forsook him, and he himself, with his remaining forces, joining battle with Antonius, was destroyed with his army.

And yet there were some who were very ready both to speak ill of Cicero, and to do him hurt for these actions; and they had for their leaders some of the magistrates of the ensuing year, as Caesar, who was one of the praetors, and Metellus and Bestia, the tribunes. These, entering upon their office some few days before Cicero's consulate expired, would not permit him to make any address to the people, but throwing the benches before the rostra, hindered his speaking, telling him he might, if he pleased, make the oath of withdrawal from office, and then come down again. Cicero, accordingly, accepting the conditions, came forward to make his withdrawal; and silence being made, he recited his oath, not in the usual, but in a new and peculiar form, namely, that he had saved his country and preserved the empire; the truth of which oath all the people confirmed with theirs. Caesar and the tribunes, all the more exasperated by this, endeavoured to create him further trouble, and for this purpose proposed a law for calling Pompey home with his army, to put an end to Cicero's usurpation. But it was a very great advantage for Cicero and the whole commonwealth that Cato was at that time one of the tribunes. For he, being of equal power with the rest and of greater reputation, could oppose their designs. He easily defeated their other projects, and in an oration to the people so highly extolled Cicero's consulate, that the greatest honours were decreed him, and he was publicly declared the Father of his Country, which title he seems to have obtained, the first man who did so, when Cato gave it to him in this address to the people.

At this time, therefore, his authority was very great in the city; but he created himself much envy, and offended very many, not by any evil action, but because he was always lauding and magnifying himself. For neither senate, nor assembly of the people, nor court of judicature could meet, in which he was not heard to talk of Catiline and Lentulus. Indeed, he also filled his books and writings

with his own praises, to such an excess as to render a
style, in itself most pleasant and delightful, nauseous and
irksome to his hearers; this ungrateful humour like a disease, always cleaving to him. Nevertheless, though he was
intemperately fond of his own glory, he was very free from
envying others, and was, on the contrary, most liberally
profuse in commending both the ancients and his contemporaries, as any one may see in his writings. And many
such sayings of his are also remembered; as that he called
Aristotle a river of flowing gold, and said of Plato's Dialogues, that if Jupiter were to speak, it would be in language like theirs. He used to call Theophrastus his special
luxury. And being asked which of Demosthenes's orations
he liked best, he answered, the longest. And yet some affected imitators of Demosthenes have complained of some
words that occur in one of his letters, to the effect that
Demosthenes sometimes falls asleep in his speeches; for-
getting the many high encomiums he continually passes
upon him, and the compliment he paid him when he named
the most elaborate of all his orations, those he wrote against
Antony, Philippics. And as for the eminent men of his
own time, either in eloquence or philosophy, there was not
one of them whom he did not, by writing or speaking fa-
vourably of him, render more illustrious. He obtained of
Caesar, when in power, the Roman citizenship for Cratippus, the Peripatetic, and got the court of Areopagus, by
public decree, to request his stay at Athens, for the instruction of their youth and the honour of their city. There are
letters extant from Cicero to Herodes, and others to his
son, in which he recommends the study of philosophy under
Cratippus. There is one in which he blames Gorgias, the
rhetorician, for enticing his son into luxury and drinking,
and, therefore, forbids him his company. And this, and
one other to Pelops, the Byzantine, are the only two of
his Greek epistles which seem to be written in anger. In
the first, he justly reflects on Gorgias, if he were what he
was thought to be, a dissolute and profligate character; but
in the other, he rather meanly expostulates and complains

with Pelops for neglecting to procure him a decree of certain honours from the Byzantines.

Another illustration of his love of praise is the way in which sometimes, to make his orations more striking, he neglected decorum and dignity. When Munatius, who had escaped conviction by his advocacy, immediately prosecuted his friend Sabinus, he said in the warmth of his resentment, "Do you suppose you were acquitted for your own merits, Munatius, and was it not that I so darkened the case, that the court could not see your guilt?" When from the rostra he had made a eulogy on Marcus Crassus, with much applause, and within a few days after again as publicly reproached him, Crassus called to him, and said, "Did not you yourself two days ago, in this same place, commend me?" "Yes," said Cicero, "I exercised my eloquence in declaiming upon a bad subject." At another time, Crassus had said that no one of his family had ever lived beyond sixty years of age, and afterwards denied it, and asked, "What should put it into my head to say so?" "It was to gain the people's favour," answered Cicero; "you knew how glad they would be to hear it." When Crassus expressed admiration of the Stoic doctrine, that *the good man is always rich*, "Do you not mean," said Cicero, "their doctrine that *all things belong to the wise?*" Crassus being generally accused of covetousness. One of Crassus's sons, who was thought so exceedingly like a man of the name of Axius as to throw some suspicion on his mother's honour, made a successful speech in the senate. Cicero, on being asked how he liked it, replied with the Greek words *Axios Crassou*.

When Crassus was about to go into Syria, he desired to leave Cicero rather his friend than his enemy, and, therefore, one day saluting him, told him he would come and sup with him, which the other as courteously received. Within a few days after, on some of Cicero's acquaintances interceding for Vatinius, as desirous of reconciliation and friendship, for he was then his enemy, "What," he replied, "does Vatinius also wish to come and sup with me?" Such was his way with Crassus. When Vatinius, who had swellings in his neck, was pleading a cause he called him the *tumid* orator; and having been told by some one that Vatinius was dead, on hearing, presently after, that he was alive, "May the rascal perish," said he, "for his news not being true."

Upon Caesar's bringing forward a law for the division of the lands in Campania amongst the soldiers, many in the senate opposed it; amongst the rest, Lucius Gellius, one of the oldest men in the house, said it should never pass whilst he lived. "Let us postpone it," said Cicero, "Gellius does not ask us to wait long." There was a man of the name of Octavius, suspected to be of African descent. He once said, when Cicero was pleading, that he could not hear him; "Yet there are holes," said Cicero, "in your ears." When Metellus Nepos told him that he had ruined more as a witness than he had saved as an advocate, "I admit," said Cicero, "that I have more truth than eloquence." To a young man who was suspected of having given a poisoned cake to his father, and who talked largely of the invectives he meant to deliver against Cicero, "Better these," replied he, "than your cakes." Publius Sextius, having amongst others retained Cicero as his advocate in a certain cause, was yet desirous to say all for himself, and would not allow anybody to speak for him; when he was about to receive his acquittal from the judges, and the ballots were passing, Cicero called to him, "Make haste, Sextius, and use your time; to-morrow you will be nobody." He cited Publius Cotta to bear testimony in a certain cause, one who affected to be thought a lawyer, though ignorant and unlearned; to whom, when he had said, "I know nothing of the matter," he answered "You think, perhaps, we ask you about a point of law." To Metellus Nepos, who, in a dispute between them, repeated several times, "Who was your father, Cicero?" he replied, "Your mother has made the answer to such a question in your case more difficult"; Nepos's mother having been of ill-repute. The son, also, was of a giddy, uncertain temper. At one time, he suddenly threw up his office of tribune, and sailed off into Syria to Pompey; and immediately after, with as little reason, came back again. He gave his tutor, Philagrus, a funeral with more than necessary attention, and then set up the stone figure of a crow over his tomb. "This," said Cicero, "is really appropriate; as he did not teach you to speak, but to fly about." When Marcus Appius, in the opening of some speech in a court of justice said that his friend had desired him to employ industry, eloquence, and fidelity in that cause, Cicero answered, "And how have you had the heart not to accede to any one of his requests?"

To use this sharp raillery against opponents and antagonists in judicial pleading seems allowable rhetoric. But he excited much ill-feeling by his readiness to attack any one for the sake of a jest. A few anecdotes of this kind may be added. Marcus Aquinius, who had two sons-in-law in exile, received from him the name of King Adrastus. Lucius Cotta, an intemperate lover of wine, was censor when Cicero stood for the consulship. Cicero, being thirsty at the election, his friends stood round about him while he was drinking. "You have reason to be afraid," he said, "lest the censor should be angry with me for drinking water." Meeting one day Voconius with his three very ugly daughters, he quoted the verse—

"He reared a race without Apollo's leave."

When Marcus Gellius, who was reputed the son of a slave, had read several letters in the senate with a very shrill and loud voice, "Wonder not," said Cicero, "he comes of the criers." When Faustus Sylla, the son of Sylla the dictator, who had, during his dictatorship, by public bills proscribed and condemned so many citizens, had so far wasted his estate, and got into debt, that he was forced to publish his bills of sale, Cicero told him that he liked these bills much better than those of his father. By this habit he made himself odious with many people.

But Clodius's faction conspired against him upon the following occasion. Clodius was a member of a noble family, in the flower of his youth, and of a bold and resolute temper. He, being in love with Pompeia, Caesar's wife, got privately into his house in the dress and attire of a music-girl; the women being at that time offering there the sacrifice which must not be seen by men, and there was no man present. Clodius, being a youth and beardless, hoped to get to Pompeia among the women without being taken notice of. But coming into a great house by night, he missed his way in the passages, and a servant belonging to Aurelia, Caesar's mother, spying him wandering up and down, inquired his name. Thus being necessitated to speak, he told her he was seeking for one of Pompeia's maids, Abra by name; and she, perceiving it not to be a woman's voice, shrieked out, and called in the women; who shutting the gates, and searching every place, at length found Clodius hidden in the chamber of the maid with whom he had come in. This matter being much talked about, Caesar put away his wife, Pompeia, and Clodius was prosecuted for profaning the holy rites.

Cicero was at this time his friend, for he had been useful to him in the conspiracy of Catiline, as one of his forwardest assistants and protectors. But when Clodius rested his defence upon this point, that he was not then at Rome, but at a distance in the country, Cicero testified that he had come to his house that day, and conversed with him on several matters; which thing was indeed true, although Cicero was thought to testify it not so much for the truth's sake as to preserve his quiet with Terentia his wife. For she bore a grudge against Clodius on account of his sister Clodia's wishing, as it was alleged, to marry Cicero, and having employed for this purpose the intervention of Tullus, a very intimate friend of Cicero's; and his frequent visits to Clodia, who lived in their neighbourhood, and the attentions he paid to her had excited Terentia's suspicions, and, being a woman of a violent temper and having the ascendant over Cicero, she urged him on to taking a part against Clodius, and delivering his testimony. Many other good and honest citizens also gave evidence against him, for perjuries, disorders, bribing the people, and debauching women. Lucullus proved, by his women-servants, that he had debauched his youngest sister when she was Lucullus's wife; and there was a general belief that he had done the same with his two other sisters, Tertia, whom Marcus Rex, and Clodia, whom Metellus Celer had married; the latter of whom was called Quadrantia, because one of her lovers had deceived her with a purse of small copper money instead of silver, the smallest copper coin being called a *quadrant*. Upon this sister's account, in particular, Clodius's character was attacked. Notwithstanding all this, when the common people united against the accusers and witnesses and the whole party, the judges were affrighted, and a guard was placed about them for their defence; and most of them wrote their sentences on the tablets in such a way that they could not well be read. It was decided, however, that there was a majority for his acquittal, and bribery was reported to have been employed; in reference to which Catulus remarked, when he next met the judges, "You were very right to ask for a guard, to prevent your money being taken from you." And when Clodius upbraided Cicero that the judges had not believed his testimony, "Yes," said he, "five-and-twenty of them trusted me and condemned you, and the other thirty did not trust you, for they did not acquit you till they had got your money."

Caesar, though cited, did not give his testimony against Clodius, and declared himself not convinced of his wife's adultery, but that he had put her away because it was fit that Caesar's house should not be only free of the evil fact, but of the fame too.

Clodius, having escaped this danger, and having got himself chosen one of the tribunes, immediately attacked Cicero, heaping up all matters and inciting all persons against him. The common people he gained over with popular laws; to each of the consuls he decreed large provinces, to Piso, Macedonia, and to Gabinius, Syria; he made a strong party among the indigent citizens, to support him in his proceedings, and had always a body of armed slaves about him. Of the three men then in greatest power, Crassus was Cicero's open enemy, Pompey indifferently made advances to both, and Caesar was going with an army into Gaul. To him,

though not his friend (what had occurred in the time of the
conspiracy having created suspicions between them), Cicero
applied, requesting an appointment as one of his lieutenants
in the province. Caesar accepted him, and Clodius, perceiving that Cicero would thus escape his tribunician authority,
professed to be inclinable to a reconciliation, laid the greatest fault upon Terentia, made always a favourable mention
of him, and addressed him with kind expressions, as one
who felt no hatred or ill-will, but who merely wished to
urge his complaints in a moderate and friendly way. By
these artifices, he so freed Cicero of all his fears, that he resigned his appointment to Caesar, and betook himself again
to political affairs. At which Caesar, being exasperated,
joined the party of Clodius against him, and wholly alien-
ated Pompey from him; he also himself declared in a public
assembly of the people, that he did not think Lentulus and
Cethegus, with their accomplices, were fairly and legally put
to death without being brought to trial. And this, indeed,
was the crime charged upon Cicero, and in this impeachment
he was summoned to answer. And so, as an accused man,
and in danger for the result, he changed his dress, and went
round with his hair untrimmed, in the attire of a suppliant,
to beg the people's grace. But Clodius met him in every
corner, having a band of abusive and daring fellows about
him, who derided Cicero for his change of dress and his
humiliation, and often, by throwing dirt and stones at him,
interrupted his supplication to the people.

However, first of all, almost the whole equestrian order
changed their dress with him, and no less than twenty thousand young gentlemen followed him with their hair untrimmed, and supplicating with him to the people. And then
the senate met, to pass a decree that the people should
change their dress as in time of public sorrow. But the consuls opposing it, and Clodius with armed men besetting the
senate-house, many of the senators ran out, crying out and
tearing their clothes. But this sight moved neither shame nor
pity; Cicero must either fly or determine it by the sword
with Clodius. He entreated Pompey to aid him, who was on
purpose gone out of the way, and was staying at his coun-

try-house in the Alban hills; and first he sent his son-in-law Piso to intercede with him, and afterwards set out to go himself. Of which Pompey being informed, would not stay to see him, being ashamed at the remembrance of the many conflicts in the commonwealth which Cicero had undergone in his behalf, and how much of his policy he had directed for his advantage. But being now Caesar's son-in-law, at his instance he had set aside all former kindness, and, slipping out at another door, avoided the interview. Thus being forsaken by Pompey, and left alone to himself, he fled to the consuls. Gabinius was rough with him, as usual, but Piso spoke more courteously, desiring him to yield and give place for a while to the fury of Clodius, and to await a change of times, and to be now, as before, his country's saviour from the peril of these troubles and commotions which Clodius was exciting.

Cicero, receiving this answer, consulted with his friends. Lucullus advised him to stay, as being sure to prevail at last; others to fly, because the people would soon desire him again, when they should have enough of the rage and madness of Clodius. This last Cicero approved. But first he took a statue of Minerva, which had been long set up and greatly honoured in his house, and carrying it to the capitol, there dedicated it, with the inscription, "To Minerva, Patroness of Rome." And receiving an escort from his friends, about the middle of the night he left the city and went by land through Lucania, intending to reach Sicily.

But as soon as it was publicly known that he was fled, Clodius proposed to the people a decree of exile, and by his own order interdicted him fire and water, prohibiting any within five hundred miles in Italy to receive him into their houses. Most people, out of respect for Cicero, paid no regard to this edict, offering him every attention, and escorting him on his way. But at Hipponium, a city of Lucania now called Vibo, one Vibius, a Sicilian by birth, who, amongst many other instances of Cicero's friendship, had been made head of the state engineers when he was consul, would not receive him into his house, sending him word he would appoint a place in the country for his reception.

Caius Vergilius, the praetor of Sicily, who had been on the most intimate terms with him, wrote to him to forbear coming into Sicily. At these things Cicero, being disheartened, went to Brundusium, whence putting forth with a prosperous wind, a contrary gale blowing from the sea carried him back to Italy the next day. He put again to sea, and having reached Dyrrachium, on his coming to shore there, it is reported that an earthquake and a convulsion in the sea happened at the same time, signs which the diviners said intimated that his exile would not be long, for these were prognostics of change. Although many visited him with respect, and the cities of Greece contended which should honour him most, he yet continued disheartened and disconsolate, like an unfortunate lover, often casting his looks back upon Italy; and, indeed, he was become so poor-spirited, so humiliated and dejected by his misfortunes, as none could have expected in a man who had devoted so much of his life to study and learning. And yet he often desired his friends not to call him orator, but philosopher, because he had made philosophy his business, and had only used rhetoric as an instrument for attaining his objects in public life. But the desire of glory has great power in washing the tinctures of philosophy out of the souls of men, and in imprinting the passions of the common people, by custom and conversation, in the minds of those that take a part in governing them, unless the politician be very careful so to engage in public affairs as to interest himself only in the affairs themselves, but not participate in the passions that are consequent to them.

Clodius, having thus driven away Cicero, fell to burning his farms and villas, and afterwards his city house, and built on the site of it a temple to Liberty. The rest of his property he exposed to sale by daily proclamation, but nobody came to buy. By these courses he became formidable to the noble citizens, and being followed by the commonalty, whom he had filled with insolence and licentiousness, he began at last to try his strength against Pompey, some of whose arrangements in the countries he conquered, he attacked. The disgrace of this made Pompey begin to reproach himself for his cowardice in deserting Cicero, and changing his mind, he now wholly set himself with his friends to contrive his return. And when Clodius opposed it, the senate made a vote that no public measure should be ratified or passed by them till Cicero was recalled. But when Lentulus was consul, the commotions grew so high upon this matter, that the tribunes were wounded in the Forum, and Quintus, Cicero's brother, was left as dead, lying unobserved amongst the slain. The people began to change in their feelings, and Annius Milo, one of their tribunes, was the first who took confidence to summon Clodius to trial for acts of violence. Many of the common people out of the neighbouring cities formed a party with Pompey, and he went with them, and drove Clodius out of the Forum, and summoned the people to pass their vote. And, it is said, the people never passed any suffrage more unanimously than this. The senate, also, striving to outdo the people, sent letters of thanks to those cities which had received Cicero with respect in his exile, and decreed that his house and his country-places, which Clodius had destroyed, should be rebuilt at the public charge.

Thus Cicero returned sixteen months after his exile, and the cities were so glad, and people so zealous to meet him, that what he boasted of afterwards, that Italy had brought him on her shoulders home to Rome, was rather less than the truth. And Crassus himself, who had been his enemy before his exile, went then voluntarily to meet him, and was reconciled, to please his son Publius, as he said, who was Cicero's affectionate admirer.

Cicero had not been long at Rome when, taking the opportunity of Clodius's absence, he went with a great company to the capitol, and there tore and defaced the tribunician tables, in which were recorded the acts done in the time of Clodius. And on Clodius calling him in question for this, he answered that he, being of the patrician order, had obtained the office of tribune against law, and therefore nothing done by him was valid. Cato was displeased at this, and opposed Cicero, not that he commended Clodius, but rather disapproved of his whole administration; yet, he contended, it was an irregular and violent course for the senate to vote the illegality of so many decrees and acts, including those of Cato's own government in Cyprus and at Byzantium. This occasioned a breach between Cato and Cicero, which, though it came not to open enmity, yet made a more reserved friendship between them.

After this, Milo killed Clodius, and, being arraigned for the murder, he procured Cicero as his advocate. The senate, fearing lest the questioning of so eminent and high-spirited a citizen as Milo might disturb the peace of the city, committed the superintendence of this and of the other trials to Pompey, who should undertake to maintain the security alike of the city and of the courts of justice. Pompey, therefore, went in the night, and occupying the high grounds about it, surrounded the Forum with soldiers. Milo, fearing lest Cicero, being disturbed by such an unusual sight, should conduct his cause the less successfully, persuaded him to come in a litter into the Forum, and there repose himself till the judges were set and the court filled. For Cicero, it seems, not only wanted courage in arms, but, in his speaking also, began with timidity, and in many cases scarcely left off trembling and shaking when he had got thoroughly into the current and the substance of his speech. Being to defend Licinius Murena against the prosecution of Cato, and being eager to outdo Hortensius, who had made his plea with great applause, he took so little rest that night, and was so disordered with thought and overwatching, that he spoke much worse than usual. And so now, on quitting his litter to commence the cause of Milo, at the sight of Pompey, posted as it were, and encamped with his troops above, and seeing arms shining round about the Forum, he was so confounded that he could hardly begin his speech for the trembling of his body and hesitance of his tongue; whereas Milo, meantime, was bold and intrepid in his demeanour, disdaining either to let his hair grow or to put on the mourning habit. And this, indeed, seems to have been one principal cause of his condemnation. Cicero, however, was thought not so much to have shown timidity for himself, as anxiety about his friend.

He was made one of the priests, whom the Romans call Augurs, in the room of Crassus the younger, dead in Parthia. Then he was appointed by lot to the province of Cilicia, and set sail thither with twelve thousand foot and two thousand six hundred horse. He had orders to bring back Cappadocia to its allegiance to Ariobarzanes, its king; which settlement he effected very completely without recourse to arms. And perceiving the Cilicians, by the great loss the Romans had suffered in Parthia, and the commotions in Syria, to have become disposed to attempt a revolt, by a gentle course of government he soothed them back into fidelity. He would accept none of the presents that were offered him by the kings; he remitted the charge of public entertainments, but daily at his own house received the ingenious and accomplished persons of the province, not sumptuously, but liberally. His house had no porter, nor was he ever found in bed by any man, but early in the morning, standing or walking before his door, he received those who came to offer their salutations. He is said never once to have ordered any of those under his command to be beaten with rods, or to have their garments rent. He never gave contumelious language in his anger, nor inflicted punishment with reproach. He detected an embezzlement, to a large amount, in the public money, and thus relieved the cities from their burdens, at the same time that he allowed those who made restitution to retain without further punishment their rights as citizens. He engaged too, in war, so far as to give a defeat to the banditti who infested Mount Amanus, for which he was saluted by his army Imperator. To Caecilius, the orator, who asked him to send him some panthers from Cilicia, to be exhibited on the theatre at Rome, he wrote, in commendation of his own actions, that there were no panthers in Cilicia, for they were all fled to Caria, in anger that in so general a peace they had become the sole objects of attack. On leaving his province, he touched at Rhodes, and tarried for some length of time at Athens, longing much to renew his old studies. He visited the eminent men of learning, and saw his former friends and companions; and after re-

ceiving in Greece the honours that were due to him, returned to the city, where everything was now just as it were
in a flame, breaking out into a civil war.

When the senate would have decreed him a triumph, he
told them he had rather, so differences were accommodated,
follow the triumphal chariot of Caesar. In private, he gave
advice to both, writing many letters to Caesar, and personally entreating Pompey; doing his best to soothe and
bring to reason both the one and the other. But when matters became incurable, and Caesar was approaching Rome,
and Pompey durst not abide it, but, with many honest citizens, left the city, Cicero as yet did not join in the flight,
and was reputed to adhere to Caesar. And it is very evident he was in his thoughts much divided, and wavered
painfully between both, for he writes in his epistles, "To
which side should I turn? Pompey has the fair and honourable plea for war; and Caesar, on the other hand, has
managed his affairs better, and is more able to secure himself and his friends. So that I know whom I should fly, not
whom I should fly to." But when Trebatius, one of Caesar's
friends, by letter signified to him that Caesar thought it
was his most desirable course to join his party, and partake
his hopes, but if he considered himself too old a man for
this, then he should retire into Greece, and stay quietly
there, out of the way of either party, Cicero, wondering
that Caesar had not written himself, gave an angry reply,
that he should not do anything unbecoming his past life.
Such is the account to be collected from his letters.

But as soon as Caesar was marched into Spain, he immediately sailed away to join Pompey. And he was welcomed by all but Cato; who, taking him privately, chid
him for coming to Pompey. As for himself, he said, it had
been indecent to forsake that part in the commonwealth
which he had chosen from the beginning; but Cicero might
have been more useful to his country and friends, if, remaining neuter, he had attended and used his influence
to moderate the result, instead of coming hither to make
himself, without reason or necessity, an enemy to Caesar,
and a partner in such great dangers.

By this language, partly, Cicero's feelings were altered, and partly, also, because Pompey made no great use of him. Although, indeed, he was himself the cause of it, by his not denying that he was sorry he had come, by his depreciating Pompey's resources, finding fault underhand with his counsels, and continually indulging in jests and sarcastic remarks on his fellow-soldiers. Though he went about in the camp with a gloomy and melancholy face himself, he was always trying to raise a laugh in others, whether they wished it or not. It may not be amiss to mention a few instances. To Domitius, on his preferring to a command one who was no soldier, and saying, in his defence, that he was a modest and prudent person, he replied, "Why did not you keep him for a tutor for your children?" On hearing Theophanes, the Lesbian, who was master of the engineers in the army, praised for the admirable way in which he had consoled the Rhodians for the loss of their fleet, "What a thing it is," he said, "to have a Greek in command!" When Caesar had been acting successfully, and in a manner blockading Pompey, Lentulus was saying it was reported that Caesar's friends were out of heart; "Because," said Cicero, "they do not wish Caesar well." To one Marcius, who had just come from Italy, and told them that there was a strong report at Rome that Pompey was blocked up, he said, "And you sailed hither to see it with your own eyes." To Nonius, encouraging them after a defeat to be of good hope, because there were seven eagles still left in Pompey's camp, "Good reason for encouragement," said Cicero, "if we were going to fight with jackdaws." Labienus insisted on some prophecies to the effect that Pompey would gain the victory; "Yes," said Cicero; "and the first step in the campaign has been losing our camp."

After the battle of Pharsalia was over, at which he was not present for want of health, and Pompey was fled, Cato, having considerable forces and a great fleet at Dyrrachium, would have had Cicero commander-in-chief, according to law and the precedence of his consular dignity. And on his refusing the command, and wholly declining to take part in their plans for continuing the war, he was in the greatest danger of being killed, young Pompey and his friends calling him traitor, and drawing their swords upon him; only that Cato interposed, and hardly rescued and brought him out of the camp.

Afterwards, arriving at Brundusium, he tarried there some time in expectation of Caesar, who was delayed by his affairs in Asia and Egypt. And when it was told him that he was arrived at Tarentum, and was coming thence by land to Brundusium, he hastened towards him, not altogether without hope, and yet in some fear of making experiment of the temper of an enemy and conqueror in the presence of many witnesses. But there was no necessity for him either to speak or do anything unworthy of himself; for Caesar, as soon as he saw him coming a good way before the rest of the company, came down to meet him, saluted him, and, leading the way, conversed with him alone for some furlongs. And from that time forward he continued to treat him with honour and respect, so that, when Cicero wrote an oration in praise of Cato, Caesar in writing an answer to it, took occasion to commend Cicero's own life and eloquence, comparing him to Pericles and Theramenes. Cicero's oration was called Cato; Caesar's, anti-Cato.

So also it is related that when Quintus Ligarius was prosecuted for having been in arms against Caesar, and Cicero had undertaken his defence, Caesar said to his friends, "Why might we not as well once more hear a speech from Cicero? Ligarius, there is no question, is a wicked man and an enemy." But when Cicero began to speak, he wonderfully moved him, and proceeded in his speech with such varied pathos, and such a charm of language, that the colour of Caesar's countenance often changed, and it was evident that all the passions of his soul were in commotion. At length, the orator touching upon the Pharsalian battle, he was so affected that his body trembled, and some of the papers he held dropped out of his hands. And thus he was overpowered, and acquitted Ligarius.

Henceforth, the commonwealth being changed into a

monarchy, Cicero withdrew himself from public affairs, and employed his leisure in instructing those young men that would, in philosophy; and by the near intercourse he thus had with some of the noblest and highest in rank, he again began to possess great influence in the city. The work and object to which he set himself was to compose and translate philosophical dialogues and to render logical and physical terms into the Roman idiom. For he it was, as it is said, who first or principally gave Latin names to *phantasia, syncatathesis, epokhe, catalepsis, atamon, ameres, kenon,* and other such technical terms, which, either by metaphors or other means of accommodation, he succeeded in making intelligible and expressible to the Romans. For his recreation, he exercised his dexterity in poetry, and when he was set to it would make five hundred verses in a night. He spent the greatest part of his time at his country-house near Tusculum. He wrote to his friends that he led the life of Laertes either jestingly, as his custom was, or rather from a feeling of ambition for public employment, which made him impatient under the present state of affairs. He rarely went to the city, unless to pay his court to Caesar. He was commonly the first amongst those who voted him honours, and sought out new terms of praise for himself and for his actions. As, for example, what he said of the statues of Pompey, which had been thrown down, and were afterwards by Caesar's orders set up again; that Caesar, by this act of humanity, had indeed set up Pompey's statues, but he had fixed and established his own.

He had a design, it is said, of writing the history of his country, combining with it much of that of Greece, and incorporating in it all the stories and legends of the past that he had collected. But his purposes were interfered with by various public and various private unhappy occurrences and misfortunes; for most of which he was himself in fault. For first of all, he put away his wife Terentia, by whom he had been neglected in the time of the war, and sent away destitute of necessaries for his journey; neither did he find her kind when he returned into Italy, for she did not join him at Brundusium, where he stayed a long time, nor would allow her young daughter, who undertook so long a journey, decent attendance, or the requisite expenses; besides, she left him a naked and empty house, and yet had involved him in many and great debts. These were alleged as the fairest reasons for the divorce. But Terentia, who denied them all, had the most unmistakable defence furnished her by her husband himself, who not long after married a young maiden for the love of her beauty, as Terentia upbraided him; or as Tiro, his emancipated slave, has written, for her riches, to discharge his debts. For the young woman was very rich, and Cicero had the custody of her estate, being left guardian in trust; and being indebted many myriads of money, he was persuaded by friends and relations to marry her, notwithstanding his disparity of age, and to use her money to satisfy his creditors. Antony, who mentions this marriage in his answer to the Philippics, reproaches him for putting away a wife with whom he had lived to old age; adding some happy strokes of sarcasm on Cicero's domestic, inactive, unsoldier-like habits. Not long after this marriage, his daughter died in childbed at Lentulus's house, to whom she had been married after the death of Piso, her former husband. The philosophers from all parts came to comfort Cicero; for his grief was so excessive, that he put away his new-married wife, because she seemed to be pleased at the death of Tullia. And thus stood Cicero's domestic affairs at this time.

He had no concern in the design that was now forming against Caesar, although, in general, he was Brutus's most principal confidant, and one who was as aggrieved at the present, and as desirous of the former state of public affairs, as any other whatsoever. But they feared his temper, as wanting courage, and his old age, in which the most daring dispositions are apt to be timorous.

As soon, therefore, as the act was committed by Brutus and Cassius, and the friends of Caesar were got together, so that there was fear the city would again be involved in a civil war, Antony, being consul, convened the senate, and made a short address recommending concord. And Cicero following with various remarks such as the occasion called for, persuaded the senate to imitate the Athenians, and decree an amnesty for what had been done in Caesar's case, and to bestow provinces on Brutus and Cassius. But neither of these things took effect. For as soon as the common people, of themselves inclined to pity, saw the dead body of Caesar borne through the market-place, and Antony showing his clothes filled with blood, and pierced through in every part with swords, enraged to a degree of frenzy, they made a search for the murderers, and with firebrands in their hands ran to their houses to burn them. They, however, being forewarned, avoided this danger; and expecting many more and greater to come, they left the city.

Antony on this was at once in exultation, and every one was in alarm with the prospect that he would make himself sole ruler, and Cicero in more alarm than any one. For Antony, seeing his influence reviving in the commonwealth and knowing how closely he was connected with Brutus, was ill-pleased to have him in the city. Besides, there had been some former jealousy between them, occasioned by the difference of their manners. Cicero, fearing the event, was inclined to go as lieutenant with Dolabella into Syria. But Hirtius and Pansa, consuls elect as successors of Antony, good men and lovers of Cicero, entreated him not to leave them, undertaking to put down Antony if he would stay in Rome. And he, neither distrusting wholly, nor trusting them, let Dolabella go without him, promising Hirtius that he would go and spend his summer at Athens, and return again when he entered upon his office. So he set out on his journey; but some delay occurring in his passage, new intelligence, as often happens, came suddenly from Rome, that Antony had made an astonishing change, and was doing all things and managing all public affairs at the will of the senate, and that there wanted nothing but his presence to bring things to a happy settlement. And therefore, blaming himself for his cowardice, he returned again to Rome, and was not deceived in his hopes at the beginning. For such multitudes flocked out to meet him, that the compliments and civilities which were paid him at the gates, and at his entrance into the city, took up almost one whole day's time.

On the morrow, Antony convened the senate, and summoned Cicero thither. He came not, but kept his bed, pretending to be ill with his journey; but the true reason seemed the fear of some design against him, upon a suspicion and intimation given him on his way to Rome. Antony, however, showed great offence at the affront, and sent soldiers, commanding them to bring him or burn his house; but many interceding and supplicating for him, he was contented to accept sureties. Ever after, when they met, they passed one another with silence, and continued on their guard, till Caesar, the younger, coming from Apollonia, entered on the first Caesar's inheritance, and was engaged in a dispute with Antony about two thousand five hundred myriads of money, which Antony detained from the estate.

Upon this, Philippus, who married the mother, and Marcellus, who married the sister of young Caesar, came with the young man to Cicero, and agreed with him that Cicero should give them the aid of his eloquence and political influence with the senate and people, and Caesar give Cicero the defence of his riches and arms. For the young man had already a great party of the soldiers of Caesar about him. And Cicero's readiness to join him was founded, it is said, on some yet stronger motives; for it seems, while Pompey and Caesar were yet alive, Cicero, in his sleep, had fancied himself engaged in calling some of the sons of the senators into the capitol, Jupiter being about, according to the dream, to declare one of them the chief ruler of Rome. The citizens, running up with curiosity, stood about the temple, and the youths, sitting in their purple-bordered robes, kept silence. On a sudden the doors opened, and the youths, arising one by one in order, passed round the god, who reviewed them all, and, to their sorrow, dismissed them; but when this one was passing by, the god stretched forth his right hand and said, "O ye Romans, this young man, when he shall be lord of Rome, shall put an end to all your civil wars." It is said that Cicero formed from his dream a distinct image of the youth, and retained it afterwards perfectly, but did not know who it was. The next day, going down into the Campus Martius, he met the boys returning from their gymnastic exercises, and the first was he, just as he had appeared to him in his dream. Being astonished at it, he asked him who were his parents. And it proved to be this young Caesar, whose father was a man of no great eminence, Octavius, and his mother, Attia, Caesar's sister's daughter; for which reason, Caesar, who had no children, made him by will the heir of his house and property. From that time, it is said that Cicero studiously noticed the youth whenever he met him, and he as kindly received the civility; and by fortune he happened to be born when Cicero was consul.

These were the reasons spoken of; but it was principally Cicero's hatred of Antony, and a temper unable to resist honour, which fastened him to Caesar, with the purpose of getting the support of Caesar's power for his own public designs. For the young man went so far in his court to him, that he called him Father; at which Brutus was so highly displeased, that, in his epistles to Atticus, he reflected on Cicero saying, it was manifest, by his courting Caesar for fear of Antony, he did not intend liberty to his country, but an indulgent master to himself. Notwithstanding, Brutus took Cicero's son, then studying philosophy at Athens, gave him a command, and employed him in various ways, with a good result. Cicero's own power at this time was at the greatest height in the city, and he did whatsoever he pleased; he completely overpowered and drove out Antony, and sent the two consuls, Hirtius and Pansa, with an army, to reduce him; and, on the other hand, persuaded the senate to allow Caesar the lictors and ensigns of a praetor, as though he were his country's defender. But after Antony was defeated in battle, and the consuls slain, the armies united, and ranged themselves with Caesar. And the senate, fearing the young man, and his extraordinary fortune, endeavoured, by honours and gifts, to call off the soldiers from him, and to lessen his power; professing there was no further need of arms now Antony was put to flight.

This giving Caesar an affright, he privately sends some

friends to entreat and persuade Cicero to procure the consular dignity for them both together; saying he should
manage the affairs as he pleased, should have the supreme
power, and govern the young man who was only desirous
of name and glory. And Caesar himself confessed that, in
fear of ruin, and in danger of being deserted, he had seasonably made use of Cicero's ambition, persuading him to
stand with him, and to accept the offer of his aid and interest for the consulship.

And now, more than at any other time, Cicero let himself be carried away and deceived, though an old man, by
the persuasion of a boy. He joined him in soliciting votes,
and procured the good-will of the senate, not without blame
at the time on the part of his friends; and he, too, soon
enough after, saw that he had ruined himself, and betrayed the liberty of his country. For the young man, once
established, and possessed of the office of consul, bade
Cicero farewell; and, reconciling himself to Antony and
Lepidus, joined his power with theirs, and divided the government, like a piece of property, with them. Thus united,
they made a schedule of above two hundred persons who
were to be put to death. But the greatest contention in all
their debates was on the question of Cicero's case. Antony
would come to no conditions, unless he should be the first
man to be killed. Lepidus held with Antony, and Caesar
opposed them both. They met secretly and by themselves,
for three days together, near the town of Bononia. The spot
was not far from the camp, with a river surrounding it.
Caesar, it is said, contended earnestly for Cicero the first
two days; but on the third day he yielded, and gave him up.
The terms of their mutual concessions were these: that
Caesar should desert Cicero, Lepidus his brother Paulus,
and Antony, Lucius Caesar, his uncle by his mother's side.
Thus they let their anger and fury take from them the sense
of humanity, and demonstrated that no beast is more savage than man when possessed with power answerable to
his rage.

Whilst these things were contriving, Cicero was with his
brother at his country-house near Tusculum; whence, hear-

ing of the proscriptions, they determined to pass to Astura, a villa of Cicero's near the sea, and to take shipping from thence for Macedonia to Brutus, of whose strength in that province news had already been heard. They travelled together in their separate litters, overwhelmed with sorrow; and often stopping on the way till their litters came together, condoled with one another. But Quintus was the more disheartened when he reflected on his want of means for his journey; for, as he said, he had brought nothing with him from home. And even Cicero himself had but a slender provision. It was judged, therefore, most expedient that Cicero should make what haste he could to fly, and Quintus return home to provide necessaries, and thus resolved, they mutually embraced, and parted with many tears.

Quintus, within a few days after, betrayed by his servants to those who came to search for him, was slain, together with his young son. But Cicero was carried to Astura, where finding a vessel, he immediately went on board her, and sailed as far as Circaeum with a prosperous gale; but when the pilots resolved immediately to set sail from thence, whether fearing the sea, or not wholly distrusting the faith of Caesar, he went on shore, and passed by land a hundred furlongs, as if he was going for Rome. But losing resolution and changing his mind, he again returned to the sea, and there spent the night in fearful and perplexed thoughts. Sometimes he resolved to go into Caesar's house privately, and there kill himself upon the altar of his household gods, to bring divine vengeance upon him; but the fear of torture put him off this course. And after passing through a variety of confused and uncertain counsels, at last he let his servants carry him by sea to Capitae, where he had a house, an agreeable place to retire to in the heat of summer, when the Etesian winds are so pleasant.

There was at that place a chapel of Apollo, not far from the seaside, from which a flight of crows rose with a great noise, and made towards Cicero's vessel, as it rowed to land, and lighting on both sides of the yard, some croaked, others pecked the ends of the ropes. This was looked upon by all as an ill-omen; and, therefore, Cicero went again ashore, and entering his house, lay down upon his bed to compose himself to rest. Many of the crows settled about the window, making a dismal cawing; but one of them alighted upon the bed where Cicero lay covered up, and with its bill by little and little pecked off the clothes from his face. His servants, seeing this, blamed themselves that they should stay to be spectators of their master's murder, and do nothing in his defence, whilst the brute creatures came to assist and take care of him in his undeserved affliction; and therefore, partly by entreaty, partly by force, they took him up, and carried him in his litter towards the seaside.

But in the meantime the assassins were come with a band of soldiers, Herennius, a centurion, and Popillius, a tribune, whom Cicero had formerly defended when prosecuted for the murder of his father. Finding the doors shut, they broke them open, and Cicero not appearing, and those within saying they knew not where he was, it is stated that a youth, who had been educated by Cicero in the liberal arts and sciences, an emancipated slave of his brother Quintus, Philologus by name, informed the tribune that the litter was on its way to the sea through the close and shady walks. The tribune, taking a few with him, ran to the place where he was to come out. And Cicero, perceiving Herennius running in the walks, commanded his servants to set down the litter; and stroking his chin, as he used to do, with his left hand, he looked steadfastly upon his murderers, his person covered with dust, his beard and hair untrimmed, and his face worn with his troubles. So that the greatest part of those that stood by covered their faces whilst Herennius slew him. And thus was he murdered, stretching forth his neck out of the litter, being now in his sixty-fourth year. Herennius cut off his head, and, by Antony's command, his hands also, by which his Philippics were written; for so Cicero styled those orations he wrote against Antony, and so they are called to this day.

When these members of Cicero were brought to Rome, Antony was holding an assembly for the choice of public officers; and when he heard it, and saw them, he cried out,

"Now let there be an end of our proscriptions." He commanded his head and hands to be fastened up over the rostra, where the orators spoke; a sight which the Roman people shuddered to behold, and they believed they saw there, not the face of Cicero, but the image of Antony's own soul. And yet amidst these actions he did justice in one thing, by delivering up Philologus to Pomponia, the wife of Quintus; who, having got his body into her power, besides other grievous punishments, made him cut off his own flesh by pieces, and roast and eat it; for so some writers have related. But Tiro, Cicero's emancipated slave, has not so much as mentioned the treachery of Philologus.

Some long time after, Caesar, I have been told, visiting one of his daughter's sons, found him with a book of Cicero's in his hand. The boy for fear endeavoured to hide it under his gown; which Caesar perceiving, took it from him, and, turning over a great part of the book standing, gave it him again, and said, "My child, this was a learned man, and a lover of his country." And immediately after he had vanquished Antony, being then consul, he made Cicero's son his colleague in the office; and under that consulship the senate took down all the statues of Antony, and abolished all the other honours that had been given him, and decreed that none of that family should thereafter bear the name of Marcus; and thus the final acts of the punishment of Antony were, by the divine powers, devolved upon the family of Cicero.

ANTONY

The grandfather of Antony was the famous pleader, whom Marius put to death for having taken part with Sylla. His father was Antony, surnamed of Crete, not very famous or distinguished in public life, but a worthy good man. Antony grew up a very beautiful youth, but by the worst of misfortunes, he fell into the acquaintance and friendship of Curio, a man abandoned to his pleasures, who, to make Antony's dependence upon him a matter of greater necessity, plunged him into a life of drinking and dissipation, and led him through a course of such extravagance that he ran, at that early age, into debt to the amount of two hundred and fifty talents. For this sum Curio became his surety; on hearing which, the elder Curio, his father, drove Antony out of his house. After this, for some short time he took part with Clodius, the most insolent and outrageous demagogue of the time, in his course of violence and disorder; but getting weary, before long, of his madness, and apprehensive of the powerful party forming against him, he left Italy and travelled into Greece, where he spent his time in military exercises and in the study of eloquence. He took most to what was called the Asiatic taste in speaking, which was then at its height, and was, in many ways, suitable to his ostentatious, vaunting temper, full of empty flourishes and unsteady efforts for glory.

He had a very good and noble appearance; his beard was well grown, his forehead large, and his nose aquiline, giving him altogether a bold, masculine look that reminded people of the faces of Hercules in paintings and sculptures.

It was, moreover, an ancient tradition, that the Antonys were descended from Hercules, by a son of his called Anton; and this opinion he thought to give credit to by the similarity of his person just mentioned, and also by the fashion of his dress. For, whenever he had to appear before large numbers, he wore his tunic girt low about the hips, a broadsword on his side, and over all a large coarse mantle. What might seem to some very insupportable, his vaunting, his raillery, his drinking in public, sitting down by the men as they were taking their food, and eating, as he stood, off the common soldiers' tables, made him the delight and pleasure of the army. In love affairs, also, he was very agreeable: he gained many friends by the assistance he gave them in theirs, and took other people's raillery upon his own with good-humour. And his generous ways, his open and lavish hand in gifts and favours to his friends and fellow-soldiers, did a great deal for him in his first advance to power, and after he had become great, long maintained his fortunes, when a thousand follies were hastening their overthrow. One instance of his liberality I must relate. He had ordered payment to one of his friends of twenty-five myriads of money or *decies*, as the Romans call it, and his steward wondering at the extravagance of the sum, laid all the silver in a heap, as he should pass by. Antony, seeing the heap, asked what it meant; his steward replied, "The money you have ordered to be given to your friend." So, perceiving the man's malice, said he, "I thought the *decies* had been much more; 'tis too little; let it be doubled." This, however, was at a later time.

When the Roman state finally broke up into two hostile factions, the aristocratical party joining Pompey, who was in the city, and the popular side seeking help from Caesar, who was at the head of an army in Gaul, Curio, the friend of Antony, having changed his party and devoted himself to Caesar, brought over Antony also to his service. And the influence which he gained with the people by his eloquence and by the money which was supplied by Caesar, enabled him to make Antony, first, tribune of the people, and then, augur. And Antony's accession to office was at once of the greatest advantage to Caesar.

So soon, then, as he had advanced and occupied Rome, and driven Pompey out of Italy, he proposed first to go against the legions that Pompey had in Spain, and then cross over and follow him with the fleet that should be prepared during his absence, in the meantime leaving the government of Rome to Lepidus, as praetor, and the command of the troops and of Italy to Antony, as tribune of the people. Antony was not long in getting the hearts of the soldiers, joining with them in their exercises, and for the most part living amongst them and making them presents to the utmost of his abilities; but with all others he was unpopular enough. He was too lazy to pay attention to the complaints of persons who were injured; he listened impatiently to petitions; and he had an ill name for familiarity with other people's wives. In short, the government of Caesar (which, so far as he was concerned himself, had the appearance of anything rather than a tyranny) got a bad repute through his friends. And of these friends, Antony, as he had the largest trust, and committed the greatest errors, was thought the most deeply in fault.

Dolabella, who was tribune, being a young man and eager for change, was now for bringing in a general measure for cancelling debts, and wanted Antony, who was his friend, and forward enough to promote any popular project, to take part with him in this step. Asinius and Trebellius were of the contrary opinion, and it so happened, at the same time, Antony was crossed by a terrible suspicion that Dolabella was too familiar with his wife; and in great trouble at this, he parted with her (she being his cousin, and daughter to Caius Antonius, colleague of Cicero), and, taking part with Asinius, came to open hostilities with Dolabella, who had seized on the forum, intending to pass his law by force. Antony, backed by a vote of the senate that Dolabella should be put down by force of arms, went down and attacked him, killing some of his, and losing some of his own men; and by this action lost

his favour with the commonalty, while with the better class
and with all well-conducted people his general course of
life made him, as Cicero says, absolutely odious, utter disgust being excited by his drinking bouts at all hours, his
wild expenses, his gross amours, the day spent in sleeping
or walking off his debauches, and the night in banquets
and at theatres, and in celebrating the nuptials of some
comedian or buffoon. It is related that, drinking all night at
the wedding of Hippias, the comedian, on the morning,
having to harangue the people, he came forward, over-
charged as he was, and vomited before them all, one of his
friends holding his gown for him. Sergius, the player, was
one of the friends who could do most with him; also
Cytheris, a woman of the same trade, whom he made much
of, and who, when he went his progress, accompanied him
in a litter, and had her equipage not in anything inferior
to his mother's; while every one, moreover, was scandalised
at the sight of the golden cups that he took with him, fitter
for the ornaments of a procession than the uses of a journey, at his having pavilions set up, and sumptuous morning
repasts laid out by river sides and in groves, at his having
chariots drawn by lions, and common women and singing
girls quartered upon the houses of serious fathers and
mothers of families. And it seemed very unreasonable that
Caesar, out of Italy, should lodge in the open field, and,
with great fatigue and danger, pursue the remainder of a
hazardous war, whilst others, by favour of his authority,
should insult the citizens with their impudent luxury.

All this appears to have aggravated party quarrels in
Rome, and to have encouraged the soldiers in acts of licence and rapacity. And, accordingly, when Caesar came
home, he acquitted Dolabella, and, being created the third
time consul, took not Antony, but Lepidus, for his colleague. Pompey's house being offered for sale, Antony
bought it, and when the price was demanded of him,
loudly complained. This, he tells us himself, and because
he thought his former services had not been recompensed
as they deserved, made him not follow Caesar with the

army into Libya. However, Caesar, by dealing gently with
his errors, seems to have succeeded in curing him of a good
deal of his folly and extravagance. He gave up his former
courses, and took a wife, Fulvia, the widow of Clodius
the demagogue, a woman not born for spinning or housewifery, nor one that could be content with ruling a private
husband, but prepared to govern a first magistrate, or give
orders to a commander-in-chief. So that Cleopatra had
great obligations to her for having taught Antony to be so
good a servant, he coming to her hands tame and broken
into entire obedience to the commands of a mistress. He
used to play all sorts of sportive, boyish tricks, to keep
Fulvia in good humour. As, for example, when Caesar,
after his victory in Spain, was on his return, Antony, among
the rest, went out to meet him; and, a rumour being spread
that Caesar was killed and the enemy marching into Italy,
he returned to Rome, and, disguising himself, came to her
by night muffled up as a servant that brought letters from
Antony. She, with great impatience, before she received
the letter, asks if Antony were well, and instead of an
answer he gives her the letter; and, as she was opening it,
took her about the neck and kissed her. This little story,
of many of the same nature, I give as a specimen.

There was nobody of any rank in Rome that did not go
some days' journey to meet Caesar on his return from
Spain; but Antony was the best received of any, admitted
to ride the whole journey with him in his carriage, while
behind came Brutus Albinus and Octavian, his niece's
son, who afterwards bore his name and reigned so long
over the Romans. Caesar being created, the fifth time, consul, without delay chose Antony for his colleague, but designing himself to give up his own consulate to Dolabella,
he acquainted the senate with his resolution. But Antony
opposed it with all his might, saying much that was bad
against Dolabella, and receiving the like language in return, till Caesar could bear with the indecency no longer,
and deferred the matter to another time. Afterwards, when
he came before the people to proclaim Dolabella, Antony

cried out that the auspices were unfavourable, so that at last Caesar, much to Dolabella's vexation, yielded and gave it up. And it is credible that Caesar was about as much disgusted with the one as the other. When some one was accusing them both to him, "It is not," said he, "these well-fed, long-haired men that I fear, but the pale and the hungry-looking"; meaning Brutus and Cassius, by whose conspiracy he afterwards fell.

And the fairest pretext for that conspiracy was furnished, without his meaning it, by Antony himself. The Romans were celebrating their festival, called the Lupercalia, when Caesar, in his triumphal habit, and seated above the rostra in the market-place, was a spectator of the sports. The custom is, that many young noblemen and of the magistracy, anointed with oil and having straps of hide in their hands, run about and strike, in sport, at every one they meet. Antony was running with the rest; but, omitting the old ceremony, twining a garland of bay round a diadem, he ran up to the rostra, and, being lifted up by his companions, would have put it upon the head of Caesar, as if by that ceremony he was declared king. Caesar seemingly refused, and drew aside to avoid it, and was applauded by the people with great shouts. Again Antony pressed it, and again he declined its acceptance. And so the dispute between them went on for some time, Antony's solicitations receiving but little encouragement from the shouts of a few friends, and Caesar's refusal being accompanied with the general applause of the people; a curious thing enough, that they should submit with patience to the fact, and yet at the same time dread the name as the destruction of their liberty. Caesar, very much discomposed at what had passed, got up from his seat, and, laying bare his neck, said he was ready to receive a stroke, if any one of them desired to give it. The crown was at last put on one of his statues, but was taken down by some of the tribunes, who were followed home by the people with shouts of applause. Caesar, however, resented it, and deposed them.

These passages gave great encouragement to Brutus and

Cassius, who, in making choice of trusty friends for such an enterprise, were thinking to engage Antony. The rest approved, except Trebonius, who told them that Antony and he had lodged together and travelled together in the last journey they took to meet Caesar, and that he had let fall several words, in a cautious way, on purpose to sound him; that Antony very well understood him, but did not encourage it; however, he had said nothing of it to Caesar, but had kept the secret faithfully. The conspirators then proposed that Antony should die with him, which Brutus would not consent to, insisting that an action undertaken in defence of right and the laws must be maintained unsullied, and pure of injustice. It was settled that Antony, whose bodily strength and high office made him formidable, should, at Caesar's entrance into the senate, when the deed was to be done, be amused outside by some of the party in a conversation about some pretended business.

So when all was proceeded with, according to their plan, and Caesar had fallen in the senate-house, Antony, at the first moment, took a servant's dress, and hid himself. But, understanding that the conspirators had assembled in the Capitol, and had no further design upon any one, he persuaded them to come down, giving them his son as a hostage. That night Cassius supped at Antony's house, and Brutus with Lepidus. Antony then convened the senate, and spoke in favour of an act of oblivion, and the appointment of Brutus and Cassius to provinces. These measures the senate passed; and resolved that all Caesar's acts should remain in force. Thus Antony went out of the senate with the highest possible reputation and esteem; for it was apparent that he had prevented a civil war, and had composed, in the wisest and most statesmanlike way, questions of the greatest difficulty and embarrassment. But these temperate counsels were soon swept away by the tide of popular applause, and the prospect, if Brutus were overthrown, of being without doubt the ruler-in-chief. As Caesar's body was conveying to the tomb, Antony, according to the custom, was making his funeral oration in the market-place, and perceiving the people to be infinitely affected with what he had said, he began to mingle with his praises language of commiseration, and horror at what had happened, and, as he was ending his speech, he took the underclothes of the dead, and held them up, showing them stains of blood and the holes of the many stabs, calling those that had done this act villains and bloody murderers. All which excited the people to such indignation, that they would not defer the funeral, but, making a pile of tables and forms in the very market-place, set fire to it; and every one, taking a brand, ran to the conspirators' houses, to attack them.

Upon this, Brutus and his whole party left the city, and Caesar's friends joined themselves to Antony. Calpurnia, Caesar's wife, lodged with him the best part of the property to the value of four thousand talents; he got also into his hands all Caesar's papers wherein were contained journals of all he had done, and draughts of what he designed to do, which Antony made good use of; for by this means he appointed what magistrates he pleased, brought whom he would into the senate, recalled some from exile, freed others out of prison, and all this as ordered so by Caesar. The Romans, in mockery, gave those who were thus benefited the name of Charonites, since, if put to prove their patents, they must have recourse to the papers of the dead. In short, Antony's behaviour in Rome was very absolute, he himself being consul and his two brothers in great place; Caius, the one, being praetor, and Lucius, the other, tribune of the people.

While matters went thus in Rome, the young Caesar, Caesar's niece's son, and by testament left his heir, arrived at Rome from Apollonia, where he was when his uncle was killed. The first thing he did was to visit Antony, as his father's friend. He spoke to him concerning the money that was in his hands, and reminded him of the legacy Caesar had made of seventy-five drachmas to every Roman citizen. Antony, at first, laughing at such discourse from so young a man, told him he wished he were in his health, and that he wanted good counsel and good friends to tell

him the burden of being executor to Caesar would sit very
uneasy upon his young shoulders. This was no answer to
him; and, when he persisted in demanding the property,
Antony went on treating him injuriously both in word and
deed, opposed him when he stood for the tribune's office,
and, when he was taking steps for the dedication of his
father's golden chair, as had been enacted, he threatened
to send him to prison if he did not give over soliciting the
people. This made the young Caesar apply himself to
Cicero, and all those that hated Antony; by them he was
recommended to the senate, while he himself courted the
people, and drew together the soldiers from their settle-
ments, till Antony got alarmed, and gave him a meeting in
the Capitol, where, after some words, they came to an accommodation.

They both met together with Lepidus in a small island,
where the conference lasted three days. The empire was
soon determined of, it being divided amongst them as if
it had been their paternal inheritance. That which gave
them all the trouble was to agree who should be put to
death, each of them desiring to destroy his enemies and
to save his friends. But, in the end, animosity to those they
hated carried the day against respect for relations and affection for friends; and Caesar sacrificed Cicero to Antony, Antony gave up his uncle Lucius Caesar, and Lepidus
received permission to murder his brother Paulus, or, as
others say, yielded his brother to them. I do not believe anything ever took place more truly savage or barbarous than
this composition, for, in this exchange of blood for blood,
they were equally guilty of the lives they surrendered and
of those they took; or, indeed, more guilty in the case of
their friends, for whose deaths they had not even the justification of hatred. To complete the reconciliation, the soldiery, coming about them, demanded that confirmation
should be given to it by some alliance of marriage; Caesar
should marry Clodia, the daughter of Fulvia, wife to Antony. This also being agreed to, three hundred persons were
put to death by proscription. Antony gave orders to those

that were to kill Cicero to cut off his head and right hand,
with which he had written his invectives against him; and,
when they were brought before him, he regarded them joyfully, actually bursting out more than once into laughter,
and, when he had satiated himself with the sight of them,
ordered them to be hung up above the speaker's place in the
forum, thinking thus to insult the dead, while in fact he
only exposed his own wanton arrogance, and his unworthi-
ness to hold the power that fortune had given him.

This triumvirate was very hateful to the Romans, and
Antony most of all bore the blame, because he was older
than Caesar, and had greater authority than Lepidus, and
withal he was no sooner settled in his affairs, but he turned
to his luxurious and dissolute way of living. Besides the ill
reputation he gained by his general behaviour, it was some
considerable disadvantage to him his living in the house of
Pompey the Great, who had been as much admired for his
temperance and his sober, citizen-like habits of life, as ever
he was for having triumphed three times. They could not
without anger see the doors of that house shut against
magistrates, officers, and envoys, who were shamefully refused admittance, while it was filled inside with players,
jugglers, and drunken flatterers, upon whom were spent
the greatest part of the wealth which violence and cruelty
procured. For they did not limit themselves to the forfei-
ture of the estates of such as were proscribed, defrauding
the widows and families, nor were they contented with laying on every possible kind of tax and imposition; but hearing that several sums of money were, as well by strangers
as citizens of Rome, deposited in the hands of the vestal
virgins, they went and took the money away by force.
When it was manifest that nothing would ever be enough
for Antony, Caesar at last called for a division of property. The army was also divided between them, upon their
march into Macedonia to make war with Brutus and Cassius, Lepidus being left with the command of the city.

However, after they had crossed the sea and engaged in
operations of war, encamping in front of the enemy, Antony

opposite Cassius, and Caesar opposite Brutus, Caesar did nothing worth relating, and all the success and victory were Antony's. In the first battle, Caesar was completely routed by Brutus, his camp taken, he himself very narrowly escaping by flight. As he himself writes in his memoirs, he retired before the battle, on account of a dream which one of his friends had. But Antony, on the other hand, defeated Cassius; though some have written that he was not actually present in the engagement, and only joined afterwards in the pursuit. Cassius was killed, at his own entreaty and order, by one of his most trusted freedmen, Pindarus, not being aware of Brutus's victory. After a few days' interval, they fought another battle, in which Brutus lost the day, and slew himself; and Caesar being sick, Antony had almost all the honour of the victory. Standing over Brutus's dead body, he uttered a few words of reproach upon him for the death of his brother Caius, who had been executed by Brutus's order in Macedonia in revenge of Cicero; but, saying presently that Hortensius was most to blame for it, he gave order for his being slain upon his brother's tomb, and, throwing his own scarlet mantle, which was of great value, upon the body of Brutus, he gave charge to one of his own freedmen to take care of his funeral. This man, as Antony came to understand, did not leave the mantle with the corpse, but kept both it and a good part of the money that should have been spent in the funeral for himself; for which he had him put to death.

But Caesar was conveyed to Rome, no one expecting that he would long survive. Antony, purposing to go to the eastern provinces to lay them under contribution, entered Greece with a large force. The promise had been made that every common soldier should receive for his pay five thousand drachmas; so it was likely there would be need of pretty severe taxing and levying to raise money. However, to the Greeks he showed at first reason and moderation enough; he gratified his love of amusement by hearing the learned men dispute, by seeing the games, and undergoing initiation; and in judicial matters he was equitable, taking pleasure in being styled a lover of Greece, but, above all, in being called a lover of Athens, to which city he made very considerable presents.

Leaving Lucius Censorinus in Greece, he crossed over into Asia, and there laid his hands on the stores of accumulated wealth, while kings waited at his door, and queens were rivalling one another, who should make him the greatest presents or appear most charming in his eyes. Thus, whilst Caesar in Rome was wearing out his strength amidst seditions and wars, Antony, with nothing to do amidst the enjoyments of peace, let his passions carry him easily back to the old course of life that was familiar to him. A set of harpers and pipers, Anaxenor and Xuthus, the dancing-man, Metrodorus, and a whole Bacchic rout of the like Asiatic exhibitors, far outdoing in licence and buffoonery the pests that had followed him out of Italy, came in and possessed the court; the thing was past patience, wealth of all kinds being wasted on objects like these. The whole of Asia was like the city in Sophocles, loaded, at one time—

"————————with incense in the air,
  Jubilant songs, and outcries of despair."

When he made his entry into Ephesus, the women met him dressed up like Bacchantes, and the men and boys like satyrs and fauns, and throughout the town nothing was to be seen but spears wreathed about with ivy, harps, flutes, and psalteries, while Antony in their songs was Bacchus, the Giver of Joy, and the Gentle. And so indeed he was to some but to far more the Devourer and the Savage; for he would deprive persons of worth and quality of their fortunes to gratify villains and flatterers, who would sometimes beg the estates of men yet living, pretending they were dead, and, obtaining a grant, take possession. He gave his cook the house of a Magnesian citizen, as a reward for a single highly successful supper, and, at last, when he was proceeding to lay a second whole tribute on Asia, Hybreas, speaking on behalf of the cities, took courage, and told him broadly, but aptly enough for Antony's taste, "if you can take two yearly tributes, you can doubtless give us a couple of summers and a double harvest time"; and put it to him in the plainest and boldest way, that Asia had raised two hundred thousand talents for his service: "If this has not been paid to you, ask your collectors for it; if it has, and is all gone, we are ruined men." These words touched Antony to the quick, who was simply ignorant of most things that were done in his name; not that he was so indolent, as he was prone to trust frankly in all about him. For there was much simplicity in his character; he was slow to see his faults, but when he did see them, was extremely repentant, and ready to ask pardon of those he had injured; prodigal in his acts of reparation, and severe in his punishments, but his generosity was much more extravagant than his severity; his raillery was sharp and insulting, but the edge of it was taken off by his readiness to submit to any kind of repartee; for he was as well contented to be rallied, as he was pleased to rally others. And this freedom of speech was, indeed, the cause of many of his disasters. He never imagined those who used so much liberty in their mirth would flatter or deceive him in business of consequence, not knowing how common it is with parasites to mix their flattery with boldness, as confectioners do their sweetmeats with something biting, to prevent the sense of satiety. Their freedoms and impertinences at table were designed expressly to give to their obsequiousness in council the air of being not complaisance, but conviction.

Such being his temper, the last and crowning mischief that could befall him came in the love of Cleopatra, to awaken and kindle to fury passions that as yet lay still and dormant in his nature, and to stifle and finally corrupt any elements that yet made resistance in him of goodness and a sound judgment. He fell into the snare thus. When making preparation for the Parthian war, he sent to command her to make her personal appearance in Cilicia, to answer an accusation, that she had given great assistance, in the late wars, to Cassius. Dellius, who was sent on this message, had no sooner seen her face, and remarked her adroitness and subtlety in speech, but he felt convinced that Antony would not so much as think of giving any molestation to a woman like this; on the contrary, she would be the first in favour with him. So he set himself at once to pay his court to the Egyptian, and gave her his advice, "to go," in the Homeric style, to Cilicia, "in her best attire," and bade her fear nothing from Antony, the gentlest and kindest of soldiers. She had some faith in the words of Dellius, but more in her own attractions; which, having formerly recommended her to Caesar and the young Cnaeus Pompey, she did not doubt might prove yet more successful with Antony. Their acquaintance was with her when a girl, young and ignorant of the world, but she was to meet Antony in the time of life when women's beauty is most splendid, and their intellects are in full maturity. She made great preparation for her journey, of money, gifts, and ornaments of value, such as so wealthy a kingdom might afford, but she brought with her her surest hopes in her own magic arts and charms.

She received several letters, both from Antony and from his friends, to summon her, but she took no account of these orders; and at last, as if in mockery of them, she came sailing up the river Cydnus, in a barge with gilded stern and outspread sails of purple, while oars of silver beat time to the music of flutes and fifes and harps. She herself lay all along under a canopy of cloth of gold, dressed as Venus in a picture, and beautiful young boys, like painted Cupids, stood on each side to fan her. Her maids were dressed like sea nymphs and graces, some steering at the rudder, some working at the ropes. The perfumes diffused themselves from the vessel to the shore, which was covered with multitudes, part following the galley up the river on either bank, part running out of the city to see the sight. The market-place was quite emptied, and Antony at last was left alone sitting upon the tribunal; while the word went through all the multitude, that Venus was come to feast with Bacchus, for the common good of Asia. On her arrival, Antony sent to invite her to supper. She thought it fitter he should come to her; so, willing to show his good-humour and courtesy, he complied, and went. He found the preparations to receive him magnificent beyond expression, but nothing so admirable as the great number of lights; for on a sudden there was let down altogether so great a number of branches with lights in them so ingeniously disposed, some in squares, and some in circles, that the whole thing was a spectacle that has seldom been equalled for beauty.

The next day, Antony invited her to supper, and was very desirous to outdo her as well in magnificence as contrivance; but he found he was altogether beaten in both, and was so well convinced of it that he was himself the first to jest and mock at his poverty of wit and his rustic awkwardness. She, perceiving that his raillery was broad and gross, and savoured more of the soldier than the courtier, rejoined in the same taste, and fell into it at once, without any sort of reluctance or reserve. For her actual beauty, it is said, was not in itself so remarkable that none could be compared with her, or that no one could see her without being struck by it, but the contact of her presence, if you lived with her, was irresistible; the attraction of her person, joining with the charm of her conversation, and the character that attended all she said or did, was something bewitching. It was a pleasure merely to hear the sound of her voice, with which, like an instrument of many strings, she could pass from one language to another; so that there were few of the barbarian nations that she answered by an interpreter; to most of them she spoke herself, as to the Aethiopians, Troglodytes, Hebrews, Arabians, Syrians, Medes, Parthians, and many others, whose language she had learnt; which was all the more surprising because most of the kings, her predecessors, scarcely gave themselves the trouble to acquire the Egyptian tongue, and several of them quite abandoned the Macedonian.

Antony was so captivated by her that, while Fulvia his

wife maintained his quarrels in Rome against Caesar by
actual force of arms, and the Parthian troops, commanded
by Labienus (the king's generals having made him commander-in-chief), were assembled in Mesopotamia, and
ready to enter Syria, he could yet suffer himself to be carried away by her to Alexandria, there to keep holiday, like
a boy, in play and diversion, squandering and fooling away
in enjoyments that most costly, as Antiphon says, of all
valuables, time. They had a sort of company, to which they
gave a particular name, calling it that of the Inimitable
Livers. The members entertained one another daily in turn,
with an extravagance of expenditure beyond measure or
belief. Philotas, a physician of Amphissa, who was at that
time a student of medicine in Alexandria, used to tell my
grandfather Lamprias that, having some acquaintance with
one of the royal cooks, he was invited by him, being a
young man, to come and see the sumptuous preparations
for supper. So he was taken into the kitchen, where he admired the prodigious variety of all things; but particularly,
seeing eight wild boars roasting whole, says he, "Surely
you have a great number of guests." The cook laughed at
his simplicity, and told him there were not above twelve
to sup, but that every dish was to be served up just roasted
to a turn, and if anything was but one minute ill-timed, it
was spoiled; "And," said he, "maybe Antony will sup just
now, maybe not this hour, maybe he will call for wine, or
begin to talk, and will put it off. So that," he continued, "it
is not one, but many suppers must be had in readiness, as
it is impossible to guess at his hour."

To return to Cleopatra; Plato admits four sorts of flattery, but she had a thousand. Were Antony serious or disposed to mirth, she had at any moment some new delight
or charm to meet his wishes; at every turn she was upon
him, and let him escape her neither by day nor by night.
She played at dice with him, drank with him, hunted with
him; and when he exercised in arms, she was there to see.
At night she would go rambling with him to disturb and
torment people at their doors and windows, dressed like

a servant-woman, for Antony also went in servant's disguise, and from these expeditions he often came home very scurvily answered, and sometimes even beaten severely, though most people guessed who it was. However, the Alexandrians in general liked it all well enough, and joined good-humouredly and kindly in his frolic and play, saying they were much obliged to Antony for acting his tragic parts at Rome, and keeping his comedy for them. It would be trifling without end to be particular in his follies, but his fishing must not be forgotten. He went out one day to angle with Cleopatra, and, being so unfortunate as to catch nothing in the presence of his mistress, he gave secret orders to the fishermen to dive under water, and put fishes that had been already taken upon his hooks; and these he drew so fast that the Egyptian perceived it. But, feigning great admiration, she told everybody how dexterous Antony was, and invited them next day to come and see him again. So, when a number of them had come on board the fishing-boats, as soon as he had let down his hook, one of her servants was beforehand with his divers, and fixed upon his hook a salted fish from Pontus. Antony, feeling his line give, drew up the prey, and when, as may be imagined, great laughter ensued, "Leave," said Cleopatra, "the fishing-rod, general, to us poor sovereigns of Pharos and Canopus; your game is cities, provinces, and kingdoms."

Whilst he was thus diverting himself and engaged in this boy's play, two despatches arrived; one from Rome, that his brother Lucius and his wife Fulvia, after many quarrels among themselves, had joined in war against Caesar, and having lost all, had fled out of Italy; the other bringing little better news, that Labienus, at the head of the Parthians, was overrunning Asia, from Euphrates and Syria, as far as Lydia and Ionia. So, scarcely at last rousing himself from sleep, and shaking off the fumes of wine, he set out to attack the Parthians, and went as far as Phoenicia; but, upon the receipt of lamentable letters from Fulvia, turned his course with two hundred ships to Italy. And, in his way, receiving such of his friends as fled from Italy, he was given to understand that Fulvia was the sole cause of the war, a woman of a restless spirit and very bold, and withal her hopes were that commotions in Italy would force Antony from Cleopatra. But it happened that Fulvia, as she was coming to meet her husband, fell sick by the way, and died at Sicyon, so that an accommodation was the more easily made. For when he reached Italy, and Caesar showed no intention of laying anything to his charge, and he on his part shifted the blame of everything on Fulvia, those that were friends to them would not suffer that the time should be spent in looking narrowly into the plea, but made a reconciliation first, and then a partition of the empire between them, taking as their boundary the Ionian Sea, the eastern provinces falling to Antony, to Caesar the western, and Africa being left to Lepidus. And an agreement was made that everyone in their turn, as they thought fit, should make their friends consuls, when they did not choose to take the offices themselves.

These terms were well approved of, but yet it was thought some closer tie would be desirable; and for this, fortune offered occasion. Caesar had an elder sister, not of the whole blood, for Attia was his mother's name, hers Ancharia. This sister, Octavia, he was extremely attached to, as indeed she was, it is said, quite a wonder of a woman. Her husband, Caius Marcellus, had died not long before, and Antony was now a widower by the death of Fulvia; for, though he did not disavow the passion he had for Cleopatra, yet he disowned anything of marriage, reason as yet, upon this point, still maintaining the debate against the charms of the Egyptian. Everybody concurred in promoting this new alliance, fully expecting that with the beauty, honour, and prudence of Octavia, when her company should, as it was certain it would, have engaged his affections, all would be kept in the safe and happy course of friendship. So, both parties being agreed, they went to Rome to celebrate the nuptials, the senate dispensing with the law by which a widow was not permitted to marry till ten months after the death of her husband.

Sextus Pompeius was in possession of Sicily, and with his ships, under the command of Menas, the pirate, and Menecrates, so infested the Italian coast that no vessels durst venture into those seas. Sextus had behaved with much humanity towards Antony, having received his mother when she fled with Fulvia, and it was therefore judged fit that he also should be received into the peace. They met near the promontory of Misenum, by the mole of the port, Pompey having his fleet at anchor close by, and Antony and Caesar their troops drawn up all along the shore. There it was concluded that Sextus should quietly enjoy the government of Sicily and Sardinia, he conditioning to scour the seas of all pirates, and to send so much corn every year to Rome.

This agreed on, they invited one another to supper, and by lot it fell to Pompey's turn to give the first entertainment, and Antony, asking where it was to be, "There," said he, pointing to the admiral-galley, a ship of six banks of oars, "that is the only house that Pompey is heir to of his father's." And this he said, reflecting upon Antony, who was then in possession of his father's house. Having fixed the ship on her anchors, and formed a bridgeway from the promontory to conduct on board of her, he gave them a cordial welcome. And when they began to grow warm, and jests were passing freely on Antony and Cleopatra's loves, Menas, the pirate, whispered Pompey, in the ear, "Shall I," said he, "cut the cables, and make you master not of Sicily only and Sardinia, but of the whole Roman empire?" Pompey, having considered a little while, returned him answer, "Menas, this might have been done without acquainting me; now we must rest content; I do not break my word." And so, having been entertained by the other two in their turns, he set sail for Sicily.

After the treaty was completed, Antony despatched Ventidius into Asia, to check the advance of the Parthians, while he, as a compliment to Caesar, accepted the office of priest to the deceased Caesar. And in any state affair and matter of consequence, they both behaved themselves with much consideration and friendliness for each other. But it annoyed Antony that in all their amusements, on any trial of skill or fortune, Caesar should be constantly victorious. He had with him an Egyptian diviner, one of those who calculate nativities, who, either to make his court to Cleopatra, or that by the rules of his art he found it to be so, openly declared to him that though the fortune that attended him was bright and glorious, yet it was overshadowed by Caesar's; and advised him to keep himself as far distant as he could from that young man; "for your Genius," said he, "dreads his; when absent from him yours is proud and brave, but in his presence unmanly and dejected"; and incidents that occurred appeared to show that the Egyptian spoke truth. For whenever they cast lots for any playful purpose, or threw dice, Antony was still the loser; and repeatedly, when they fought game-cocks or quails, Caesar's had the victory. This gave Antony a secret displeasure, and made him put the more confidence in the skill of his Egyptian. So, leaving the management of his home affairs to Caesar, he left Italy, and took Octavia, who had lately borne him a daughter, along with him into Greece.

When at length an agreement was made between them, that Caesar should give Antony two of his legions to serve him in the Parthian war, and that Antony should in return leave with him a hundred armed galleys, Caesar went immediately to make war with Pompey to conquer Sicily. And Antony, leaving in Caesar's charge his wife and children, and his children by his former wife Fulvia, set sail for Asia.

But the mischief that thus long had lain still, the passion for Cleopatra, which better thoughts had seemed to have lulled and charmed into oblivion, upon his approach to Syria gathered strength again, and broke out into a flame. And, in fine, like Plato's restive and rebellious horse of the human soul, flinging off all good and wholesome counsel, and breaking fairly loose, he sends Fonteius Capito to bring Cleopatra into Syria. To whom at her arrival he made no small or trifling present, Phoenicia, Coele-Syria, Cyprus, great part of Cilicia, that side of Judaea which produces balm, that part of Arabia where the Nabathaeans extend to the outer sea; profuse gifts which much displeased the Romans. For although he had invested several private persons in great governments and kingdoms, and bereaved many kings of theirs, as Antigonus of Judaea, whose head he caused to be struck off (the first example of that punishment being inflicted on a king), yet nothing stung the Romans like the shame of these honours paid to Cleopatra. Their dissatisfaction was augmented also by his acknowledging as his own the twin children he had by her, giving them the names of Alexander and Cleopatra, and adding, as their surnames, the titles of Sun and Moon. But he, who knew how to put a good colour on the most dishonest action, would say that the greatness of the Roman empire consisted more in giving than in taking kingdoms, and that the way to carry noble blood through the world was by begetting in every place a new line and series of kings; his own ancestor had thus been born of Hercules; Hercules had not limited his hopes of progeny to a single womb, nor feared any law like Solon's or any audit of procreation, but had freely let nature take her will in the foundation and first commencement of many families.

Octavia, in Rome, being desirous to see Antony, asked Caesar's leave to go to him; which he gave her, not so much, say most authors, to gratify his sister, as to obtain a fair pretence to begin the war upon her dishonourable reception. She no sooner arrived at Athens, but by letters from Antony she was informed of his new expedition, and his will that she should await him there. And, though she were much displeased, not being ignorant of the real reason of this usage, yet she wrote to him to know to what place he would be pleased she should send the things she had brought with her for his use; for she had brought clothes for his soldiers, baggage, cattle, money, and presents for his friends and officers, and two thousand chosen soldiers sumptuously armed, to form praetorian cohorts. This message was brought from Octavia to Antony by

Niger, one of his friends, who added to it the praises she deserved so well. Cleopatra, feeling her rival already, as it
were, at hand, was seized with fear, lest if to her noble
life and her high alliance, she once could add the charm
of daily habit and affectionate intercourse, she should become irresistible, and be his absolute mistress forever. So
she feigned to be dying for love of Antony, bringing her
body down by slender diet; when he entered the room, she
fixed her eyes upon him in a rapture, and when he left,
seemed to languish and half faint away. She took great pains
that he should see her in tears, and, as soon as he noticed
it, hastily dried them up and turned away, as if it were her
wish that he should know nothing of it. All this was acting
while he prepared for Media; and Cleopatra's creatures
were not slow to forward the design, upbraiding Antony
with his unfeeling, hard-hearted temper, thus letting a
woman perish whose soul depended upon him and him
alone. Octavia, it was true, was his wife, and had been
married to him because it was found convenient for the
affairs of her brother that it should be so, and she had the
honour of the title; but Cleopatra, the sovereign queen of
many nations, had been contented with the name of his
mistress, nor did she shun or despise the character whilst
she might see him, might live with him, and enjoy him; if
she were bereaved of this, she would not survive the loss.
In fine, they so melted and unmanned him that, fully believing she would die if he forsook her, he put off the war
and returned to Alexandria, deferring his Median expedition until next summer, though news came of the Parthians
being all in confusion with intestine disputes. Nevertheless,
he did some time after go into that country, and made an
alliance with the King of Media, by marriage of a son of
his by Cleopatra to the king's daughter, who was yet very
young; and so returned, with his thoughts taken up about
the civil war.

When Octavia returned from Athens, Caesar, who considered she had been injuriously treated, commanded her
to live in a separate house; but she refused to leave the

house of her husband, and entreated him, unless he had already resolved, upon other motives, to make war with Antony, that he would on her account let it alone; it would be intolerable to have it said of the two greatest commanders in the world that they had involved the Roman people in a civil war, the one out of passion for, the other out of resentment about, a woman. And her behaviour proved her words to be sincere. She remained in Antony's house as if he were at home in it, and took the noblest and most generous care, not only of his children by her, but of those by Fulvia also. She received all the friends of Antony that came to Rome to seek office or upon any business, and did her utmost to prefer their requests to Caesar; yet this her honourable deportment did but, without her meaning it, damage the reputation of Antony; the wrong he did to such a woman made him hated. Nor was the division he made among his sons at Alexandria less unpopular; it seemed a theatrical piece of insolence and contempt of his country. For assembling the people in the exercise ground, and causing two golden thrones to be placed on a platform of silver, the one for him and the other for Cleopatra, and at their feet lower thrones for their children, he proclaimed Cleopatra Queen of Egypt, Cyprus, Libya, and Coele-Syria, and with her conjointly Caesarion, the reputed son of the former Caesar, who left Cleopatra with child. His own sons by Cleopatra were to have the style of king of kings; to Alexander he gave Armenia and Media, with Parthia, so soon as it should be overcome; to Ptolemy, Phoenicia, Syria, and Cilicia. Alexander was brought out before the people in Median costume, the tiara and upright peak, and Ptolemy, in boots and mantle and Macedonian cap done about with the diadem; for this was the habit of the successors of Alexander, as the other was of the Medes and Armenians. And as soon as they had saluted their parents, the one was received by a guard of Macedonians, the other by one of Armenians. Cleopatra was then, as at other times when she appeared in public, dressed in the habit of the goddess Isis, and gave audience to the people under the name of the New Isis.

Caesar, relating these things in the senate, and often complaining to the people, excited men's minds against Antony, and Antony also sent messages of accusation against Caesar. The principal of his charges were these: first, that he had not made any division with him of Sicily, which was lately taken from Pompey; secondly, that he had retained the ships he had lent him for the war; thirdly, that, after deposing Lepidus, their colleague, he had taken for himself the army, governments, and revenues formerly appropriated to him; and lastly, that he had parcelled out almost all Italy amongst his own soldiers, and left nothing for his. Caesar's answer was as follows: that he had put Lepidus out of government because of his own misconduct; that what he had got in war he would divide with Antony, so soon as Antony gave him a share of Armenia; that Antony's soldiers had no claims in Italy, being in possession of Media and Parthia, the acquisitions which their brave actions under their general had added to the Roman empire.

Antony was in Armenia when this answer came to him, and immediately sent Canidius with sixteen legions towards the sea; but he, in the company of Cleopatra, went to Ephesus, whither ships were coming in from all quarters to form the navy, consisting, vessels of burden included, of eight hundred vessels, of which Cleopatra furnished two hundred, together with twenty thousand talents, and provision for the whole army during the war. Antony, on the advice of Domitius and some others, bade Cleopatra return into Egypt, there to expect the event of the war; but she, dreading some new reconciliation by Octavia's means, prevailed with Canidius, by a large sum of money, to speak in her favour with Antony, pointing out to him that it was not just that one that bore so great a part in the charge of the war should be robbed of her share of glory in the carrying it on; nor would it be politic to disoblige the Egyptians, who were so considerable a part of his naval forces; nor did he see how she was inferior in prudence to any of the kings that were serving with him; she had long governed a great kingdom by herself alone, and long lived with him, and gained experience in public affairs. These arguments (so

the fate that destined all to Caesar would have it) prevailed; and when all their forces had met, they sailed together to Samos, and held high festivities. For, as it was
ordered that all kings, princes, and governors, all nations
and cities within the limits of Syria, the Maeotid Lake, Armenia, and Illyria, should bring or cause to be brought all
munitions necessary for war, so was it also proclaimed that
all stage-players should make their appearance at Samos;
so that, while pretty nearly the whole world was filled with
groans and lamentations, this one island for some days re-
sounded with piping and harping, theatres filling, and chor-
uses playing. Every city sent an ox as its contribution to
the sacrifice, and the kings that accompanied Antony com-
peted who should make the most magnificent feasts and the
greatest presents; and men began to ask themselves, what
would be done to celebrate the victory, when they went to
such an expense of festivity at the opening of the war.

This over, he gave Priene to his players for a habitation,
and set sail for Athens, where fresh sports and play-acting
employed him. Cleopatra, jealous of the honours Octavia
had received at Athens (for Octavia was much beloved by
the Athenians), courted the favour of the people with all
sorts of attentions. The Athenians, in requital, having decreed her public honours, deputed several of the citizens
to wait upon her at her house; amongst whom went Antony as one, he being an Athenian citizen, and he it was
that made the speech. He sent orders to Rome to have Octavia removed out of his house. She left it, we are told,
accompanied by all his children, except the eldest by Fulvia, who was then with his father, weeping and grieving
that she must be looked upon as one of the causes of the
war. But the Romans pitied, not so much her, as Antony
himself, and more particularly those who had seen Cleopatra, whom they could report to have no way the advantage of Octavia either in youth or in beauty.

The speed and extent of Antony's preparations alarmed
Caesar, who feared he might be forced to fight the decisive
battle that summer. For he wanted many necessaries, and

the people grudged very much to pay the taxes; freemen being called upon to pay a fourth part of their incomes, and freed slaves an eighth of their property, so that there were loud outcries against him, and disturbances throughout all Italy. And this is looked upon as one of the greatest of Antony's oversights, that he did not then press the war. For he allowed time at once for Caesar to make his preparations and for the commotions to pass over. For while people were having their money called for, they were mutinous and violent; but, having paid it, they held their peace. Titius and Plancus, men of consular dignity and friends to Antony, having been ill-used by Cleopatra, whom they had most resisted in her design of being present in the war, came over to Caesar and gave information of the contents of Antony's will, with which they were acquainted. It was deposited in the hands of the vestal virgins, who refused to deliver it up, and sent Caesar word, if he pleased, he should come and seize it himself, which he did. And, reading it over to himself, he noted those places that were most for his purpose, and, having summoned the senate, read them publicly. Many were scandalised at the proceeding, thinking it out of reason and equity to call a man to account for what was not to be until after his death. Caesar specially pressed what Antony said in his will about his burial; for he had ordered that even if he died in the city of Rome, his body, after being carried in state through the forum, should be sent to Cleopatra at Alexandria. Calvisius, a dependant of Caesar's, urged other charges in connection with Cleopatra against Antony; that he had given her the library of Pergamus, containing two hundred thousand distinct volumes; that at a great banquet, in the presence of many guests, he had risen up and rubbed her feet, to fulfil some wager or promise; that he had suffered the Ephesians to salute her as their queen; that he had frequently at the public audience of kings and princes received amorous messages written in tablets made of onyx and crystal, and read them openly on the tribunal; that when Furnius, a man of great authority and eloquence among the Romans, was pleading, Cleopatra happening to pass by in her chair, Antony started up and left them in the middle of their cause, to follow at her side and attend her home.

Calvisius, however, was looked upon as the inventor of most of these stories. Antony's friends went up and down the city to gain him credit, and sent one of themselves, Geminius, to him, to beg him to take heed and not allow himself to be deprived by vote of his authority, and proclaimed a public enemy to the Roman state. But Geminius no sooner arrived in Greece but he was looked upon as one of Octavia's spies; at their suppers he was made a continual butt for mockery, and was put to sit in the least honourable places; all of which he bore very well, seeking only an occasion of speaking with Antony. So at supper, being told to say what business he came about, he answered he would keep the rest for a soberer hour, but one thing he had to say, whether full or fasting, that all would go well if Cleopatra would return to Egypt. And on Antony showing his anger at it, "You have done well, Geminius," said Cleopatra, "to tell your secret without being put to the rack." So Geminius, after a few days, took occasion to make his escape and go to Rome. Many more of Antony's friends were driven from him by the insolent usage they had from Cleopatra's flatterers.

As soon as Caesar had completed his preparations, he had a decree made declaring war on Cleopatra, and depriving Antony of the authority which he had let a woman exercise in his place. Caesar added that he had drunk potions that had bereaved him of his senses, and that the generals they would have to fight with would be Mardion the eunuch, Pothinus, Iras, Cleopatra's hairdressing girl, and Charmion, who were Antony's chief state-councillors.

These prodigies are said to have announced the war. Pisaurum, where Antony had settled a colony, on the Adriatic sea, was swallowed up by an earthquake; sweat ran from one of the marble statues of Antony at Alba for many days together, and though frequently wiped off, did not stop. When he himself was in the city of Patrae, the temple of Hercules was struck by lightning, and, at Athens, the figure of Bacchus was torn by a violent wind out of the Battle of the Giants, and laid flat upon the theatre; with both which deities Antony claimed connection, professing to be descended from Hercules, and from his imitating Bacchus in his way of living having received the name of young Bacchus. The same whirlwind at Athens also brought down, from amongst many others which were not disturbed, the colossal statues of Fumenes and Attalus, which were inscribed with Antony's name. And in Cleopatra's admiral-galley, which was called the Antonias, a most inauspicious omen occurred. Some swallows had built in the stern of the galley, but other swallows came, beat the first away, and destroyed their nests.

When the armaments gathered for the war, Antony had no less than five hundred ships of war, including numerous galleys of eight and ten banks of oars, as richly ornamented as if they were meant for a triumph. He had a hundred thousand foot and twelve thousand horse. He had vassal kings attending, Bocchus of Libya, Tarcondemus of the Upper Cilicia, Archelaus of Cappadocia, Philadelphus of Paphlagonia, Mithridates of Commagene, and Sadalas of Thrace; all these were with him in person. Out of Pontus Polemon sent him considerable forces, as did also Malchus from Arabia, Herod the Jew, and Amyntas, King of Lycaonia and Galatia; also the Median king sent some troops to join him. Caesar had two hundred and fifty galleys of war, eighty thousand foot, and horse about equal to the enemy. Antony's empire extended from Euphrates and Armenia to the Ionian sea and the Illyrians; Caesar's, from Illyria to the westward ocean, and from the ocean all along the Tuscan and Sicilian sea. Of Africa, Caesar had all the coast opposite to Italy, Gaul, and Spain, as far as the Pillars of Hercules, and Antony the provinces from Cyrene to Aethiopia.

But so wholly was he now the mere appendage to the person of Cleopatra that, although he was much superior to the enemy in land-forces, yet, out of complaisance to his mistress, he wished the victory to be gained by sea, and that, too, when he could not but see how, for want of sailors, his captains, all through unhappy Greece, were pressing every description of men, common travellers and ass-drivers, harvest labourers and boys, and for all this the vessels had not their complements, but remained, most of them, ill-manned and badly rowed. Caesar, on the other side, had ships that were built not for size or show, but for service, not pompous galleys, but light, swift, and perfectly manned; and from his headquarters at Tarentum and Brundusium he sent messages to Antony not to protract the war, but come out with his forces; he would give him secure roadsteads and ports for his fleet, and, for his land army to disembark and pitch their camp, he would leave him as much ground in Italy, inland from the sea, as a horse could traverse in a single course. Antony, on the other side, with the like bold language, challenged him to a single combat, though he were much the older; and, that being refused, proposed to meet him in the Pharsalian fields, where Caesar and Pompey had fought before. But whilst Antony lay with his fleet near Actium, where now stands Nicopolis, Caesar seized his opportunity and crossed the Ionian sea, securing himself at a place in Epirus called the Ladle. And when those about Antony were much disturbed, their land forces being a good way off, "Indeed," said Cleopatra, in mockery, "we may well be frightened if Caesar has got hold of the Ladle!"

On the morrow, Antony, seeing the enemy sailing up, and fearing lest his ships might be taken for want of the soldiers to go on board of them, armed all the rowers, and made a show upon the decks of being in readiness to fight; the oars were mounted as if waiting to be put in motion, and the vessels themselves drawn up to face the enemy on either side of the channel of Actium, as though they were properly manned and ready for an engagement. And Caesar, deceived by this stratagem, retired. He was also thought to have shown considerable skill in cutting off the

water from the enemy by some lines of trenches and forts,
water not being plentiful anywhere else, nor very good.

The fleet was so unfortunate in everything that was undertaken, and so unready on every occasion, that Antony
was driven again to put his confidence in the land forces.
Canidius, too, who commanded the legions, when he saw
how things stood, changed his opinion, and now was of
advice that Cleopatra should be sent back, and that, retiring into Thrace or Macedonia, the quarrel should be decided in a land fight. For Dicomes, also, the King of the
Getae, promised to come and join him with a great army,
and it would not be any kind of disparagement to him to
yield the sea to Caesar, who, in the Sicilian wars, had
had such long practice in shipfighting; on the contrary, it
would be simply ridiculous for Antony, who was by land
the most experienced commander living, to make no use
of his well-disciplined and numerous infantry, scattering
and wasting his forces by parcelling them out in the ships.
But for all this, Cleopatra prevailed that a sea-fight should
determine all, having already an eye to flight, and ordering
all her affairs, not so as to assist in gaining a victory, but
to escape with the greatest safety from the first commencement of a defeat.

When it was resolved to stand to a fight at sea, they set
fire to all the Egyptian ships except sixty; and of these the
best and largest, from ten banks down to three, he manned
with twenty thousand full-armed men and two thousand
archers. Here it is related that a foot captain, one that had
fought often under Antony, and had his body all mangled
with wounds, exclaimed, "O my general, what have our
wounds and swords done to displease you, that you should
give your confidence to rotten timbers? Let Egyptians and
Phoenicians contend at sea, give us the land, where we
know well how to die upon the spot or gain the victory."
To which he answered nothing, but, by his look and motion of his hand seeming to bid him be of good courage,
passed forwards, having already, it would seem, no very
sure hopes, since when the masters proposed leaving the

sails behind them, he commanded they should be put aboard, "For we must not," said he, "let one enemy escape."

That day and the three following the sea was so rough they could not engage. But on the fifth there was a calm, and they fought; Antony commanding with Publicola the right, and Coelius the left squadron, Marcus Octavius and Marcus Insteius the centre. Caesar gave the charge of the left to Agrippa, commanding in person on the right. As for the land forces, Canidius was general for Antony, Taurus for Caesar; both armies remaining drawn up in order along the shore. Antony in a small boat went from one ship to another, encouraging his soldiers, and bidding them stand firm and fight as steadily on their large ships as if they were on land. The masters he ordered that they should receive the enemy lying still as if they were at anchor, and maintain the entrance of the port, which was a narrow and difficult passage. Of Caesar they relate that, leaving his tent and going round, while it was yet dark, to visit the ships, he met a man driving an ass, and asked him his name. He answered him that his own name was "Fortunate, and my ass," says he, "is called Conqueror." And afterwards, when he disposed the beaks of the ships in that place in token of his victory, the statue of this man and his ass in bronze were placed amongst them. After examining the rest of his fleet, he went in a boat to the right wing, and looked with much admiration at the enemy lying perfectly still in the straits, in all appearance as if they had been at anchor. For some considerable length of time he actually thought they were so, and kept his own ships at rest, at a distance of about eight furlongs from them. But about noon a breeze sprang up from the sea, and Antony's men, weary of expecting the enemy so long, and trusting to their large tall vessels, as if they had been invincible, began to advance the left squadron. Caesar was overjoyed to see them move, and ordered his own right squadron to retire, that he might entice them out to sea as far as he could, his design being to sail round and round, and so with his light and well-manned galleys to attack these huge vessels, which their size and their want of men made slow to move and difficult to manage.

When they engaged, there was no charging or striking of one ship by another, because Antony's, by reason of their great bulk, were incapable of the rapidity required to make the stroke effectual, and on the other side, Caesar's durst not charge head to head on Antony's, which were all armed with solid masses and spikes of brass; nor did they like even to run in on their sides, which were so strongly built with great squared pieces of timber, fastened together with iron bolts, that their vessels' beaks would easily have been shattered upon them. So that the engagement resembled a land fight, or, to speak yet more properly, the attack and defence of a fortified place; for there were always three or four vessels of Caesar's about one of Antony's, pressing them with spears, javelins, poles, and several inventions of fire, which they flung among them, Antony's men using catapults also, to pour down missiles from wooden towers. Agrippa drawing out the squadron under his command to outflank the enemy, Publicola was obliged to observe his motions, and gradually to break off from the middle squadron, where some confusion and alarm ensued, while Arruntius engaged them. But the fortune of the day was still undecided, and the battle equal, when on a sudden Cleopatra's sixty ships were seen hoisting sail and making out to sea in full flight, right through the ships that were engaged. For they were placed behind the great ships, which, in breaking through, they put into disorder. The enemy was astonished to see them sailing off with a fair wind towards Peloponnesus. Here it was that Antony showed to all the world that he was no longer actuated by the thoughts and motives of a commander or a man, or indeed by his own judgment at all, and what was once said as a jest, that the soul of a lover lives in some one else's body, he proved to be a serious truth. For, as if he had been born part of her, and must move with her wheresoever she went, as soon as he saw her ship sailing away, he abandoned all that were fighting and spending their lives for him, and put himself aboard a galley of five banks of oars, taking with him only Alexander of Syria and Scellias, to follow her that had so well begun his ruin and would hereafter accomplish it.

She, perceiving him to follow, gave the signal to come aboard. So, as soon as he came up with them, he was taken into the ship. But without seeing her or letting himself be seen by her, he went forward by himself, and sat alone, without a word, in the ship's prow, covering his face with his two hands. Thus he remained for three days, either in anger with Cleopatra, or wishing not to upbraid her, at the end of which they touched at Taenarus. Here the women of their company succeeded first in bringing them to speak, and afterwards to eat and sleep together. And, by this time, several of the ships of burden and some of his friends began to come in to him from the rout, bringing news of his fleet's being quite destroyed, but that the land forces, they thought, still stood firm. So that he sent messengers to Canidius to march the army with all speed through Macedonia into Asia. And, designing himself to go from Taenarus into Africa, he gave one of the merchant ships, laden with a large sum of money, and vessels of silver and gold of great value, belonging to the royal collections, to his friends, desiring them to share it amongst them, and provide for their own safety. They refusing his kindness with tears in their eyes, he comforted them with all the goodness and humanity imaginable, entreating them to leave him, and wrote letters in their behalf to Theophilus, his steward, at Corinth, that he would provide for their security, and keep them concealed till such time as they could make their peace with Caesar.

But at Actium, his fleet, after a long resistance to Caesar, and suffering the most damage from a heavy sea that set in right ahead, scarcely at four in the afternoon, gave up the contest, with the loss of not more than five thousand killed, but of three hundred ships taken, as Caesar himself has recorded. Only a few had known of Antony's flight; and those who were told of it could not at first give any belief to so incredible a thing as that a general who had nineteen entire legions and twelve thousand horse upon the seashore, could abandon all and fly away; and he, above all, who had so often experienced both good and evil fortune, and had in a thousand wars and battles been inured to changes. His soldiers, however, would not give up their desires and expectations, still fancying he would appear from some part or other, and showed such a generous fidelity to his service that, when they were thoroughly assured that he was fled in earnest, they kept themselves in a body seven days, making no account of the messages that Caesar sent to them. But at last, seeing that Canidius himself, who commanded them, was fled from the camp by night, and that all their officers had quite abandoned them, they gave way, and made their submission to the conqueror.

When Antony came into Africa, he sent on Cleopatra from Paraetonium into Egypt, and stayed himself in the most entire solitude. But when the officer who commanded for him in Africa, to whose care he had committed all his forces there, took them over to Caesar, he resolved to kill himself, but was hindered by his friends. And coming to Alexandria, he found Cleopatra busied in a most bold and wonderful enterprise. Over the small space of land which divides the Red Sea from the sea near Egypt, which may be considered also the boundary between Asia and Africa, and in the narrowest place is not much above three hundred furlongs across, over this neck of land Cleopatra had formed a project of dragging her fleet and setting it afloat in the Arabian Gulf, thus with her soldiers and her treasure to secure herself a home on the other side, where she might live in peace far away from war and slavery. But the first galleys which were carried over being burnt by the Arabians of Petra, and Antony not knowing but that the army before Actium still held together, she desisted from her enterprise, and gave orders for the fortifying all the approaches to Egypt. But Antony, leaving the city and the conversation of his friends, built him a dwelling-place in the water, near Pharos, upon a little mole which he cast up in the sea, and there, secluding himself from the company of mankind, said he desired nothing but to live the life of Timon; as indeed, his case was the same, and the ingratitude and injuries which he suffered from those he had esteemed his friends made him hate and distrust all mankind.

This Timon was a citizen of Athens, and lived much about the Peloponnesian war, as may be seen by the comedies of Aristophanes and Plato, in which he is ridiculed as hater and enemy of mankind. He avoided and repelled the approaches of every one, but embraced with kisses and the greatest show of affection Alcibiades, then in his hot youth. And when Apemantus was astonished, and demanded the reason, he replied that he knew this young man would one day do infinite mischief to the Athenians. He never admitted any one into his company, except at times this Apemantus, who was of the same sort of temper, and was an imitator of his way of life. At the celebration of the festival of flagons, these two kept the feast together, and Apemantus, saying to him, "What a pleasant party, Timon!" "It would be," he answered, "if you were away." One day he got up in a full assembly on the speaker's place, and when there was a dead silence and great wonder at so unusual a sight, he said, "Ye men of Athens, I have a little plot of ground, and in it grows a fig-tree, on which many citizens have been pleased to hang themselves; and now, having resolved to build in that place, I wish to announce it publicly, that any of you who may be desirous may go and hang yourselves before I cut it down." He died and was buried at Halae, near the sea, where it so happened that, after his burial, a land-slip took place on the point of the shore, and the sea, flowing in, surrounded his tomb, and made it inaccessible to the foot of man. It bore this inscription:—

"Here am I laid, my life of misery done.
 Ask not my name, I curse you every one."

And this epitaph was made by himself while yet alive; that which is more generally known is by Callimachus:—

"Timon, the misanthrope, am I below.
  Go, and revile me, traveller, only go."

Thus much of Timon, of whom much more might be said. Canidius now came, bringing word in person of the loss of the army before Actium. Then he received news that Herod of Judaea was gone over to Caesar with some legions and cohorts, and that the other kings and princes were in like manner deserting him, and that, out of Egypt, nothing stood by him. All this, however, seemed not to disturb him, but, as if he were glad to put away all hope, that with it he might be rid of all care, and leaving his habitation by the sea, which he called the Timoneum, he was received by Cleopatra in the palace, and set the whole city into a course of feasting, drinking, and presents. The son of Caesar and Cleopatra was registered among the youths, and Antyllus, his own son by Fulvia, received the gown without the purple border given to those that are come of age; in honour of which the citizens of Alexandria did nothing but feast and revel for many days. They themselves broke up the Order of the Inimitable Livers, and constituted another in its place, not inferior in splendour, luxury, and sumptuosity, calling it that of the Diers Together. For all those that said they would die with Antony and Cleopatra gave in their names, for the present passing their time in all manner of pleasures and a regular succession of banquets. But Cleopatra was busied in making a collection of all varieties of poisonous drugs, and, in order to see which of them were the least painful in the operation, she had them tried upon prisoners condemned to die. But, finding that the quick poisons always worked with sharp pains, and that the less painful were slow, she next tried venomous animals, and watching with her own eyes whilst they were applied, one creature to the body of another. This was her daily practice, and she pretty well satisfied herself that nothing was comparable to the bite of the asp, which, without convulsion or groaning, brought on a heavy drowsiness and lethargy, with a gentle sweat on

the face, the senses being stupefied by degrees; the patient,
in appearance, being sensible of no pain, but rather troubled to be disturbed or awakened like those that are in a
profound natural sleep.

At the same time, they sent ambassadors to Caesar into
Asia, Cleopatra asking for the kingdom of Egypt for her
children, and Antony, that he might have leave to live as
a private man in Egypt, or, if that were thought too much,
that he might retire to Athens. Caesar would not listen to
any proposals for Antony, but he made answer to Cleopatra, that there was no reasonable favour which she might
not expect, if she put Antony to death, or expelled him
from Egypt. The winter being over, he began his march,
he himself by Syria, and his captains through Africa. Pelusium being taken, there went a report as if it had been
delivered up to Caesar by Seleucus, not without the consent
of Cleopatra; but she, to justify herself, gave up into Antony's hands the wife and children of Seleucus to be put
to death. She had caused to be built, joining to the temple
of Isis, several tombs and monuments of wonderful height,
and very remarkable for the workmanship; thither she removed her treasure, her gold, silver, emeralds, pearls, ebony,
ivory, cinnamon, and, after all, a great quantity of torch-
wood and tow. Upon which Caesar began to fear lest she
should, in a desperate fit, set all these riches on fire; and,
therefore, while he was marching toward the city with his
army, he omitted no occasion of giving her new assurances
of his good intentions. He took up his position in the Hippo-
drome, where Antony made a fierce sally upon him, routed
the horse, and beat them back into their trenches, and so returned with great satisfaction to the palace, where, meeting
Cleopatra, armed as he was, he kissed her, and commended
to her favour one of his men, who had most signalised
himself in the fight, to whom she made a present of a breastplate and helmet of gold; which he having received went
that very night and deserted to Caesar.

After this, Antony sent a new challenge to Caesar to fight
him hand-to-hand; who made him answer that he might

find several other ways to end his life; and he, considering with himself that he could not die more honourably than in battle, resolved to make an effort both by land and sea. At supper, it is said, he bade his servants help him freely, and pour him out wine plentifully, since to-morrow, perhaps, they should not do the same, but be servants to a new master, whilst he should lie on the ground, a dead corpse, and nothing. His friends that were about him wept to hear him talk so; which he perceiving, told them he would not lead them to a battle in which he expected rather an honourable death than either safety or victory. That night, it is related, about the middle of it, when the whole city was in a deep silence and general sadness, expecting the event of the next day, on a sudden was heard the sound of all sorts of instruments, and voices singing in tune, and the cry of a crowd of people shouting and dancing, like a troop of bacchanals on its way. This tumultuous procession seemed to take its course right through the middle of the city to the gate nearest the enemy; here it became the loudest, and suddenly passed out. People who reflected considered this to signify that Bacchus, the god whom Antony had always made it his study to copy and imitate, had now forsaken him.

As soon as it was light, he marched his infantry out of the city, and posted them upon a rising ground, from whence he saw his fleet make up to the enemy. There he stood in expectation of the event; but as soon as the fleets came near to one another, his men saluted Caesar's with their oars; and on their responding, the whole body of the ships, forming into a single fleet, rowed up direct to the city. Antony had no sooner seen this, but the horse deserted him, and went over to Caesar; and his foot being defeated, he retired into the city, crying out that Cleopatra had betrayed him to the enemies he had made for her sake. She, being afraid lest in his fury and despair he might do her a mischief, fled to her monument, and letting down the falling doors, which were strong with bars and bolts, she sent messengers who should tell Antony she was dead. He, believing it, cried out, "Now, Antony, why delay longer? Fate has snatched away the only pretext for which you could say you desired yet to live." Going into his chamber, and there loosening and opening his coat of armour, "I am not," said he, "troubled, Cleopatra, to be at present bereaved of you, for I shall soon be with you; but it distresses me that so great a general should be found of a tardier courage than a woman." He had a faithful servant, whose name was Eros; he had engaged him formerly to kill him when he should think it necessary, and now he put him to his promise. Eros drew his sword, as designing to kill him, but, suddenly turning round, he slew himself. And as he fell dead at his feet, "It is well done, Eros," said Antony; "you show your master how to do what you had not the heart to do yourself"; and so he ran himself into the belly, and laid himself upon the couch. The wound, however, was not immediately mortal; and the flow of blood ceasing when he lay down, presently he came to himself, and entreated those that were about him to put him out of his pain; but they all fled out of the chamber, and left him crying out and struggling, until Diomede, Cleopatra's secretary, came to him, having orders from her to bring him into the monument.

When he understood she was alive, he eagerly gave order to the servants to take him up, and in their arms was carried to the door of the building. Cleopatra would not open the door, but, looking from a sort of window, she let down ropes and cords, to which Antony was fastened; and she and her two women, the only persons she had allowed to enter the monument, drew him up. Those that were present say that nothing was ever more sad than this spectacle, to see Antony, covered all over with blood and just expiring, thus drawn up, still holding up his hands to her, and lifting up his body with the little force he had left. As, indeed, it was no easy task for the women; and Cleopatra, with all her force, clinging to the rope, and straining with her head to the ground, with difficulty pulled him up, while those below encouraged her with their cries, and joined in all her efforts and anxiety. When she had got him up, she laid him on the bed, tearing all her clothes, which she spread upon him; and, beating her breast with her hands, lacerating herself, and disfiguring her own face with the blood from his wounds, she called him her lord, her husband, her emperor, and seemed to have pretty nearly forgotten all her own evils, she was so intent upon his misfortunes. Antony, stopping her lamentations as well as he could, called for wine to drink, either that he was thirsty, or that he imagined that it might put him the sooner out of pain. When he had drunk, he advised her to bring her own affairs, so far as might be honourably done, to a safe conclusion, and that, among all the friends of Caesar, she should rely on Proculeius; that she should not pity him in this last turn of fate, but rather rejoice for him in remembrance of his past happiness, who had been of all men the most illustrious and powerful, and in the end had fallen not ignobly, a Roman by a Roman overcome.

Just as he breathed his last, Proculeius arrived from Caesar; for when Antony gave himself his wound, and was carried into Cleopatra, one of his guards, Dercetaeus, took up Antony's sword and hid it; and, when he saw his opportunity, stole away to Caesar, and brought him the first news of Antony's death, and withal showed him the bloody sword. Caesar, upon this, retired into the inner part of his tent, and giving some tears to the death of one that had been nearly allied to him in marriage, his colleague in empire, and companion in so many wars and dangers, he came out to his friends, and, bringing with him many letters, he read to them with how much reason and moderation he had always addressed himself to Antony, and in return what overbearing and arrogant answers he received. Then he sent Proculeius to use his utmost endeavours to get Cleopatra alive into his power; for he was afraid of losing a great treasure, and, besides, she would be no small addition to the glory of his triumph. She, however, was careful not to put herself in Proculeius's power; but from within her monument, he standing on the outside of a door, on the level of the ground, which was strongly barred, but so that they might well enough hear one another's voice, she held a conference with him; she demanding that her kingdom might be given to her children, and he binding her to be of good courage, and trust Caesar in everything.

Having taken particular notice of the place, he returned to Caesar, and Gallus was sent to parley with her the second time; who, being come to the door, on purpose prolonged the conference, while Proculeius fixed his scaling-ladders in the window through which the women had pulled up Antony. And so entering, with two men to follow him, he went straight down to the door where Cleopatra was discoursing with Gallus. One of the two women who were shut up in the monument with her cried out, "Miserable Cleopatra, you are taken prisoner!" Upon which she turned quickly, and, looking at Proculeius, drew out her dagger which she had with her to stab herself. But Proculeius ran up quickly, and seizing her with both his hands, "For shame," said he, "Cleopatra; you wrong yourself and Caesar much, who would rob him of so fair an occasion of showing his clemency, and would make the world believe the most gentle of commanders to be a faithless and implacable enemy." And so, taking the dagger out of her hand, he also shook her dress to see if there were any poison hid in it. After this, Caesar sent Epaphroditus, one of his freedmen, with orders to treat her with all the gentleness and civility possible, but to take the strictest precautions to keep her alive.

Many kings and great commanders made petition to Caesar for the body of Antony, to give him his funeral rites; but he would not take away his corpse from Cleopatra by whose hands he was buried with royal splendour and magnificence, it being granted to her to employ what she pleased on his funeral. In this extremity of grief and sorrow, and having inflamed and ulcerated her breasts with beating them, she fell into a high fever, and was very glad of the occasion, hoping, under this pretext, to abstain from food, and so to die in quiet without interference. She had her own physician, Olympus, to whom she told the truth, and asked his advice and help to put an end to herself, as Olympus himself has told us, in a narrative which he wrote of these events. But Caesar, suspecting her purpose, took to menacing language about her children, and excited her fears for them, before which engines her purpose shook and gave way, so that she suffered those about her to give her what meat or medicine they pleased.

Some few days after, Caesar himself came to make her a visit and comfort her. She lay then upon her pallet-bed in undress, and, on his entering, sprang up from off her bed, having nothing on but the one garment next her body, and flung herself at his feet, her hair and face looking wild and disfigured, her voice quivering, and her eyes sunk in her head. The marks of the blows she had given herself were visible about her bosom, and altogether her whole person seemed no less afflicted than her soul. But, for all this, her old charm, and the boldness of her youthful beauty, had not wholly left her, and, in spite of her present condition, still sparkled from within, and let itself appear in all the movements of her countenance. Caesar, desiring her to repose herself, sat down by her; and, on this opportunity, she said something to justify her actions, attributing what she had done to the necessity she was under, and to her fear of Antony; and when Caesar, on each point, made his objections, and she found herself confuted, she broke off at once into language of entreaty and deprecation, as if she desired nothing more than to prolong her life. And at last, having by her a list of her treasure, she gave it into his hands; and when Seleucus, one of her stewards, who was by, pointed out that various articles were omitted, and charged her with secreting them, she flew up and caught him by the hair, and struck him several blows on the face. Caesar smiling and withholding her, "Is it not very hard, Caesar," said she, "when you do me the honour to visit me in this condition I am in, that I should be accused by one of my own servants of laying by some women's toys, not meant to adorn, be sure, my unhappy self, but that I might have some little present by me to make your Octavia and your Livia, that by their intercession I might hope to find you in some measure disposed to mercy?" Caesar was pleased to hear her talk thus, being now assured that she was desirous to live. And, therefore, letting her know that the things she had laid by she might dispose of as she pleased, and his usage of her should be honourable above her expectation, he went away, well satisfied that he had overreached her, but, in fact, was himself deceived.

There was a young man of distinction among Caesar's companions named Cornelius Dolabella. He was not without a certain tenderness for Cleopatra, and sent her word privately, as she had besought him to do, that Caesar was about to return through Syria, and that she and her children were to be sent on within three days. When she understood this, she made her request to Caesar that he would be pleased to permit her to make oblations to the departed Antony; which being granted, she ordered herself to be carried to the place where he was buried, and there, accompanied by her women, she embraced his tomb with tears in her eyes, and spoke in this manner: "O, dearest Antony," said she, "it is not long since that with these hands I buried you; then they were free, now I am a captive, and pay these last duties to you with a guard upon me, for fear that my just griefs and sorrows should impair my servile body, and make it less fit to appear in their triumph over you. No further offerings or libations expect from me; these are the last honours that Cleopatra can pay your memory, for she is to be hurried away far from you. Nothing could part us whilst we lived, but death seems to threaten to divide us. You, a Roman born, have found a grave in Egypt; I, an Egyptian, am to seek that favour, and none but that, in your country. But if the gods below, with whom you now are, either can or will do anything (since those above have betrayed us), suffer not your living wife to be abandoned; let me not be led in triumph to your shame, but hide me and bury me here with you, since, amongst all my bitter misfortunes, nothing has afflicted me like this brief time that I have lived away from you."

Having made these lamentations, crowning the tomb with garlands and kissing it, she gave orders to prepare her a bath, and, coming out of the bath, she lay down and made a sumptuous meal. And a country fellow brought her a little basket, which the guards intercepting and asking what it was, the fellow put the leaves which lay uppermost aside, and showed them it was full of figs; and on their admiring the largeness and beauty of the figs, he laughed, and invited them to take some, which they refused, and, suspecting nothing, bade him carry them in. After her repast, Cleopatra sent to Caesar a letter which she had written and sealed; and, putting everybody out of the monument but her two women, she shut the doors. Caesar, opening her letter, and finding pathetic prayers and entreaties that she might be buried in the same tomb with Antony, soon guessed what was doing. At first he was going himself in all haste, but changing his mind, he sent others to see. The thing had been quickly done. The messengers came at full speed, and found the guards apprehensive of nothing; but on opening the doors they saw her stone-dead, lying upon a bed of gold, set out in all her royal ornaments. Iras, one of her women, lay dying at her feet, and Charmion, just ready to fall, scarce able to hold up her head, was adjusting her mistress's diadem. And when one that came in said angrily, "Was this well done of your lady, Charmion?" "Extremely well," she answered, "and as became the descendant of so many kings"; and as she said this, she fell down dead by the bedside.

Some relate that an asp was brought in amongst those figs and covered with the leaves, and that Cleopatra had arranged that it might settle on her before she knew, but, when she took away some of the figs and saw it, she said, "So here it is," and held out her bare arm to be bitten. Others say that it was kept in a vase, and that she vexed and pricked it with a golden spindle till it seized her arm. But what really took place is known to no one, since it was also said that she carried poison in a hollow bodkin, about which she wound her hair; yet there was not so much as a spot found, or any symptom of poison upon her body, nor was the asp seen within the monument; only something like the trail of it was said to have been noticed on the sand by the sea, on the part towards which the building faced and where the windows were. Some relate that two faint puncture-marks were found on Cleopatra's arm, and to this account Caesar seems to have given credit; for in his triumph there was carried a figure of Cleopatra, with an asp clinging to her. Such are the various accounts. But Caesar, though much disappointed by her death, yet could not but admire the greatness of her spirit, and gave order that her body should be buried by Antony with royal splendour and magnificence. Her women, also, received honourable burial by his directions. Cleopatra had lived nine-and-thirty years, during twenty-two of which she had reigned as queen, and for fourteen had been Antony's partner in his empire. Antony, according to some authorities, was fifty-three, according to others, fifty-six years old. His statues were all thrown down, but those of Cleopatra were left untouched; for Archibius, one of her friends, gave Caesar two thousand talents to save them from the fate of Antony's.

INDEX OF NAMES

THE DECLINE
AND FALL OF
THE ROMAN EMPIRE

BY EDWARD GIBBON

One of the greatest histories of all time in a highly readable abridgment by Frank C. Bourne.

The panoramic history of the Roman Empire from the end of its golden age to its final political and physical disintegration some twelve centuries later: from the reign of the emperor Trajan to the Fall of the West, from the age of Justinian to that of Charlemagne.

THE DECLINE AND FALL OF THE ROMAN EMPIRE is unquestionably the foremost study of its kind ever written.

AN ORIGINAL LAUREL EDITION 95c